ENCHANTED

BOOK 2

THINGS WE LOST IN THE NIGHT

A Memoir of Love and Music in the 60s with
Stark Naked and the Car Thieves

LARRY J. DUNLAP

Author of Amazon Best Seller in Biographies of Pop Artists
NIGHT PEOPLE

Copyright © 2018 by Larry J. Dunlap

Claremont Village Press
5352 Algarrobo Street, #P
Laguna Woods, CA 92637 USA
www.claremontvillagepress.com

Thank you for buying an authorized edition of this book and for complying with copyright laws by not reproducing, scanning, or distributing any part of it in any form without permission, except in the case of brief quotations embodied in critical reviews and certain other noncommercial uses permitted by copyright law. You are supporting authors and allowing publishers to publish books for every reader. Note that all song and book titles, and lyric fragments are the property of their respective copyright holders. For reprint permission requests, contact the publisher at info@cvppress.com.

Publisher's Note: The author has attempted to recreate events, locales, and conversations from his memories of them. In certain places, time has been compressed to fit the years this book covers. Interactions between the author and friends, band members, acquaintances, family members, celebrities, and others in this book, etc., are as true as the author's memory recollects. Liberties have been taken with dialogue, as remembering word-for-word what was said fifty-plus years ago is impossible. But the actual events and connections that instigated the dialogue happened, and the conversations convey the truth as the author recalls it. In a very few instances, not material to the story, the author may have changed the names of individuals and places in order to maintain their anonymity. In times of rapid change, however, ensuring all information provided is entirely accurate and up-to-date at all times is not always possible. Therefore, the author and publisher accept no responsibility for inaccuracies or omissions, and specifically disclaim any liability, loss, or risk, personal, professional, or otherwise, which may be incurred as a consequence, directly or indirectly, of the information provided in this book.

Developmental editing - Katie Stirling/John C. Clair
Line/Copy editing - Katie Stirling
Proofreaders - Erin Hart Wisti, Kristi Bartmess Warren
Cover design by Claremont Press
Author photograph by Studio 1921, Montclair, CA

First Edition 2019

ISBN 13: 978-0-9906279-3-7 (Paperback Edition)
ISBN 978-0-9906279-4-4 (Kindle Edition)
ISBN 13: 978-0-9906279-5-1 (EPUB Edition)

Dunlap, Larry J.
Enchanted, Book 2: Things We Lost in the Night, A Memoir of Love and Music in the '60s with Stark Naked and the Car Thieves / [by Larry J. Dunlap].
pages cm.

STARK NAKED AND THE CAR THIEVES
Photo taken before leaving for Hawaii 1968
Top: Dave Dunn, Leonard Souza, Mickey Borden
Bottom: Mac Brown, Larry Dunlap, Les Silvey

ALSO BY LARRY J. DUNLAP

NIGHT PEOPLE, *Book 1 of Things We Lost in the Night, A Memoir of Love and Music in the 60s with Stark Naked and the Car Thieves*

Dedicated to my sister
CHERYL MARIE GENTRY
always the smartest one

MY CHILDREN &
my band brothers
DAVID DUNN, MACARTHUR J. BROWN, and LES SILVEY
including Joan Brown & the members of
The Aristocats, The Reflections, The Checkmates,
and
Stark Naked and the Car Thieves

in memoriam
SHERI (SCHRUHL) MOLINE-RILEY
1952 - 2016

Always and especially, my one true thing
LAURIE

Write like you're clinging to the edge of a cliff, white knuckles, on your last breath, and you've got just one last thing to say, like you're a bird flying over us and you can see everything, and please, for God's sake, tell us something that will save us from ourselves. Take a deep breath and tell us your deepest, darkest secret, so we can wipe our brow and know that we're not alone.

— Alan W. Watts

INTRODUCTION

For information about how this memoir is constructed and the style choices, including—and especially—using quote marks for conversations that happened fifty or more years ago, please refer to the preface of the first book, Night People. *The same explanation pertains here.*

In August of 2011 I began working on this story of four young men from the Midwest setting out for California in 1965 in an implausible attempt to reinvent themselves as a rock and roll band. It was meant to be a simple written account for friends and family members who hadn't known of our accomplishments as singers, entertainers and musicians in the six years that followed. Our struggles and successes in that era of cultural and historical change had bonded us as close as brothers.

We'd remained in close contact over the 40 plus years since, often reminiscing about our times together, which gave me a good foundation of tales and sketches to work with. In stitching these together with my memories, I was surprised to find that our experience had been much more unique and interesting than even we had realized. I wanted to complete the narrative; I'd begun to wonder if it might be of interest to a wider audience.

While my bandmates and I generally remembered the broader aspects of our story similarly, the devil was in the details. We could not always agree on them. I couldn't relate events other than the way I remembered them, but I realized that if I continued the way I'd planned the implication would be my bandmates agreed with everything I wrote. The solution was for me to tell the band's story *through my eyes*, from my point of view – in other words – a memoir. Memoir is generally accepted as an author's feelings and opinions based on their own memories of an event, or events, over a specific period of time. With that in mind, coupled with what my friends and I remembered in accord, and as much established fact as I could find, I filled seven loose-leaf notebooks, a file drawer, and several gigabytes of computer memory with research.

The longer I worked on the story and improved as a creative writer, the more I appreciated the value of a personal view. Readers would easier relate to the story if I could capably describe the emotions and experiences as I felt them in the story. But there was something I hadn't considered when I began this venture. Authenticity would require me to reveal my personal feelings. I would have to expose my own failures, losses, and poor decisions. The most traumatic events in my life had taken place in my last months in the band. Since then, I'd done my best to push them away into a hidden corner of my mind. I would need to exhume and expose my deepest feelings and, no matter how confused and conflicted I'd been, answer for the questionable actions I'd taken and mistakes I'd made, some of them intensely embarrassing. Because they are as central to the band's story as they are to mine.

In that long and torturous remembering I have come to realize the story has changed again; to what it had always been from the beginning — A LOVE STORY.

Table of Contents

TITLE PAGE i
COPYRIGHT ii
FRONTISPIECE iii
DEDICATION v
EPIGRAPH vi
INTRODUCTION vii
TABLE OF CONTENTS ix
PART I 1
   MARIE (Prologue) 3
   1 THE LEMON TREE 7
   2 ISLAND GIRL 11
   3 THE BUS STOP BENCH 17
   4 SANDY BEACH 25
   5 LOVE AND DEATH 37
   6 RUMORS OF WAR 47
   7 SMOKE DREAMS 55
   8 BUNNY'S TALE 63
   9 TURNED OUT 71
   10 BLUE HAWAII 77
   11 DOIN' TIME IN PARADISE 85
   12 THE STARK NAKED GIRL 93
   13 LOOK BACK IN LOVE 99
   IMAGES - PART I 105

PART II 107
   14 HOMECOMING 109
   15 JUNIOR PROM 115
   16 THE WAY THINGS WERE 125
   17 PEANUT BUTTER COOKIES 135
   18 RAT FINK CONFESSIONAL 145
   19 RACE DAY 153

20 ALOHA NO AU IA 'OE 159
21 CALIFORNIA DREAMING 165
22 THERESA 171
23 HOME ON THE ROAD 177
24 A TRIP TO THE DESERT 185
25 THE CAT AND THE FAMILY STONE 191
26 THREE DOG NIGHT 197
27 OKRA AND THE WINGNUTS 203
28 IT'S A GIRL 211
29 LIBERACE'S TAILOR 221
30 DEER PARK 228
31 THINGS CHANGE 235
IMAGES - PART II 241

PART III 245

32 THE SKY ROOM 247
33 TRYING TO GET IT RIGHT 253
34 STARRY VEGAS NIGHTS 257
35 RING DAY 267
36 MIXED EMOTIONS 273
37 LATE NIGHT WITH LENNY 281
38 COPY 'CATS 287
39 CHASING THE MUSE 297
40 A FOOT ON THE BRIDGE 303
41 AN APPLIED PHILOSOPHY 309
42 SMOKELESS 315
43 THE TWENTY-FIVE YEAR PHONE CALL 323
44 VEGAS BLUES 331
45 FUN DAYS 337
46 KEOKI 345
47 HOT VEGAS NIGHTS 349
48 REUNITED 355
49 WHISPERS IN THE WIND 361

50 ROOM WITH A VIEW 365
51 THE INTERNATIONAL CROWN ROOM 373
52 BAD MICKEY 379
53 DISTURBING ELVIS 387
54 A HAWAIIAN IN HOOSIERVILLE 393
55 BACK TO THE RAT 401
56 TELEPATHY 409
IMAGES - PART III 415

PART IV 419
57 A HAWAIIAN HEARTACHE 421
58 THE GREETER 429
59 FOUR SAFE WORDS 435
60 ENTURBULATED 443
61 THE SAINT AND THE SINNER 449
62 RIDING WITH ELVIS 455
63 SKY ROOM FOLLIES 459
64 ROBO-VOICE AND THE FORCE FIELD 467
65 BEDMATES 475
66 A HOUSE ON STILTS 481
67 A COUNTERFEIT HAWAIIAN 487
68 CASTAWAY 491
69 BURNED 495
70 PARADISE REVISITED 501
71 SLOW MOTION NOTICE 509
72 NORTHWEST PASSAGE 515
73 REVENGE SEX 521
74 AREA 51 529
75 CONSPIRACY 535
76 THE LAST CAT 541
77 MIDNIGHT ON THE MOJAVE 551
IMAGES - PART IV 557
AFTERMATH (Epilogue) 559

ACKNOWLEDGMENTS 569
BEFORE YOU GO..571

PART I

If you intend to write as truthfully as you can, your days as a member of polite society are numbered, anyway.

—STEPHEN KING

MARIE (Prologue)

One day I will find the right words and they will be simple
—Jack Kerouac

March 25, 1968
North Hollywood, California

I DIDN'T SAY GOODBYE. I shouldered a carry-on bag, and half-carried, half-dragged one of the two cheap pressed-board J.C. Penney trunks I kept everything in, out to the car. Marie had offered to keep the other one for me even though I'd insisted I wouldn't be back. We'd had this conversation before, and I hadn't been able to make it stick, maybe she was counting on that. There were only a few disintegrating paperbacks, some old clothes, used-up toiletries and other odd items in it. It was an easy sacrifice if believing I might return for them made it easier for her.

She'd been my confidant, friend, and part-time lover for the best part of three years. I'd met her after a grant of divorce decree I'd never wanted, arrived from my soon-to-be ex-wife in Indianapolis. Marie's affection and avid love-making had soothed my scorched emotions then. And our continued intimacies had helped blanket the complex stew of emotions left over from the loss of my first love and our two little boys.

I'd slipped into a passionate attachment to Marie, perhaps even a dependency until the disparity between our deeper feelings became awkwardly apparent. I couldn't commit to a long-term exclusive relationship with her or anyone, and told her so. At first, she'd walked away, but then she'd accepted that when we were together, we were together, and when we weren't—there might be others.

As our musical and performance skills improved and our popularity grew in the East Bay, we signed a year-long contract at the Galaxie in San Francisco's North Beach. She never came to the City to see us, content to spend my off-nights with me in my Berkeley apartment.

I assumed our relationship would fade naturally when the band's fortunes took us south to Hollywood and Las Vegas. Instead, her visits lasted weeks, and sometimes months. She never expressed unhappiness about our circumstances, but I was never unaware of what she wanted.

We couldn't continue this way; I knew that, but I hadn't found a way to break it off. She fit perfectly into the band's little society; the wives loved and approved of her, she was comfortable to be with and our intimacy easy and satisfying—I couldn't bring myself to end it.

A couple of months ago I was driving home in a cannabis-induced melancholic fog from the nightclub where we were playing. I was immersed in one of my favorite eight-track's, *The Mamas & the Papas* second album. This time, John Phillips' *I Saw Her Again Last Night,* struck home and brought me to tears. His desperate and guilty voice singing about a guy seeing a girl he knew he shouldn't, forced me to see my own selfishness, and revealed the insecurity and loneliness I feared without Marie. I couldn't hide from it anymore; I had to let her find someone who could give her what I could not.

After our recent appearance in Las Vegas the time arrived. I'd gotten too attached to an English showgirl from the Lido show at the Stardust whose visa was about to run out. Things had nearly gone too far. I couldn't reconcile my actions with who I thought I was. We'd be leaving for Hawaii soon, two months in Honolulu followed by a month in Indianapolis. It should be long enough to deaden the ache of separation for both of us.

Before I could tell her, Marie brought me her own news: she'd moved from Northern California to an apartment in the San Fernando Valley near the Rag Doll, our home club in LA. She wanted me to consider it home.

Despite tears and incandescent sex, my resolve didn't break, though I'd let it get severely bent. She realized I was serious this time; I meant this to be the end.

She asked me to stay in her apartment with her until I left for Honolulu. It felt like an adult way to bring our relationship to a close, and I agreed. With the amount of fanfare our upcoming record release, *Look Back In Love*, was receiving, the band was busy during the days with meetings, photo shoots, and PR interviews. But in the nights, Marie and I took refuge in usually tender, and sometimes frenzied, lovemaking. And sometimes, in wrapping ourselves in bittersweet nostalgia. Her final request was simple: "Don't say goodbye. When you have to go, just go. Please. Make it seem like it's just another day."

1 THE LEMON TREE

> We live in a world where lemonade is made from artificial flavoring and furniture polish is made from real lemons.
> —Alfred Newman, MAD Magazine

March 25, 1968
Waikiki, Honolulu, Hawaii

THE NONDESCRIPT NIGHTCLUB tucked into the Diamond Head edge of Waikiki—where Liliuokalani Avenue T-boned Kalakaua at the ocean—was not impressive. But inside the Lemon Tree's street-side lanai, the late afternoon view oozed with tropical ambiance. Curious breezes frisked past me, anxious to explore the corners and crannies of the building's single-story interior. Across the street, beyond Kalakaua's flowing traffic, lazy waves rolled and broke onto a white sand beach. Flowering bushes undulated, and coconut palms soared into a crystal azure sky. I resisted an urge to call Marie and describe the incredible moving picture postcard in front of me. Kuhio Beach's tingling promise of imminent adventure crept into my consciousness. It made up for many missing amenities.

Earlier, Stan Alapa and his girlfriend, Shirley, who owned the Lemon Tree, welcomed us at the Honolulu Airport. A ukulele band played the aloha song while grass-skirted girls draped us with leis and hugs. We loaded our luggage into a passenger van with help from our new employers. Two jumbo-sized young men, whom the normal-sized Stan claimed were his brothers, filled a matching panel van with our equipment. We were driven to the far side of Honolulu and left off in front of a ramshackle pile of rooms whimsically named the Surfboard Hotel. Though it seemed likely that a strong wind would blow it away to the other side of the island, it was expected to be our home for the next nine weeks. In its defense, it offered a convenient exit across a narrow alleyway into the nightclub's back door and easy access to the beach. And I appreciated the privacy of individual rooms for each of us. Despite its lack of charm, something about it seemed right for an island adventure. Not all my band brothers agreed.

"This place is a fucking dump," Dave, our lead singer spat out. "No way am I staying here." His luggage lay tumbled at his feet in the cramped lobby. The rest of us had been stashing our bags in our rooms and, at our employers' suggestion, changing into casual beachwear for a welcoming lunch next door.

"What's got your shorts in a bunch, bro?" Mac Brown asked, concern in his gravelly voice. Mac handled our emcee duties and sang lead on our R&B tunes. He flicked a cigarette butt out the door across two narrow steps to the sidewalk.

Les Silvey stalked in, a grimace etched on his deceptively innocent face. Our new bass player, Mickey Borden, followed him. They were both in shorts and tees. I hoped Mickey would work out better than the last two bass players I'd had to contend with, but—so far, so good.

"No TV," Les said, his frown deepening. "This place is a real pit."

"Not even room phones," Mickey added.

Both stood about six-feet-tall, but Les, our guitar player, was dark haired and could have been a male model while Mickey's physique seemed carved out of oak and his pale blond hair hung in a loose Prince Valiant cut.

"Television?" Leonard twisted his rubbery features into a puzzled grin. "You guys are going to sit here watching TV? Look at this place; we're in frickin' heaven."

"Sure, pretty easy for you to say." Les rested his guitar case on a chair arm. "You know people here. You're not staying in this rat's nest with the rest of us."

Leonard Souza did know people here. Before we'd found him drumming behind a topless snake-dancer at Big Al's in North Beach, he'd been stationed here in the Navy for two years. Oahu was a second home to him, and he already looked the part in his flip-flops, swimsuit, and an open Hawaiian shirt. He, his wife, and little Lenny would be staying with local friends for the duration.

"Now wait a minute, you guys. Just hold on." I waved everyone quiet and glanced at Dave. "Tell us man, what's bugging you?"

"Bugging me?" he fumed, eyes bulging. "Holy Mother of God! There's a cockroach the size of a German Shepherd up there—that's what's bugging me. I could've saddled the damn thing and rode it around the room. Roaches!" Dave glared at us as we struggled to hide our grins. "Roaches and rats, two of God's creatures I cannot abide. You guys stay if you want, but I'm not spending a single night here. The Surfboard Hotel, what a joke! This place can kiss my rosy red asshole adios."

Mac scratched at the stubble his face had sprouted between jobs. "So, what you gonna do, man? Rooms are pretty fuckin basic, give you that, but they are what comes with the gig." His soft drawl spoke of a rugged adolescence growing up in the OTR, Cincinnati's Over-the-Rhine, neighborhood. He told me he'd learned to run like the wind; as the only white kid in an all-black high school, he'd had to sprint to and from classes every day. At least, he'd added with a grin, until he'd joined one of the street-corner singing groups around Washington Park.

"Guy at the counter says there are apartments for rent a few blocks from here. He calls it the "jungle," but I'd rather pay for a place there than stay in this infested shit-hole. Gotta leave my stuff somewhere while I go check it out. And," Dave's frustration turned into a challenging glower. "Anybody got a problem with that?"

"Come on, bub," Mac said, easing him around. He hefted one of Dave's suitcases. "We'll drop 'em in my room. I can handle the sound check. You go on; find yourself a place; that's what you wanna do."

We might have preferred playing at one of the flashy, luxurious Waikiki nightspots like the Outrigger or in the International Marketplace nearer Honolulu's famous tourist beaches, but we'd survived too many rough times over the last three years to let it bother us. With a name like Stark Naked and the Car Thieves, it wouldn't be the first time we'd had to prove ourselves. Anyway, *Look Back In Love* would be out any day now. *Billboard Magazine* had picked it to jump high on its Hot 100 chart. Our producer, personal managers, booking agent, even the president of Bell Records assured us we had a smash hit on our hands.

At the club, we witnessed a courtesy no other engagement had extended. Our equipment was being manhandled to the stage by Stan Alapa's two humongous brothers, who we'd learned, were Samoan *hanai* brothers—*hanai* being a kind of an informal adoption between local families. A third, slightly smaller *hanai* brother, Dewey, had spread an assortment of local delicacies on a bar looking over the incredible beach across the street. I skipped the raw fish dishes, sticking with fruit, rice, Portuguese sweet bread, and cooked meat on a stick. As the band's leader, I felt an obligation to keep up with the conversation, but I found myself insistently drawn to the murmuring rumble and crack of the surf across the street. I'd discovered the Pacific Ocean's calming influence over me at San Francisco's Half Moon Bay. Despite the spectacular setting, or maybe because of it, a sense of rootlessness rolled over me. I drifted to the stage to release my Hammond B3 organ from its shipping crate.

Dave was back in time for our final sound check. His temper could boil up quickly but, as I'd known since we'd become best friends singing together in high school, it cooled as fast. That evening, with Dave and Leonard sheltered elsewhere, the rest of us settled into our modest accommodations in the Surfboard Hotel. I could hardly wait for the next day to begin

.

2 ISLAND GIRL

I'm hungry for a juicy life. I lean out my window at night and I can taste it out there, just waiting for me.
—Brigid Lowry, "Guitar Highway Rose"

March 26, 1968
Honolulu, Hawaii

I PUSHED THROUGH the hotel's back door, across the narrow alley, to emerge next to the Lemon Tree's stage an hour early Tuesday night. Several tables already held customers. I'd been unimpressed by the simplicity of the club, but it probably meant the Lemon Tree was a hangout for the locals living around here. It certainly wasn't a tourist trap like the fancy resorts on the other end of Waikiki. And, as we'd learned in Las Vegas, there were advantages to playing for the locals. Our audience, if they liked us, would welcome us into their island culture, something I looked forward to.

The nightclub, larger than it appeared from outside, was a plain rectangular box, open on one of the short ends to the street-side lanai on Kalakaua and the beach beyond. The front wall, made of folding panels, could be closed when necessary. The bar was located in front so it could serve the lanai when the wall was open, as well as the room. On the opposite wall was our stage. It was large but nothing fancy. It stood high enough for us to easily see over the dance floor no matter how crowded it became. Along both of the long sides, two rows of wooden columns, set about six feet in from the walls, supported the roof.

The place was nearly full before we took the stage. Though there were plenty of locals, as expected, I was surprised to see just as many blue, green, brown, tan, and several shades of camo, military uniforms. Hawaii was one of the main R&R, Rest & Relaxation, destinations for service men and women serving in Vietnam. The local residents welcomed us wholeheartedly but our music, our very presence, meant more to the soldiers, sailors, and airmen than just a night-long party.

Some drank with a steady precision meant to suppress grim memories and anxiety; they weren't here for our show. But for most of these young warriors, far from home and fresh from the terror and horror of life-and-death struggle, the songs we played made an indelible impression. Every tune stirred vivid memories, if only for a moment, of home, families, friends, lovers, and spouses for them.

By the beginning of our first weekend, we'd become more attuned to the heightened emotions at the Lemon Tree. We'd played in San Francisco East Bay clubs where tensions ran high between Hell's Angels and Mexican locals. This was a different kind of stress brought on by a sense of imminent life-threatening danger. Here, in Honolulu, the war in Vietnam was in-your-face real, not a mainland protest movement you could go home from afterward.

The war's violence was at a fever pitch when we arrived. American forces had been pouring into Schofield Barracks, Hickam Air Force Base, and the Marine base near Mokapu in response to the surprise North Vietnamese Tet offensive two months earlier. It wasn't the peaceful island getaway the incongruous ukulele music and charming flower necklaces at the airport had implied.

After our second set, I surveyed the noisy, jammed to the rafters room, looking for a spot to relax. We'd closed with Otis Redding's rollicking R&B rocker *Can't Turn You Loose,* and the room buzzed in response. In the back, out toward the lanai, I caught a glimpse of someone, a girl, tossing back long, luscious, dark hair in the jam-packed room. Curious, I jumped down from the stage for a better view.

I'd hoped to meet someone here who would help ease my jittery feelings from ending things with Marie. I'd shared so many experiences with her; she'd brought me into the warmth of her family's home in the Decoto barrio near where we'd played in Hayward. She'd helped me develop a taste for her culture's spicy food; we'd feasted on lobster fresh from the ocean in San Francisco—she'd rolled my first joint. Our drawn-out goodbye had been an emotional drain on both of us.

But I'd decided before leaving LA; I wouldn't take the chance of developing a long-term relationship again. It was unreasonable to expect them to work. We lived like nomads, rarely in a town more than a few weeks. I hadn't meant to hurt her and didn't want it to happen again.

On the other hand, and despite appearances, my instincts were monogamous—at least as much as circumstances permitted. From now on I would look for one compatible girlfriend, someone who'd enjoy a straightforward, companionable, and if the vibes were right, physical relationship, for as long as we were wherever we were playing. No expectations beyond that. If I couldn't find anyone, the search would probably still be fun—and the next city only a few weeks away. I would avoid attachments, I promised myself, keep things simple and fun.

I worked my way through smoky and crowded tables for a closer look at whoever owned that sumptuous tossed hair. Walking through the mass of boisterous soldiers here had taken some getting used to. Grinning servicemen jumped to their feet to shake my hand or pound me on the shoulder. I smiled, shook hands, listened to their names, and sometimes shared a hug as I progressed, until . . . my breath caught. I saw her laughing and talking with a girlfriend. I'd hoped she might be attractive, but she was way beyond that. She was an exotic heart-stopping beauty.

Jesus, God in heaven. What should I do? Guys would be all over a girl like her. She's already got somebody in her life; she has to have. She might even be married. Damn it! I hated getting rejected and willed myself to walk away—but I didn't. What if, in a million to one chance, she wasn't? How many times has a sixth sense told you in a glance you've seen someone special, and you failed to get up the nerve to say something? You pass each other without a word and the moment is gone forever. You never get over wondering, what might have happened.

If I walked away now, it would be like that. I wouldn't try later, and I'd hate myself forever. *But she's probably out of my league. She'll take one look and—* Don't think, keep moving. *So what, if it was only a slim chance? What was there to lose? I was just looking for someone to be with while we were in Hawaii. And if this was her, every second lost, I risked losing out to some other guy, even— heaven help me—one of my band buddies.* Well, in fairness, only a couple of them. We did have a pact—more guidelines really—going back to our earliest days. As the leader of the group, I'd insisted we set rules so clashes over girls wouldn't affect the band. If one of us showed interest in a girl, and if she responded, the others would steer clear. So far, it had worked.

But wait, this is wrong. I don't walk-up on a girl without at least an inviting smile. Meeting someone is always more natural. She usually knows somebody where we're working, and I get introduced—that's happened. Or maybe she's a girlfriend of a girl going out with one of the other guys or, sometimes— sometimes a girl has asked to meet me. Whatever I don't . . . I stopped. Here I was, standing like an idiot in front of her table.

She was focused on the crowd behind her as though searching for someone. Her sleeveless teal dress, garnished with large orchid blossoms and bamboo shoots, harmonized perfectly with her golden shoulders and slender arms. My heart slid south, my throat dry as the Mojave Desert.

"Uhhh," I finally croaked out. "Hi. Would you guys be okay with me buying you drinks?"

The cute, smaller girl eyed me suspiciously for a moment. "Guess if you buyin', I take one virgin Piña Colada. I'm Charlene." She turned to the one I wanted to meet, who either hadn't noticed me or, more likely, was ignoring me. "Theresa girl, what kine drink you like?"

Theresa. What an elegant name! It moved effortlessly through my consciousness. *Okay, quit it! Just hold on. She's gorgeous, sure—on the outside. She might be mean as a water moccasin, or brainlessly silly, like lights-on-but- no-one's-ever-coming-to-the-door, silly.*

"I'm just having Seven-Up." Her voice was low and rich. No matter what happened, I would never forget it. Her huge, wide-set eyes flickered up from under her lids for a moment before flicking off into the crowd again, scanning for someone, anyone probably, who wasn't me. *Oh God, she's truly stunning . . . and she doesn't sound silly. . . Verdict's still out on mean, though.*

I gave the waitress our order, adding a Coke for me.

"Would you mind if I sit with you?" The girls glanced at each other and Theresa shrugged with indifference.

"You're in the band, aren't you?" she accused when I was seated. I was forced to admit it. With a wry twist of her full lips, she dismissed me again, gazing away uninterested. *Well, no more than I'd expected. As soon as the drinks arrive, I'll make some lame excuse and slink away.*

"I've only been here a few days," I said, needing to fill the awkward pause while we waited. "It was weird, you know, getting off the plane. Had this weird feeling between footsteps. Lifted a foot, and before I could get it down, it was like walking in invisible quicksand."

"You stay island time now," Charlene diagnosed with an emphatic nod. I worried Theresa might get a crick in her neck; she looked away from me so purposefully.

"We've been playing in California and Las Vegas for the last few years. Thought those places were exotic. But this, being here is unreal, almost more than I can get my head around." I glanced toward the dark beach, moonlight rippling over the water less than a football field away. "I mean, look at that incredible beach over there. I hang out there as much as I can since we got here. Have to be careful, I sunburn easily. What's so surprising though, there's almost never anyone there. Sometimes, I go over there at night on my breaks to get away. If I walk far enough along behind those bushes and the palms, the club and traffic noise disappears. I feel like I'm all alone, a million miles away. . ." My smile slipped as I realized how touristy I must sound.

"Good thing I don't moonburn, I guess."

Charlene gave me a dark gaze. "You go over der at night-time, you betta watch out fo dem flyin' cockaroaches. Dey giants, lot bigger den da reglar ones. Big enuff fo carry you away."

Theresa tried to suppress a giggle as she turned to watch me parse through Charlene's dire warning. At least I was entertaining her.

I glanced into her eyes. The centers of her liquid, chocolate pupils swallowed the light. Her tan face, flawless without makeup, maybe a touch of mascara, a hint of eyeliner—maybe, but maybe not—sent shivers tingling down my spine. I silently prayed to any deity paying attention to change her mind and let her like me.

The drinks appeared, and our waitress smiled and said *mahalo*. I reconsidered my inclination to leave and didn't.

"*Pupule haoles*," Charlene said, in a caustic, weary tone. I took a moment trying to make sense of that.

"What's poo-poo-lay how-lees?"

Theresa hid another giggle behind a slender, cinnamon hand, but it couldn't hide her generous mouth's mischievous grin. "A *haole* is a white person." Her sudden, wide smile revealed her true face, one made for laughter. "Charlene called you a crazy white person." I couldn't help but snicker; Charlene sounded like a three-year-old.

"Guess I do sound kinda nutty. You guys could help me fit in here, though, so I won't sound so deranged."

Theresa poked her friend. "What now girl, got no mo nothin' rude fo say?" she taunted her.

Leonard banged a drum too soon. Much as I wanted to sit here entranced, I had to go play music. "Can I come back and talk to you in a few minutes?"

"We have to go," Theresa said.

Charlene turned to her. "We go stay, little bit more, sistah?" she pleaded. Theresa shook her head vigorously.

"No sistah. Said we must go. Now."

"Will you come back tomorrow, Saturday night?"

Charlene gazed at Theresa; when she said nothing, Charlene shrugged.

"Don't know, *haole*. *Pēlā paha*, maybe. Aloha."

Making my way back toward the stage, I realized I hadn't even told her my name. I looked back, but they were gone.

3 THE BUS STOP BENCH

If you don't know where you are, you don't know who you are.
—Wendell Berry

March 30, 1968
Honolulu, Hawaii

WE BEGAN WITH some of our more laid-back tunes Saturday night: *Get On Up*, a perky, little R&B dance number done in falsetto; *California Girls*, the Beach Boys' anthem that could have as easily been about Hawaiian girls; *The Way You Look Tonight*, us sounding so much like the Lettermen people had believed we were at Caesars Palace; and then *Comme Si Bella*, an Italian love song Frankie Valli recorded with the Romans before they became the Four Seasons. Our original vocal group in Indianapolis had learned this song's four-part harmony when we were in high school, and I still loved singing it. The title translates to something like "You Are So Beautiful," and for a moment, I thought of Pat, once my childhood sweetheart, now an estranged wife. I quickly put that thought away and wondered instead if the girl from last night would come in.

"Hey guys," Leonard stage-whispered, "we gotta get rockin'. These soldier-boys wanna boogie." Les nodded, and I retreated to the B3. I'd sung the first four songs up front with Dave, Mac, and Les. Dave was lean, and a little over six feet tall. Mac and I, at five-foot-eight, bookended him though Mac was skinny as a post and I was stocky. With Les, our poster boy on guitar at one end, and Mickey the Viking warrior on the other, I thought we made a pretty impressive front line. When we worked like this, it emphasized the four of us from the Midwest as the vocal core of the group. But for the get-down R&B groove of the Soul Survivors' *Expressway to Your Heart*, we needed the funky sound of the B3. Leonard gave me just enough time to slide onto the bench and rip into the tune, adjusting drawbars and the rotation speed of the Leslie speakers on the fly. We flew through the rest of the set, but by the end, Theresa and her friend hadn't appeared.

Standing on stage with the lights low before the next set, Mac caught me searching cocktail tables filling below us. "Checkin for that smoking-hot babe you was with last night, ain't you? You expectin her to come in tonight?"

"Theresa." I surveyed the crowd. "Her name's Theresa. I'm not sure. Maybe. We sat together for a whole break. That might mean something."

"Saw 'em leavin right after, too. More like you scared 'em off, stalkin 'em the way you did." He laughed, teasing me. "You looked like me huntin on the last day of deer season."

"Yeah. You're probably right." I turned back, disappointed. "She. . . They're not coming back. I must have been too pushy."

"Nope. Guess you musta done all right," His eye had caught something over my shoulder. "She and her foxy little friend are pullin out chairs at a table right now."

I spotted them, settling in nearer to the stage tonight. I grinned at Mac. He smiled and gave me a little headshake. Leonard clicked his sticks, and we were off into our first tune. After we'd cooked through Stevie Wonder's *Uptight*, I sang the McCoys' *Hang On Sloopy*. After playing mainly dance numbers, we closed the set with *Here, There and Everywhere*, one of my favorite Beatles' tunes. We'd learned this magical song just before leaving for Hawaii. I thought the harmony Les, Dave, and I interweaved caught the wistful mood of Paul McCartney's unusual chord changes. His lyrics of how a man can become a better person when he makes the woman he cares for happy held a personal wish for me.

"Hi," I said to Theresa when I came to their table. "Glad you came in." She nodded and turned away. It seemed to be her way of hiding her feelings. Tonight, she wore a beige sundress imprinted with creamy-white hibiscus blossoms, umber bamboo branches, and viridian ferns that accentuated her amber skin. She'd slipped a small plastic watch halfway up her left forearm, and a thin silver ring circled her tanned pinky finger.

Charlene tossed her head in Theresa's direction. "I tink you only like us come back so you can talk wid her." Charlene was a petite, vivacious girl, but she was right. I couldn't take my eyes off Theresa or prevent a silly grin whenever our eyes met. Seeing my face redden, the teeniest of smiles escaped before she gazed away again.

By the time our drinks arrived, the three of us were laughing and teasing the way we had Friday night. All too soon I'd have to go back on stage.

"On my next break," I said, "would you guys like to sit out on the lanai? Might be quieter out there." The roaring crowd of mostly drunk servicemen was ferociously loud.

Charlene offered her own suggestion. "Maybe betta you two do that. I'm stay, make sure dis table no grow legs and walk away."

When I came back to their table, I extended my hand to Theresa, aware I'd be touching her for the first time. She didn't seem the slightest bit nervous when she rested her warm, slim-fingered hand in mine, though she seemed even more preoccupied in avoiding my eyes. She gently withdrew her hand as she stood, and I followed her out to the club's porch-like lanai. In flat, woven sandals, she was only a couple of inches shorter than me.

Not finding a table outside, we crossed Kalakaua at the corner to a bench where the bus stopped. We sat backward on the wooden plank, facing the ocean through an opening between two guarding palms. The river of vehicles behind us separated us from the nightclub as we listened to the lazy rumble of surf creaming against the shore. A breeze slipped by, fluttering strands of her hair, and setting off a sibilant hiss among fingerlings in the palm leaves above. The half-moon had slipped past its zenith. Despite the distant lights of Waikiki and Honolulu, a million stars jeweled the sky. *It's just another night sky to her*, I thought, wondering what I could say to connect with her.

After a few moments, I understood she was waiting, giving me a chance, and I was wasting the opportunity. I had to say something, regardless of what idiotic thing might come out.

"How long will you stay tonight?"

She glanced up from her hands clasped on her lap and smiled out toward the water.

"Why do you ask that?"

Small fluorescent combers rolled up the deserted shoreline before receding away into nothingness. I tried to think of some witty response. Witty can often come out of my mouth more like smartass so— I went with the simple truth.

"Because I'm being stupid, letting time slip away when our breaks are so short. Especially considering how much I hoped you'd come in tonight, so I'd get another chance to talk with you again. And," I admitted, "it's the first thing that popped into my head."

She nodded as though I'd said something profound and paused for a long moment. "I can't be late. I have to be home before two o'clock."

"But you can stay until I'm off again, can't you? I'd like more time with you. I mean, it would take a lot of pressure off trying to be charming in these short stretches."

She glanced in my direction. "Why would you want to charm a local girl like me?" she said with a gentle, self-deprecating smile.

Without thinking, I answered her simple question with a deeper truth. "I could tell you how breathtaking I think you are; it would be easy because it's so true. But if I understand what I think— what I hope— you're asking, it's because I think you could connect me to the beauty of this incredible place," I gestured around us, "if you wanted to.

"This will sound weird, but when we travel to someplace for the first time, I'm not comfortable until I can get physically oriented. Sometimes I can do it by walking around outside, but usually, it takes getting in the car and driving around until I can locate myself in the world. I don't think that's gonna work here. But sitting here beside you, the way I am right now, I feel, in some small way, I can sense what it's like to be here."

Speaking unfiltered truth to someone I barely knew probably wasn't the smartest idea. Even to me, it sounded a little strange, but I sincerely wanted to connect to the person I hoped to meet in this way. "So, no matter what happens, thanks for that."

Theresa smiled, nodding as if making a decision. She shook her hair away from her eyes and gazed directly at me for the first time. Her eyes, bottomless umber pools, searched mine before she turned away with a smile. "I would meet you here—on our bench—on your next break if you like."

Back on stage, in the only sane spot left in the raving madhouse of fragmented noise and frantic movement that surrounded us, we worked through our setlist. In a rare and special moment during Spencer Davis's *Gimme Some Lovin'* when Leonard pounded his drums without accompaniment, he found and set a relentless rhythm. Mickey pounced on it with a driving metronomic bass line. I jumped in, staccato rhythm chords reinforcing the groove and setting the stage for Les. His solo didn't disappoint, shooting us off into a euphoric twenty-minute jailbreak jam. Les signaled me to solo a couple of times, and I danced my fingers across the keys giving it my best and wishing I'd practiced my scales more. The frantic pace fed our reeling warriors fervor to slam-dance across the floor.

Reading the crowd, we followed with *Louie, Louie* and then broke from the list, picking Wilson Pickett's arrangement of *Land of a Thousand Dances*. We preferred Wilson Pickett's quicker, funkier beat over The Headhunter's original recording; this was the song we'd played in the Hayward dive bar days when things got rough at the Town Club. We tried to work ourselves into another wicked jam but somehow squandered the chance and never reached our previous plateau of musical unity. The drunk and disorderly were too far-gone to recognize nuance anyway, we consoled ourselves with knowing that we'd at least helped them dance away their cares for another night.

I clambered through the deafening racket, past the table where the girls had been—now crowded with marines who gave me toothy smiles, ooh-rahs, and hoppy beer breath. Out on the lanai, the extended crowd overflowed onto the sidewalk, where some stayed erect by hanging onto the lanai's wrought iron railings. Across the street, Theresa waited at the bus stop bench for me.

"Getting pretty rowdy," I said, walking up, fascinated by how perfectly she fit the moonlit backdrop behind her. "I'm a little concerned for you and Charlene." We moved to the opposite side of the bench to sit.

"It's okay. Shirley and Stan and Stan's brother Dewey watch out for us here. Charlene is under their wing at the bar right now."

"Much as I wish you would stay, I'm glad you're leaving. I'd feel terrible if anything happened to you."

Her face softened as she tried to read mine. "What color are your eyes? I thought they were green at first, but now they seem bluish-gray . . . with a gold ring around them."

"Hazel. They change color sometimes. I think it depends on the light. My dad's got a gray eye and a blue one that seems green sometimes; guess mine came out more like that one."

She let me take one of her hands. The touch of her skin was electric. "Tell me something about you," I asked. "Do you live around here? What's your life like?"

She delicately retrieved her hand before she spoke. "It's nothing exciting. I live on Ewa side of Pearl Harbor in Waipahu, near the sugar plantation, not around here. As for my life, I'm like most people here I guess. We go to the water, to the dances and parties, we surf—"

"You're a surfer girl?" I imagined her in a bikini on a surfboard. "Do you surf on beaches like this one?" The palm trees above swayed in the moonlight of what I now considered to be our beach.

Her eyes widened as she grinned. "Oh, no. Kuhio Beach isn't good for surfing. A breakwater across there"—she pointed northwest toward the lights—"makes sure the tourists in Waikiki don't drown. I go to different beaches closer to my house, mostly at Tracks, near Nanakuli. The people are friendly there, and the surf is almost always good. You can choose breaks where the waves are not too dangerous."

"Next time we sing *Surfer Girl*, I'll be thinking of you."

She smiled and turned away again.

"When will you be back? When will I see you again?"

Her brow furrowed. "I don't know. Maybe next weekend. I don't have a car. I can only come when Charlene brings me."

"Can you give me your phone number? Could I call or meet you somewhere, so I'd have more than a few minutes at a time to get to know you? I don't have a car either, but I'm sure I can find a way to come get you. I could take you out to lunch or something. You could show me around."

She hesitated. "No, I can't give you my number." That didn't sound promising. She saw my smile slip. "You can give me yours if you like. I could call you. Would that be okay?"

"Sure. That would be perfect." I searched my suit's pockets for the scrap of paper I'd gotten with my room key from our roach hotel. It had the name of the hotel printed on it so she could look up the number.

She took it from me and said, "I have to go now. And you must go play. I haven't told you before, but I love your music. I love hearing you sing." She ducked her head and skipped through traffic across Kalakaua. With a quick wave, she disappeared into the crowded lanai near the bar.

4 SANDY BEACH

I must not fear. Fear is the mind-killer. Fear is the little-death that brings total obliteration.
—Frank Herbert, Dune, Bene Gesserit Fear Litany

April 1, 1968
Sandy Beach, Hawaii

ABOUT TEN IN the morning on our first day off, Leonard wedged open my room's paint-cracked and poorly-fitted door. A hint of the ocean's aroma wafted in. "Hey man, you wanna go for a ride?"

My eyes drifted up from the pages of *The Carpetbaggers*, a novel I'd fallen asleep reading last night. I hadn't been awake long, but Leonard, hyperactive by nature, was always up and about before the rest of us. A startlingly wide grin cracked his mournful Portuguese face.

"You've got a car?" I perked up. "Where do you want to go?"

"You said you wanted to see the island. Everybody else seems more interested in sleeping." In a powder-blue aloha shirt, flowered surf shorts, and a puka-shell necklace setting off his dark skin, he looked like he'd lived in the islands all his life instead of just his Navy hitch.

The thought of the inviting tropical setting outside made my dingy little room seem even more dark and cramped. And getting to understand more about this tiny island in the middle of the Pacific Ocean would help me learn more about Theresa. "Damn right I do. Let's go."

Memorizing the page number, I tossed aside Harold Robbins's relentless trashing of movie stars and Hollywood for later. It was getting pretty racy. I laced myself into the hand-made board shorts I'd splurged on from a local Waikiki surf shop. The green, white, and yellow canvas suit was stiff and tight as a second skin, especially snug around the family jewels. I figured wearing my new shorts whenever possible would loosen things down there. I pulled on a red-and-white-striped tee and grabbed sunglasses; stepping into slaps, I was ready to ride.

Leonard waited outside at the curb behind the wheel of a pink 1956 Ford convertible he'd scored from his local friends. Enveloped in another unbelievable day, we drove north on Kalakaua toward Diamond Head, the volcanic landmark on this end of Oahu.

We rode on with the top down, the wind ruffling our hair, drenched in sunlight and warmth. Leonard found a road that took us to a highway around the southern edge of Diamond Head where amazing shoreline vistas flew by my side of the car. I could have ridden like this all day. As we skirted along the ocean, Leonard pointed to the right. "Hanauma Bay. We gotta go snorkeling there while we're here. The guys will love it."

"Snorkeling? Like scuba diving?"

"No, a snorkel is a simple tube thing to breathe through while your head is under water. Scuba takes oxygen tanks, and you have to be certified. Navy trained me in scuba diving as part of my lifeguard training here. But snorkeling is better for Hanauma Bay. It's shallow, and underwater, behind the reef, it's clear as glass; there's no surf to whip up all the sand and junk."

A few minutes later, I stared at massive swells pounding against the beaches below. We'd passed Blowhole a few minutes ago, where Leonard had pointed out how the heavy surf drove into a lava-rock vent and forced ocean water up in a vertical shower. The waves seemed even higher here.

"God, this is dramatic," I said. Just past a sign reading Sandy Beach Park, a rugged dirt track angled off to parallel the beach. "Can we drive by the shore? I can't believe how cool this is."

We bumped along, staring at immense waves cresting white as they lifted, pausing at their peak, before thundering across the empty beach. Only a few cars were parked in the rough swaths cut into the shoreline brush. Leonard maneuvered into an open spot a few feet from the beach where waves rode in like a herd of gigantic sea animals stampeding out of the ocean.

"God in heaven, will you look at that? I never imagined seeing anything like this." As the waves roared in, foamy water retreating from the shore forced them into towering, crackling, translucent walls before gravity forced them to disintegrate. Lacy streamers of spindrift lingered behind the collapsing surge. I opened the door. "Let's get closer."

Leonard attempted to appear complacent, but I could tell he was impressed. "Those monsters are fifteen, sixteen feet high, maybe more."

"Look." Farther down the beach, I spotted dots like raisins in a sweet roll in the turbulent water. "Those flyspecks out there are people's heads," I said, astonished.

"Probably Kanaka body surfers. A longboard can get caught in a big wave and smack you on the head. It's probably safer in surf like this to make yourself flat and ride in on your stomach."

As Leonard spoke, one figure, another, and then another floated up, stroking the water. Beneath them, a massive watery fist lifted their bodies on its back.

"Kanakas?" I was just able to make out when the embedded riders stopped swimming and stiffened, arms tucked to their sides. Their bodies rose higher, sped faster, until the top of the wave, outrunning its base, caved toward the shore in slow motion. Its passengers fell, lost in the tumbling flood.

"Local Hawaiians, native Hawaiians. Whatever that means—not a lot of genuine Hawaiians anymore. Some locals call themselves Kanakas because they don't like mainlanders. They say the US turned their islands into a state so they could steal them."

"There are Hawaiians who hate us? Honestly?"

He nodded. "They can be dangerous. Lotta Navy guys got beat up when I was stationed here."

I looked along the shoreline to see more bodies riding in to scatter like bits of confetti in a crashing wave.

"Well, what they're doing is so damned cool, man. I want to do it, too. Got to be such a rush." I needed to experience how it felt to rise up and fly on the water toward the shore.

Leonard stared at me aghast. "You're not serious, are you?"

"Of course, I am." His perplexed expression questioned my sanity. "If they can do it, why can't I? Leonard, this is water. I used to run the stuff in my bathtub in Indiana. I dance around in showers of it every day. Hell, I've even been known to drink it. What's to be afraid of?" I gazed at the wild scene, entranced by the loud cracks and rumbling crashes of the waves as they smacked the wet sand.

"Do you have any idea of how to body surf? Cause I don't. I was a competition high diver here—in swimming pools." The combers kept getting bigger, more dramatic. I was anxious to get out in them before they got smaller.

"Well, any advice at all?" I shouted over the thundering ocean. "Anything you think I should know?"

"Yeah, you should stay on the beach." Leonard shook his head as he took in the massive surf. "Okay first, you have to be far enough out to catch the waves where they begin, where the ocean is smooth. Otherwise, they'll be going too fast. The main thing, when you see a wave forming, you need to swim hard. You have to be going as fast or faster than the wave as it gets to you. Once you're traveling with the wave, you tuck everything in and ride. But man, I've never been in anything like this kind of surf. I seriously don't think you should be doing this."

Unfazed, my shirt off, I turned toward the water. "Would you bring a towel from the car for when I get back?"

"If you're going to do this," he hollered after me, "maybe you should go watch the locals first." I glanced in their direction. Beach blankets and tatami mats laid out on the sand marked their territory. No, I didn't want to do that. If I embarrassed myself, I wanted as few people watching as possible.

"I'm only going to walk down to look at the surf," I said over my shoulder. "I won't go in if I think it's dangerous."

He nodded uncertainly.

At the ocean's edge, I studied the sea's retreat as it reared back in towering waves that hesitated, waiting for the salty, white rivulets left behind to catch up, before crashing in front of me and misting my face. The rush of water surged past my shins before slithering back to dislodge the sand beneath my feet. I watched several waves until it came to me in a flash—I knew how to do it. I got it— "grokked it" as Heinlein's Valentine Smith would say—naturally inferred the way the mechanics worked. If I ran out along with the retreating water, I could crash through the first wave at an angle and ride out in the swell that formed afterward. Easy.

I dashed forward, following the outrush, before I'd even made the decision. I might chicken out if I thought too long but more important, I felt the timing, sensed the split second when the wall of water would hesitate and weaken, and sprinted to meet it under the hulking wave's rising shadow. At the last minute, not daring to falter, I half-dove, half-jumped into and through the smooth panel of water wobbling in front of me. I didn't fear water. With no anticipation of danger, I only thought about which way the flow of foaming water would go. So far, so good. I rode up in a liquid elevator, the silent wave sweeping me along as it receded into the ocean, rocking me like a baby in a cradle. Kind of cool how the water carried me so smoothly out toward the sweet spot where the waves were born.

I pulled in a deep breath preparing to fight through the next soaring wave, but this swell subsided too, lifting me again until I seemed to be floating on the back of a powerful surging animal. What a creepy thought!

Distracting myself, I thought of Stan, the Lemon Tree owner, encouraging us to surf at the baby beach on Waikiki. A touristy and dumb experience as it turned out. I'd played a lot of sports and thought of myself as pretty athletic, but I'd only managed to get upright on the loaner board for a few seconds, one time. I was convinced, that similar to bike riding, speed would've made balancing on a surfboard easier. I was sure I would have done better in real waves and planned to try it soon, but now I wondered why I shouldn't choose body surfing instead.

The ocean's gentleness out here surprised me, though the sun's rays reflecting off the water in the shoreline's direction glared painfully into my eyes. Except for the muffled sound of surf pounding away at the distant shore, the sea around me was eerily silent. I slapped the water just to hear a noise. A receding wave subtly shifted me farther into the ocean. The view in that direction revealed nothing but an empty horizon. I glanced back to the beach to reorient myself and found I'd drifted farther than I realized. Leonard looked like a tiny mannequin.

Behind me, an incoming swell messed with my equilibrium for a moment. *I should begin body surfing back to shore*, I decided, until I noticed humpbacked swells still rising between me and where the ocean smoothed out, and the waves originated. It hadn't seemed so far when seen from the shore.

I thought about going farther out; it wouldn't be hard; the water wasn't so wild here. But . . . I didn't like the creepy feeling of the waves silently rising beneath me. The sensation made me suddenly aware there was nothing but water beneath me for a long way down, and, though I tried to shove the apprehension away—maybe not so empty. Creatures swam and crawled down there, probably some of them with sharp teeth. My imagination began to freak me out. I would definitely rather be back on the shore right now. Besides, I was getting a little tired. I should hitch a shorter ride on one of these waves and go back in. Enough for the first day, right?

I was flippering around toward the beach when I caught sight of Leonard's frantic gestures toward where the locals bodysurfed. A surge lifted me momentarily, and I glanced that way. There were no longer any surfers in the waves; the last of them were walking out of the water—leaving me alone out here in this enormous fucking ocean.

Don't panic you idiot, don't panic; as *Frank Herbert says in* Dune, "Fear is the little death." I had to stay calm, but I needed to get to shore now.

I glanced behind me trying to gauge the billows coming at me and started swimming. The wave behind me rose, and I flew up into sunlight for a moment before the resulting ripple left me behind in gurgling, frothy aftermath.

I tried to set a stroke, swimming ahead of the next giant wave in the set. It rose, quietly lifting me for a moment, before dropping me as I paddled in vain. Even so, I must be closer to shore. As the hump of water flew ahead of me, the following wave billowed higher than the last, its energy massive.

Knowing this might be my final chance to hitch a ride in, I gave everything left of my failing strength to catch the roaring behemoth surging around me. Helpless in the torrent, I rode up and up until the wave suddenly failed to support me. I fell several feet to land on hands and knees in shallow water rippling over a patch of rocky ground. Walls of water twice my height threatened from front and back. Though I was still too far away to see the shore, I struggled to plant my feet for a desperate sprint against the current toward land. Before I could move, a mountain of water drove me into the sea floor, pummeling and somersaulting me in the chaotic flow like lost driftwood. As the immense pressure passed over me, a reverse action—a wave in front of me, repulsed at the shore—formed for its return to the ocean. I'd fallen into a trough where powerful forces exploding beneath the monster surf pulled me in every direction.

I hoped to snatch a breath at the first hint of sunlight as the roller receded, but the opportunity never came. The outgoing wave caught and tumbled me across the ocean floor. With any sense of orientation beaten out of me in the confused, sand-filled flood, I lost track of which way to struggle toward precious air.

I wasn't going to get out of this.

I was really, actually going to die.

The realization came too suddenly to scare me. Jumbled wisps of emotions swarmed my consciousness: the sting of regret—Pat, our little boys—a sharp pinch of loss; this amazing girl I'd just met; the band. I would become a cautionary joke. I could almost hear Les: "What an idiot, you must have gone swimming with Larry." I grew more light-headed. Knuckles brushed against sandy bottom, and I reached to grip the sea floor with frantic fingers that were ripped away instantly. I was so disoriented, it seemed as if everything around me revolved instead of my body being rolled and turned. I didn't want to die, but I'd spent all my energy. Soon my lungs would force me to breathe seawater. Parts of me were going numb, shutting down, and I was close to losing consciousness.

But something stubborn inside refused to be reasonable. If my rational mind couldn't figure out where to go, my reptilian brain decided going anywhere else beat drowning. My limbs flailed as if electrified. My back bumped the bottom as I was driven down to the bottom again; this time I seized the sandy soil beneath me in a death grip. My toes dug in, my knees locked, and my butt cheeks clenched.

The sand moved, dragging me along wherever the current chose to go. If it ran the wrong direction, that would be it. Out of time, my lungs forced themselves open as the water broke to bright light and open air. I gasped desperately and struggled to my knees. I knew I wasn't safe, not yet—another mounting wave was rushing to capture and roll me out across the sea floor again. I would never survive that.

With rubbery legs and thrashing, lead-heavy arms, I scrambled onto the shore like a mad crab before they gave out. Wicked little wavelets washed mischievously up to my waist before reluctantly fading into the foam where I lay retching, choking, every muscle quivering. At the last possible moment, the capricious ocean had chosen to let me live.

Leonard hurried to the surf line and dragged me up the beach before throwing a towel across my back and falling beside me.

"You almost drowned," he yelled into my face as if I'd somehow missed that. I couldn't answer. My lungs pumped like bellows trying to suck in air. "Didn't you see the locals getting out? When the Kanakas leave the water, the surf is seriously dangerous."

Did someone knock Leonard silly? They hadn't left the waves until I was already way out there. But I couldn't answer. I lay in the sand, chest heaving, the physical reactions to being alive racking my system.

Sometime later, an hour, or maybe only ten minutes, I choked out, "Why the fuck didn't they help me? I'm probably nothing but a stupid asshole *haole* to them, but goddamn it, I almost drowned on their goddamned beach right in front of them."

Truthfully, I didn't believe for a second anyone could've helped me out of that raging flood. *And why should they risk their lives to save mine anyway?* But I wasn't in a frame of mind to accept responsibility for my own idiocy yet.

"For that matter, what about you? You're supposed to be a goddamned lifeguard, for chrissake." That sounded asinine even as the words escaped my mouth.

Leonard sat back on his heels, his head lowered. I glared north toward the local surfers, sitting on their tatami mats now, knowing they must think I'm the stupidest, most idiotic tourist they'd ever seen. Maybe so, but I was one of the luckiest ones, too. I pushed over onto my elbows and stared into the blind, grasping waves. I feared them. I understood their power now; I would never be tempted to go into them again, even little ones. I fell back, gazing into the neon-blue sky.

I didn't say much to Leonard as he maneuvered us back onto the highway and headed toward the Pali Highway through Oahu's central mountains. "Fastest way to Honolulu," he yelled over to me, "way faster than the way we came."

My disassociated and preoccupied mind ran through what had nearly happened over and over. After a few miles, Leonard broke through my soul-searching when he slowed to turn off the highway telling me we needed gas to get home. The rough exit took us into Waimanalo, a small beach town of wood-framed buildings that looked like a giant had dropped a Hollywood western movie set into a tropical jungle. He pulled into a station on the corner of a street running down to the shoreline. While he dealt with an attendant insisting Leonard pump his own gas, I got out to ease my tortured joints as well as loosen the stiffened, salt-infused bathing suit painfully chafing my genitals. I'd limped a few steps onto the empty road when I heard shouts coming from the street.

"What?" I called out, shading my eyes trying to make out what the brown man in shorts and a faded, surf-logo Tee shirt was yelling at me.

"I said, get in your fuckin' car, *haole*. Dis no place foh you go wanderin' round."

"Oh." I stood shocked, still not sure if he meant me.

"Guess you nevah heah me den, hah brah? I said, get your fucking ass outta heah. You like get all buss up or wat?"

Conserving as much dignity as possible, I lurched back to the convertible as Leonard put a hand on the door. "Leonard," I thumbed behind me. "I think this guy's got some kind of problem with us."

"Yeah, him and some of his friends." His eyes focused behind me. A rumbling roar caused me to look back. A couple of motorcycles pulled up next to the man, and more were rolling out of an alleyway farther up the street.

We vaulted into our seats and fishtailed out of the station back onto the narrow road out of town. The bikers shadowed us to the highway before turning back.

Leonard glanced at me. "Those are the kind of Kanakas we need to avoid."

Once we were back on the road, Leonard looked for a town called Kailua, where we turned inland on the Pali Highway toward the mountains. He shook his head and glanced my way once in a while as the road bored a path through thick jungle foliage, full of unsettling movement in the gusting breezes. As we switchbacked toward the heights, clouds scudding across the sky created a dramatic checkerboard of light and dark over the leeward side of the island.

Though it was still a sunlit afternoon where we were, the cloud-smothered mountaintop ahead threatened enough for us to stop and raise the convertible's roof. I'd been grateful for the wind and noise making conversation difficult. But even with the car closed up, we didn't speak. I was lost in my thoughts. I'd never thought about dying before this had happened. What if my luck had failed in those giant waves today? What difference would me dying have made to anyone? What difference does me living mean to anyone? Who would care? What would they think of such a foolish way to go? My parents, my sister. My band-brothers. What about Pat, my boys? *I have got to be better prepared. I can't be surprised like this. I get it: death can come between one heartbeat and the next; everything stops forever without warning. I have to be more aware.* I would never be able to think of death, or life, the way I had before.

The view from the Pali highway of sheer cliffs draped in brilliant, variegated greens broke through my brooding rumination. The mountain hid its treacherous, jagged rock walls behind delicate, feathered camouflage. The beauties of this island paradise concealed menace at every turn. At any other time, the height alone would've paralyzed me, but after Sandy Beach and Waimanalo's Kanakas, I was flat scared out.

Leonard waved out the window. "You're frickin' lucky you're getting to see this, you know." We gazed down on a cloud top in a distant valley, where rain fell below it in a spectacular, rainbow-producing shower. I wondered what new calamity it was inflicting on the land beneath it.

We entered and exited a pair of tunnels near the top of the Pali, and Leonard negotiated the descending zigzag road through intermittent showers. Foliage, thinner on this side of the mountain, slipped by our windows as we skirted east around Honolulu toward the distant ocean. I sensed Leonard's attempt to read me, his anger gone, long lines carved on his face.

"You do know I couldn't have saved you, don't you? If I'd gone into the surf after you, I would have drowned along with you. You do know that, right?" I nodded dreamily. I knew. I'd never actually blamed him. What had happened was my fault; my lack of impulse control and sheer idiocy had nearly killed me. I should have absolved him then, but soul-seared, still somewhere between this life and the next, I couldn't bring myself to speak.

"I was so scared," he mumbled, glancing toward me as he drove. "More scared than I've ever been for myself. More scared than you, I bet. I was sure I would have to tell everybody—including your new girlfriend—you wouldn't be coming back to the band."

5 LOVE AND DEATH

. . . there is no nakedness that compares to being naked in front of someone for the first time.
—John Irving

April 2, 1968
Waikiki, Honolulu, Hawaii

SKIN SUN-SCORCHED AND SALT-DRIED, body aching from a pummeling to the edge of eternity, I hung on the railing pulling myself up the few steps to the Surfboard's lobby. The desk clerk waved me to a stop to hand over a telephone message: "If you would like to see Theresa and Charlene tomorrow, please call number below." In an instant, my mood changed.

The one good thing about my room was the shower. Not fancy, but scads of hot water. I pushed it to the limit before collapsing across the bed. When I was able to drag myself downstairs to call Charlene on the lobby phone, I got great news.

"Aloha, Larry. Theresa wan know if you like go to hula show at Kapiolani Park tomorrow, den go after to zoo?"

"That would be fantastic. God yes, I would love that."

"So . . . why not you ask Dave come too if he like?" I told her I'd see if he was available. I knew he was interested in another girl, but Dave's attentions rarely lasted more than a few days, it wouldn't hurt to check.

"The park is close, you know, you guys can walk from Lemon Tree. Just go couple blocks Diamond Head on Kalakaua. We goin' wait for you in front of the grandstand at one o'clock, ah?"

I knew Kapiolani Park was close. My first night here I'd been startled out of bed by shrill screams in the wee hours of morning. I'd rushed down to alert the night clerk of the heartrending wails from screaming children outside. Unconcerned, he explained I was hearing cries from peacocks wandering through the park at night. They still woke me sometimes, but I could usually get back to sleep.

After a quick dinner, I hit the sack, sleeping twelve hours straight before waking stiff and sore in the same position I'd fallen asleep. I managed to get rehearsal pushed back to four, so I'd have more time. And I'd checked with Dave. He thought Charlene was cute, but he'd grown attached to a server at the club named Eileen.

The brisk walk along Kalakaua in the brilliant afternoon worked away most of the lingering physical effects from yesterday. Good, I didn't want to hobble around in front of the girls and be forced to admit what a doofus I'd been. As I hiked along the sidewalk, my senses seemed to expand, and flickers of electricity rippled across my nerve endings. Cries from the roaming peacocks mixed with exotic bird song and the traffic noise from Kalakaua felt exaggerated, over-vivid, and loud.

Cutting through the park, I thought I'd never seen anything more stunning than how the low-spreading canopies of banyan and pink-blossomed monkeypod trees cast inky shade across the emerald lawn. I seemed to be observing and hearing through an enhanced set of senses. I shivered in the warm sunshine remembering how lucky I'd been yesterday. I couldn't fully explain my expanded consciousness, but I hungered to embrace the gift of life I'd nearly lost.

Theresa waited near the entrance of the arena, more lovely than ever in a creamy, pale, mid-thigh sundress. Her long, dark hair spread across one shoulder, in motion from the gentle onshore breeze. Charlene seemed elfin beside her in colorful shorts and a twisted yellow halter-top. Her face fell when she realized I was alone. Dave sent his apologies, I told her, but couldn't make it. I didn't have the heart to tell her he was interested in someone else.

We chose a vantage point halfway up the bleachers on one side of the three-sided, open-air grandstand. Tourists from all over the world joined families of locals in seats around us. We chattered together until Hawaiian ladies of every dimension, age, and beauty poured out of thatched huts and enclosures on the fourth side of the amphitheater. The women had arrayed themselves in a variety of grass skirts, colorful tops, and leis, most with fresh red, blue, or yellow blooms in their hair. The only thing in common was their broad smiles as their hips swayed in rhythm to a ukulele band. Even the most overweight and oldest worked their posteriors in erotic wiggles.

"I know this is the public cultural center, but . . . uh, this seems pretty—well, X-rated."

"Most *haoles* notice only the hips," Theresa acknowledged. "But you should keep your eyes on the wahines' hands. The hands are telling a story." There was a kind of symmetry to the way their hands and arms moved, but any living and breathing male's attention would have gone directly to their swiveling bottoms.

"Do you see the wavy movement of their palms and fingers? That is the ocean's waves, and that one means an outrigger canoe. Theu are telling of how Polynesians spread across the ocean."

"I think I see what you mean." I knew this was a cultural thing, but the originator of this dance had to have been an excellent marketer determined to make sure the men and boys paid attention to their unwritten history.

"Traditionally, hula dancers don't wear tops." She leaned in to speak softly. "So maybe you wouldn't always watch their bottoms then, ah?"

"What have they got on under those grass skirts?" I asked in the spirit of the moment, knowing what the kilt-wearing ancestors of my Irish island heritage wore—or didn't. She laughed, a strong lusty laugh I instantly treasured.

"I think I will leave that to your imagination."

We enjoyed the show for a little while before I asked without thinking, "Do you dance like this, Theresa?" I liked the sound of saying her name. "Can you do the hula?"

"Of course, we learn it in classes about our culture in school. I can also do the ote'a, a Tahitian dance. Now that is truly sexy; hips move very fast."

"Will you dance like that for me sometime?" My face turned red; *why had I said that?* We're from different cultures. Without consciously meaning to, I might have made a very intimate request.

Her tanned skin didn't betray a blush, but she glanced shyly away. "I might."

I was relieved I hadn't offended her, but I secretly thought to watch her move that way would answer a fervent prayer.

"That would be the best day ever," I murmured.

After the hula show, the three of us wandered past food booths and tables spread out in a part of the park sheltered by a band of koa trees. Among them grew ferns and bushes filled with thick bunches of hibiscuses.

The scent of kalua pork made it my first choice, and I found some chicken baked in taro leaves, called laulau. Once I unpacked the steaming meat from its leafy envelope, I savored its smoky flavor. Fish wasn't high on my menu favorites, especially not raw as served in several dishes the girls tempted me to taste. Fortunately, a chunk of toasted butterfish fillet tasted much better than I expected. My taste buds were exploding with new flavors, not every one of them good. Theresa convinced me to try poi—a sour, soupy paste she said real Hawaiians ate at every meal, even breakfast. When I thought she wasn't looking, I dumped the purple mess into a bush.

We strolled along Kalakaua toward the zoo. I don't care much for zoos, the caged animals make me uncomfortable, but I wanted to stay near the target of my affection. At times, when it felt natural, we held hands as we wandered through the habitats. Charlene moped along behind. Theresa's growing warmth toward me kept me with her until the last minute.

When it came time to leave for rehearsal, she gave me her usual "aloha."

"It's a little confusing," I said, stretching out my last minutes with her. "Everyone here says aloha for both hello and goodbye. Seems to mean a lot of other things, too."

She smiled, and I thought again how much I hungered to make her smile like that all the time. "My Hawaiian grandmother told me 'alo,' the first part, is saying, 'from me, from my center.'" She gestured in a graceful, continuous motion, starting from her heart, up past her mouth and toward me, "and 'ha' means 'the breath of life.'" She shook her hair left and right, away from her face.

"Together, aloha means a willingness to share life with a person, like wishing someone good luck, only much more. More than there are words for."

I nodded but guessed I'd missed a lot in translation.

"Your grandmother is Hawaiian? Leonard told me there aren't many pure Hawaiians left anymore."

"Yes, it is true. I'm hapa Hawaiian, but my grandmother was a 100 percent native-Hawaiian woman, and my grandfather, Portuguese. And I have some Filipino, too, like Charlene."

"Yeah, dat's me," Charlene added. "One pure Filipina girl."

I couldn't delay any longer, but I had to ask what I'd wanted to know from the moment I'd seen her again. "Will you come to the Lemon Tree again soon? Maybe this weekend?"

"I will see if this girl will go." Theresa glanced at her friend, eyes crinkling with amusement. "If she will bring us, then yes." Charlene managed a tight grin and nodded. I finally forced myself to leave for rehearsal, wishing the weekend could start tomorrow.

The heightened sense of reality I'd experienced during the week—as though textures, colors, and sounds held a profound meaning—was amplified Friday night. Fascinated, I spent every possible moment with Theresa, and she encouraged my attention. I was disappointed that she was gone after we'd finished for the night, but she'd assured me she would be back tomorrow night.

When Theresa returned the next night, an animal heat drew me to her at every opportunity. She responded in subtle touches and glances. Charlene, shut out by our focused attention to each other, sulked in private.

Late in the night, when I couldn't find Theresa on the lanai or at the bus stop, I wasn't sure where to look. I wondered if she'd left, until . . . I caught her inviting gesture through the gap between the coconut palms and low palm grass separating Kalakaua and the beach. Smiling, she watched me cross the street before slipping out of sight behind the sheltering vegetation. I followed her into a secluded spot away from the lights. Here, behind the foliage, the metronomic slap of water rippling in stereo along the shoreline, muted the chaotic club and traffic noise.

Moonlight, flickering over Theresa's shadowed figure, heightened my awareness of her kneeling on the sand. A nervous smile of anticipation played across her face as she swept a beach towel across the sand several times before laying it out. "So we can be sure there are no flying cockroaches," she said with the hint of a smile, her expressive hands inviting me to join her.

"Oh, right," For a moment I was unsure what she meant, and then I smiled remembering Charlene's warning the night we met. As I moved down beside her, she leaned back on an elbow, wide eyes on me. Sand beneath the towel retained enough heat from the day's sun to warm us. The full moon silvered Theresa's features, the fallen palm fronds, and deserted beach; a fresh, coastal breeze rode over us from the murmuring and cresting surf a few yards away. Just days earlier, I'd learned to fear those waves, but here, they were caged, and I let myself be whisked into exotic fantasy.

I leaned to kiss her as she lifted her face to mine. The richness of her cushioned lips, open and welcoming, surprised and overwhelmed me. In an instant, our tongues touched, and it was as though we'd shared them with each other for all our lives.

Her breath caught for a moment as I dared to caress her untethered breasts, abundant and firm beneath her light dress. She leaned into me as sensitive nipples peaked through the thin fabric beneath my palms and fingers. As our kiss extended, my palm swept unimpeded across her taut stomach, under her gathered dress, to lightly grasp her waist. Searching, testing fingertips, left unsupervised by either of us, brushed under the thin cotton to span her flaring hip, and moved lower to cup her bottom.

Senses overwhelmed by shapes and textures, my hand continued its measured slide across the skin-carpeted curve of her taut cheek to where it joined the long muscle of her thigh; in sudden reflex, I pulled her into an embrace so passionate my breath caught until I wasn't sure if I would breathe again. Coconut, mingled with fresh flowers and a hint of spicy perspiration, scented her skin as we worked her panties over her ankles with them somehow ending up in my inside jacket pocket. She helped shuck me from my suit pants and briefs, allowing mischievous caresses from an intrusive breeze to cool my heated exposure.

Her thighs separated, inviting, as she lay back against the toweled sand. I moved over her, hard and heavy with painful throbs that matched my heartbeat. Her knees lifted, opening. Her eyes locked on mine, but her stare was inward as if observing her own physical reactions. I willed myself to enter her gently, but her body was ready. Her mouth widened into an O as I slid into complete, snug perfection. We froze, anchored in a moment outside of time, willing ourselves to capture sensations too intense for containment in mere memory.

In that moment, Theresa's eyes changed, reaching deep into mine as her face relaxed into an expression of tenderness, hope, and optimism I can hardly describe and will never forget—an emotion so pure, tears started at the corners of my eyes. In some mysterious way, I felt I'd entered the whole island through this lovely girl—as if I were interacting with everything around me: the beach, the whispering vegetation, the zephyring breeze, even the protective moon cloaking us in our private world.

Our bodies' natural rhythms took over, and her hands guided me, holding me to her in the supernatural naturalness of the Hawaiian night. Never had anything felt so right, as though an omniscient creator gazed down fondly on us, two of his human creatures consumed in the most ancient and powerful of rituals. With lips pressed together, breathing as one, we clung to each other, pressing as much skin against each other as possible. Our kiss broke as her eyes flew wide, searching mine for something. I don't know what expression she read on my face; I concentrated solely on drinking her in through every pore. Her smile grew. Had we been transported to Times Square in that instant, nothing could've stopped the primal motion driving me into Theresa's center.

In this elevated state, I felt as though I'd ascended toward the heavens; my whole existence in this world tilted on its axis. Whatever had happened in my life before, whatever it had taken for me to be in this moment, in this unbelievable place, with this extraordinary girl, it was a bedrock instant in my timeline, as vital as birth or death, a moment I had always been meant to reach, and in it—my soul was quieted.

I could hear her breathing in my ear, the catch as each new sensation lifted and shook her. As she peaked, her hands and arms locked to my hips; she threw her shoulders back, tilting her hips to pull us deeper into consummate harmony.

I existed entirely in this moment, my perception of past and future reduced to insignificance.

If I'd died then, which didn't seem impossible in the torrent of completion, my life would have been fulfilled and perfect. As we slid to our sides, still entwined, I savored the ecstasy of being alive. The thought of my life almost ending in the waves a few days earlier flickered through my awareness, and I had a moment of heartbreak for any other selves in parallel universes who might have drowned in their ocean's violent chaos and missed this night. If death meant to come for me here and now, I was ready, this experience marked and impressed in my memory with every ounce of effort I had to give.

Live music from across the street returned us to reality. The band had started without me. We parted gently, and I stood to help Theresa to her feet. Smiling, examining each other in a new light, she straightened her dress while I slipped into my suit pants. Theresa left me with a tender kiss before gliding across Kalakaua Avenue, beach towel and my room key in hand so she could shower and wait for me. Alone, the leaves in the palms above clicked and hissed like snakes in the stiffening breeze. The sensation of experiencing a momentous, once-in-a-lifetime event shivered through me and left me not entirely unaware of a fading, unspoken, commitment wrung from me by this island.

Pulling on my suit coat, I scurried through the riotous atmosphere in the club where I tried to sneak onstage to rejoin the band for the final songs of the night.

"Hey, I recognize that look," Mac said with a ridiculous grin as I slipped past him. "Bro has just been laid." I blushed neon. Les, strapped into his guitar, wanting to frown because I'd missed part of the set, but he couldn't hide a smirk.

"Yep, it's obvious." Dave shook his head in mock dismay. "We could turn off the lights; let you light the place up, man."

I opened my mouth to say something, but Leonard's sticks clicked out a tempo. I set the B3's drawbars for super funky with my left hand while my right slammed chord rhythms behind Mac dancing across the stage singing, Sam and Dave's *I Thank You. You guys are right on the money tonight*, I thought with a secret smile.

I cruised through our songs on automatic, attempting to connect the transcendent event I'd experienced to the reality surrounding me. We ended the night with Vanilla Fudge's hard rock remake of *Keep Me Hanging On*. I usually loved playing this song with the B3 cranked to the max, but I couldn't help wondering if my erotic fantasy had been no more than an illusion. The powerful ending of the staccato drum, bass, and guitar hits that overrode the eerie drama of the melody from the keyboard through the changing speeds of the organ's revolving Leslie speakers couldn't come soon enough. As the last note died, I flipped the organ's power switch off, slammed down the keyboard cover and dashed out of the back door, across the alley, and into the hotel.

Theresa's presence, fresh from the shower, damp hair glistening, her fawn-colored skin glowing, had transformed my over-bright, dingy little room into a romantic hideaway. We knew we would make love again. My craving for her had only intensified. We didn't speak of our encounter on the beach. I thought about saying something but didn't; words were flimsy messengers for what our bodies had already told each other.

Not surprisingly, since Theresa wore only a towel, our naked selves were unveiled within moments. Lying across my simple bed, shy but provocative, she invited my inspection. I looked down on her, drinking in her physical beauty. Her mixed European and Hawaiian ancestors had bequeathed her flawless skin—island-bronzed, except where a skimpy bikini had hidden beige strips and tiny patches from the sun. With her clothes on she was stunning; unclothed, she was fantasy made flesh. Her lean, youthful body was richly succulent—naturally rouged tips centered on proud breasts, waist tapering to hips wider than apparent in the loose sundresses I'd seen her in.

Her huge, dark eyes slid to the part of me that had invaded her. She glanced up to assure I was okay with her attention and then, with curiosity, reached out a tentative hand to weigh and stroke. I shivered, and moved a hand along her inner thigh, through the sumptuous thatch of silky black hair, still shiny and moist from the shower. I gasped at the silken richness hidden within. I tried to pull away long enough to run through the shower, but she raised her leg to replace my hand with the part of me she held.

We never considered turning off the harsh overhead light in the room. Instead, we studied each other in its illumination like scientists researching sensuality, reading expressions and slight eye movements to combine with our own powerful responses of where and how to please and be pleased. I didn't have skin or extremities enough to experience simultaneously all that I hungered for of her. Though our joining wasn't as mystical, hidden here away from the moon, our physicality reached greater heights as our bodies explored and dared to learn and demand more from one another.

I slid alongside her, spent for the moment but far from sated. Our hands drifted along each other's skin, comforting and soothing—touch-remembering—as perspiration dissipated.

"We've hardly said two words," I whispered to her. I caught a glimpse of her smile in profile, but she said nothing, and we lay quiescent.

"I have to go," she sighed at last. "Charlene will be waiting for me, not so patiently, I am sure."

I gently placed my hand on the side of her face. "Theresa, I want to see you again. Soon."

Her kiss on my palm was gentle yet full of promise. "I know. I want to be with you, too. Soon." She slipped out of bed and into the bathroom before returning to shrug into her dress and sandals, combing fingers through her hair.

"I've lost my underwear," she said with a little frown as her eyes searched my tiny room, "unless you've seen them."

"Oh." I'd been watching, mesmerized, as she dressed. "Oh, wait. I have them." I emptied out my coat pocket. Within moments, she'd gone, leaving me with ephemeral memories of the dream girl and a dream night just passed.

6 RUMORS OF WAR

Monsters don't sleep under your bed; they sleep inside your head.
—Theonette van Niekerk

April 17, 1968
Waikiki, Honolulu, Hawaii

"I SHOULDN'T BE HERE," the young sergeant whispered. "Shouldn't be here man. Got to get back." He gulped at a beer staring at nothing. It was a weeknight, which meant Theresa wasn't here, thank God, though I missed the physical way we were learning more about each other. The Lemon Tree was encouraging servicemen to participate as judges in a wet Tee shirt contest. Not the kind of demeaning event I'd generally want the band to be part of, but we relaxed our standards when it came to these guys. Mac, our charismatic R&B lead singer, was most involved, escorting soldiers to the stage to interact with a collection of young (and some not so young) female volunteers recruited from the audience by the club's master of ceremonies. The competition's rules, to the degree they existed, were ambiguous.

The girls competed in a thin Lemon Tree Tee shirt with nothing on underneath. A soldier splashed a gallon of cold water over each girl's chest, making sure to drench her thoroughly. From there, it seemed to be a popularity contest. Regulations allowed contestants to stretch the now translucent shirt to reveal nipple details and emphasize the erotic contours of the heft of their breasts through the thin cotton. Most simply flipped the Tee shirt up to compete *au natural*. The emcee made a half-hearted attempt to convince the girls to pull their shirts down, copping feels in the process, which went over huge with the well-oiled soldiers, sailors, marines, and airmen.

When an Army sergeant nominated by the crowd had been reluctant to take part in the mock contest, Mac went to encourage him. When he realized the soldier was agitated, and in some sort of distress, he brought him to the table I shared with Dave and Mickey in the quieter edge of the room where we were trying to stay out of the way. Anxiety rippled off him like heat from an open fire. The sergeant's unfocused eyes glittered as he continued to mumble, "Shouldn't be here, shouldn't be here, man."

Mac motioned to Donna, the nearest cocktail waitress, and asked her to bring him a rocks glass half full of Jack Daniels straight up, with water on the side.

"Put it on my tab, willya sweetheart?" He flashed her a brief smile. The young soldier was shorter than me and in dress cammies. Though I was sure he was in his mid-twenties, his face held the etched lines of an older man. He was jumpy as an over-wound super ball, and Mac did his best to settle him but, every once in a while, a tight little shudder ran through the young man.

"Now look soldier, this here's medicine." Mac put the drink into his hand and helped him find his mouth. "Consider this hair off the dog that shoulda bit you." The young warrior shot back the whiskey, and his eyes bugged before he swallowed. He grabbed the water glass Mac handed him and gulped it down.

In a minute, his color improved, and he seemed aware of us for the first time. His wild eyes searched beyond us for someone or something. Mac signaled Donna for another of the same.

"What's up sergeant?" Mac leaned in to examine his eyes. "You better now?"

He glared at Mac for a second, panting. "I shouldn't be here, sir. Need to get back to Nam. Oliver needs me. Me and Oliver—only ones left."

"Wanna tell us what happened?"

The soldier buried his face in his hands. For a minute, I didn't think he was going to speak again. "We was in the bush, recon, got pretty far from the LZ. Surprise firefight, got all separated. I don't know, support snafu probably. Had those all the time, guys who were supposed to know where we were in the shit didn't have no idea in actual fact. We was cut off, in the wrong goddamn place. Whole motherfucking squad shot up right in front of me. Oh, Jesus." His eyes squeezed out tears that ran back from his eyes as his head tilted, seeing something no one else could in the dim recesses of the Lemon Tree ceiling. I visualized automatic weapons' fire cutting his men to pieces in some remote jungle.

Donna returned, and Mac pressed another rocks glass into the young man's hand.

"Only Oliver and me. That's all. Chopper smoked us a new LZ to get us out. Just him and me alive in that field." He let out a sob and chugged the whiskey again. I could tell he wanted to feel it burn all the way down. "Oliver says, 'take Sergeant Sloan here, take him, he's the one needs to go to Hawaii. He's the one needs some R and R.'" He looked at us pleading. "I don't need no goddamn R and R. It's comin' on the wet season, mud up to your balls. I need to get back, take care of my guys—well, Oliver anyway. Can't help the others. Goddamnit, can't be stuck out here in the world leavin' Oliver to go into the shit without me. Can't have that. Wouldn't be right."

Behind us, the emcee caressed another breast and said something suggestive into the mic; the girl giggled and jiggled. Her backers in the audience went wild. All we knew to do for Mac's soldier, or any of the others, was listen to their stories and play our music for them.

Our personal manager, Jimmy O'Neill, had been a well-known deejay in LA before becoming the emcee of the popular, though short-lived, ABC Television show *Shindig!* He'd discovered us at a club in North Hollywood and worked out of Seymour Heller's office in West Hollywood. Seymour managed Liberace and a number of other celebrities. It was exciting having such famous representation, and another reason for optimism when it came to our career. Jimmy's part-time assistant and full-time girlfriend, Eve, tried to keep us stocked with publicity photos for us to give to the servicemen, but no matter how many we received, there were never enough. Mac spent a lot of his nights rushing around getting us to autograph them for different guys.

One night, he walked up to me with a guy in his greens. "This here is Jim McAfee with the 821st—umm, what's your unit again?"

Jim grinned. "Combat Security Police, we're Air Force special cops."

Mac, all business-like, handed me one of our publicity photos. "Sign the back, Larry. Got to get everyone's John Henry on here 'fore my main man, here, goes home."

"John Hancock," I said.

"Yeah, we're gettin him, too. Come on Jim, let's go."

These young men captured a special place in Mac's generous heart. He seemed to be tucking some soldier under his wing all the time. He hadn't told us much, but I'd heard him mention he'd been in the 101st Airborne as a teenager before the conflict in Vietnam had begun sinking under its own weight.

As the nights went by, many of the boys and men wanted to talk to us, to say hi, tell us their names and hometowns. They often treated us like long-lost friends they needed to remind what they'd been doing the last time they'd heard a song we played. It seemed like every song we knew brought back an important moment to someone. Hard-boiled combatants burst into tears hearing *Brown Eyed Girl* or the Box Tops' *The Letter*, or even some raucous Stones' tune, as their comrades threw arms around them in commiseration. Popular rock music was the background score of their young lives and a few notes from the Four Seasons, Otis Redding, the Beach Boys, Sam and Dave, or the Beatles could reanimate intense memories for them. We didn't talk among ourselves about the raw emotions our music exposed in these soldiers, but we showed and communicated it in the way we played and in the expressions on our faces. The response of these boys and young men validated the real reason why we lived the lives we did: the joy we received from affecting our audiences by singing and playing the music we loved for them. And our appreciation of the freedom they were protecting.

One guy, an information officer, told me the average age of the guys fighting this war on the ground was nineteen. Meaning most soldiers out in those jungles couldn't vote and legally weren't allowed to sit and drink in this nightclub. Most of them over there in the killing fields with their lives on the line were boys. And though they may have initially come as liberators, he said, some people back home are accusing them of being invaders. They didn't seem to understand that these boys were being commanded to burn down forests, farms, and plantations, or kill every single moving thing where and when some general thought it needful.

As the weeks went by, I realized I recognized these guys, these marauders, these raiders. They were the fuckups from my Junior Prom who upchucked off the balcony of the Indiana Roof Ballroom in downtown Indianapolis. They'd showered with me in PE, played grabass, climbed ropes, shot baskets, and all the other stuff teenagers do. There were good ones, bad ones, and just plain goofy ones. Someone decided to turn them into an army, so here they were, scared stiff, fighting like demons to despoil and kill people they'd dehumanized as gooks or slants before they killed them, or got killed themselves. Their leaders told them they had to.

I thought a lot of people would feel differently about the war if they saw our nation's warriors for what they were—just a bunch of boys from their cities, towns, and villages trying to survive a nightmare. You could be pissed at our government for what they were being made to do, for putting them in harm's way, but you'd have to take your hat off to their bravery in doing the best they could.

I thought about this bubble we occupied on this island dreamland, like an airlock between the war in Vietnam and their homes on the mainland—not a part of the war, but so close that guys in our club any given night might be fresh from a rice paddy or jungle recon the day before. I couldn't imagine how disorienting fighting like this must be—coming in only hours from mortal danger in a primitive alien culture in a land as far as possible from where they'd grown up to the sudden nightlife of Waikiki in the middle of a sparkling-clean Pacific Ocean. I could see how it might feel like the afterlife to some of them. No wonder our songs affected our soldier boys so profoundly.

It had been less than a year ago I'd received my induction notice into the Army. We were playing at a club in Downey, California, weeks before our first record was released. It was never far from my mind how scared I'd been in the Long Beach induction center where buses waited to whisk me, and hundreds of others young men and boys, to Texas to turn us into cannon fodder. The band had already left for Las Vegas, my replacement contacted and waiting there, before I even entered the warehouse-sized building. No one but Marie had believed the Hollywood attorney, who my new friends at the Pink Carousel had found for me, could save me from conscription. If he hadn't, it could have easily been me in uniform here in this nightclub.

The relief from my dramatic escape from induction last summer came from knowing I wouldn't be forced out of my band, my family of brothers. The longer we stayed among these soldiers, the more I came to terms with the odd realization that if things had broken differently, some of them might have become my brothers, instead. Or worse, I could have been one of those brothers who came home in a sack.

Many young people skipped off to Canada or found other ways to avoid going to fight in Vietnam—an action in normal times, considered treasonous. Many Americans despised the Vietnam War so vigorously that they felt forced to stand against a government who demanded the nation's youth risk death or maiming in a tiny, primitive country's civil war on the opposite side of the world. Television, for the first time, was ripping away the heroic facade of war portrayed by John Wayne and Audie Murphy.

I numbered among those draft dodgers, I suppose, but not in political protest. I was far too immersed in my precious life to have opinions about the events roiling the nation. Too ignorant to even be afraid. If I'd been pressed to answer whether we should have been fighting in Vietnam back then, I probably would have answered yes. If our president, our government, said we needed to fight in some godforsaken part of the world, I would have trusted there was a good reason. That was before coming here, seeing for myself the unending river of wasted lives the decisions of our country's leaders were producing. Five hundred soldiers a week were dying in Vietnam while we were here, which didn't count how many had been wounded physically, mentally, and spiritually.

Around me here were young men, recently recovered from physical wounds, suffering from anguish, fatigue, and in many cases, conspicuous mental illness. It wasn't unusual to see a soldier sit alone, face full of tears, or talking to some invisible companion. Moral compasses swung wildly between the conflicting values they'd learned from parents, teachers, and religion and the practical demands of survival in a brutal environment. Many masked their terror behind arrogant bravery and binge drinking, and there were those whose humanity seemed entirely burned away.

I pitied them and tried hard to understand what they were going through. In all honesty, though, I was glad as hell I wasn't one of them. I felt a survivor's remorse for my actions but would never regret them. If I'd known what the Army had in store for me when that induction notice arrived, I'd have been willing to do far more than I had to avoid the barbaric experiences these young men and boys were desperately trying to survive.

7 SMOKE DREAMS

Reality leaves a lot to the imagination.
—John Lennon

April 19, 1968
Waikiki, Honolulu, Hawaii

FROM THE MOMENT she'd shown interest in me I'd hoped Theresa would become my lover and companion while I was in Hawaii. Since the overwhelmingly romantic night on the beach with her, I'd had no room for thoughts of anyone else. Over the following weeks, she came to see me most weekend afternoons, staying until well after my nights onstage ended. She was animated and playful now; it was hard to believe she was the same girl who'd been so reserved when I first tried to catch her attention.

We hungered for each other's affection, urgently making love as soon as we could, and, as often as time permitted, in tender passion afterward. Though her uninhibited enthusiasm was unlimited, I got the impression what she experienced with me was new and fresh to her—an endearing quality. She was eager to learn what turned on either or both of us, which seemed to be almost everything. As we became more comfortable in sharing ourselves, her growing confidence and inventiveness consistently left me breathless, and her enjoyment in making my desires hers, captivating. When we weren't indulgently feasting on sex, we laughed and talked about everything under the sun, which meant she was an excellent listener. I hadn't learned much about her life when she wasn't with me. There was no reason to ask a lot of questions; she was my island fantasy girl. Our time together was just an incredible interlude during an amazing few months far from home on the mainland.

After the last show Friday night, Theresa sat perched on the bed with a knowing grin. "I found a bag of grass in your nightstand." She'd come to the room early to get out of the smoky club and shower before I got back at the end of the night. Her little makeup purse lay open on the weathered dresser. Something was appealing about her looking around, making herself at home in my room. I smiled tentatively, unsure of her reaction.

"More than willing to share but I didn't know. . ."

"Didn't know if I knew about marijuana?" she interrupted. "Really? Growing up on an island where Maui Wowie grows wild everywhere?" She pulled open the drawer in the nightstand and tossed me the baggie with a mischievous grin. "Go ahead, roll one. I've smoked lots of this before."

"Maybe not like this. This weed is wicked; it's called ganje." I hefted the plastic bag. "A lot stronger than anything I've ever smoked before. Guy Mac got it from last Wednesday says it's being brought back from Vietnam in soldiers' backpacks. When Mac and Dave and I went out in the alley behind the club to try it out, this guy rolled the skinniest joint you could imagine. Including him, we each got two hits. Two hits off this toothpick of a joint, and I could barely remember my name." I shrugged off my shirt and kicked off my shoes. "Haven't gotten high since we left LA, don't think any of us have. Didn't dare bring any grass with us on the plane. Could be why we got so loaded from this stuff." By now I was down to my undershorts.

"When we started the set, I was so stoned I didn't recognize the keys on my B3's keyboard, and Mac and Dave couldn't remember the words to the first songs. Les was royally pissed off. Nobody's supposed to get high at the gig, but it hadn't happened on purpose. Mac just wanted a little taste of what the guy was selling before he bought some, Dave and I were tagging along.

"When Les realized we were stoned, he did his best to embarrass us on stage as punishment for breaking the rules. But it didn't work. We were too out of it to be shamed, and nobody in the place cared anyway as long as we played music. So instead, the whole thing got hilarious. When the set ended, and we could explain what happened, Les thought about it for a minute and asked Mac to get him some, too."

Unimpressed by my story, Theresa told me she would take her chances, so I rolled a slender joint for us to share. I was a little self-conscious of how my joint humped in the middle as if a tiny white snake had swallowed a small marble.

"Rollin' it slim," I said, lighting and handing the rough cylinder to her. "Cause you might want to go easy with this stuff." She twisted it in her slim fingers, examining my skill.

"Not too good at this, are you?"

"So take off for style points. It smokes, you know. That's what counts." She took a big hit and gave me a tolerant smile as I pulled off my shorts and joined her on the bed.

"I found something else in there." She held the smoke in, gesturing at the nightstand as she exhaled.

"Oh, what else?"

She opened the nightstand's bottom drawer, smiling, and lifted out a decrepit and yellowing paperback book titled *Forbidden Love*. I took it from her.

"I've never opened that drawer before." On the cover, an illustration displayed two bare-chested men embraced in a kiss. I flipped through the pages.

"Uh, pretty sure this is gay porn, must have been left behind by a previous resident." There'd been indications of a thriving homosexual community living in the raggedy hotel before Stan and Shirley bought the place. Little by little, management had been encouraging them to leave. I quickly closed the tattered paperback before any of it triggered my yuk reaction.

"What's the matter? I thought it might be funny to look at." Theresa passed the smoldering joint back.

"You do know it's about men having sex with each other, don't you?"

"Guess that would bother you more than me, ah?" Grinning, she took the paperback from me and opened it to mid-book.

"Oh!" she said, after another hit on our shared smoke. "You've got to hear this." She read out loud in a teasing voice as though she was reciting in class. I tried to close my ears, worried what she was reading might ruin the mood.

She stopped reading long enough to give me a long glance. She returned to the disintegrating paperback and spoke more carefully — the love scene she'd been reading described a man fellating another man. If you could get past the gender thing, it was intense and clinically graphic. Every so often she paused to look at me. She noticed I'd gone embarrassingly erect, which I'd been trying to hide.

She studied me for a moment. "Would you want me to do what I'm reading to you?"

"Ah, umm. Well yeah, sure. What man wouldn't?"

"All of it, even the end part?"

"Emphatically yes. I mean, only if you wanted to, though."

"It sounds interesting," she said, putting the book aside. "If I can do it right, it seems to me you will like it a lot." She playfully tapped my erection to watch it bob back, already shockingly comfortable in our intimacy. "Let's finish smoking, and I will surely try."

The love-making that followed ripened into another erotic fantasy, full of sensual impressions impossible to forget, details tender beyond remembering. A couple of times over the weekend I caught her re-reading sections of *Forbidden Love*, and soon, very soon, as the days and especially the nights went by, she'd perfected techniques I'd only heard about and surpassed anything similar I'd ever experienced.

Despite the lack of a lesbian sex manual, we both delighted in my explorations of her exquisite body. My eyes exulted her female curves, my running hands swept around and across her buoyant breasts, teasing nipples stiffened with fingertips and lips; I savored the dense and silky pelt furnishing the crease between her legs, redolent with a personal perfume that would've aroused me if I'd been a dead man. We lost ourselves in ecstasies of discovery and exploration.

One afternoon she asked me to hold up my palm so she could put her hand against mine, thumb to thumb, little finger to little finger.

"Do you think my hands are too big?" she asked.

"Too big? No, they're perfect." The tips of her long slender fingers matched mine, her middle finger, maybe a touch longer. I could easily visualize them caressing me. "Why?"

"Some people think Hawaiians have big hands and feet." She popped up a naked foot and wriggled the toes. "I am only hapa-Hawaiian, so maybe mine aren't so much. I wanted to know if you thought so."

Often, in the late afternoon, we found time to slip out to the club's lanai and look out to our beach and watch the shadows grow long as dusk descended over the island. These hours of quiet conversation, gentle laughter, and affectionate comfort-touching were coming to mean as much to me as our lovemaking. I was experiencing with Theresa a freestyle way of life in a Hawaii most visitors would never see. On the girlfriend front, things were working out better than I could have dreamed.

On sun-hazy weekend afternoons, we sometimes walked along Kalakaua toward Waikiki, checking out the sidewalk shops. One of Theresa's favorite treats was "shave ice"—thin ice chips in a paper cone flavored with tropical flavors like pineapple, mango, guava, and passion fruit. I liked them too, but I didn't care for every treat she did.

Several of us caught a ride to the Ala Moana Shopping Center to see the Saturday matinee showing of *2001*, a movie adapted from Arthur C. Clarke's stories. Stoned to the gills, we nearly left our skulls during one of the character's transformation through a monolith. I couldn't stop talking about it. That hadn't been some schlock horror crap up on the movie screen that some idiot called science fiction. It was the real deal, from Arthur C. Clarke, one of my favorite science fiction author's books.

Afterward, Theresa wanted to visit the Crack Seed Store, where her favorite treats, salty dried plums called *li hing mui*, were sold. A small bag of these dried-up lumps would last her several days. She chewed them like a ballplayer chews tobacco, a lump in her cheek for an hour or more. I asked to try one, but she refused, assuring me I wouldn't like them, and she didn't want to waste any. I dogged her until she finally gave in. The hard, dried fruit required mastication and lots of saliva to release a sweet and sour, but mostly salty flavor so strong it brought me to tears. I was determined to like it even though I was forced to spit it out on my palm every couple of minutes. My valiant effort continued until I finally gave up and hawked the soggy mess into the gutter. I kept her in stitches laughing at the faces I made. Though I laughed along with her, I didn't ask for another one.

Without question, Hawaii was a distraction to the band, and as the bandleader, I'd been woefully derelict in my duties. The desk clerk had to come to my room with two telegrams he'd waited days for me to pick up. In the first, dated several days earlier, Jimmy wrote that he'd gotten Mac instead of me when he called and asked him to have me phone the office in LA, collect. Uh oh, that was the day we discovered and smoked ganje, which explained why Mac forgot to tell me. The second, from two days earlier, read: "Rumor has it, Larry Dunlap alive and well in Honolulu. Please confirm immediately."

When I got Jimmy on the line, he told me he'd guaranteed us a spot on the *Steve Allen Show*, though no specific date had been set yet. Also, we'd be doing a TV special with the Grass Roots, and another was in the works with Billy Joe Royal. Last, he wanted me to consider accepting dates at the Factory and other influential Hollywood clubs after Hawaii to promote *Look Back In Love* rather than going to Indianapolis. Exciting stuff, but as far as rescheduling Indiana, no dice, it would be the first time in three years since some of us had seen our families and friends—too many people would be disappointed.

"And oh, before you hang up, Larry," Jimmy said, "you should know that Eddie growled at me. He wants to know when he's getting the finished arrangements for the new tunes you're supposed to record when you get back to LA." Hawaiian time held us in its grip; I promised him we'd get back to work on this enchanted island of Circe soon.

Theresa and I settled into a routine. I hungered for Friday and Saturday late afternoons and nights with Theresa, letting everything else take a backseat. We struggled as a band to maintain our professionalism in the midst of the giant beach party taking place at the Lemon Tree every night. We tried to stick with wearing matching outfits on weekends, but on weeknights we'd gone native, playing in aloha shirts and long shorts, and bathing suits or shorts and tank tops at Saturday afternoon jam sessions. Mac often kept an unlit Camel behind his ear unless it was working in an ashtray next to a drink on a table by the stage.

I grew elongated sideburns down to my jawbone in furry isosceles triangles; they came in bright red in weird contrast to my dirty-blond mop-top. I kept them anyway; I thought they looked kind of Beatle-y. Since the constant breezes blew my hair every which way, I didn't bother with haircuts, rarely even a comb. Nobody seemed to mind.

Rehearsals went unscheduled as, beguiled by sun, sand, and sea, we snorkeled at Hanauma Bay and visited North Shore, the Hawaiian Cultural Center, and other island highlights. There was no demand from our mostly military audience to learn new songs; their musical preferences were time-warped by memories of home. Our club owners, Stan and Shirley always had some event on tap—informal luaus, lunches, or dinners—with standing invitations for us.

We visited the Nooney Rickett Five, friends of ours from Indianapolis when they performed in the International Marketplace. Our bands had hung out together in San Francisco during our year in North Beach. Most of us were having a fine old time, except for Mickey, who'd begun showing signs of distress at being stuck on a small island in the middle of a big ocean—a kind of geographic claustrophobia locals called rock fever. I thought it was probably caused by homesickness for his wife, Lora, and little boy, Mikey. But I wasn't homesick. I loved Hawaii.

8 BUNNY'S TALE

Be wary then; best safety lies in fear.
—Shakespeare, *Hamlet*

April 26, 1968
Waikiki, Honolulu, Hawaii

THE FOLLOWING FRIDAY, Theresa and I sat alone on the Lemon Tree lanai sipping fruit juices with our feet up. She'd twisted her lustrous hair back into a bun; a pale sundress covered her bikini. On her feet were braided leather sandals I'd found for her in a Waikiki shop. I wore an unbuttoned short-sleeved shirt over my canvas board shorts. Except for occasional pedestrian and light traffic on Kalakaua, we enjoyed the afternoon's solitude. Our chairs were pulled close so we could touch while we watched cloud shapes shed shadows across the rippling ocean in the approaching dusk. As usual, the warm breezes ruffled our hair, carrying indecipherable secrets from far away. I turned and smiled at Theresa, content to be by her side.

"Larry," she said, a tentative tone in her voice. "Would you mind if I stay with you tomorrow night? All night?"

"You mean you and me sleeping tucked tight together until morning?" We spent hours entwined together in my narrow bed, napping in the afternoons, but we'd never tried a sleepover.

"Yes." She grinned. "I like it when we fit together like two spoons. I get so comfortable, sometimes it's hard to make myself leave."

"That would be amazing. I would love snuggling with you all night, sweetheart." Waking up in each other's arms seemed a natural progression in our relationship. I liked the idea and hoped this would lead to her staying all night more often.

"Great," she said. "That will help a lot." She jumped up and pulled me to my feet. "Let's go for something to eat at the noodle shop." I loved the way she concentrated on every item on the menu before making a choice, how enthusiastically she enjoyed eating, slurping her noodles and voraciously spearing every morsel on her plate or in her bowl. She'd steal bits from me and offer me tastes of her choices. Every day was an adventure.

There was something odd about her response to my exuberant agreement to a sleepover that tickled my brain, but it didn't percolate through until the next day. How would sleeping all night with me help her? I hadn't decided whether I would mention it or not when she came to my room Saturday afternoon with her overnight case.

Ravenous for each other, the decision about whether to ask her about how I was helping her got postponed again until we lay nestled together.

"Theresa, is there some reason why you need to stay here all night? I mean, besides the obvious. You made sleeping here sound like I'd be doing you a favor."

She sat up, slipped on her bikini bottoms and rustled into her sundress as she moved to sit at the little table. "You know I like being curled up with you. I've wanted to let myself go to sleep instead of leaving, even if I never said so."

I swung my feet to the floor looking for my boxers. I was missing something. "I'm looking forward to tonight, but if there's some other reason you need to be here, I'm okay with that, too."

Theresa gazed at her fingers twining together on the table, reluctant to acknowledge I'd said anything.

"Look, I want you to be here. The way you asked seemed strange, that's all. I can't help being curious."

Her face twisted away from me. "I don't want to say, but I don't want to lie to you either." Her swollen eyes reproached me. "Someone is coming tomorrow to take me to the mainland. I have to go meet them."

I held back shock and surprise, and yes, disappointment. Sleeping together in each other's arms, the new experience of waking together, wasn't the reason she was here.

This would also mean goodbye; our unbelievable fantasy would end. But aside from that—someone coming to take her away—it sounded all wrong. I wasn't good at probing questions, especially when I feared the answers, but I had to ask them. Though she was embarrassed to tell me, eventually it came out. Before we met, she'd been seeing a musician in a band who'd played at the Lemon Tree previously. Though our fragile relationship was evolving, I didn't know much about her life beyond the hours we were together. I had no right to be jealous, but these revelations produced bruises I felt on many levels.

"I'm going to have my own apartment on the mainland," she said, voice small with the sort of fragile hope you deceive yourself with when the rent's due, and you're praying your lottery ticket will hit. "In San Francisco. And I'll have a good job—as a model. I do model sometimes, you know, at Liberty House."

I sighed from somewhere around my heels. "Theresa . . . who, in what band, honey? Who promised you this?" I worried at this question the way a tongue harries a sore tooth.

"What difference would that make?"

I hadn't been able to keep myself from asking about this nameless musician. I wanted to ask how she felt about him, but she was right, what difference did it make? Except to make me feel crappy about being a musician.

Her eyes dulled, and she glanced away. "He said he would get me a good job on the mainland."

"What's supposed to happen? There's someone you're supposed to meet?"

"A woman will be here Sunday morning to take me and some other girls to California. He said he would try to come, too, if he could. If not, the woman would arrange a place for us to stay until he could come to help me pick out my apartment." She pulled at a strand of her hair as the fantasy she'd let herself believe unraveled with every word she spoke. "She would get us easy work in the beginning so we could get on our feet." She spoke in a plaintive tone, like a disappointed child.

My heart made my stomach ache through a difficult discussion for us both. She told me she'd only been with him the last couple of weeks he'd played here, but she was the one he loved, even though other girls were offered trips to the mainland, too. I'd heard enough. In rising panic, I realized the undeniable truth. Theresa was being recruited into the sex trade. How could such awful things be happening in this incredible place?

I'd learned about sex trafficking from Bunny, a girl Mac shared a faded mini-mansion with in Indianapolis in late 1964, three and a half years ago. After Dave and I saw Mac performing in a slick nightclub band from Cincinnati, we discovered he'd left his group and was living with two girls in a large house on North Meridian Street near downtown, not far from the Governor's Mansion. We needed a singer, so I decided there was nothing to lose in asking Mac if he'd like to sing in my vocal group, the Reflections. From the moment he'd introduced me to Bunny, who I'd assumed was his girlfriend, I'd been morbidly fascinated by her thinly veiled profession.

I'd never considered the existence of a dark underbelly to the Wonder-Bread town my friends and I often disparaged as "Indianoplace." Mac's comments more than hinted at Bunny's ambiguous celebrity in the shadowy under-city where she consorted with vice detectives, corrupt police, judges, and high officials in city and state government. She must have known countless sordid stories if she ever dared tell them. I hinted to Mac about my interest in more details, but he was reluctant to elaborate. One thing he did say: "Never ask a working girl why she does what she does—'bout the worst thing you can ask."

My wife, Pat, met Bunny in the normal course of events when Mac joined the group. I hadn't yet figured out what to tell my innocent, young wife about Bunny; I was still trying to wrap my mind around who she was myself. Pat naturally assumed as I had at first, that she was Mac's girlfriend, similar to the other girlfriends of the guys I'd sung with and known from school. Soon, she'd struck up a friendship I'd never seen coming. On a fateful fall night, Bunny invited Pat to join her in a secret field trip to Cincinnati to check out a suspected rival for Mac's affection. To say the outing ended badly is to suggest the Civil War was a minor scuffle.

Not long afterward, I dropped by the mansion to pick Mac up for rehearsal. Bunny and I sat together in the mansion's sitting room while I waited for him. I'd never had a real conversation with her before. She turned the topic to Pat.

"You know, Larry, I love your sweet wife. I never met anyone so smart and still so innocent," she told me. "We had such fun talks on the phone. I never had a girlfriend to say silly girl stuff to before. I suppose I knew she didn't understand what I do for a living." Bunny's sideways glance revealed her vulnerability. I couldn't help but sympathize with her wistful desire to connect with someone who lived a normal life, as she saw it.

"I guess we can't be friends anymore now that Pat knows what I am. I'll miss that very much."

"I can't say for sure how she feels, Bunny," I said, realizing what she was asking. "I think she's a little embarrassed about being in the middle of what happened, but she's not mad at anybody." Bunny's suspected rival had turned out to be Mac's wife, a personal detail he'd failed to mention to her, or us.

She nodded. "I sound like a stupid school girl, and God knows, I've never been one of those." She stared away from me, despondent. I understood Mac's convoluted relationship with Bunny much better now, of course, but in those early days, Bunny had displayed a proprietary affection for Mac I assumed he reciprocated. I'm sure what she discovered in Cincinnati, and the ferocious fights with Mac that followed, disheartened her more, but her regret for the loss of her short-lived friendship with Pat was touching.

"Do you know how someone becomes what I am?" she asked softly. The delicate lines etched beneath her eyes were beginning to concede her age and experience.

"No, Bunny, I don't." I itched with curiosity. I couldn't deny my lascivious desire to hear what choices had brought her to this life.

She nodded and paused before going on. "I was an orphan." She sighed with regret. "An orphan in Chicago. Found out my folks hailed from Tennessee originally, never figured out how I got to Chicago, though. As a kid, you don't have a way to measure how bad a place is." Her eyes drilled into me, but a glimmer of the little girl she might have been shined in them somewhere. "I never remember being happy as a child." She straightened the skirt of her long, flowing day dress and reached for a cigarette. Bunny's hair was done up in tight blonde curls, but I'd seen her real hair—buzz-cut short for wigs she used to help create erotic illusions in her professional roles.

"I was such a pretty little thing, you see, so cute, and I craved the attention I got from that as a youngster. Until I turned thirteen and my ass was sold to the Chicago mob so they could turn me out." I bit back a shocked expression at the casual way she uttered that brutal statement.

"I can't say the mob picked me out of the child welfare system exactly, but the bosses musta paid off whoever the hell did. Of course, I didn't understand this then. They started me out right away, taught me everything about sucking and fucking every which way, men and women both, sometimes together." She spoke matter-of-factly, just reciting the truth of it. "The training was simple. They'd treat me nice if I did everything they told me to and starve and beat the shit out of me if I didn't. Only good thing about that, they didn't use drugs. I was prime beef; they wanted me to last a long time." She took a lengthy drag on her cigarette.

"My trainers passed me around for a while, banging various people in the organization. Not for too long, though, they wanted me young and relatively unspoiled. I was being tested for aptitude, and well. . . I took pride in doing what I'd been taught." She stopped speaking, and with exacting deliberation tapped ash into a thick glass ashtray. Her laugh came harsh and painful.

"What the hell did I know? I was just a goddamned kid. A girl like Pat, now, she was probably in junior high when she was that young." She sighed again. This disclosure was costing her; I reconsidered whether I should let her revisit all this for the sake of my curiosity.

"Being put out on the street was the next step in my professional career. Like some sorta graduation, I guess you could say. I didn't like that, but they didn't put me out on the stroll for public consumption to, say, turn a car trick for some weirdo in a pickup truck, oh no. I was far too valuable, though they did threaten me with it. Better things were planned for me, so some wise guy stayed with me to chase off any cars that tried to stop and proposition me. They dressed me in tight, white, up-my-ass shorts, a halter-top made of a shiny piece of string, and five-inch pumps. Everything I had was out there on display." She licked her lips and crossed her legs, collecting her thoughts.

"The street scene didn't last long. I was nearly fifteen. At least I thought so. By then I realized nobody knew or cared about my exact age, they told me how old I was, and I believed 'em. What the fuck difference did it make anyway? Not long after what I thought was my fifteenth birthday, I got a present. My handlers arranged for the Chicago cops to pick me up in a blue and white for solicitation and give me a vacation in juvie hall for a few days." Her eyes, dim and cold, challenged me. I knew what she wanted me to ask, so I did.

"Why would they want you arrested? You said they had big plans for you."

"Yeah, and those plans didn't involve me ever getting away from them. That's one of the ways they protected their investment in me. See, by getting me busted as a hooker, even as a minor, I had a record. I'd never be able to work at any other kind of job. They used the Chicago police department to designate me as 'fuck-for-hire' for the rest of my life. That was now my permanent résumé for any cop, in reality, almost anyone, to look up. Don't seem to be no expiration date on taking money for sex. And after I was legal, they got me busted a few more times—just to be on the safe side."

"How did you end up here? With all this? In this huge mansion and all?"

She shot to her feet, waving her arms wildly. "All this?" Her laugh was maniacal. "All fucking this? All goddamn-it-to-hell this? You think this is mine?"

Her face wobbled as she groaned, pulling her lips into a bitter grimace. "Larry, this place ain't mine. I don't own a goddamn thing. Chicago owns this place, Chicago owns me. My name isn't even my own. Chicago gave me my name because one of my trainers thought I looked like a Playboy bunny. Nothing here belongs to me—least of all me—me doesn't even belong to me."

Bunny's conversation came to me in a flash as I sat with Theresa. I'd grown more and more regretful of my meddling curiosity as my sympathy for Bunny grew, but I also understood she would despise me if I let any pity show. I was forced to sit with nothing to say as she fled from the room. I hoped what I was about to tell Theresa would count in Bunny's favor whenever such things were toted up.

9 TURNED OUT

The person who ignores slavery [human trafficking] justifies it by quickly deducting the victim is a willing participant hampered by misfortune.

—D'Andred Lampkin

April 27, 1968
Waikiki, Honolulu, Hawaii

"LISTEN, THERESA," I SAID, desperate for her to understand. "You're being turned out. You can't let this happen to you."

"What does that mean?"

"Turned out, is an ugly expression for luring or forcing girls into having sex for money. This guy you knew is trying to use your affection, and phony promises he'll never keep, to capture you. And I don't think he's working alone. I knew a girl who got caught up in this kind of evil, and she told me how it works. They'll make you have sex with people you would never want to have sex with, and in ways you would never want to do it. If they have the right connections, they'll arrange to get you arrested so you'll have a record as a prostitute and you'll never be able to do anything else. And they will hurt you without pity—maybe even use drugs—to make you do exactly what they want. Your life will be over if you do this."

She averted her eyes. "I wouldn't have to do anything I didn't want to. And I could get away if I had to. I know I could. All I want is to leave this island. On the mainland, I could get away."

I moved close to her and forced her to look into my eyes. "You won't escape from them. They might let you think you can, but you won't be able to. Theresa, going with these people won't be the beginning for you. It will be the end of you. They want to turn you into a sex slave." I pulled her close. She curled into me, sobbing.

"I don't like scaring you this way but believe me, this is extremely dangerous," I whispered in desperation. "Please, Theresa. You have to believe me."

She lifted her eyes to mine, and I saw her misery and confusion. She glanced from one of my eyes to the other. Whatever she saw made her say, "I can't stay here, Larry. There's nothing for me here. I have to leave this place."

I ached to tell her I didn't want her to go anywhere away from me, that I'd be here for her always, but I choked on the thought. My emotions were running wild, I didn't dare promise things I couldn't deliver, so I only said, "But you do understand this isn't the right way, don't you? You'll give up this crazy, dangerous plan, right? You won't try to go with them tomorrow, okay?"

She wouldn't agree right away, but her stubborn resolve was breaking down. When I detailed more of the depravity she was facing, she finally shook her head. "No. I won't leave with them, but I want to go to the pickup place. Robert is supposed to be there with the woman. I made a promise, and so did he. I want to tell him in person. I want to slap his face for his lies."

"You shouldn't go tomorrow; you shouldn't risk it. You don't have any idea who or what will be waiting for you out there." Even as I said this, I was ashamed to admit I didn't want any part of such a confrontation myself.

"I don't care. I must go see." She was adamant. This wasn't part of the simple and fun part of the plan. I was getting involved in something that happened before I'd come to Hawaii. After all, how much of this was any of my business anyway? But how could I live with myself if I let her face these deceivers alone?

"Okay," I said, fears and reservations ringing in my head. "Guess we'll have to go tell them you're not going anywhere tomorrow morning."

Sunday morning revealed a Honolulu cloaked and hidden from the usual sunshine by a thick fog obscuring every familiar sight. The moist air was still and unpleasantly cool, making me sneeze and cough; no trade winds blew for the first time I could remember since being here. I gave Theresa a questioning glance.

"Kona winds," Theresa said. "They blow smoke from volcanoes on the big island over Oahu sometimes."

"Well, if we needed it to be more creepy, it is."

We walked hand-in-hand down Liliuokalani to the corner, everything across the street, including our beach, lost in the gloom of an alien city. We cautiously made our way along a strangely malignant Kalakaua as barely visible vehicles whooshed past us. At a corner, where I struggled to make out Lewers Street on the sign above us, we waited apprehensively. I peered at my watch. The fog had delayed us—it was five minutes past eight. Theresa leaned against me, shivering. I felt rather than saw movement in the cross street to my right.

"Theresa? Are you Theresa, is that you girl? Come over this way so I can see you."

I stepped in front of Theresa as an obese woman's form in a long robe or shapeless dress that must have been cut from a tablecloth materialized out of the mist.

"Who are you? What you here foah, mista?" She tried to peer around me. "Is Theresa there behind you? You come out now, Theresa." She fumbled in a large handbag. "I have airplane ticket for you girl." She waved a rectangular ticket envelope in front of her.

My revulsion brought on shudders. I worried someone might jump out of the fog at us. I'd figured I could deal with some musician and a woman in broad daylight on a major street in Waikiki. I hadn't counted on this dark and gloomy morning. Major mistake on my part not to ask any of the guys to come with us. *Especially, Mickey*, I thought. *If the fighting pride of Prineville, Oregon, were here, nobody would dare threaten us. Where is this Robert asshole anyway?* I thought, my head on a swivel.

"Where is Robert?" Theresa called out.

"He cannot come. He is playing the music. He sent me, Roxanna, to get you, to bring you to him. Along with the other girls." She gestured to either side, and three or four shapes appeared beside her, pallid forms, thin and solemn as if waiting for Charon's ferry. "You see? We are all going to big happiness on the other side of the ocean. You want to come, no?"

Theresa yanked on my arm and whispered. "Larry, get me out of here. Please."

"Get away from us, woman, before someone calls the police," I screamed, though in the thick air it didn't sound near as menacing as I'd intended. "Get out of here you hag, you vulture. You girls. You should get away from this evil woman."

Roxanna took a step toward me screeching. "You come here to me Theresa; you come here now. You been bought and paid for girl." She took another step, her tone wheedling. "You come, be safe with me. You will have happiest life ever."

Loathing everything about this creature, I shouted, "I told you to get away, you ugly bitch. Theresa is not coming with you. Not now, not ever."

The woman reached into her purse again. Only God knew if her hand would come out holding a weapon. "You must come, girl, otherwise other people will come for you. You agreed, so now you must come."

I spoke from the side of my mouth without turning, counting on my voice not carrying beyond Theresa in this murk. "Quick, turn around and walk back the way we came, but don't get out of my sight. Stay within a few feet of me; I'll be right behind you."

"Send anybody you want," I yelled at the corpulent apparition, adrenaline wobbling my voice. I stepped backward, one foot at a time. "They'll have to come through me." We melted back into the fog. I grabbed Theresa's wrist. Praying a car wasn't coming, we sprinted across Kalakaua. I pulled her along behind me, and soon the shrill voice shrieking her name faded behind us. I didn't feel secure until we were behind the dubious safety of my locked door where I held this precious girl in my arms as she sobbed on my shoulder.

As a result of our expedition, we'd crossed an unspoken threshold. Sunday night we slept wrapped around each other like puppies. Though close to my height, she snuggled into me, the crown of her head beneath my chin in a possessive way we never had before. When we woke, the experience we'd gone through squeezed my heart, and I could barely stand to let her out of my sight.

Her eyes never seemed to leave me, and we needed to touch each other throughout the day.

We took lunch out to our beach where Theresa told me things I hadn't known. She'd already told me she was only nineteen. When we met, I'd assumed she was at least twenty-one and hadn't given much thought to the difference in our ages. I hadn't realized the Lemon Tree was an eighteen and older club, not serving alcohol to anyone under twenty-one. I was twenty-six. Instead of Theresa being five or fewer years younger than me, there were nearly seven years between us. It was a disparity I'd set aside, considering how well things were going between us. But now that our souls had crossed into new territory, I guess she wanted me to know more about her.

She lived with her family and three brothers, one older and two younger, in a little town above Pearl Harbor called Waipahu. She worked at her mother's restaurant on some afternoons, and occasionally as a clerk or model at a Hawaiian department store. Her folks hadn't known she'd been coming to the Lemon Tree with Charlene on weekends. She didn't like sneaking around behind their back, she said, but she didn't think she could tell them what she was doing with a musician in a nightclub in Waikiki, either.

"Theresa, did you consider what you would have put your parents through if you'd gone with that woman? It would've broken their hearts, wouldn't it?"

She looked troubled. "I would have written them when I got there. I would have let them know."

We sat in silence. "What will your mom and dad think about you not coming home for the last two nights?"

"They think I am with Charlene." Her eyes weighed me for a moment. "But now I think I'm going to tell them the truth, that I was here with you." I nodded uncertainly. I wasn't exactly sure what that meant for our future. My erotic fantasy adventure wasn't over as I'd feared, but it had become a lot less fantasy and a lot more real.

10 BLUE HAWAII

It's no use to go back to yesterday because I was a different person then.
—Lewis Carroll - Alice, *Alice in Wonderland*

April 30, 1968
Waikiki, Honolulu, Hawaii

A COUPLE OF the guys noticed my moodiness Tuesday night, but I didn't tell them why. The harrowing experience Theresa and I had gone through Sunday had changed things. The girl was burrowing a home in my heart; a part of me was panicked, another elated.

"Hey bruddah, whaddup?" Dewey waggled the Hawaiian Shaka sign at me, a fist with thumb and little finger extended. "What you wan drink, ah?"

Stan's Lemon Tree was a family affair. Dewey, with help from Stan, was the brother who held down the head bartender job. I sat at the bar—something I normally didn't do, but I wanted to be away from everyone while I tried to let my chaotic emotions sort themselves out.

"Come on, my bruddah, I'm buy. What you like?" Dewey leaned widespread arms on the bar as his face widened in an infectious grin.

What the hell, a drink might get me onto a different page. "What are those cool-looking blue drinks I see people order? They almost glow, I've never seen those anywhere else."

"Ahhh. Blue Hawaii. Very special Hawaiian drink. Invented by famous bartender at Hawaii Hilton. We make 'em wit Blue Curacao liquor, three kinds rum, all layered just so, and plenty fresh juice. You will like *nui loa*. You want one of dose, I make for you myself."

While Dewey set off to build this amazing-looking drink, I considered the flaws in my dating plan.

It wasn't the perfect solution I'd hoped for. I hadn't counted on getting to know so much about my fantasy girlfriend. Conflicting emotions fogged the simple pleasures I'd been experiencing with her. I was already a little apprehensive about the bittersweet pain I knew parting with Theresa would cause, but something serious was happening now that I wasn't sure how to process.

I was still shuffling through my brown mood when Dewey interrupted to whip a napkin onto the bar and settle a huge, double-rocks glass on it with great care. Light reflected through deep, neon-blue liquid overtopping the glass to surface tension.

"No umbrella or limes on dis, leave mo room fo rum." He smiled proudly as he gently slid the glowing, azure creation across the bar to me. "*E luana*, my *haole* friend."

My first sip surprised me. This drink not only looked spectacular, it tasted good. I took another healthy swallow. No, it was fantastic. When I drank liquor, I drank for the effect of the booze, not because I expected my taste buds to enjoy the experience. The flavor of exotic fruit juices and a smoky-sweet tang that must have come from the different kinds of rum, plus a clove-like hint of spice, filled my mouth.

As Dewey drifted toward the other end of the bar, I hollered at him. "Hey man, insane drink. Had no idea. Thanks, my Kanaka friend."

He laughed. "Okay bruddah, but I'm no Kanaka, me. I'm Samoan. When you finish dat one, though, you come back. I give you nudda one, goin break yo mouf."

He spoke English every bit as well as I did, but he liked to switch back and forth between pidgin and what he called "proper English" when he was playing his role behind the bar.

I strolled back to the stage, feeling pretty groovy, and rested the remainder of my drink on the B3. I got way into the music this set, singing my ass off, too.

I finished my Blue Hawaii between songs, sure that Leonard, Mickey, and I'd been attached through our musical souls. We'd cooked the rhythm section. The other guys must have thought so too—they grinned like the baboons at the Honolulu Zoo.

The thick, blue, neon goodness was helping me turn a corner about my Hawaiian girlfriend. Some of my mood had come from knowing she'd been with another guy in another band, one that played here, in this club. But that wasn't what was most important. I shuddered, wondering how any human being could trick another into the depraved and evil thing he'd had in store for her. How could he live with himself? How much money does a monster get for destroying a girl's life, selling her into slavery? What was the going rate for that? And how, I thought with guilty outrage, how could Theresa have ever agreed to this? What made her so desperate to leave? I could barely think about her doing the things we did together with someone else, let alone this vicious animal and the horrors she could have faced in the future.

My slightly-alcohol-tinged new reasoning attempted to lecture me: *You're such a fucking idiot. Why are you reliving this? It's over. She's got a chance at a much happier life now, thanks to you. Whatever happened before you came here is in Theresa's past and has nothing to do with you. Why pick the whole thing to pieces? She's arguably one of the most gorgeous, sexy girls in Hawaii. She wants to be with you while you're here, and you certainly deserve to get the girl. Can't you stop trying to analyze everything for a change and just enjoy being with her? Doesn't everyone say, "If it feels good, do it"—and Theresa does feel undeniably, incredibly, good, doesn't she?*

There must be some Hawaiian word for the concept of living in the moment. t's such an island-ish concept. I wished Theresa was here to tell me the word. But since she wasn't, the next best thing would be to go see Dewey again before I went back to the stage for the . . . hmm, what set was this? Oh yeah, the third.

The second Blue Hawaii was better than the first. I smacked my lips at the sweet, smoky tang after the first swallow, but a racket from the other guys interrupted my appreciation. I remembered I played—and maybe even sang— on this number, so I decided I better get with it on the keyboards. I might be a few bars late, but right there was middle C. I spread my fingers into the right chords and dropped them onto the keys. *Nope, wrong chord, wrong sound too, need more stops out. Okay, got that, oh wait, goddamn chord changed, got to move my little finger out to a major seventh, like so. Check out those fingers of mine, popping up and down on the keys. Is that cool or what?*

The drink, the set, and I finished at approximately the same time. Guess I'd been good again 'cause everybody laughed with me, 'cept Les. There was a gleam in his eye, but he wasn't smiling. I clapped him on the shoulder.

"Hey now, Bear," I said, using the nickname the girls who'd let us sleep on their floor had tagged him with when we first got to California. "Don' worry 'bout me gettin' it goin' now. Jes' had a tiny little setback there for a minute, I'll be bringing it next set."

I'd gotten a little paranoid. I was pretty sure the band thought I'd had enough to drink. In fact, someone might have even said, too much. How could anyone have enough of these astonishing drinks? They made everything so clear. People ought to be able to get a prescription for Blue Hawaii libations. Help anybody get a new perspective on life. I took my empty glass to a table in the far corner of the club where nobody from the band would notice and got Eileen's attention, a waitress Dave was dating, and I knew, to order a Blue Hawaii. She took my empty and returned before I expected, asking me for five dollars. Goddamn, first one I'd had to pay for, these fuckers didn't come cheap. I took another heavenly swallow.

I had to admit the keys were a little fuzzy, but I wasn't worried, my mind was clear as a bell. I'd taken the ingenious precaution of getting to the stage early so I could set the drawbars on my B3 for the first song ahead of time. Extra carefully, so as not to slosh a drop, I used both hands to gently set my fresh blue elixir on the organ. Crap, couldn't set 'em right if I didn't know what we were going to play first. I stumbled around the dark stage looking for the setlist Leonard kept on top of his bass drum. When I put it back, the damn thing slipped past the edge of the drum and down behind the drum pedal. *Crap! Well, Leonard will find it.* I scrambled back to the bench, but by then I'd forgotten the song. *Crap!*

I couldn't remember a lot of our final set. I figured I probably had some good moments, but I'd gotten confused a couple of times, too. I might have been supposed to go up to the front mic, but I forget on which song. Seemed to be a surprisingly short set. I wondered if someone had snuck sips out of my blue drink. The glass sat dead empty on my B3, and I didn't remember getting a swallow. Les might have dumped it out when I wasn't looking. He didn't seem too happy with me.

I staggered off the stage, relieved the night was over so I could concentrate on blue drinks and not have to wonder which damn song was next. I didn't think I'd be able to play that well after another one anyway. Not a very positive attitude, I know, but still I didn't think so.

"Larry, in a few minutes we're going to the Outrigger to see Dick Jensen, you with us?" We'd first met Dick and the Imports at the Hullabaloo Afterhours in Hollywood last year. He was here playing at the Royal Hawaiian Hotel and their hours ran later than ours.

I nodded, not entirely positive who'd asked. "Sure am. Going with my brothers. I love you guys, and I go where you go. Everywhere we go, I go, too." But before we went, I had to get another drink, which I'd come to think of as medicine. I found another table and explained I wanted the blue drink with Hawaii in the name, which my new waitress found hilarious. She said she'd have to hurry to get my order in before last call, so I let her go while I congratulated myself on how funny I was. I was still laughing when the bright-blue glass arrived. I had to pee, but I took a generous swallow first. It was a considerable achievement to get the main vein drained—*damn I should be doing standup comedy*. Soon, I was back to savoring this rockin' drink. I probably wouldn't be able to get another one, I thought sadly. . . *Say, I bet they have them wherever it is we're going.*

"Come on Larry, we're going to walk. It's only a few blocks. . . Hey, you too fucked up to go?" I smiled and shook my head waving them on as I drained the glass. I stood, taking a moment to get my bearings. Everyone had disappeared out the front door, past the lanai, so I followed a bunch of people out onto Kalakaua into the soft Waikiki night air.

The scene around me was from a fantasy world. The aroma from the flowers and pretty things blooming everywhere floored me. What an achingly beautiful place I'm in. I sniffled at the thought of how many people I knew who might never get to see or experience these things. I had to try and remember times like these in case I died. What did Les always say? "These are the good times, and we're having 'em." I guess I'd gotten ahead of everyone or something because Dave and Mac came up on each side of me from behind.

"You okay, man?" Mac asked. "Come on Dave, think our fearless leader needs a little assistance." They grabbed me under the shoulders and duck-walked me between them. Did seem as if I walked straighter. *I'm not heavy, they're my brothers*, I giggled. I'm still funny. I wanted to thank them but decided to focus on moving my legs instead.

"Don' think I wan' go in," I told them, shaking my head carefully because otherwise, I got dizzy. We were outside of someplace where an awful racket came from inside. I felt sensitive to sound; tires hissing behind me on the street made my skin crawl. Dave and Mac tried to encourage me to come in, but I held my palm up to them. "Think I better go home, though I'd 'preciate you pointing me in the right direction." I burped up a little Blue Hawaii, not tasting so good the second time around. "Not exactly sure where home is from here."

My world had become a little shifty, revolving around me faster than I could keep up. Dave and Mac let go of me while they discussed something I couldn't follow, so I threw my arms around the pole I was leaning on and examined a spot where a bit of yellow paint had worn off the metal. Focusing on the imperfection seemed to help me orient myself. But my legs gave way, and I slid down the pole to the sidewalk, forced to search for another smudge or splotch to stop everything from whirling.

Mac's face loomed in front of me like a mustachioed balloon in the streetlight's glare. "Listen man. We want to go inside, but like you said, you're too messed up to go in with us. But we can't take you back right now, so we're leavin you here for jes a few quick minutes. We'll be right back. You'll be safe here."

My brothers sat me straddling the pole on the sidewalk. They pulled my arms around each side, so my hands touched each other. "Put your fingers together like this. Now hold on to the pole and don't let go until we come back, got it?"

I carefully laced my fingers together. The pole reassuringly cooled my warm cheek. I was aware of the rings on my fingers and thought about pulling my fingers apart long enough to put them in my pocket so they wouldn't get stolen. But I couldn't control them individually; they were good and stuck. Well, helpful to know they wouldn't release themselves by accident anyway, so I didn't have to worry about falling over. I glanced up to show my buddies I'd figured out how to lock my fingers together, but they were gone.

Some other people came by, and I tried to smile at them, but they seemed horrified to see me sitting on the pavement hugging a pole. I wondered why. I was still in my suit. My tie was in my pocket, but I couldn't have looked that terrible. I must have fallen asleep because when I woke up Dave was trying to get my fingers unhooked from each other— but then everything went black again.

I came back to the world holding on to something white and cold. A stomach full of seething acid insisted on exiting my body. I barely had time to lean forward before a stream of thick, steaming, brown liquid gushed out through my mouth, each nostril and maybe even my eyes and ears. Once wasn't enough; in a couple of seconds my stomach rose again, expelling more noxious and sticky, burning fluid, and I let out a pitiful moan. These parts of my body weren't made for stuff to come out of; it made them hurt. I grunted and hurled and slept, rinsed, repeated. Someone came in and flushed the white thing, and I realized I was nuzzling my hotel-room toilet. I didn't care. I was ready to die. Anything to stop the retching.

Eventually, when I'd vomited up everything including most of my internal organs, I curled up into a ball on the linoleum floor. Ten minutes, ten days, or it might've been ten years later, I crawled into the shower. Someone had gotten my clothes off me. Leaning on the walls, I managed to tug socks and underwear over my ankles. I drenched myself until the ends of my fingers wrinkled. Grabbing a towel, I pulled it after me, falling into bed wet, to sleep away most of the next day.

11 DOIN' TIME IN PARADISE

There's something therapeutic about nudity... Take away the Gucci or Levi's and we're all the same.
—Kevin Bacon

May 5, 1968
Waikiki, Honolulu, Hawaii

SINCE FACING DOWN a sex-traffic collector together, Theresa stayed in my room most nights as we immersed ourselves in a life out of time filled with simple pleasures, constant smiles, and sensual lovemaking whenever we felt like it. She made me feel as though I lived here, even if it was only a fantasy. She'd seemed so exotic when we first met, but the more we were together, the more we were simply two lovers falling into a comfortable rhythm. If she were from any other state in the union, you'd have to consider her a country girl: born, raised, and living in a small town distant from the big city. While there were little things unusual about her, like her love of dried, salty fruit and seeds, in most ways she thought, laughed, and worried about the same stuff all girls did. As I'd hoped from the beginning, I was experiencing many of the different faces of Hawaii through our relationship, though I'd have to admit they'd turned out to be surprisingly different from what I'd expected. I soon came face to face with another.

Early one morning we were aroused by screaming police sirens coming near before ceasing abruptly. Theresa was spooned tightly behind me, her arm around my waist, palm against my chest. We didn't leap out of bed in concern, instead snuggling into our shared warmth, waiting for the racket to end so we could drift back to sleep. Sirens in the night were not unusual on this end of Waikiki, usually amounting to nothing more than public drunkenness.

When the rising volume of thumping noises and loud voices, one of them female, penetrated the room's thin wall, I realized the police were inside the hotel. Theresa raised her head. "The girl's voice, I think I know who she is."

I disentangled myself to pull on my board shorts, a handy tank top, and slip into slaps. About all I wore when not performing, and sometimes even on stage. Theresa, now in sundress and slaps, followed me to peer out into the corridor from our half-opened door. The commotion seemed to be coming from one of the basement rooms below.

Outside, I looked down the stairwell, trying to sort out voices in the confusion. Flashing red, yellow, and white streaks of light from the cop cars cascaded into the darkened lobby and the open corridor below us.

"You bastard, you asshole, you don't get to use me and throw me away like a used Kleenex, you son of a bitch. You don't deserve to live, you piece of shit," and much more shrill invective spewed from a half-sobbing female voice.

"Her name is Grace . . . something. . ." Theresa whispered in my ear. "She's been hanging around in the Lemon Tree a lot recently. Acting kind of crazy, if it's her."

"A brunette? Skinny? Sort of cute, in a sexy, pouty sorta way?"

"You would be the one to say if she is sexy." I sensed a little smile in her voice. "But yes, I guess you could describe her that way. She told me she was living out of her car. That could make anyone grumpy."

A male shout broke through the chaotic din below. "Get her out of here. She's nuts. She was going to shoot me."

I took cautious steps down to the basement-level rooms. A uniformed police officer stood outside looking in through the open door. I found a spot close enough to peer inside without drawing attention to myself. In the hotel room similar to mine, except for the casement windows, another policeman held his hands out toward each party, doing his best to defuse the situation.

The slender brunette, who I'd thought of as trouble looking for somewhere to happen, sat half-crouched on a chair, her tangled hair wild as a feral cat with its fur up, her flushed face glowering and twisted in rage. The officer questioned the man whose face I couldn't see. "Do you want to press charges? We can take her in, and you can make a full statement in the morning."

He shook his head. "No, I don't care about that. I just want her outta here. She's out of her goddamn mind."

"Gracelynn," Theresa whispered, peering over my shoulder. "Her name's Gracelynn."

Gracelynn leaned toward the policeman. "He hit me. I had to defend myself," she shouted. Her runny mascara made her staring eyes seem mad and witchy.

"That's crap. I didn't hit you." He held out his palms to the cop. "I tried to get her out. She was acting crazy, so I pushed her through the doorway."

"Nobody pushes me, you bastard. Nobody, you fucker. You never lay hands on me again, you hear me?"

"Okay, okay, c'mon young lady. You have to leave. This man is registered in this room, and you're not. He says get out, you gotta go."

"He can't tell me where to go. Don't listen to him. He's tossing me out because he's an unfeeling asshole." She raged at the policeman until, in a sudden change of mood, she seemed to wilt. "I can't walk out in the middle of the night, can I? I don't have anywhere to go. Why is everything so unfair? Especially for the woman?"

"Are you married to this man, ma'am?" the officer asked, showing great restraint.

The two combatants both shouted no at the same time.

"Well then, you don't have any standing here, ma'am. If he says you have to leave, you have to leave. I should be arresting you for threatening him with a firearm, but I'll just take it with me if you walk out of this room quietly."

I felt Theresa breathing behind me, caught up in the drama.

"Oh, I'll go," Gracelynn said, scaling her rage back up to ten. She glanced around wildly. "I'll go. Almighty God, yes, I'll go. I'll go out to the ocean and swim right-the-fuck back home, that's what I'll do," she howled. "Fuck all of you. I don't have to live this way. You don't get to treat me like this." She pushed the officers aside, running past them and us, wailing, "I'll fucking leave, right fucking now." I caught a glimpse of the man's dark gaze giving nothing away as he followed the girl's break out of the door. He seemed familiar. He looked a lot like one of the part-time bartenders at the club.

Theresa gave me an enigmatic glance and turned to race up the stairs after the fleeing girl.

I shrugged and chased after my girlfriend.

Out on the street, I glanced toward Kuhio beach in time to see Gracelynn fly across Kalakaua without looking. Theresa lost a little ground checking for traffic, though there was none at this hour in the morning. I dashed after them. The girl ran out onto the beach, flailing her arms as if she intended to rush out into the surf before turning to scurry along the packed sand toward the lights of Waikiki. Theresa sprinted close on her heels while I trailed behind. Gracelynn soon tired and veered toward the water; running in sand is hard work. Theresa reached out to grab her arm, and Gracelynn collapsed like a jumble of sticks. Theresa held her down, but she didn't look like she had it in her to get up anyway.

I fell to my knees next to them, panting. Theresa tried to sooth the girl's incoherence until her deep sobs subsided into heavy breathing. She rolled onto her back, arms and legs flopped wide, and stared into the starry, morning-edged sky.

Theresa glanced at me and shook her head in pity for this lost girl.

Gracelynn, finally calmed enough to make some sense, wanted to go to her car parked a few blocks away. While we walked along the sidewalk, her rambling story came out in odd bits and pieces. She tried to explain that though she was a little short right now, she would be getting plenty of money next week, and how, through some disagreement with her landlord, she'd been forced out of her apartment before the lease ended. Anger issues again. She would get a new place to live when her allowance got here.

"I only asked the guy if I could stay until then, but he thought I was trying to move in on him," she said. It was an abrupt change of topic, but I figured she meant the guy in the hotel room. "It wasn't like that," she repeated a couple of times, peering through her fingers at Theresa. "I really did like him, though."

Her troubles had started, it seemed, when she was stopped for drunk driving somewhere in her home state—Massachusetts, I think—more than a year ago.

But that wasn't the most significant part of her problem. Not only had she been charged with a DUI, they also tacked on resisting arrest and threatening an officer when she violently pummeled and threatened the arresting patrolman. Not even her influential family could keep her out of court, where she continued to be aggressive and defiant. Her father had somehow gotten her pending prison sentence or confinement in a sanitarium commuted to two years' probation in Honolulu. *How the hell did that work?*

Gracelynn's powder-blue 1968 Ford Thunderbird with a white Landau top and white leather interior stuffed with clothes and belongings was right where she said it would be. She noticed our puzzled gaze.

"Yeah, I know," she said, frown deepening. "Daddy shipped my car here to get me to stay. But it doesn't help; I hate this fucking rock!" Dawn was in the air if not quite in the sky when she drove off on Kuhio Avenue toward Honolulu.

Theresa and I strolled back to the hotel hand in hand. "Why did you go after her that way?"

"I felt bad for her." She kept her eyes on the sidewalk in front of us. "I couldn't stand by and not try to help. I know what it's like to feel helpless."

"Never heard of exchanging prison sentences for an extended vacation in Hawaii. Is it even legal? Seems pretty ass-backward to me." Some of our guys were experiencing rock fever. I could see how someone like Gracelynn might consider Hawaii a prison.

"The things you *haoles* do to us Hawaiian persons," Theresa said, with a rueful smile.

At the hotel, the police were gone, and the room where the ruckus had begun closed and quiet. Seemed like a good idea to let things be. We went back to our room and made love, admiring each other in the soft morning light, and slept until noon.

After a late breakfast, I came back to a note on my door. A package from Eve had arrived from Los Angeles. I left the reference copy of our new single, *Look Back In Love*, in Les's mail slot and took the rest, including publicity photos and a letter from Jimmy, to my room.

At rehearsal a few hours later, Les turned on the portable turntable so the four of us could listen to the final version of our new record. Since we'd planned vocal work today, Mickey and Leonard were excused. Outside, the breezy tropical afternoon sent airy messengers into the nightclub to tempt us. I daydreamed of being out there under the palms with Theresa after an interlude in our room. Too often, though, we'd given in to the island's siren song when there was work we needed to do. Anyway, we were going to hear the final mix on our new record, although the sour look on Les's face concerned me.

"Before we get started, I'm going to play the *Look Back In Love* reference single we received from LA this morning." He mumbled under his breath as he fitted the record with the little plastic piece that let a 45-rpm record play on a 78-rpm spindle. "Eddie Cobb and What-The-Fuck Productions strike again. Larry, have you listened to this yet?"

"No. But Jimmy sent a page torn out of last Saturday's *Billboard Magazine*." I unfolded and held the torn sheet out for them to see. "*Billboard* is picking *Look Back In Love* to reach the top sixty in the Hot 100. That's pretty hot shit, right?"

"Great. Hope it's true. But I wouldn't get too excited until you hear both sides of this." Les slid the disk onto the turntable's spindle, set it in motion, and positioned the needle to drop into the beginning grooves. The speaker amplified record hiss, then . . . the sound of canned applause rattled through our ears until someone started playing bongo drums, joined by a piano arpeggio, and some guys on the record who were not us shouting, "Hey! Hey! Hey!" I glanced at Les in baffled consternation. His impassive expression said, yeah, I know. Finally, the opening chorus lyric: "Look back in love, not in anger." Chimes or tubular bells rang over our harmony, already dropped into deep echo. Outside of the attempt to create a wall of sound from our background voices, the song continued. It ended with more clapping and whistles drowning the outro.

"Holy Christ. Is Eddie on some kind of serious drugs or something?" I said, stunned.

"Why is there all the clapping?" Dave asked in shocked astonishment. "You guys know anything about that?"

Les shook his head as he flipped the record over, and the first notes of *Contact* broke into our concerned discussion. The song sounded decent at first, though there was a weird underwater warbling effect added to Craig's dominating bass line. Dave's voice was clear, the background voices okay, though, as usual, blurred from too liberal use of the echo slider. At the end of the verse, where we hit the first chord of a cool, rolling vocal progression Les had designed for us, the harmony muddied into meaningless, reverberating noise. Instead of lifting the background harmony up around Dave's lead, Eddie had dropped our voices even further into echo. The effect of individual voices moving in independent parts through the mosaic of changes was entirely gone. Crap. Out of nowhere, a clarinet riff out of the *Thousand and One Nights* began to weave through the tune. I couldn't help yelling out, "When did we hire a goddamned snake charmer?" All of us tried to speak at once as the music faded away.

Les listened to our frenzied babble and shrugged. "Have to hope these new tunes we're supposed to work on don't get the same treatment."

"That's another thing. Jimmy's letter also says Eddie thinks we're goofing off. He's pissed because we didn't get the arrangements back to him when he wanted them." I read from the letter: "I sense a dangerous waning in Ed's initial enthusiasm about recording this group. . ." That shut us up, it was true. The Hawaii vibe was responsible for sucking a lot of the ambition out of us, no question. We'd given little attention to the work Les had done on these songs before we left LA. But in all fairness, considering how Eddie added extraneous instruments, and the way he multi-tracked and slapped rumbling echo over our original harmony, it was difficult to work up enthusiasm for an assignment that wouldn't make any difference anyway. Just as he'd done on our first record, our background voices had been reduced to some weird, Phil Spector wall-of-sound experiment. Once we were out of the studio and back working in the clubs, our opinions in the creative process were no longer considered.

Apparently, Eddie didn't trust our strength: our voices. Our vocals were what defined us, made us who we were, they always had. Les was an excellent guitarist, but the instruments in our band were there to frame Dave and the signature harmonies we created. If Eddie didn't believe in our vocals enough to help us develop them for the studio... *That's a big problem*, I thought. If true, he shouldn't be producing us. *The Pleasure of Your Company*, our first record, it's flip side, *Maria, Love and Music*, and now this one, didn't represent what we were capable of, what we strove to be known for—not as far as I was concerned.

Despite our disappointment, we buckled down to polishing Les's vocal harmonies for the next three songs we'd been assigned. It was hard to be optimistic; I didn't care as much for these songs as the ones we'd already recorded. The lyrics to *Can't Stop Thinking About the Good Times* felt awkward, and the bridge dragged. *The Merry-Go-Round Is Slowing You Down* offered the most promise—Les had worked out a cool round for us to do in the chorus—but the arrangement didn't feel complete yet. Maybe he planned to finish it in the studio. I liked that Mac would be featured in our latest batch of songs, but I thought *Now a Taste of Tears* was a terrible song choice for him and didn't fit the band's style. We needed to find him an upbeat Sam-and-Dave-style R&B tune where we could put cool, lush, signature-white-boy vocals behind him, and maybe add some tight, but not emphasized, horn hits. Full on horns wouldn't be us.

We were forced to work with what Eddie gave us. There was no other choice—if Eddie didn't produce us, who would? We were signed with Greengrass Productions for multiple years to come, and not only was he a partner, but he was also the company's only producer. If we complained too much, I wouldn't put it past Eddie's partner, Ray Harris, and the enforcer, to drop us into the deep freeze. I took what solace I could in what Jimmy's letter told us. Bell Records, who distributed our production company's label, Sunburst, assured him *Look Back In Love* would be a fantastic success. Key top-forty radio programmers in several major US markets had previewed *Look Back In Love* and were sure the record would climb into national radio's top ten. Maybe we were wrong, maybe we were too critical, and it would be a big hit anyway. And if it was, maybe it would give us a little more leverage in the studio.

12 THE STARK NAKED GIRL

Girls do not dress for boys. They dress for themselves and, of course, each other. If girls dressed for boys, they'd just walk around naked at all times.

—Betsey Johnson

May 15, 1968
Waikiki, Honolulu, Hawaii

IT SEEMED LIKE every night there were soldiers maddened by the extraordinary stresses of war in the Lemon Tree, but one particular night topped them all. The wet Tee shirt emcee had graduated from dueling breasts to a goldfish-swallowing challenge. The rules for this contest were even less clear. It gave us a longer than usual break, one I would've preferred to spend with Theresa if she were here, but she hadn't come to Honolulu today.

We'd bunched up at a couple of tables behind one of the interior columns where we waited out this tasteless event. I half-heartedly watched the developing antics on stage. Five guys in various uniforms stood in awkward poses around a bosomy girl and a table. On the table, in a squared-off globe, doomed goldfish swam in placid ignorance of their fate.

"Man, I hate these idiotic contests, but this one's barbaric." I tried hard not to think about those poor little creatures being absorbed alive in a human belly. I'd seen stomach acid up close recently and could testify to the inhumanity of their fate. I glanced at my buddies.

"The night we went to see Dick Jensen? I completely blacked out, man. Halfway remember Dave unhooking me from a streetlight, after that, nothing until I woke up hanging on the wheel of the porcelain bus." I sipped a Seven-Up spiced with mango juice. I didn't see Stan or Shirley anywhere and wanted to hope they didn't realize what a terrible idea this debacle was.

"You were out of it," Dave agreed. "Haven't seen you that drunk since Saint Louis, but you can't blame us." He tapped Mac on the shoulder. "We were pretty wasted ourselves. Wouldn't have left you out on the street like that otherwise."

"You don't remember nothin?" Mac said. "You was white as a ghost, but you laughed and joked with us while we walked you back to your room. Knew you was gonna be sick, man, so I parked you at the thunderbowl. Couldn't stay. Had to get to my own room 'fore I fell on my ass my ownself."

"Kinda worries me. Never been so drunk I couldn't remember afterward. Don't want to do that again, ever. Loved those Blue Hawaiis going down, but fuck! Can't recommend 'em coming back up. Not touching another one."

"What gets you sick," Leonard gestured toward my glass, "is the sweet fruit juice and syrup. Same thing with Mai Tais, Singapore Slings, all them tropical rum drinks." While Leonard rarely drank himself, he was fascinated with the process of drink making.

Our attention was drawn to the stage where a guy in an Army Ranger's dark-green beret had interrupted the proceedings with a noisy, uninvited scramble over the front of the stage. He staggered to the microphone to drunkenly declare he intended to compete for all the Special Forces guys, which brought delighted ooh-rahs and howls from various spots in the crowd. The emcee reluctantly agreed to a sixth contestant and continued asking them introductory questions, eliciting applause along with whistles and shouts, for their branches of service, hometowns, girlfriends, and so on.

"Time to begin the contest," the emcee announced but paused when the girl stage-whispered something to him off-mic. "We have a little problem it seems. There's only five goldfish, and we've got six contestants now." The pretty girl paraded around with the fishbowl held high, demonstrating the dilemma. So, he continued, they'd been forced to find another fish one of the contenders would have to swallow. He paused dramatically as a second pretty girl carrying a similar fishbowl entered stage left, only this bowl contained a fat, foot-long, gold and white carp.

The emcee told us afterward the whole thing had been a setup, a gag. It was obvious no one could swallow that fish, he said. The idea was to bring it out long enough to get a big laugh from the crowd and then take it off stage. But, when the inebriated ranger stepped forward and yelled, "This is for all my brothers-in-arms wherever they serve," and swept a fist into the second girl's bowl to capture the big carp, the script changed.

Uncertain what to do, she let him trap the fish against the flat side of the glass where he could wedge it out to grab it in both hands. The fish flipped and flopped. It seemed certain the squirming creature would pop out of his hands to slither across the floor. To avoid that, he shoved the wriggling thing into his mouth head first as far as he could, which turned out to be halfway, its tail whipping madly. The crowd of drunk servicemen went wild in appreciation of the gesture, simultaneously laughing themselves to their knees at the spectacle of a man with a fish's tail flapping out of his mouth. Unable to gobble the thing whole, as I guess he'd intended, he decided to bite down on the fish.

My memory holds graphic proof that human teeth aren't nearly sharp enough to chomp through a live, foot-long fish. He tried hard to force his ivories through the writhing fish, blood pulsing out from between his lips. Failing to bite the fish in two, the ranger grabbed the frantically flopping tail to yank and tear at it. Over the next several minutes, entrails and fish guts stretched to bursting, messily exploded as he finally managed to rip it apart. The laughter turned to groans when the tailed chunk finally separated, leaving gruesome spaghetti and globs of tissue hanging out of his mouth. Many in the crowd of soldiers stood paralyzed, though a few of the most alcohol-impaired hollered encouragement. Most turned away in disgust. He glared out at his audience, defiantly swinging his head from left to right, the fish's reflexes in its tail still powerful enough to rock his fist as he held it high in a gesture of some kind of victory. His bared teeth were smeared with grisly scales and gory fish guts.

Then things got worse. He made a valiant attempt to finish swallowing the head section, already halfway down his throat. For or a moment, as his Adam's apple bobbed, it seemed he might get it down until something twitched enough to set off his gag reflex. His eyes bugged and rolled back as he projectile-vomited a fish head and a spray of everything else in his stomach into the crowd. Those gathered near the stage got drenched with a hot, nauseous slurry I smelled from where we sat, as I tried to contain my own stomach's contents. The horde of warriors responded in everything from revulsion, to exultation, to sympathy-barfing themselves, though the majority hastily left to find their fun elsewhere.

The riot reigned while a futile attempt was made to bring some order to the stage. The ranger still managed to get off a weak V-for-victory sign before being surrounded and shouldered off by a circle of his special-ops buddies wearing various military dress and undress uniforms. Despite efforts to clean up the unholy mess, the place stank like a downtown Honolulu fishing wharf. Dewey and the other Alapa brothers promised us the stage and dance floor would be washed and entirely disinfected before work the next night. Not surprisingly, and to my great relief, management didn't schedule any more contests during the final weeks of our engagement.

"Here are some ideas I've been working on for *Look Back In Love*," David Cornwall said. His film production company, who had been hired to do one of the first videos of the Beatles in the US, was pitching us a film concept for our new record—us! A little Stark Naked and the Car Thieves music movie! Yes, for us! Cool, or what?

The lanky, blond-haired guy was a little geeky and carried a camera eyepiece with him wherever he went, but he seemed to know what he was doing. In his latest letter, Jimmy O'Neill, our manager, informed us that Bell Records' West Coast promotional director was so sure our new record was going to top the charts, he wanted us to find some local company to do a short film for *Look Back In Love*. Something like the Monkees' TV show or the Beatles' *Hard Day's Night*. The label would pick up the tab.

"We've got these model cars, perfect replicas of full-sized ones," David Cornwall continued. "Listen, these aren't toys." He glanced at us to make sure we understood. He palmed an area on a large table in his office inside his Honolulu production studio. "We'll bring our camera right down on the sand at an angle that will make them seem real but a little out of focus, because"—he struck a serious pose pointing up and away to somewhere only he could see—"you guys will be the focal point farther along the beach, as if you're off in the distance. One by one you'll race in, reach down, grab these cars and run off camera." His swooping hands illustrated his vision. "It will look like you're in perfect proportion to real cars until you grow and grow; we'll be pulling focus with you as your hand reaches out, and—bam! You're these giant car thieves ripping cars out of the sand and running off. Beach car thieving." He responded to our enthusiastic applause with a wide grin before continuing.

"Got another idea, too. Near Waianae, there's a valley full of junked automobiles. We think we can get some great shots of you popping in and out from behind the cars, all kinds of gags we can shoot there." He leaned back against his desk. "Like what we've got so far?"

It was unanimous. "Hell yeah. When can we start?" This was going to be fantastic!

"Only one thing missing." David Cornwall pushed his chair back against a credenza. "You ever hear the phrase, 'sex sells?' We need a pretty girl to make this film complete." He pointed at Theresa, sitting with me on a bench against the wall. "How about her?"

Theresa smiled in surprise, flattered. "Me? I don't know. . ." She glanced at me with a questioning smile. I had to nod. It was a great idea. "I don't have any experience at anything like this. I've only done a little modeling. I was in the Junior Miss Hawaii contest, but I didn't win. I was only runner-up."

"All you have to do is be as pretty as you are right now. We'll do the rest." David walked toward her saying, "I'm thinking we'll get a shot of you coming out of the ocean in your bikini for the beach scene. You'll be excited about what the guys are doing, and we'll get great reaction shots. And we'll get some of you around the wrecked cars, too. You'll be incredible."

We were out-of-our-skins thrilled about shooting a film for our record. Only the most important recording artists had them. I wrote Jimmy to tell him everything was ready to go as soon as I got back to the hotel and sent it off special delivery. We waited all week for the confirmation we needed to get David Cornwall started. Finally, Jimmy's return letter arrived. So far, he'd been unable to get anybody to guarantee payment, but no one was saying no, either. He'd telegrammed Larry Uttal, the president of Bell Records, directly, he wrote, and expected approval any minute.

Time was running out. In little more than a week, we'd be gone. In closing, Jimmy left me a sliver of hope. Even if he couldn't get a green light in time, he wrote, if the video got made, he was sure the bill would get paid one way or another. It was too big an opportunity to let get away. Not precisely a go-ahead, but if we wanted a film shot in this incredible setting, I needed to work something out with David Cornwall right now. Leonard drove me into Honolulu to talk with him.

"David, our manager, has been told that the president of Bell Records, our record label, has approved payment for this project. And, he told me, even if there was a problem, which there won't be, our management company will foot the bill. *Look Back In Love* is already breaking big on the East Coast. If we don't do this in the next few days, we'll be gone, and we won't be able to shoot the amazing concept you've developed for us in Hawaii."

David had gotten excited about the project, too. He agreed to shoot the video on speculation, but only the raw footage, he said, no editing, not until he'd gotten at least a signed work order from our record company or management company. Though we wouldn't be here for the edit, we had no doubts the finished product would be incredible.

A few days before the end of our run at the Lemon Tree, we ran up and down the beach, making faces and acting like crazy people while we grabbed miniature cars. The camera previews were fabulous, and the shots in the automobile junkyard in the afternoon looked like something the Monkees or the Beatles would do. Theresa, gorgeous in a short white sundress, appeared in a few of the junkyard scenes, but we didn't do her beach scenes. David Cornwell wanted all the band's shots on the beach in the same angle of sunlight, so her pickups were scheduled for next week after we were gone.

I tried desperately not to think about that. Right now, Theresa was my girl. But when the plane returning us to our old life took off, she no longer would be. But after this film, she would always be connected to the band. She would always be the Stark Naked Girl. How would I deal with that? I forced myself to think of my long-term plan; there would be another someone in another town. There had to be. I had to let her go. For both our sakes. I had to.

13 LOOK BACK IN LOVE

> *In Sleep we lie all naked and alone, in Sleep we are united at the heart of night and darkness, and we are strange and beautiful asleep; for we are dying the darkness and we know no death.*
> —Thomas Wolfe

May 26, 1968
Honolulu, Hawaii

THE MOMENT THERESA and I dreaded had arrived. The biggest of Stan's Samoan brothers, Leo, helped us pack our equipment and heavy luggage into the van he would drive. Theresa and I would ride with the other guys in Stan's passenger van. Charlene planned to meet us at the airport and drive her home afterward.

Over the last several weeks, Theresa had essentially been living with me, glorifying my tawdry little hotel room nearly every day. The closer departure came, the more she made each moment precious to me. I could barely conceive of a future without her in it. *I can always work out a way for her to visit me in California*, I thought, knowing I couldn't. *Maybe we'll get back here someday*, I lied to myself. Mickey, and now Mac and Dave, suffered from rock fever—they never wanted to return—and Les seemed indifferent. *Just don't say anything stupid, don't let your emotions get away from you. Don't make promises you can't keep. Don't make this harder than it already is.*

Theresa and I had barely spoken all morning, picking through a breakfast of Portuguese sweet bread, eggs, and fresh pineapple. We'd repeated last night's desperate passion with equally bittersweet fervor when we woke in each other's embrace. Intimacy between us had expanded far beyond sex. We'd submerged ourselves in each other, feeling what the other felt whether we spoke or not, knowing every passing moment brought us nearer to the end.

Theresa, gorgeous in a pale-yellow sundress, got bear hugs from Stan and Shirley before stepping into the passenger van. I sat next to the window and put an arm around her as she rested her head on my shoulder and closed her eyes. As we pulled away from the curb, Stan tuned the radio to KPOI for us in hopes of hearing *Look Back In Love*. Our record was at the top the island's primary rock station's playlist and ranked the most requested on stations all across Hawaii this week. Paradise showered us with golden sunlight through the van's open window. Leonard and I seemed to be the only ones who would regret leaving, the rest of the band teased and taunted one another as brothers do, excited and eager to catch our flight.

At the departure gate, Theresa and I were a bundle of nerves. We'd tried to prepare for this difficult moment, but it was impossible. There didn't seem to be anything we could say we hadn't already expressed in a far better way. When I got back from ticketing, Theresa and Charlene had disappeared. As boarding drew nearer, I wondered if she'd lost her nerve and decided not to see me off after all. Desperately sad but a little relieved, I understood. Maybe it was for the best. As boarding for our flight was announced, Theresa appeared. I turned and there she was, a few steps away, a pink blossom tucked over her left ear in her loose, flowing hair, the perfect image of a Hawaiian dream girl. I didn't know then that the flower over her left ear signified she was taken. What I did know, was she left me breathless. Her eyes seemed to drink me into her memory as they brimmed up and over. She held out the largest, most gorgeous lei I'd ever seen. I took a step and leaned down so she could drape it around my neck. It was moist and dense, surrounding me in a heady, languid aroma. How many orchids must have sacrificed their flattened, matte-pink and white petals to create this weighty floral ring? It had to have cost her a fortune.

She crushed through the flowers to kiss me. Theresa's lips, as familiar as my own, warmed by tears and banked emotion, burned into mine in a tenderness I would never forget. I took the lei off and gave it to Charlene so I could pull Theresa into a full embrace. I could have held her this way forever, our fevered mouths and bodies pressed into one another. The guys understood and went out onto the tarmac, leaving us a private moment. Stepping back, she stared into me. Her eyes told me she was trying to get something out. I met this heavenly girl's passionate gaze while trying to control my own feelings as she gulped for air. Her head rocked with emotions that threatened to reduce us both to a puddle. Behind us, Charlene wept as though her own heart was breaking.

"*Aloha no au ia 'oe*," Theresa breathed out before giving me a heartsick glance and darting away from the boarding gate. Charlene pushed the flowered ring at me and hurried into the crowd after her. Dazed, I followed the line weaving out to the rolling stairs, trying to absorb Theresa's parting words. I understood aloha, of course, but I could only guess at the meaning of the rest of her fervent declaration. I desperately wished I'd thought of something as moving to say to her.

The cabin attendants oohed and aahed over my lei before packing it into a thick plastic bag to keep it fresh all the way to Indiana. My assigned seat was in the middle of the massive plane with the others, but a sympathetic flight attendant let me use her jump seat with a window view before takeoff. I hoped Theresa had gone to a terminal window, I was desperate for one more glimpse of her. I caught a dim view of her figure in one of the windows, her face hidden by her dark cascading hair, fluttering as she shook with emotion. I knew it was her; I could see Charlene trying to console her. I choked and bawled as quietly as I could, here where none of my friends could see me. I couldn't take my eyes from her through the sun-shaded window until the plane revolved and I had to move. Surrounded by my band brothers, I tried to pull myself together, tried to reel in the panicky feeling that I was making the mistake of a lifetime.

Listening to the excited banter generated by the adventure of us flying together for the second time eventually pulled me out of my misery. Those of us returning to homes in Indianapolis savored and discussed the pros and cons of White Castle between Steak and Shake burgers. The three of us from Indianapolis reminisced about cruising our high school circuit of drive-in restaurants from the Tee Pee by the state fairgrounds, to Knobby's near Dave's house in Broad Ripple, all the way out to Al Green's on East Washington for their deep-fried, foot-long, pork tenderloin sandwiches. Dave brought up the Ron-D-Vue drive-in restaurant, a rumored hangout for gangs and loose girls from the wrong side of the tracks. Those of us who had been there retold colorful stories of events that had supposedly happened there.

Leonard and Mickey were far less enthusiastic about visiting the heartland. It wouldn't be like Hollywood or Las Vegas, we told them, but we promised to make sure they had fun in our hometown.

After a while, we settled down. Some took naps or attempted to wheedle more liquor from the attendants. Some of us took turns sneaking into the bathroom to smoke our imported grass; we'd been unable to resist bringing as much as we dared back to the mainland in our luggage, and we'd also stashed a few pre-rolled joints in our carry-on bags. After a while, most guys quietly grooved to the music in their headphones. I tried to immerse myself in Jack Vance's *The Five Gold Bands*, the first half of a ragged and dog-eared Ace double-book I'd picked up second hand in Waikiki, but Theresa's face, holding back tears and whispering her sweet, Hawaiian, soft-voweled farewell, wouldn't leave my mind.

I thought about the tiny photo of her and me captured in a little souvenir viewer in my carryon luggage. I pulled the traveling case out of the overhead rack and rummaged around for it so I could see her again. We were in the back of Leonard's car a couple of days after our romantic night on the beach. It was a brilliant sunwashed afternoon just before everyone in the band had lined up in cars for an excursion around the island to North Shore. Leonard's wife, Paula, though out of view, was in front of me in the passenger seat. One of Theresa's friends from school who was working as a tourist photographer in Waikiki had taken the picture and for a small price would have a tiny copy inserted into a souvenir key-chain viewer. I'd ordered one for each of us.

I as I peered in at her face smiling out at me, I imagined what Theresa would think of Disneyland and smiled. Showing her Knott's Berry Farm and Griffith's Park, the Santa Monica Pier, the view from the Observatory, and other fabulous places in Southern California would be crazy fun. Enjoying them through her fresh eyes would be like discovering them all over again. *Just a visit to the mainland for a few weeks maybe . . . to ease the transition for us, right? What better vacation than for your lover to be your guide?* I was walking too close to the edge. With a sinking stomach, I knew if I kept thinking this way, I would lose the struggle against asking Theresa to come to me.

I put the plastic viewer away and tried to sweep away such dangerous thoughts. I intended to get back to my book—Jack Vance was one of my favorite authors—when my sneaky memory reminded me of times when I was immersed in a book, and Theresa would want my attention. I could almost feel her hand steal between my thighs to massage and harden me, knowing I wouldn't be able to focus on the words for long and would soon give in to her lustful demands. These moments had become common, hugely anticipated contests, as she would go to any lewd extreme to distract me from anything I was involved in while I tried in delicious anticipation to prolong the tempting and unbearable sexual tension she built between us.

Have to stop this, I thought with a gasp, struggling to eradicate the vivid pictures my imagination was producing. My body and mind remembered far too much. The odds were astronomically high I would never see her again. I didn't even have a phone number. We hadn't promised to wait for each other. Wait for what? Wait for when? I hadn't even said I would write. How would that go? Pen pals? Until she found someone else and utterly destroyed me when she wrote to tell me? Her vulnerability, the way she had come to trust my affection, endeared her to me beyond explaining. What would become of her? I worried, momentarily panic-struck. How could she have fallen for that sex-ring scam? My god, what would happen to her? *Stop it!* I had to stop thinking this way. She was responsible for making her own decisions now. I wasn't her guy anymore; it was over.

I'd find someone new in Indianapolis anyway. If not, we'd be back in LA soon, and after that to Las Vegas. There'd be lots of opportunities ahead—let her go.

Part I
images

Sandy Beach

Larry & Theresa

Kuhio Beach

Marie

PART II

"Words cast spells. That's why it's called Spelling. Words are energy: use them wisely."
—U<small>NKNOWN</small>

14 HOMECOMING

It's a funny thing coming home. Nothing changes. Everything looks the same, feels the same, even smells the same. You realize what's changed, is you.
—Eric Roth

May 27, 1968
Indianapolis, Indiana

IT WAS EARLY morning when the pilot announced our controlled fall out of an inky-black sky. Ten hours of flying against the clock and a two-hour layover in LA had taken me more than four thousand miles away from the amazing Hawaiian girl who'd been as much a part of my days and nights as breathing. Our two months together already was taking on the surrealistic quality of a long, impossible dream.

Ghosts of the past had driven my decision to leave her behind, fears I might eventually hurt her—and she, me. Theresa would've come with me if I'd asked, I was sure. But I had stuck with the plan I'd made before arriving in Hawaii—I wouldn't take a relationship to the next city.

In the final weeks, I had surrendered to the moment, trying not to examine my feelings too closely. I'd known our fantasy would end, and it would be painful. We'd told ourselves we loved each other, and in the moment, no doubt we did. In truth, I'd fallen hard for her. But I refused to let my resolve unravel. Love or not, I was determined to avoid any potential catastrophe that could damage our lives and those of the people around us in an ever-widening circle. *No.* No more losing hostages to fate as I had with Pat and our children. No more hurting someone the way I had Marie. Accept this pain now instead of worse later.

Our jet angled lower and the roar of air-drag increased. I pushed the ache I felt away. I'd been so caught up in leaving Theresa that I hadn't given much thought to the implications of my return. I'd left this city a failure. I hoped time and experience had given me new perspectives to make peace with some of it.

My life had resembled a slow-motion train wreck in the days and weeks before I'd left on the plane to Oakland. But I hadn't left to escape the emotional firestorm that erupted after Pat's threat of divorce. I was simply responding to a call for help from my friends. I'd had no idea how long I'd be gone, but it wasn't likely it would be long; I'd only taken a few clothes and a little cash. I didn't want to go, but Dave and Mac had considered my presence so crucial they'd wangled first-class airfare to get me there. I felt obligated, and the miraculous way events had fallen together despite my opposition seemed to signify destiny.

After I arrived, we'd worked day and nights to beat the odds against us. Even now it seemed impossible that, naive and inexperienced as we were, our makeshift band would catch a toehold. Even more surprising, we'd risen to success on the West Coast. We were knocking on the door of national prominence: *Look Back In Love*, was ready to break-out on the East Coast. I was a different person now. I was returning as the leader of a respected and polished rock-and-roll band. My expectations and confidence couldn't have been higher.

A faint click advanced the minute hand of the clock over the kitchen sink. I was aware of the wall phone with an extra-long cord coiled behind where I sat at the kitchen table; the refrigerator Dad could open while sitting in his chair; the washer and dryer in an alcove to the right. Glare from the overhead light fixture staved off the gloom of an overcast afternoon and pooled on the table's surface. Sitting here, in my chair, felt like I'd never left this house. Sun-washed Honolulu seemed like a picturesque weed dream, someplace I might have read about in a book. A few minutes later, my mother discovered me.

"Larry. I didn't realize you were up. Didn't expect a peep out of you for hours."

"Couldn't sleep." I yawned until my jaw cracked. "Everything's a blur. Barely remember breakfast or coming home." In the pre-dawn dark, Weir Cook

Airport had been over-bright, bustling with arrivals for the five-hundred-mile Memorial Day race that was bringing more than a quarter of a million visitors to Indianapolis. I vaguely remembered Dave, Les, and me hugging family at the luggage carousel—Mac already off to board his flight to Cincinnati. *It's midnight in Honolulu, my body time,* I thought, wondering if Theresa was asleep.

Dad had driven us through a murky blanket of fog to a buffet breakfast in Castleton Square before a dreary ride to our ranch-style house off Kessler Boulevard on the northwest side of town. Cheryl had rushed away with school friends, while my father hurried to a golf date with a tool-and-die maker, an important policyholder from Southport. I'd fallen, as if shot, into the same single bed I'd slept in the night before I'd left, expecting to wake in time for dinner refreshed and alert. Instead, I woke glassy-eyed and displaced. I'd slept less than four hours.

"Can I make something for you?" Mom offered. "I can heat up some soup."

"Is there any juice? That might help."

She filled a tumbler with orange juice and sat across the table, where she always had, peering at me. Her smile widened as if she'd recognized something. As though reading my mind, she said, "This is nice, isn't it? Mother and son, together again."

I grinned, feeling my first sense of homecoming, and gulped down half the glass.

"So, what do you want to do? Are you going back to bed?"

"Don't think I can. I'm still halfway between here and Honolulu. Guess it's the jet lag. It's disorienting flying so far so fast."

"Well, you're here now. You can relax."

"Can't tell you how much I've been looking forward to coming home, seeing everybody." I worked up a crooked smile. "But being here makes me think about . . . things. . . I can't exactly explain. Seems so long ago in one way." I whooshed out my breath. "Like I never left in others. Been through a lot of changes, Mom." She examined me.

"You don't seem so different. Hair's kind of wild and those peculiar-looking red sideburns of yours remind me of the color my hair used to be." She grinned, fluffing a waved permanent hairstyle still showing abundant fire since the last time I'd seen her. "And those bell-bottom trousers that look like sailor pants, that's the new style, I guess. Otherwise, same guy."

"Can I ask you something?"

"Of course. What do you want to know?"

"Maybe I'm not supposed to know, but. . . Where are they, Mom? The boys . . . and Pat?" I knew they weren't here anymore, I wasn't stupid, but I felt strangely vulnerable and couldn't shake the irrational sensation that she was still here waiting with David and Danny. "I wasn't told when they left or where they'd gone."

My mother's face fell, her hands wriggled together in her lap like little animals taking comfort from each other. "She took them to Kentucky so her sister Katie could help with the boys while she finished her senior year at Austin Peay. She left not long after she . . . she came back. . ."

. . . *from California.* Pat had come to make amends, to try and find a way back to where we'd been before she'd thrown us over a cliff—*for God's sake, she'd already divorced me.* But that hadn't really mattered, despite the divorce, we both felt joined to each other for life. Only I couldn't go back to being her mother's punching bag. Threatening me with what her mother wanted, a divorce, and then going through with it had let the genie out of the bottle; I didn't know how to recapture it. I knew I'd failed her when I couldn't figure out a future with all of us in it together. The memory of our final moments at the Oakland airport, when she'd walked away from the indescribable ruin our lives had become, seared that guilt into my consciousness.

When Pat threatened to cut off contact between our sons and my mother and sister, I'd been forced to let her new husband adopt them. But that wasn't the entire reason I didn't fight it. I gave them up for her because it was what she wanted. And because I couldn't give her what she really wanted—us back the way it had been before it fell apart. But I hadn't expected her to shut me out of my sons' lives. Or that she, or someone in her camp, would demand a pact of silence.

"Not telling you . . . was . . . part of the deal, I guess you could say." Mom had chosen her words carefully. "I'm not exactly sure where they are now. Her husband, Jim, is in the Air Force and they go where he's stationed. I think they're in North Carolina, but they're going to move soon." She shifted restlessly in her chair and answered a question I hadn't asked: "He does love her, you know. And he's wonderful with the boys."

I clamped down on emotions I'd given up the right to feel. *North Carolina!* I couldn't imagine Pat and my two sons anywhere but here.

"I haven't received a letter from her recently, but she calls me when she comes here to see her family, and we try to get together."

There was a lot left unspoken. My mother didn't offer to show me her letters and I would never ask. It was hard to believe my mother and sister had been so successful in keeping news of them from me. But in fairness, they might have thought that would make it easier for me. They may have been right. Either way, it had changed my relationships with Mom and Cheryl forever.

Pat had rescued my teenage life when I was a junior in high school, but it hadn't been only me who adored her. She was a sensationally cute and bright, blonde doll who'd captured my family's hearts, too. Cheryl accepted her as a de facto big sister; Mom and Dad loved and enveloped her into the Dunlap clan well before we were married. While we were in high school, she'd grown so attached to my family, she'd told me in confidence she preferred them over her own much of the time. My folks believed and expected, in time, we'd eventually marry. But everything went over-the-cliff crazy when Pat announced her unexpected pregnancy. After we were married, we'd set up housekeeping in the tiny two-bedroom apartment at the back of this house until our first son was born. Mom had originally designed it for my grandmother and her father, Frank, when the house had been built. Unfortunately, Grandma Marion hadn't lived long enough to see these rooms, and my great-grandfather had passed on not long after we'd moved here to Bevedere Drive.

I'd never doubted my family's love; I think they saw me as a pretty decent guy, if headstrong, with a head-in-the-clouds attitude and a resistance to authority that, in some weird way, was part of my allure to Pat. They were frustrated when I always seemed to choose the most unrealistic path through life, while I was always surprised they thought I saw a different choice.

"Think I need to get out," I swept my palm across my face and rubbed my forehead. "Get grounded. Look around a little."

"Take my car. Let me fix you something first, though. You must be starving."

"Not hungry, Mom. Just need to get my brain accustomed to being in Indianapolis again."

I took the back route to Indiana 421 south, turning east and north past the Delt house. Dave and I had been rushed and accepted into the first Delta Tau Delta pledge class at their new off-campus location in 1960. At our first rush party, he and I and another rushee named Mickey had ferried beer from the back of a shuttling pickup truck to ever-rejuvenating pyramids of cases covering the fraternity's long dining room table all night long.

On campus, I drove past the Greek sororities and fraternities opposite the Butler mall, and east again to coast across the basketball arena parking lot. It had been renamed Hinkle Fieldhouse after longtime coach Tony Hinkle. I'd ached to play on the hardwood of this storied arena. The imposing brick building was the mecca of high school basketball in Indiana, and famous in college sports nationally.

With forty-foot windows and a vaulted cathedral ceiling so lofty it produced its own weather, it allowed God himself to follow ferocious games on the court below. By the time I'd gotten to Butler, I'd given up hope of playing on my school's teams. Instead, I had double-majored in cutting classes to chain-smoke, while playing ruthless bridge in the student union building and sneaking out with Dave to sing with my Aristocat buddies rather than studying.

Pat's family home was a few blocks south of the fieldhouse. Crunching across the gravel brought back memories of my first date with her, which I'd also been sure would be my last, and how we'd ended up here at the end of the night. I did a U-turn and eased to a stop in the southeastern corner looking back over the Fieldhouse lot. It had been the night of my Junior Prom, and it seemed huge. That was before I'd been to Disneyland where their parking lot must have its own zip code. Gazing at the residential streets and university campus bordering the wide expanse, I let the bright moment of memory from ten years past wash out the gray afternoon.

15 JUNIOR PROM

I don't want to repeat my innocence. I want the pleasure of losing it again.
—F. Scott Fitzgerald

May 3, 1958
Indianapolis, Indiana

AFTER HASTY SMITH had joined my embryonic singing group, he took it upon himself to make sure I knew how to sing, which included introducing me into our church choir at North Methodist. When he realized I'd been struck by the vision of a certain soprano, a freshman girl he'd known in elementary school, he'd arranged to get her telephone number for me, and Pat and I became companionable phone friends.

But Hasty wasn't going to leave it at that. He continued to push our relationship forward whenever the Aristocats got together to sing. He bugged me about asking her out, especially with Junior Prom right around the corner. Though he was a freshman, he'd already made the golf team and was in demand for all the school functions I'd despised and made every effort to avoid in my two and a half years at Shortridge. But Junior Prom was different; even my parents made it a big deal for me to attend this affair. My dad had even hinted he might let me take our Dodge sedan to the dance. He knew I'd do anything to drive the family car.

"You shouldn't be nervous about asking her out," Hasty reassured me. Of course, this was one of the most popular guys in his class talking. "She told me she likes you. Ask her to the prom, I know she'll want to go. Look, you two can double with Em and me if you want. And if you drive, I'll pay for the gas." The concept of parents driving us to pick up our dates made us both cringe.

Em was Emily Hyer, Hasty's new girlfriend. After seeing her, me and the other two guys in the Aristocats had to agree, she had the most divinely shaped ass any of us had ever gazed upon. During my Latin and Greek derivatives class, I coined the term, callipygian—beautiful buttocks—to describe her lush rear contour. Hasty pretended to be offended by my characterization of his new girlfriend's posterior.

What he hadn't told me was he'd broken up with Pat so he could date Emily. I probably wouldn't have believed him, though. Emily had a breathtaking bottom, no doubt, but Pat was much prettier, had a cute, slim figure, and was not only exceptionally smart but the coolest person I'd ever met. And in secret, I sacrilegiously cherished Pat's backend and thought it every bit as shapely in its own special way.

In my next phone call to Pat, I tried to find a way to casually bring up the prom. "So, here's the thing, I'm a junior, you know. That means I pretty much have to go to this special dance for juniors that's coming up. I mean, I don't think I'm allowed to become a senior if I don't get my junior card punched there; something to consider if you're not doing anything else that night."

After a pause, Pat said, "Are you asking me to Junior Prom? I'm not sure you are, but just in case you are, I'd love to go with you."

I wiped my sweaty palms on my jeans, changing hands on the receiver. "Seriously though, if you don't want to go, I won't be offended. Look, if you do, it would be fantastic. Absolutely amazing. But honestly, you don't have to say yes. I mean it. You don't have to go."

It would kill me if she turned me down, but Junior Prom was a big deal, and I could understand if she might not want to be seen with me at something so . . . so public. More importantly, I didn't want her to stop talking with me on the phone. Maybe most people wouldn't consider a phone conversation a real date, but at least I could fantasize about her while her voice was in my ear.

"It'll be wonderful," she said. "All my girlfriends are hoping they'll get to go. I think I'll be the first one who's been asked. The prom's going to be at the

Indiana Roof Ballroom, you know, on the Circle. I've never been there, but I've heard there are little twinkling lights in the ceiling, almost as if you're outside on a summer night, except no mosquitoes." I loved the tinkling sound of her voice.

"One thing you'll like, you won't have to be nervous about going out alone with me. Hasty says he'll double date with us. Of course, that could be because I might get to drive to the dance, but my dad hasn't said if I can use the car for sure yet." While my dad let me drive as long as he was in the passenger seat, he'd only let me solo our '55 two-toned green Dodge sedan down to the end of our driveway and back to the garage door. If he decided I could, this would be my first time out alone in the car.

"Hasty wants to double with us? You and me?"

"Yeah. He says we need to figure out where we should rent tuxes, and he's checking out a pretty fancy restaurant over on 52nd and College, and there are flowers and corsages and stuff. I didn't want to tell you he was coming before I asked you, in case you didn't want to go. You two are such good friends, I didn't want you to feel any pressure."

"Who is Hasty taking?" Pat said, trying to sound unconcerned.

"Emily Hyer. Do you know her? She's in your class at school."

"No, but I'm sure I'm going to. I think it's terrific we're going together, Larry. We're going to have the most amazing time."

Dinner at the Hawthorne Room was excruciating and confusing. Hasty and Emily chattered with each other constantly, including Pat and I only on occasion. Pat seemed irritated by their intimacy. Sometimes, when she thought they were looking, she was animated, laughing and reaching out to thrill me with light touches on my arm.

The Indiana Roof, the state's most regal ballroom, was set above the Indiana Theater on the downtown circle across from the Soldiers and Sailors Monument. Structures with doorways and balconies and painted grapevines running along staircase railings and up stucco walls created a convincing impression of an evening in an open village marketplace somewhere in Europe. Circulating air invigorated the spacious hall with an outdoorsy atmosphere that made the room seem even larger. A perpetual summer sky of stars twinkled above us in the cavernous ceiling. But below, the noise and chaos of hundreds of teenagers made it nerve-wracking.

Most of the night was a blur. Hasty and Emily spent most of the time on the dance floor. When they came to our table, Pat tried to avoid looking at their casual ease with one another. When they were away, she ignored me, and we gazed everywhere but at each other through plastic smiles. Stolen glances at my confusing, if dazzling, companion left me speechless for most of the evening. I escorted Pat to the dance floor a few times, and though I could dribble through a crowd on a basketball court, the intricacies of the foxtrot and waltz were daunting. My mother had insisted I learn ballroom dancing, so I didn't trip over her feet more than a couple of times. Somewhere during the evening, we had our picture taken under an arch of flowers. We were both warm and flushed: me, from the pleasure of this breathtaking girl on my arm; Pat, probably because of the dancing.

Afterward, we drove north on Meridian with the windows down, and Pat seemed to relax as our evening drew to an end. I planned to turn east on 38th to take Emily home when Hasty spoke up from the back.

"Hey, Larry. You don't have to take us home right away, do you? Em and I don't want to go yet."

My wristwatch said quarter till eleven. I wouldn't be late until midnight. I glanced at Pat. I'd tried desperately to please her all night, but I still didn't have a clue of what she wanted. She was so different from the girl on the phone.

"We can drive around for a while I suppose," Pat said, the spring breeze in her hair. I felt her eyes on me in the dim interior.

"Well, okay." I paused. "Where should we go?"

"Let's cruise the Butler campus," Pat suggested.

Good. Butler was close to Pat's house. Despite how badly the evening had gone, I wanted to be with her as long as possible, but I didn't want to be late getting the car home either. I loved driving and didn't want anything to spoil being trusted with the car in the future.

I passed 38th and took us west on 49th to one of the smaller streets leading to Pat's neighborhood and the fieldhouse parking lot. I lifted my foot off the accelerator and let the Dodge idle to a stop. Maybe she would like to walk down to the football stadium or the Bell Tower in Holcomb Gardens.

"I want to drive," Pat said as I turned to ask.

"What? You want to drive?"

"Yes. I want to drive the car." The interior went silent. I couldn't believe what I was hearing.

"You can't drive, you don't have a license. Are you even fifteen?"

"I'm a freshman—of course, I am. Anyway, I know how to drive a car. Hasty, tell him it's okay."

The whites of Hasty's eyes gleamed from the back seat, but he said nothing.

"Look, Pat, I don't think this is a good idea. If something happened, I'd get in so much trouble."

"What could happen? It's just a big, old parking lot. No one's around, there's nothing to hit. Let me drive it around in here."

I felt myself weakening. I badly wanted to please this enchanting, mercurial girl. I glanced anxiously behind me, but no help came from the backseat, not until Emily gave us her opinion.

"I say let her drive." *Thanks, Emily.*

"Okay, then I say let her drive, too." Hasty gave Emily a conspiratorial grin. Not difficult to tell whose spell he was under.

My eyes filled with dread while Pat's gazed back in anticipation. Moonlight shimmered in her golden hair, and her sky-blue eyes were wide with excitement. *How could I say no?* I shut off the engine.

Once out of the car, I was enveloped in one of those fabulous Midwestern spring evenings, bright with moon and stars, the kind of night that makes people write poems and compose songs about Indiana. The gigantic parking lot, illuminated in pale light shining down from the universe, appeared curved by the surface of the earth. I scanned 360 degrees and, seeing no hint of anyone, sighed.

Pat waited at the driver-side door. I waved her in and climbed in the passenger side.

"Adjust the seat with the bar in the front underneath," I told her. She was five-two, so the seat needed to go as far forward as possible. "Check the side and rearview mirrors." I sounded like my driver training instructor. "Hands at ten and two." She tilted her head toward me in question.

"Like a clock. Left hand at ten o'clock and right at two." She complied.

"Okay, I'm ready to go."

"Give it a little gas and turn the ignition key, when the engine turns over, let go." The engine roared and the starter whined in protest as she held the key too long. She lifted her foot and the car settled into an idle.

"Okay. That's okay." My fancy white dress shirt was beginning to stick to my skin under the tuxedo coat. "Shift into drive."

"How do I do that?"

"You said you knew how to drive a car."

"I do. Theoretically. After all, I'm too young to have a license." She gave me a mischievous grin.

God, this is so crazy, I thought, eyes to heaven. "The gear shift is on the steering column." I tapped the lever. "Pull it toward you a little and move it until the little arrow is over the D. D stands for Drive."

Pat clunked out of Park and got the transmission into gear. "Check the hand brake; it's below the dashboard on the left. Okay, now you're ready—but wait, wait." The idling car began to roll. "Keep your foot on the brakes, Pat." The car jerked violently as she stomped the brake pedal.

I got a hand on the dash in time to keep from crashing into it. Hasty and Em laughed uproariously in the back. "Now, listen. We should not be doing this. I should have my head examined. Listen, carefully, with just a light touch of your right toe, press down the accelerator until you get going a little and then steer the car toward the campus. Slow. All right?"

Pat nodded.

"Let's go."

She stepped on the gas, and the car's front end popped up sending gravel spitting out behind the rear wheels.

"Whoa, whoa. What are you doing?"

Pat tromped the brakes. Realizing that made the car bounce, she stomped the gas again. We jerked and weaved across the expanse in jumps and stops to my consternation and Hasty's and Emily's demented glee. Pat grimaced in exasperated concentration as we neared the end of the lot.

"Okay, okay. Brake to a stop. I'll take the wheel." I said, relieved to end the adventure without getting caught, somehow wrecking the car, or giving this mystifyingly lovely girl any reason to hate me.

"I want to drive back."

Oh, crap.

"Please," she pleaded. "I'm sure I can do it better now, let me go back to the other side of the parking lot."

"All right. Turn the wheel and this time go easy on the gas. Don't let the car get all jerky." She turned the car in short fits and starts until we faced the right general direction. The fieldhouse wall loomed out of the dark to the left. Pat put her foot in it. The car accelerated into a fishtail, but Pat kept her foot on the gas. She leaned forward, her face flushed with enthusiasm, staring through the windshield as she gripped the steering wheel. She must have decided to eliminate the jerky ride by standing on the accelerator.

"Slow down, slow down, Pat. Too fast!" In moments, we were nearing sixty as we flew across the open space. She hit the brakes, and the Dodge slid to a near stop, still rocking and rolling.

Hastings tapped me. "Uh oh," he said, thumbing over his shoulder. A police car had entered the other end of the parking lot behind us and was turning in our direction. An exit directly in front of us led out into the residential side streets.

"Pat, quick, steer the car out of the parking lot and into the street straight ahead. Don't go fast but go." Pat got the car out of the lot and into the side street without too much herky-jerky movement.

"Turn left at the corner and pull over." She did, sort of—only one wheel climbed over the curb. So far, the patrol car wasn't in sight. "Okay, jump out. We've got to change places."

I drove ahead a few blocks before turning into a dark alley between streets. Hastings, Emily, and Pat strained to see if the police had followed us. I pulled into a spot horizontal to a closed garage door and turned off the lights. We slumped into our seats, huddled and silent, while we waited.

I glanced at Pat; she stared straight ahead. After a few minutes, noises emerged from the back. Taking advantage of the moment, Hastings and Emily had begun making out. Little moans and kissy noises grew louder. Pat angrily motioned me to her side of the bench seat.

"Put your arm around me," she whispered. I did, and she leaned toward me. I thought she wanted to kiss, so I started to move my mouth toward hers. "Stop it, just stop it," she said in a fierce whisper. "I didn't tell you to do that." I drew back in confusion.

I waited for whatever signal came next. She eyed me warily and slid closer in distaste. She forced herself against me and closed her eyes as she brought her lips to mine, and I was lost for a moment. My arms went around her until I heard, "No, no, no. I don't want that. You can kiss me, but I didn't say you could grope me." Grope her? How would I have dared? I waited again. The moans and groans from the back intensified.

"It wasn't me who wanted us to park, you know," Pat accused me loud enough to carry to Hasty and Emily. "It wasn't my idea." No reply from the back and I couldn't think how to respond. "Oh, all right then." She moved back and tilted her head for me to kiss her. We kissed several times, and though her attention was on the back seat, mine was on her lips and sweet breath that felt and tasted like heaven. I didn't know if she meant to, or if she could fake it, but her mouth softened and slid open as she responded to my passionate kisses. I'd never kissed anyone like this before. I was ecstatic we'd decided to drive around instead of going home. I decided I'd happily risk all my driving privileges to stay here doing this with her until dawn.

She abruptly pushed me away. "I have to go home. Right now. I was supposed to be in by eleven thirty, and it's almost midnight." *Omigod.* In five minutes I was going to be late turning into my own driveway!

"Gotta go, you guys," I said, turning the ignition. "I'm taking Em home first."

Hastings's muffled voice from the back objected, "No, no. Take Pat first. She only lives a few blocks away."

"Yes, Larry. Take me first. I'm late." She was angry again, and I didn't know why.

A couple of minutes later, I walked Pat to her house where she let herself in and closed the door behind her without a word. Confused, I came back to the car. Make out sounds still emerged from the back seat while I pushed the speed limit east. After Hastings gave Emily a long, romantic smooch at her door, he sat beside me on the way to his house.

"What happened?" I craned my neck to get eyes on him.

He leaned back in pleasure. "Well, you were right about Em's ass. It is truly magnificent, I mean it sure feels like it is."

"Ah. Well, no. I meant with Pat. She didn't even say goodnight when I took her to her door. I think she's mad at me about something."

"No, I don't think so. In fact, I'm sure she's not. She was probably worried about being out late, that's all." I didn't think that was it. I was pretty sure this had been my first and only date with her.

I didn't pull the car into our narrow driveway on Salem Street until twelve-thirty. In the faint hope everyone was sleeping, I left the car next to the side door instead of opening the creaky garage door and putting it away. Dad was waiting in the living room. Though he didn't mention anything about me being late, I had to field questions about prom night without revealing that a fifteen-year-old girl had drag-raced the family sedan across the Butler Fieldhouse parking lot. I wanted to live to see morning. It might have been worse—Pat had lied. Her birthday wasn't until October. She wouldn't turn fifteen for months.

16 THE WAY THINGS WERE

All the art of living lies in a fine mingling of letting go and holding on.
—Havelock Ellis

May 27, 1968
Indianapolis, Indiana

I SAT IN MY mom's car with the engine idling, basking in the sweet memory of how insanely crazy I'd been about Pat. I hadn't seen any point in calling her after the prom. I'd figured she'd never want to talk to me again after I'd gotten her so upset and irritated. A few days later she'd asked Hasty why I hadn't phoned, as if nothing out of the ordinary had happened. Before long, we were dating regularly, our mutual affection and commitment snowballing so rapidly we were together every minute we could arrange. Pat, the amazingly cute socialite cheerleader, who cared about me had dramatically rearranged my life.

Her complete acceptance of the singing, science-fiction-reading, board-game-playing, cartoon-drawing, basketball weirdo that was me, caused my confidence in me to grow, too. She introduced me to her friends, who were the popular kids in the freshman class, and they welcomed me as though I were one of them. She'd given me a place to fit in for the first time in my teenage life.

I gazed around at the homes bordering the parking lot and university campus. A couple of years later, when Pat was a junior and I was a college freshman, we'd conceived our first son in this quiet neighborhood on a magical spring evening like this one. He'd been so eager to arrive he'd shown up ahead of schedule—his mother and I hadn't had a chance to finish school and get married yet. Before leaving, I drove through the quiet streets hoping to pass the spot where one of our sweet couplings had lit the spark of love we'd named David.

Back home, my mind still stuck ten years in the past, the sound of Mom rinsing and stacking dishes broke through. "Did you drive over to North Central?" She spoke over the clatter of plates and pans without turning her head. "It's a shame you couldn't be here to see Cheryl graduate. She loved it there."

I rubbed a forearm. "Not me. It was a brand new high school when I transferred in. Being a senior in the first senior class made it not mean anything, I hardly knew anyone. The best thing I remember about moving out here from Salem Street—I got my first car." I grinned remembering the 1951 straight-stick four-door Ford sedan my dad had bartered for an overdue insurance premium, a bribe meant to help me accept the move. I'd cherished that car and the independence it brought.

"Don't forget, you had a real bedroom here." I had to smile. Mom loved this house; she'd worked with the builder, slaved over the blueprints, planning every inch of the home she believed our family would inhabit forever.

"Oh, the dungeon wasn't so terrible," I said with a straight face. My mother peered over her shoulder with a facetious grin.

When my grandmother and great-grandfather had come from New York to live with us, we'd become a four-generation clan, the three bedrooms in our Salem Street house no longer enough. I'd been relocated to the semi-finished space in the basement behind the furnace room. The one concession I'd wrung out of the deal: I got to choose what color it would be painted. I went with battleship gray.

My cellar bedroom, nicknamed the dungeon, had served as everything from the control room of an interstellar spaceship, to a deep-sea submarine, to a neighborhood clubhouse before it became my vocal group's rehearsal room. But getting to my room was spooky, especially at night. It required indomitable courage to cross beneath the furnace's menacing, multi-tentacled heating ducts in the dark to reach it, and the light switch inside.

"I wanted to graduate from Shortridge, Mom, but man, how that school intimidated me."

"It was difficult for you sometimes, I know," she turned toward me for a moment, "but aren't you forgetting how you and John Clair got the chess club going again and started playing in masters tournaments? And you organized your vocal group there, sang in the school choir and the Madrigal Singers, and some of the musicals. And you and Pat, of course—"

"Yeah," I interrupted, "but I had to leave her behind just as we were getting ready for my senior year. And the guys in the Aristocats." Before we moved, Pat and I had made plans for a fantastic year together. Remembering how terrified we'd been about being separated and losing each other, I pulled a crumpled pack of smokes out of my shirt pocket and slapped my pockets looking for my lighter.

Mom noticed and said, "Don't drop ashes all over the table. I keep an ashtray on top of the refrigerator for your father." I found the Elk's Club ashtray and set it in front of me.

"We were so worried about losing each other. . ." My voice trailed off. I glanced at Mom. I'd almost blurted out how that was when we'd begun the exhilarating exploration of each other's bodies.

She turned to lean back against the sink. "Shortridge was changing, and we wanted Cheryl to go to a great high school; plus, we got a great deal on building this house. We weren't the only ones who moved, you know. The Clairs only live about a mile from us. And after Pat's sophomore year, her folks bought a house on the east side. She had to adjust to a new school, too."

I remembered. Pat had made an immediate impact at Warren Central. Even though she was a transfer, she'd been elected Junior Prom Queen and head cheerleader. I was at Butler then, and her success made me feel we were slipping away from each other. She worried too, and we wondered how we could stay together with so many forces pulling us apart. That was before our desperate love-making changed the direction of our lives forever.

"Anyway," I said, changing the subject, "after driving through Butler, I cruised over to Carrollton." I inhaled and dropped ashes into the ashtray. "That might have been a mistake."

The south half of the semi-detached rental our little family had once inhabited on Carrollton Avenue was a ten-minute drive from the Butler campus under a slate-metal sky so close it made me hunch my shoulders. I pulled to the curb and a rude awakening. I don't know exactly what I'd expected, but not this. On our side of the double, a forlorn, sway-backed screen door hung loose. There was no suspended swing, no hint of a child's tricycle or playpen on the raw concrete porch. No sign lingered of the nascent Dunlap tribe who'd sheltered here. It seemed too small and tawdry to comfortably house a family of four, but I didn't remember it that way.

Memories popped up and blew away like dandelion seeds: a morning food fight featuring weaponized-oatmeal with little David. Pat and I in the downstairs bedroom, snuggled together in the nights. Bundling kids in stiff little snowsuits for car trips to celebrate joyful Christmases and happy birthdays. We'd shared many tender moments surrounded by our boys. But underlying them all was the unrelenting sting of my in-law's disdain.

I'd hesitated on our wedding day sensing we might never be able to overcome the scarlet letter our parents, especially hers, had pinned on us. But neither of us had been ashamed. We'd always planned on being married anyway. So, we played our parts in the grand marriage performance they'd arranged. Her family's plan demanded that we enroll at Murray State in Kentucky as soon as we could travel with our new baby. Dave Dunn had entered Murray State at the same time Pat and I did, but he dropped out after the first semester. Five semesters in a row later, which included the traumatic birth of our second precious son, Dan, we'd returned home under a crippling cloud of contempt from her family because we'd left school before graduating.

Back in Indianapolis, adulthood had settled over me like a shroud. Singing was pretty much over, there wasn't a group anymore, and the pressure was on to support a family. I took a big job underwriting commercial property and casualty insurance for three southern states at Grain Dealers Mutual. My mom and dad had considered it a fantastic opportunity, but it was far beyond my responsibility level, and the crushing amount of minutiae overwhelmed me. It had, however, allowed me to move my little family out of my parent's house into this rented duplex. When I couldn't stand that job anymore, I applied for a position at Aetna underwriting auto insurance; it was so boring I hated it worse. I drove for Red Cab for a while, tried construction, sold mortgages, delivered glass and paint for a windshield company, sold advertising for an FM radio station.

Meanwhile Dave and I continued to stay in touch as he drifted between employed to mostly unemployed. We commiserated with one another until, little by little, we quietly resurrected the Aristocats. Singing seemed to be our only way to achieve some sort of self-esteem.

In Kentucky at Murray State, Pat had performed with Dave and me in a short-lived vocal group doing Skyliners songs, like *This I Swear*, and *Since I Don't Have You*, featuring her exquisite soprano voice. But she didn't take it seriously when we asked her to sing with us again.

By the end of 1964, the year before I left for California, a series of events that had actually begun a year earlier, aggravated the animosity between me and my in-laws. In late December of 1963, the Universe had setup a practical joke for the Reflections, as our vocal group was now named—a hit record! We didn't know it at the time, but one of the radio stations in Chicago had begun playing our recording *In the Still of the Night*. In the first week of January 1964, WLS in Chicago, one of the three biggest radio stations in the country, had picked our record to push.

We hadn't even known the song had been released. Our producer, Jan Hutchens, had recorded us singing it on a whim. We finally found out when he called to tell me the Reflections were expected in Chicago the following weekend to do personal appearances to promote the record.

The first week the record came out, we'd hit WLS radio's Top Forty chart at number twenty-seven. By Friday of the next week, we'd risen to number sixteen and were being heard every hour on the hour in more than twenty states. We were on our way to a national breakout! At the same time, you know those guys from England? The Beatles? Well, they were on the WLS chart with *I Want to Hold Your Hand*, twenty-four spots below us!

In Chicago we were stars. A glitzy Rush Street restaurant hosted a special dinner for us in their VIP room the night we arrived. The next day we began a chauffeured tour to high schools all over town to sing and sign autographs at sock hops emceed by WLS personalities.

We were awestruck and astonished at the number of screaming kids we played for until WLS' programmer, Dick Biondi, warned us not to get too used to the limelight; the record stores had suddenly begun reporting zero sales of our record. We were sent to Ran-Dee Records, who distributed our producer's Tigre label, to find out more. They loved *In the Still of the Night*, they'd said. The entire first pressing had sold out in two days! Everyone was clamoring for copies, but the master tape had gone missing. Without it, they couldn't press more records.

By the first of February, we'd fallen out of the Top Forty, and our roller coaster ride was over—and no radio station in Indianapolis had even aired our song, not once. Our producer, Jan, rushed us into the studio to record another song for release, but it was already too late. Less than two weeks later, on the second Sunday in February of 1964, we watched Ed Sullivan introduce the Beatles to a live audience of shrieking girls, and wondered about what might have been.

Jan Hutchens' studio, which had been held together by rubber bands and paper clips, closed. The disappointment of our near miss took its toll. We'd loved recording, but there were no other studios in Indianapolis. Worse, our contracts with Jan Hutchens remained in force and would be for years to come. There didn't appear to be a way forward. Once again, the vocal group fell into decline.

In the spring semester of 1963, I picked up a long-term contract at an elementary school as a fourth-grade substitute teacher. I adored the kids in my class, and they helped me as much or more than I helped them as I struggled with what had happened.

Perry Baldwin, one of the original Aristocats, dispirited by the experience, quit to spend more time with the girl he intended to marry. With the Vietnam War expanding and the future bleak for the Reflections, Dave enlisted in a four-month Army program that included basic training. Chuck Tunnah, our bass singer, seemed to vanish into thin air.

In early fall, I was involved in a harrowing incident meant to force Jan Hutchens to release us from our recording contracts. It turned deadly when the father of Jan's featured girl singer threatened to shoot him with a 45-caliber pistol he'd kept from his days in the OSS, for having sex with his underage daughter. At the time, I wasn't sure if Jan, or I, as the only witness to the encounter, would survive. In the end, Jan had been severely beaten, and the young singer's contract and ours, returned. One of the Reflections' roadblocks had been removed.

When Dave got back from the Army, like a bad weed after a hard winter, the urge to resurrect the Reflections roused us to locate Chuck. After we'd been unable to convince Perry to rejoin us, destiny led us to Mac Brown. And a couple of months later on New Year's Eve, Mac changed everything.

At the last minute, Pat and I had decided to invite a few friends over for New Year's Eve to help discard 1964 and join us in hopes of a better year to come. Each time we opened the front door to welcome in guests, the harsh winter wind blew directly into our living room. Outside, a moon-silvered world patched with glistening old snow, made it seem as though they stepped in from an unfinished painting. Coats, hats, and scarves overwhelmed a chair near the door while we gathered in warm spots away from the draft. The front rooms smelled of liquor, boots, cigarette smoke, and fresh, crunchy Chex mix.

Our little boys, tow-headed like their mom, were suited up in footie pajamas with trapdoors. David ran from room to room, arms out, buzzing like a little blue airplane. Danny, snugged in yellow, cooed and grinned from ear to ear as he was dandled from one lap to another, receiving congratulations on becoming two years old today. Pat and I shared a bottle of Bacardi dark rum and Pepsis. *The Skyliners* first album, one of Pat's favorites, played on a portable stereo that was gradually being drowned out by laughter and conversation.

I'd given up substitute teaching at the end of the school year to take a dead-end job selling ads for the once-dominant *Indianapolis Times*. Though Scripps-Howard hated losing its Mid-west anchor newspaper, it had finally succumbed to its powerful upstart rival, the *Star-News*, and announced it would close its doors in the upcoming year. At the end of summer, the city school district called Pat back to substitute teach, and though she worked most days—between us—we barely scraped by.

I hated how the recent years had worn on her. What we'd seen as the Reflections near miss to become a nationally recognized recording group, Pat's mother had seen as another failure of her daughter's unrealistic dreamer, loser husband. Maybe it would have helped if our record had been on the radio in

Indianapolis, but I didn't think so. Even if I had helped Jonas Salk invent the Polio vaccine over at the Eli Lilly labs, she would have still considered me unworthy of being a part of her family.

But here tonight, on the cusp of 1965, my wife was lighthearted and happy with her friends. She gave me brief contented smiles as we passed each other like tugboats in a harbor, ferrying glasses of ice, ashtrays and mostly useless coasters to our guests. Pat and her girlfriends had gravitated around the table near the kitchen's natural warmth. I could see her from my spot on the couch laughing with her schoolmates from Warren Central and Shortridge. She was still the gorgeous high school cheerleader and Junior Prom Queen. Even after giving birth to two baby boys, she'd maintained the same girlish figure, and was more stunning in my eyes at twenty-one than when I'd fallen for her in high school.

Me, and the guys in my group congregated around our fake fireplace where an electric space heater crouched inside. Dave and Chuck, reclined with me on the sagging couch while our newest member, Mac, perched on one of the two overstuffed chairs. Les Silvey, who'd dropped by earlier, was already gone. He had entered our orbit when he and players from his guitar band, the MGs, backed us on some amateur recording. In return, we'd sung vocal backup for him at some local sock hops. An association that had brought both of our groups to Jan Hutchens' recording studio.

After returning from a bed-check of the kids Pat had requested, I rejoined my friends. I didn't know if it was the rum and Pepsi or seeing our little guys lying in their cribs so innocently that had shaken me. I leaned into the couch cushions pulling myself together before I could follow the conversation. Before I'd slipped away, we'd been talking about singing and recording, but now the discussion had turned to another common topic, complaints about finding work, or more accurately, the need for money. Dave was saying mournfully, "Come Monday, I'll be out pounding the pavement again."

"Thought you was driving' for some milk company?" Chuck said. Chuck Tunnah, our bass singer, was an inch or two over six feet and gawky like he hadn't grown all the way into his skeleton. He wore his hair swept back in a heavily Butch-Waxed DA with a curl draped artfully onto his forehead; his narrow chin and vee-shaped mouth gave him a devilish smile like the Joker in Batman. I thought he was a pretty nice guy at heart, but he was a master at social self-destruction.

"I was, but not as a regular milkman," Dave said. "I was doing special deliveries for Borden Milk. Permanent route never came up, so I was laid off."

"Seem to remember you saying," Chuck gave him his signature devil grin, "you were makin' special deliveries to some lady when you were in her neighborhood."

There were big "whoaaas" from us.

Dave grinned. "Yeah, well there were some perks with that job I'm gonna miss. When I had a delivery out her way I'd drop by her place, give or get something a little special. She wasn't the youngest thing, but she was damn sure pretty, in great shape, and had these fantastic boobs." He demonstrated with his hands in front of his chest.

I tapped a cigarette out of a pack and leaned to Dave for a light.

"Got me a job, I suppose," Mac said. "Ain't no other thing to call it. But as to whether I want to stay with it, I'd have to say no."

"Don't see why," Chuck said, a little too drunk to weigh his words. "As I see it your main job is to fuck Bunny and be her pretty boy." He slurped the Crown Royal Mac had shared with him out of a re-purposed jelly jar.

"Ya know, you big dumb son of a bitch," Mac said without raising his voice, but giving Chuck a hard grin, "in most any other place and at another time, you'd be pickin your teeth outta your ass right now."

Then he paused, sat back slowly and spoke in a pensive tone. "On the other hand, maybe what Charlie the Tuna says is right. On the one side, I got me a damn fine car, a Pon-ti-ack Bon-nee-ville convertible, fine clothes, and a big ole mansion to live in." Mac turned to Chuck with a slow, wicked grin. "So, what do you got going on, Tuna-man?"

"Hey. Don't mean no harm by it," Chuck held out a palm in peace. "But I'm still saying . . . I'd trade with you any day, and twice on Sundays. I believe I could style around all day doing what you do, and I don't think I'd have any trouble with your night shift either."

Mac examined Chuck like a bug on the sidewalk. "On the other side, I got to watch my ass all the time. Bunny has damn near killed me, two times with a knife and once with a pistol." He gave us a little headshake of chagrin. "She's got a suspicious nature. Plus, there is some pressure in being the coolest white man on the Meridian Street circuit. And it can get burdensome, constantly tryin on and choosin new clothes, new shoes, gettin new jewels, and rings and watches and shit . . . but I got to do it cause my main job is upholdin Bunny's reputation on the street, you see."

"Yeah, that's tough work, Mac," Dave got up from the couch to stretch.

"Here's the thing," Mac said, ignoring Dave. "I hear all you guys sayin you're outta work and need money." He paused for effect. "But what I see is a bunch of talented guys, guys who sing their asses off, better singers than we were in the Casinos. Can't help wonderin why."

"I don't get it." Dave thought about it for a moment. "What are you saying?"

"I'm sayin, my brother, we could get us an act together that'd shame the Casinos—if we put our minds to it. Get us some work right away. That's what I'm sayin." Mac stood, walked off a step to get out the kinks, and then turned back. "In a week, maybe two, I could get us ready to play in clubs around here. Like the Rat Fink." He paused for a moment. "I got another idea; I should call Dottie O'Brien."

"Dottie who?" I said.

"She is the agent who booked the Casinos into Indianapolis at the Rat Fink. And I bet," Mac snapped his fingers, "she would book us in a New York minute."

"The Casinos are a band," I said. "They play instruments. We're singers. We don't play any instruments."

"And we've hardly ever sung in front of anyone," Dave added.

"The Casinos had Joe, he was our guitar player, and he figured out the music for the players and the singers while me and Glen worked out the moves." He thought for a minute. "Hey, whataya think about this?" He looked over his shoulder at us. "What if Les Silvey would be our Joe. Maybe somebody oughta ask him."

17 PEANUT BUTTER COOKIES

Man cannot live by bread alone; he must have peanut butter
—James A. Garfield

January 1, 1965
Indianapolis, Indiana

OUR FIRST KISS OF 19665 was warm, wet, and flavored with rum. Afterward Pat and I gazed at each other with little sleepy smiles tinged with a touch of dismay. The reality of life as young parents without established career paths and the resulting financial struggle continued to push our expectations lower. But she never seemed to lose faith in me or our situation. Some of Pat's friends came over to buss the guys when the clock struck midnight so maybe all wasn't lost for them.

"What are you and your ruffian buddies talking about in there," she said, smiling. "Hope it's more innocent than our girl talk."

"Usual stuff, especially about finding a way to make money though. Nobody seems to be able to find a job." I had reason to be worried. The *Times* had announced it would close its doors this year, though no one knew when. I might be checking the classifieds myself any day now.

"So, nothing new. Seems like Chuck and Dave are always looking for jobs," her lips wrinkled in a wry smile, "but Mac always seems to have enough money."

"Umm. Well, yeah." I said with my own twisted grin. "But, I guess he's not all that happy with his situation. He thinks the Reflections could make money performing the way he used to. Thinks he could get us into clubs like the one where we met him."

"He wants you guys to sing . . . in bars? . . . for a living?" She looked a little surprised and concerned.

"No, no, of course not. That would be crazy. He just means we could make a few extra bucks in places around town on weekends or whatever. Nothing to worry about, just a bunch of drunk talk. Mac's new, he doesn't get it yet, we're not a band like the Casinos. We don't play instruments, we don't know how to dance. We don't know how to do anything but sing."

After New Year's, events took off in peristaltic waves. Mac phoned to tell me he'd talked to the booking agent in Nashville he'd mentioned and told her he was in a new band who wanted to play in and around Indianapolis. He said she'd asked, "How good are they, Mac?" And he'd told her, "Twice as good as the Casinos, Dottie," and she said she'd take his word, and could he have us ready in six weeks? She had something in mind. It would have to be out of town because the band had to be tight before she could promise decent bookings in Indianapolis. He'd already called Dave and Chuck who he said were enthusiastically on board. He'd even talked Les about playing guitar. And apparently, he was willing.

At our first rehearsal, Mac took over. He explained we would need ten songs arranged as two five-song shows; we'd begin there. First, we'd choose as many songs as we could from those we already knew, and he had suggestions for others to consider. As soon as we agreed on the song list, he would work out some simple choreography for them. Les would learn the chord changes and look for a drummer and bass player willing to go out of town for a couple of weeks. Despite my reservations, I let myself be swept along in the momentum.

It was much different to learn and sing while Mac coached us on dance moves and moving smoothly into formations from one number to the next. We had the added pressure of a deadline; Dottie O'Brien had confirmed a date in Birmingham, Alabama. One day at rehearsal the stress took its toll; Chuck and Dave nearly came to blows. Chuck had a tendency of releasing tension by joking and teasing, which Dave read as a contentious unwillingness to focus. Their relationship had always been somewhat strained, Dave often referring to him as our "lead bass singer," not meant as a compliment.

When this dispute exploded into World War III, Dave demanded either he or Chuck would have to go. I'd hoped it would blow over because, without a doubt, we'd choose Dave. It didn't, and our longtime bass singer's run with our living-room singing group, extending back to high school, was over.

With our commitment to play at some place called the Boom Boom Room in Birmingham almost upon us, we were in a panic. We had no idea who could replace Chuck, and no time for auditions—and Dave refused to relent. As a last resort, we asked Les to take his place.

There were a lot of reasons why this could work. He already knew the songs, had a decent voice, and he was a good-looking guy; he'd look great in our lineup. But we'd lose him as a musician, he'd couldn't play guitar and perform the dance steps Mac was teaching us. I didn't think he'd be willing to give that up. Though Les had a good voice, he wasn't a natural bass, and I'd gotten the distinct impression he saw himself as a single artist, ala Ricky Nelson, from the amateur recordings we'd done together. Surprising me, he accepted on the spot—with one caveat. On his twenty-first birthday, three months away, he was leaving for California—unless, he grudgingly agreed, we had something great going. We decided we'd deal with April when it came, but for now, he picked up Chuck's parts easily and told us he was sure he could find a replacement guitarist. We were back on track.

I gazed up the inclined lawn to the porch of the little half-house we'd made our home. Just a few weeks before our world would fall apart, I'd waved goodbye to her standing there on the top step. As Dave pulled away to take us to Alabama, Pat cradled two-year-old Danny on her hip, and four-year-old David leaned into her knees. Had anyone ever suggested that, in any future, this would be the last time I'd see my little family together, I would never have believed them. As it turned out, the timing couldn't have been worse. Two nights earlier, before I left with Dave, Pat and I had been arrested and taken to jail in the wee hours of Sunday morning—complicating everything.

We'd gone to Susie's Twist Lounge Saturday night. Susie's was a downtown dive where our new backup band was closing to work with us. Les had found his replacement in the Zeb Miley Trio who'd agreed to back us up and play their regular dance music when we weren't doing our little 5-song shows. Zeb played guitar, Johnnie Lamb played keyboards and kicked bass, and Scott Skinner was their drummer. It seemed to be a perfect solution: the seven of us were now known as the Checkmates.

Pat had never been to a nightclub. It was a rare walk on the wild side for a couple of young parents, and her eyes had been lit with the excitement all night long. As planned, we tried out some of our show songs during the last set that night and were well-received. After helping Zeb Miley's guys pack and load their equipment, we were invited to a nearby wrap-party for the band. When got there, at about 2:30 AM, the number of partygoers was far beyond the capacity of the host's single-bedroom apartment. The overflow had spilled out onto the parking lot below. When the police arrived to try and herd everyone indoors, an argument broke out resulting in those outside scattering to the four winds, while inside the apartment, all of us, including my sweet, young wife, were detained, separated by gender, and swept into police vans. We were being arrested for something we hadn't even known had happened. I'd expected us to be set free at the courthouse. Instead, the guys had been pitched into the drunk tank. I didn't know how Pat had been treated.

Monday afternoon, two days later, after a judge had fined the guys fifty dollars each for violating an old blue law called "Visiting a Dive," I was released, not knowing that Pat had been jailed and that her parents had bailed her out later Sunday morning. When I got home, I was glad to hear she'd been let out sooner than me, but there hadn't been time to discuss anything more before Dave came to get me for our drive to Alabama. I hadn't known that her parents had worked her over, still reeling and vulnerable from her terrifying experience, how her mother had insisted she and the boys move in with them, then and there.

Birmingham was my first trip to the South, and it was nothing short of a nightmare from the moment we arrived. We nearly starved during the first few days due to a misunderstanding over the contractually provided meals in the club's restaurant. We'd only been allowed one meal a day and went hungry the rest of the day until the club finally agreed to open meal tabs to be redeemed from our paychecks. Though the room was full every night, the crowd booed and yelled at us and hated our Four Seasons and Beach Boys tunes, and especially our R&B music.

Nightly, we were saved from mayhem by Zeb Miley's county-music-styled rendition of *Ghost Riders in the Sky*. We were forced to play it four or five times a night to keep the rowdiest from overrunning the stage. In our final week, a man threatened us with a gun, claiming someone in the band had slept with his wife, or maybe girlfriend—it wasn't exactly clear. We all claimed innocence, and though I knew where I'd been on my breaks, I couldn't be sure of everyone else.

It was a relief to arrive in downtown St. Louis, where Dottie had told Mac we were expected to play at the Can Can Room for two more weeks of seasoning. I knew the guys needed the money, I did too, but I wanted to get back to Indianapolis soon.

The hotel room I shared in downtown St. Louis with Dave, Mac, and Les had huge high ceilings with age-darkened crown molding and faded blue-patterned wallpaper. The place was so ancient, Abraham Lincoln might have stayed here. It was an unusually cold March, and the rooms were drafty and chilly. Steam heaters in the room hissed occasionally and produced momentary blasts of hot vapor, but they fell impotently silent in the nights when the temperatures dropped to near zero. I could never get warm enough. We asked for extra blankets after the first night, but the maid service took them away every day; if we forgot to ask for them during the day, it was hard to find someone to get them for us in the early morning hours.

I scrambled into some pants and picked up the phone receiver Dave laying on a table by a tall window. "Pat? Is that you, honey? Give me a second." I gripped the receiver between my chin and shoulder while I pulled on a shirt. It was even colder on this side of the room next to the windows, and my teeth were about to chatter. "Just got out of the shower, jeez, it's freezing here. Thankfully there's a good shower so there's at least one place I can warm up."

"It's cold here, too. How's your show going? Better than Birmingham I hope."

"At least the people here like our music, which is a positive change. I thought the people in the Boom Boom Room were going to jump us right on the stage and beat the hell out of us. Don't have quite the same sense of personal danger here.

"We did have some excitement a few days ago. We started doing this new song, *Last Night*, though it's actually an instrumental and we just shout out a few words more than sing. Mac found this crummy old sax, and Dave got a trombone from somewhere, and they toot out a couple of notes while we march around the club. Les takes his unplugged guitar with him and pretends to play it. It's pretty hokey, but people think it's cool."

"What about you? Did you have something to play?"

"Claves. I thought they were just two pieces of wood, now I understand are considered ancient and revered South American musical instruments. We got in a lot of trouble because of that stupid song. A guy from the Musician's Union came in and told us we couldn't go on stage again unless we paid $150 each to join the union here. When we tried to explain we were only singers, he referred to this one song where we all played instruments, including me. Dave had to drive us to Indianapolis to get cheaper union cards, and right back afterward to make the first show the next night. Man, was I beat.

"Sorry, honey, but I had to spend some of the money I'm sending home; thirty-five bucks on a union card and a few more to chip in for gas."

There was a pause, "That's part of why I'm calling,"

"Okay, but first, how are the boys? Anything exciting to report?"

"They are fine, except they miss their daddy. That would be you, of course. I heard you had come back to do something with a union, but you didn't think to come by to see us," she accused, "not even for one minute."

Wow, she sounds upset. "I . . . we didn't have time to do anything. Dave had to drive us right back to be here in time for Thursday night's show. You know I would have come to the house if I could have."

"Is that right?" she said. "Well, you could've come home last weekend. St. Louis isn't that far away."

My heart sank. She knew I didn't have a car, though. I'd left ours with her. I guess I could've asked Dave if he would let me use his car. I hadn't thought of that. "But honey, some of the locals offered to take us over to East St. Louis after work Saturday night to someplace called the Opal Club to see live jazz. We heard the most amazing musicians you could ever imagine until the sun came up Sunday morning. This incredible trio in this dump of a club played this incredible music. I got a taste of the real blues there, honey."

I visualized the long, lean bass player leaning his back against the dirty side wall of a makeshift stage, eyes closed like he was asleep, a cigarette dangling from his lips, never missing a beat, playing the most perfect bass lines I'd ever heard. And the incredible Hammond B3 player who'd made that organ scream and moan. And Les—he'd thought the guitar player was the best he'd ever seen live. I'd forgotten to be sleepy until we were back in our room. I'd found myself thinking, while we were crossing the river back to Missouri. Despite all their talent and what little money we got paid, we probably still made more than they did. I knew it was because we were white, and they weren't. It had made me feel guilty.

"And that was more important?" Pat broke in. I couldn't remember hearing such a shrill tone in her voice before. I struggled with how to respond.

"Well no, not more important, of course not, but I had to go, when would I ever get another chance like that? I mean . . ." *This was not going well.*

"Larry, everything is more important to you than us, your family. You have been gone for weeks now, and I barely hear from you. I don't know if you are okay or not. I can't live like this. The boys can't either."

Silence and quiet sounds that could be muffled sobs.

"I . . . uh. I'm sorry. I didn't realize . . ."

"That's the problem. You don't realize. I don't think you ever will. I have something to tell you, but it's so hard. . ." Her strained voice trailed off.

Uh oh, we're in new territory, I thought. I'd never heard her like this.

"Larry," she said, steeling a voice made scratchy by emotion. "You have to come home right now. I mean right now. Tonight." She sighed and hiccupped. "If you won't . . . my mother will give me the money to get a divorce."

"What?" The words she spoke in those few sentences were full of explosive content. First was Pat brought up her mother, referring to my unconquerable and implacable foe. I had never fully understood hatred and contempt until I'd crossed paths with this woman. I feared and loathed her. Then she'd said divorce. It might as well have been a word in a foreign language. *Divorce* couldn't apply to us. The possibility had never entered my consciousness. Her family had always made life difficult for us, sure, but the one true constant between us was our determination to be together no matter what we faced. Not only were we husband and wife, lovers, and parents to our children, we were also each other's best friends, companions, helpers, confessors—whatever we needed to be. I couldn't imagine an existence without her.

I felt rather than heard the last piece of telling information in her statement. My wife had given me an ultimatum. I was being ordered home like a kid late for dinner! She knew what a demand like that would mean to me. She knew if there was anything I'd be constitutionally bound to reject, it would be an ultimatum. We'd always treated each other as equals. If she could *command* me, or me her, for that matter, the balance between us would be gone.

"What?" I said again, fumbling for something to say. So many reactions and responses came to mind I was unable to choose. Sensing the importance of the moment, I searched desperately for the right words in the deafening silence that followed.

"They promised to put me back in school if I leave you," she whimpered. "I'd rather have you home, but you have to decide." I knew Pat was desperate to get a college degree. Everyone in her family, except her young brother, had graduated and gone on to post-grad studies, and she was less than a year away from her diploma. *In fact, it was probably my fault she didn't already have it.*

"Your mother. Your mother will buy you a divorce from me?" I looked around the crappy hotel room and the four squeezed-in single beds. Nobody seemed to be paying attention to my conversation.

"I can't leave the band in the lurch, Pat," I tried to keep my voice low so no one could hear what we were talking about. "You can't demand that from me. And to get your mother involved in our life—what are you thinking? You know she's been waiting for an opportunity to get rid of me." My mind was reeling.

"Is that what you really want? A divorce?" The word felt strange on my tongue when I said it. I couldn't possibly be having this conversation with her. We were connected by our souls, we were the same person. No matter what either of us did, we'd always be together. This was insanity. Yet I could not stop myself from pushing, from probing the wound. "I can't believe you'd do this. You're going to let your mother help you divorce me?"

"If you don't come home now, Larry," *her voice sounded tired. She probably hasn't been sleeping well,* "then yes, I'm going to file for divorce."

Fucking A! Jesus H. Christ! What should I say? What should I do?

"If you want a divorce, you just go right to hell and get it," I hissed and banged the phone into the cradle.

Ten days later, after being fired in the middle of opening night at a club in Fort Wayne, the Checkmates expired with barely a whimper, and it seemed that the Reflections had, too. We'd hardly talked to each another on the ride back to Indianapolis. I couldn't go home, so I'd asked Dave to drop me off at my parents, who'd been willing to take me in. After returning from that disastrous four-week and one-night road trip a little less than three years ago, I'd awoken this morning in the same bedroom I'd stayed in that night.

My eyes streamed in dismay as I sat in the car realizing that no trace of the events that loomed so large in my memories, remained. It was as though we'd never existed. Everything was gone except the stinging pain. In some desperate, bewildering way, I craved Pat's understanding, her absolution—ludicrously, her approval. *Oh my God! I am so crazy! What I need is an exceptionally good shrink.*

"I'm sorry coming back hasn't been as comfortable for you as you'd hoped," Mom said. "But I'm glad you were able to be here a few days before your . . . um . . . work starts, so you could do a little sightseeing and visit with your family."

I nodded, still distracted. *What would I have thought of me sitting here, now, in this chair?* Shocked I was making a living as a singer on the West Coast? For sure. But much more shocked to find I was no longer married to Pat, and no longer father to my two sons. Had it been worth it? Was what I had now a fair trade for all I'd left behind and lost? Would I change, could I have changed, what had happened? I'd never come up with a satisfactory answer, and I didn't have one now.

I sat brooding, trying to absorb all the feelings and memories I'd awakened when a fragrant plate of recently-baked peanut butter cookies slid across the table along with an ice-cold glass of milk. Beyond the cone of light from the fixture above the kitchen table, my mom smiled gently and abandoned me to my what-ifs.

18 RAT FINK CONFESSIONAL

> *You must learn from the mistakes of others. You can't possibly live long enough to make them all yourself.*
> —Samuel Levenson

May 29, 1968
Indianapolis, Indiana

WALKING INTO THE Rat Fink on North Meridian was a voyage into the past. In the fall of 1964, Dave had noticed a newspaper announcement that Neil Sedaka, one of my favorite recording artists, was appearing here and we decided to go. It was my first time in a nightclub, and I was filled with excitement. We'd entered through a storefront on the west side of Meridian, the city's major north-south artery, a couple of miles north of downtown. With its own front lounge and bar, a coat check concession, showroom, and curtain-drawn stage, the nightclub had given me the impression of worldly sophistication. Subtle lighting created an atmosphere of drama and mystery, as though we'd been transported into a famous nightspot in an old movie.

But instead of Neil Sedaka performing, we'd discovered Mac Brown singing and dancing with the Casinos, a band from his home town, Cincinnati.

When we'd heard Mac wasn't going back to Cincinnati with the Casinos, I'd come back a few days later hoping to find a way to contact him. We needed another singer to replace Perry so the Reflections could sing again, and I hoped I could interest him. But it was a long shot; after all, he was a professional.

It had shocked me that afternoon to see how unsparingly the sunlight exposed the truth of what had seemed so urbane at night. The rooms were probably glamorous once, maybe as far back as live burlesque, but even three years ago, their worn and rundown condition had been masked in the dim lighting. Tackiness and rough repairs, blanketed by layers of grime and dust, were exposed everywhere. In the lounge behind the begrimed plate glass window, several lonely looking tables in front of the bar were occupying a cracked linoleum floor unsuccessfully posing as marble.

I'd gotten the attention of the elderly daytime bartender wiping the bar's dispensers and surfaces with a dirty rag. The sound of running water and rattling glassware emanated from the kitchen behind him. He refused to answer my questions, waving me instead toward a pretty young girl who appeared to be supervising the coat check room by the showroom's threadbare velvet curtains. She smelled of spring flowers, a welcome change from the odor of stale beer. While she concentrated on filing her nails, I'd tried to explain why I wanted to find Mac Brown.

Now, all these years later, here I was sitting next to Mac, sipping a Coca Cola, and feeling the déjà vu peculiarity of the circumstances. He nursed a brew, a cigarette hanging precariously from the corner of his mouth. There was a miasmic sense of time failing to pass in this place; nothing had changed except added layers of dust and dirt. I sneezed.

Dave brushed through the showroom's open curtain. He spotted us at one of the rickety tables and joined us.

"Hey, what's shakin'?"

"Been reminiscing about when I came in here looking for this guy." I shifted my gaze toward Mac. "While we were setting up, I mentioned the night we came in here to see somebody famous but instead, we found him."

"Told him I remembered him dancing around on this same stage way back when," Dave pulled out an unsteady chair, "except the place seemed bigger and not such a dump." He glanced around. "No, I take it back. After playing at Caesars Palace, the truth is, this place was crappy then and a whole hell of a lot worse now."

"Point of view is everything," I said.

Mac grinned at me. "Will never forget the day you came to the house tryin to find me. Scared the shit outta them girls."

Les's guitar riffs from Del Shannon's *Runaway* filtered out from the showroom. Hadn't heard that tune in forever.

"The daytime bartender didn't want to talk to me," I said, thinking back. "Must have figured you owed somebody money, or I was an upset husband or boyfriend or something. Pointed me toward the pretty young thing sitting behind the Dutch door of the coat check closet." I shot a glance toward the narrow door next to the showroom entrance. "I was so naïve. I mean, come on; that should've been an obvious clue. Why is a coat check girl working in the middle of the day? It wasn't like the Rat Fink had matinees."

Mac and I traded grins. "Yeah, that would be that little fox, Darlene."

"Not surprising you would remember her name."

"Bunny's contact person here at the club. Her job to call when somebody wanted to set somethin up."

"So, this girl, Darlene, calls ahead to get Bunny's okay before she gives me directions. When I get to this huge house a few blocks north on Meridian, the other girl who lived with Bunny lets me in. She's in a bathrobe, got her hair wrapped in a towel like she's just finished washing it."

"Phyllis," Mac interjected.

"Right. I wait a while in the living room of this mansion, which looks a little strange, hardly any pictures on the wall, furniture nice but more modern than the house and not particularly well arranged."

"Interior decoratin was not those girls' main talent," Mac said. Dave grinned.

"So, in comes this guy in dress slacks, barefoot and shirtless, toweling off his hair, like he's just hopped out of the tub or something." I settled into visualizing that day. "I'm wondering why everybody's taking showers and baths in the middle of the afternoon. Funny thing, Mac, I couldn't exactly remember your face, not until I actually saw you."

"Didn't know who you was either 'til I come in the livin room, see you there on the couch. Remembered you and another guy had bought me a drink at the club."

"Told him you and I were in a local vocal group, Dave, and how we heard there'd been a fight and he'd quit his band and wondered what he'd think about singing with us now if he planned to stay in Indianapolis."

Mac shook his head and reset his feet. "Gene Hughes was bein an asshole that night. Guy had such a big head. Wanted to change the band's name to Gene fucking Hughes and the Casinos. Wanted to pay us like sidemen, the son of a bitch. Told him to go fuck himself! But the actual fight took place between me and his brother Glen, who was more like a brother to me than he was to Glen. He was supposed to have my back. Me and Glen took a couple of shots at each other. I hit him, he never touched me. No big thing, though, just scufflin." Mac lit up his million-dollar smile. "Knew I was gonna get fired, so I quit right on the spot before Gene could fire me."

"Then a blonde girl with her hair in a brush cut comes in," I continued, "fresh from a bath, too. Finally, Mac takes pity on my confusion and says, 'Look, man, you don't seem to get it, you are in the best and most expensive fancy house in the Midwest outside of Chicago. This here's Bunny and Phyllis's whorehouse.'"

"You was lookin kinda dumb. Had to come out and say somethin. Bunny didn't like me callin the place that, though. Girls called themselves call girls." Mac shrugged. "But it was what it was."

Dave had grinned all the way through our conversation. "Heard most of that already, but interesting hearing it from you," he said to Mac. "Larry and I came from a pretty straight-laced background. We didn't have any idea about what goes on in this part of town."

Before Mac put out his cigarette, I used it to light mine.

"Hey, man," Dave asked me, "can I bum a smoke? Left mine in the machine." We grinned like monkeys.

"Left 'em in the machine? Who you kidding?" Mac chuckled. "Thought you quit smoking?" I pulled out a pack of Chesterfield Kings and offered Dave one. Mac took one, too.

"Did. Probably will again, once I finish this one." Dave wedged his flip-top Zippo out of his jeans and flicked it lit with his thumb and little finger. Soon we sat wreathed in a smoky haze.

"And here we are again, fellas." I glanced around the shabby room. "We've come full circle."

"Oh my god," Mac said, doing his own 360. "Love seein the folks and all, but Jesus, can't wait to get my ass back to Vegas." We vehemently agreed.

Les waved as he shepherded Leonard and Mickey past us out the door. He was dropping them off on his way home at a motel farther south on Meridian. They'd come straight to the club from the airport after taking an extra day with their families on the West Coast. Dave stood and told us he'd see us tonight, before leaving for his mom's house in Broad Ripple. I waited with Mac while he finished his beer.

"You staying with Mickey and Leonard at the motel?" I asked.

"Nah. Stayin with some local friends while we're workin here. Goin to Cincy on my days off."

We sat companionably quiet until Mac, who must have read my mind, spoke. "You're thinking about your girl, Theresa, ain't ya?"

I nodded. I'd been thinking about the miniature photo of her and me in the little plastic viewer in my pocket. It had been taken in the back of Leonard's car a couple of days after our romantic night on the beach. I knew I was peeking into it too often. My hand twitched wanting to reach for it. Instead, I brushed my hand across the table so grimy I wished I hadn't.

"Been thinking about a lot of things. Indianapolis doesn't feel as much like home as I expected. I mean, it's weird. I look around, and almost nothing's changed in most ways. But I guess I have. It's like I'm a stranger visiting someone else's life. Fucked up so many things I never meant to here."

"You think I didn't?" He scowled for a moment before going on. "How come you didn't bring her back with you? Pretty sure she woulda come."

"I'm trying not to get stuck on anyone. It was hard breaking up with Marie before we left for Hawaii. Every time I get involved in some long-term thing, it ends up difficult for both of us. I decided I should move on after every gig, try to meet somebody new in the next city."

"Ain't gonna be easy findin another one like her. Hate to be the one to tell you, brother, but you two was like teenagers. We used to laugh our asses off, the way you two was always glued together. You were hilarious."

"Not that funny."

"Kinda was."

I managed a weak smile. "Okay, maybe we were." I rubbed a palm against the back of my head weighing what I was about to tell Mac.

"I told Theresa about Bunny, how she'd been turned into a working girl." I wrinkled up my lip, remembering our conversation. "Think it might've saved her life, Mac."

He drew a breath. "Didn't think you knew much about that."

"One day when I came by to get you for practice, Bunny was alone with me while you were getting ready or something. It was right after she'd met Pat and convinced her to go on that field trip to Cincinnati to find a non-existent girlfriend of yours." Maybe my tone was a little too sarcastic. But my poor naïve wife had no idea what she'd gotten herself into.

"Yeah, well, that was a total fuck up." Mac shuffled his feet and tipped forward, elbows on knees, studying the floor. "It was a complicated time for Joan and me," he mumbled.

"I know, I'm sorry. Shouldn't have mentioned it." We'd been through this before.

"Bunny told me she felt bad about losing Pat as a friend after the whole thing blew up. I think she hoped I could help her fix things with Pat, or at least, explain it to her. She said she'd liked the idea of having a normal girlfriend, someone, *not in the life*, as she called it. To her, Pat's life, the way she'd been raised and lived as a wife and mother was a fantasy, something she could never have. I felt terrible for her after I heard all the crap she'd been through." We both stared at the floor until I spoke.

"Somebody tried to turn Theresa out in Hawaii."

"What?" Mac sat back in shock. "You gotta be shittin me?"

I nodded, remembering how horrified and fearful I'd been for her. "That's why I told her about Bunny. Happened a couple of weeks after I met her. There was some guy in a band who played there before we did. The son of a bitch promised her a job as a model with her own apartment on the mainland. San Francisco, I think."

"You know who it was?"

"She didn't say, and I couldn't bring myself to cross-examine her."

"Goddammit, bro. I never knew any of this shit." Wasn't easy to startle Mac, but this news did. "I don't get that at all. Not Theresa."

"She thought she could outsmart them, get away or something. She had no idea what she was dealing with. I told her Bunny's story in all the blunt, brutal detail Bunny told me. The next morning, I went with her to run off whoever was coming to collect her. It was so foggy on Kalakaua, we couldn't see across the street. Spooky as hell. There was a woman out there who'd come to collect her, and she had other girls with her. I felt horrible for them and wished I could've helped, but I had no idea who else might be there in the fog. If I'd been smart enough to ask some of you guys, like Mickey, for instance, to come with me, we might've . . . I don't know, tried to get them away."

"Why didn't you say something, man? You know we all got you and your girl's back."

"Thought I could handle it myself. Didn't expect the fog." As much as anything, I hadn't told them because I'd burned with embarrassment for Theresa, and for myself, God help me. I'd never understood what demons drove her to make such a drastic decision.

"It's not exactly a secret," I continued, "but I haven't mentioned it to anyone but Dave." I studied Mac for a minute. "If I remember right, Bunny came to see us at the Pussycat the last time we were in Vegas, before Hawaii. Don't think she stayed long. Did you talk to her?"

"Not much. Her health's not too good, but she wouldn't say why. Said she'd come in to say goodbye." We sat quietly for a minute. I could tell Mac wanted nothing more to do with that part of his life.

"Well, if you should ever see Bunny again, ever talk to her, or if you find her address so I could write to her, I'd like her to know what she told me probably saved someone's life."

19 RACE DAY

Never take life seriously. Nobody gets out alive anyway.
—Unknown

May 29, 1968
Indianapolis, Indiana

OTHER THAN A simple ad in the Indianapolis Star, George Saliba, who owned the Rat Fink Lounge, hadn't done much promotion for our engagement, but with the town full of partygoers on the night before the big race, it was no surprise opening night was jammed. It amazed me all over again what strategic lighting and a great crowd could do to make the Rat Fink seem much classier than it actually was.

I started the night wearing the opulent, double-orchid lei Theresa had given me in Honolulu. It was fun for a while until it got sad. The opalescent orchid petals had begun drying out, it wasn't as heavy, and the flowers no longer gave off perfume. Hawaii had distracted us, we hadn't added many new songs to our playlist there, but the incentive of performing for friends and family helped us sing and play the old ones as though they were fresh.

After one set, Leonard staggered into a group of us with a shocked look on his face. "Omigod, that guy Michelle." He grabbed a cocktail napkin off a table and twisted it into his ear, grimacing with effort.

"What happened?" I said laughing at his antics. Leonard always looked for an opportunity to clown around.

"George's brother. I jumped off the stage there in front of him. When he sees me, he sticks his finger in his mouth, pulls it out with a big smile, and jams it in my ear. Yuckity, yuck, yuck, yuck."

"Michelle's Wet Willie," Mac said. Michelle Saliba, George's younger brother, was a strange man who seemed to pop out of dark corners in the club at odd times. "It's his favorite trick. Gotta keep your eye out for him. He'll try to stick a wet finger in the ear of everyone in the band." He grinned at Leonard, twirling his fingers at his temple. "He's harmless, but he ain't quite right in the head either."

Rumors flew through the nightclub that Paul Newman had brought a film crew to the Speedway to shoot footage for a movie about the 500, and some of them said they were coming to the Rat Fink. Whether any of the crew came in, Paul Newman didn't, but the possibility still ginned up the excitement.

Louisville had its Kentucky Derby's "Run for the Roses," but here in Indianapolis, we treasured our "Greatest Spectacle in Racing," the 500-mile race. It was a quintessential Midwestern event: a combination long-distance auto race and week-long rolling party. The line of parked cars waiting for the track to open started on the first day of May. By the last few nights before the race, the line was three lanes wide and two miles long, beginning in Indianapolis and running to the track's entrance in Speedway, Indiana, a mile and a half west. It was like a stationary New Orleans parade, without the floats and necklaces, but all the booze. For several years beginning in high school, I'd been involved in parking a car in the long line of vehicles along 16th Street as headquarters for the rampaging all-night street parties during race week. More than a few of the people waiting in line never made it to the race. Some were so hung over the next morning they drove away when the cars began to move, others did the same; they had only come for the before-party anyway. It seemed as though the event touched every city resident in some way or another. For a few years, my dad worked in the Pagoda at the 500 helping track and post the driver positions for spectators during the race.

The storm threatening the race failed to materialize, allowing Dad to prepare his traditional Indiana Memorial Day barbecue before the big event. We invited Leonard and Mickey and sat outside in lawn chairs guzzling beer while Dad grilled thick, aged, marinated slabs of beef on the backyard grill, enhanced by fresh-picked corn on the cob, sweetened by roasting in the husk, and baked potatoes the size of melons. Homemade pecan and Dutch-apple pies waited on a side table. As we were slicing into cold chunks of watermelon, the rumble of racecars starting their engines at the track five miles distant carried out to our neighborhood in the heavy air.

I sprinted inside to turn on the radio I'd pre-tuned to catch Sid Collins make his introductions of the pit reporters and the track announcers in the four turns, the main straightaway, and the backstretch as the parade laps began. The race wasn't on live television. Each commentator gave a "words-eye view" from their vantage point: I could close my eyes and visualize it all in front of me. Dad told me ABC Wide World of Sports didn't plan to show highlights of the race until the weekend after next. That was okay by me, listening to Sid Collins's familiar voice narrate the 500 at the Brickyard live, let me revisit my childhood, curled on the rug in front of our floor-model radio. As soon as I was old enough, I'd finagled a way into the infield for races with a portable radio so I could listen to the broadcast on WIBC. The track was so huge, you needed a way to follow the action all around the two-and-a-half-mile oval.

Len Sutton, the veteran driver who co-hosted the broadcast, mentioned a driver who'd been killed doing practice laps early in the month. Danger was the spice that heightened the spectacle of the race, but I was torn by it. This wasn't an adventure movie, death was real here. Drivers weren't stuntmen who could dust themselves off and walk away.

When I was in eighth grade, one of my all-time favorites, Bill Vukovich, whose family now owned a house a couple of blocks from ours, had been killed in a horrific crash that appeared to behead him as his car went over the guard rail upside down. It was shown over and over again on television. Bill's son, Billy Vukovich, was in today's race. I couldn't comprehend how he could climb into a car and compete at the highest and most dangerous level of racing after what had happened to his father.

I loved the race for all its pageantry and adventure, but I didn't know if I'd ever go to another one in person after the 1963 race. I'd been standing on the infield grass across from the grandstands on the main straightaway, peering over the heads of the crowd, as all thirty-three cars bunched together and roared into the first turn on the second lap. Suddenly, Eddie Sachs smashed into Dave McDonald's car at about 150 miles an hour. McDonald had spun off the wall coming out of the fourth turn to end up slowly moving in the center of the track. The force of Sachs's collision erupted into a thirty-foot fireball so hot, parts of each racecar welded together, incinerating both drivers in front of us. Horrified, I watched Eddie Sachs's arms wave aimlessly through the sheet of flame engulfing his car. Ash from the accident swirled high on waves of heated air that stung, even from that distance, as if the midday summer sun was shining directly into my staring face. The fire crew removed McDonald from his car into an ambulance, but the Sachs car was pulled into Gasoline Alley with the cockpit covered. I imagined them having to remove him with a shovel. By then, I was retching from the unforgettable smell of roasting human flesh, burning rubber, stinking hot metal, and the claustrophobic feeling of being trapped in a crowd of a quarter-million people.

I rushed, stumbling, out of the Speedway before the race could be restarted. I shuddered with the certainty that the white ash drifting in the air contained ashes from the drivers' bodies and had fallen onto my face, my skin, and hair. I hurried home to shower and scrub for an hour. I was troubled by the memories for a long time. Even so, I tried not to miss the event on radio, or later, television. I knew I could always turn off a radio or TV.

As the green flag dropped for the running start, the cars took off with a roar, but within the first nine laps, Jim Hurtubise, who I'd picked to follow because he drove one of the notorious Novis, my favorite cars, was already out with engine trouble. We could hear the rumble and whine of the race cars here, but when a Novi took the track, it's deep-throated V8 roar and rising shriek as it flew into the straightaways sounded like all the furies in hell had been loosed—it filled our neighborhood. It was the most powerful car ever built to race at the 500 but also the most difficult to control or keep running. Most believed the engine had too much force for the chassis it was strapped to, which was why these cars were best known for leading in races they failed to finish. True to form, both Novis were out of the race with 19 laps left to go. While Mickey and Leonard and my family came to sit with me for a few minutes at a time, I hardly paid attention to them as I listened rapturously until Bobby Unser took the checkered flag.

20 ALOHA NO AU IA 'OE

Ua ola loko i ke aloha—he alii ka la'i, he ha Ku'ulani na. Life is an echo—what you give out comes back.
  —Wise Hawaiian Saying

May 29, 1968
Indianapolis, Indiana

THE NEXT WEEKEND, one of Dave's high school friends and his wife came into the club bringing along another classmate named Mary Jo. She lit up Dave's eyes and made him smile. They'd met at school, and Dave had been interested in her though apparently, nothing had come from it back then. She seemed sweet and a little shy, attractive, but much different from the bombshells he was usually drawn to. He spent every minute he could with her, and she sparkled in response.

Watching Dave meet someone who affected him that way accentuated the loss and defeat that dogged me. I seemed to have slipped back into a skin of inadequacy I'd hoped never to wear again.

Stop wallowing around in the past! I reprimanded myself. *So you have regrets for things that happened here; what good can come from that now? Move on, find a way to make the future better.*

As though waiting for this moment, the obvious jumped out at me—I'd been deliriously happy with Theresa in the islands. I'd been denying myself the possibility of that feeling that joy again! I worried those two amazing months had resulted from the life-changing experiences and the incredible sun-showered setting surrounding us there. Would—could it even be possible for our relationship to be as magical anywhere else? Where there was no time limit? Was there a chance we cared enough for each other to risk everything I feared? Enough to go against my own resolve? The only way to know would be to try it somewhere else—like California.

The decision was made the way a padlock clicks into place, though I had a sneaking suspicion it might have been made before I'd even left Hawaii, and I just hadn't let myself admit it. Theresa speaking those final words in Hawaiian rose clear in my mind—*Aloha no au ia ʻoe*—I truly love you. I took the plastic key-ring viewer out, still warm from my pocket, and closed an eye to peer again at the two of us together. Though I looked as dorky as ever in my red-and-white-striped tee, the tropical sun seemed to emphasize the knowing promise in Theresa's enigmatic smile.

For God's sake, Larry, what are you waiting for? Freight trains can come out of the night, someone can run a stop sign, life can change in a heartbeat. You have a chance to be righteously happy—take it. Nothing's guaranteed, regrets are forever, you've been getting hit in the head with that lesson from the moment you came back here!

For a moment I panicked; *what if I've waited too long?* What if she'd met someone else before I could ask her? As soon as the night ended, I rushed like a dog off its leash to find a quiet place to call Hawaii.

Theresa's airmailed letter arrived at the end of the week.

My dearest darling Larry, I am so happy to have received your phone call. You made me the happiest girl in the world. I'm sorry for crying so much on the phone. But, darling, I was so happy to hear from you and to know that you do still love me. I really thought I wasn't going to hear from you at all. I would wait for the mail to come, hoping to get a letter from you. When nothing came I would sit in my room and cry like a baby.

Do you remember the picture Carol took of you and me in the car when Leonard was going to drive us around the island? Well I have that picture and would look at it every night before I went to bed, and it would make me think of how much fun we had. Then in the morning after I woke up I would look at it again. I can't wait to be with you, darling. You just don't know how much I love you . . .

She'd sent five pages full of declarations of love and promised to come to California. I'd thought she would, she'd said so on the phone, but it seemed more real handwritten in a letter. Knowing I was going to see her soon made a dramatic improvement in my attitude. Her long list of questions about how I felt about being home and if I liked playing here only reminded me of how difficult it was going to be to wait.

Letters from Jimmy and his assistant, Eve, arrived and included playlist reports from radio station programmers from Spokane to Nashville claiming, *Look Back In Love* was their "pick to hit" or "most requested" by listeners. *Billboard Magazine* kept us in their Top 60 Pop Spotlight section along with famous bands like The First Edition, Procol Harum, and Cream.

Before leaving Hawaii, I'd asked the office to send promo material and deejay copies of *Look Back In Love* to the local Indianapolis stations and to let them know where we would be appearing. But none of them played our record. No one here had ever heard of us.

When I asked Jimmy why they hadn't been contacted, he told me the office had sent them everything I'd asked him to; if I didn't believe him, he could show me the receipts. Either he or Eve had called the stations daily and left messages, he said, but their calls weren't returned. Not the kind of reception I'd hoped to get in my hometown.

The three of us from Indianapolis took pride in our Hoosier heritage. Personally, I believed my Midwestern upbringing had helped me navigate the pitfalls and temptations we'd encountered, and, despite my inquisitive nature, kept me from getting into too much trouble. But our hometown wouldn't return the respect. Beginning with our short-lived recording career as the Reflections, when Chicago, the big city nearest us, had been on the verge of making us national hit recording artists, we'd been ignored here—our records never receiving a second of airtime; not a word in the local press or in the smallest of local publications. Indianapolis radio seemed to consider us a Groucho Marx punch line: Why, they seemed to say, would we want to play music by a group from Indianapolis? If they were any good, they'd be from someplace else.

Now it was happening again. Not only was WIBC, our main rock station here not playing *Look Back In Love*, I doubted they would unless they were forced to when and if broke into the national top ten. This city refused to give me the affirmation I longed for. *Hey Indianapolis, gimme a break will ya? We're here! We're makin' it! I'm not just some chipped-tooth shithead buried in the back of the goddamned Shortridge and North Central yearbook anymore!*

I wondered if Dave and Les's return home had been as disheartening for them as it had for me. It didn't seem so, but Mac's appearance was a triumphant moment for him as his many admirers from Cincinnati made the trek to Indianapolis to see him. Leonard and Mickey kept their complaints about being here to a minimum and made some friends in the club, but offstage they hardly knew what to do with themselves. Especially our hyperactive drummer; nothing seemed to catch his interest.

Earlier this year, in February, my father had come to the West Coast for an insurance conference and stopped in Las Vegas in time to see our closing night at the Pussycat A' Go Go. He was the first person in my family to hear us and loved the show. To see his pride in our performance was one of the highlights of my life. But the Rat Fink Lounge with its down-at-the-heels atmosphere and sketchy sound system was a long step down from a club on the Las Vegas Strip. Our music overwhelmed my mom. I watched her try to smile her way through two hours, but we played too loud and hurt her ears. Dad took her home early. They tried another night but didn't stay long.

My sister Cheryl, though well shy of twenty-one, had wangled herself a bartender's license through her part-time job in a restaurant in Bloomington and used it to get in. She bubbled over with enthusiasm and seemed to be having the time of her life. Most of her friends couldn't get in though, so after a while, she didn't come anymore. I liked having her there, but I always felt I had to keep an eye out for her, to make sure she was safe in this joint. Other than these personal moments, we could have been performing anywhere—except the weather would have probably been better.

The arrival of Theresa's letter inspired and lifted my expectations for the future. I'd begun to feel life was getting back to normal when more promising record-promotion reports arrived. A cloud was lifting, the planets coming into alignment, everything was going to be okay. I blazed Wednesday night, lustily singing my leads, focusing on getting my harmony parts perfect. I should have known, though—destiny rarely shows its cards in advance.

21 CALIFORNIA DREAMING

You never run out of things that can go wrong.
—Edward A. Murphy

June 9, 1968
Indianapolis, Indiana

I WATCHED MY DAD wade through the thick Sunday edition of the *Indianapolis Star*, animated by the view from my mom's upholstered glider in the wood-paneled family room. The afternoon sun splayed rays through partially drawn horizontal blinds on the windows.

"You seem a little skittish." He glanced at me from the devastation around him. He'd ravaged through the Sunday paper the way Sherman went through Georgia.

"It's the news about Bobby Kennedy's murder in LA. It hit us hard."

His head swiveled toward me. "An awful shock, for certain, but what in the world would it have to do with you boys?"

"Robert Kennedy's death was a tragedy, Dad. But when the brother of an American president who's been assassinated, who's also running for president is assassinated, it's too much. It's too coincidental. It feels like our country is under attack but from where? From who? It's scary. It's hard to know what to think. I haven't paid much attention to politics since John Kennedy was . . ." I stopped the glider and sat forward.

"It has also affected us in another way. The guy in our management office who coordinates promotion with our record label sent me a note; the bad political news wiped us off the airwaves. Nobody thinks our record will recover. Also means they won't pay the bill for the little music movie we did in Honolulu. I wish you could've seen it. Jeez, wish I could have." Jimmy's optimism that someone in our management office would take care of the film's cost had proved to be wrong. I pushed into the cushions to make the glider glide again.

"Sorry to hear that, of course." He shook out a page and folded it into a square showing a story he wanted to read. "Seems to me you're anxious to shake our Indiana dust off your heels and get back to California."

"Well . . ." I hesitated, not sure how far I wanted to get into this. "I met a girl in Honolulu who's coming to LA to see me. She was in our little movie. Can hardly wait to see her."

"Oh?" Dad showed me his steely-eyed look, giving away little of what he was thinking. "What about the girl in Las Vegas? Jan, wasn't it? The English girl who performed in one of the hotel shows? I thought you were pretty interested in her." I hung my head, though I couldn't say why. I found it easy to feel defensive around him.

"I was. I did. I mean, I liked Jan a lot, but . . . we decided it would be better to end it. I didn't know when the band would get back to Vegas, and her visa was running out. Looked like she'd be moving back to England soon." I paused. "Wasn't meant to be, I guess."

I slowed the rocker I'd unconsciously pumped up to about thirty miles an hour. "Anyway, except for family, I don't know anybody here anymore. A lot's changed in three years—at least for me."

"Three years can be a long time. Thought you'd be back here much sooner. Have to admit," he chuckled, "thought it likely I'd see you back here shortly after you left." He sipped a little coffee as his eyes roved over another page. "Or that you'd at least come home to visit your mother and sister."

"I was so messed up when I left, I didn't have a clue what to expect. After I got there and realized what we were up against, I'd thought we'd be on the road home in a couple days, too. We had less than a week to put the band together, Dave lost his voice . . . I can't begin to tell you how many obstacles we had to overcome to turn ourselves into a working band. And I'd have an even harder time explaining how we managed to hang on until we got good enough to be called decent. We were never secure until we signed a year-long contract in San Francisco." I tried to catch my dad's eyes, but the paper continued to snap and rustle as he worked his way through it.

"We had to make it work. I think we all felt that way. I know I did; I felt something inside me would die if we didn't. I knew it when I got off the plane, the air smelled different, the sunlight brighter, ocean breezes . . . like I was right where I was supposed to have been all along."

Dad's two-toned eyes, one icy blue, the other pale gray today, came to rest on mine and his eyebrows raised in an unasked question.

"We're always traveling, you know. Almost never stay more than four weeks anywhere. I wouldn't have believed I could exist this way. We live our lives on the opposite side of the clock from most people." I felt my mouth twist in a wry smile. "When Pat came to see us, she told me we were night people.

"I'm uncomfortable in crowds now—unless they're on the other side of a stage. Hate waiting in lines. I'm used to buying groceries at open-all-night stores when they're mostly deserted. We go to movies in the afternoons or on our off nights when theaters are half-empty, amusement parks like Knottsberry Farm or Disneyland on weekdays. That's my life now."

He nodded. "When I saw you boys in Las Vegas, I felt a touch of that. It's seductive that wanderlust, that sense of adventure." He gave me a foxy grin. "But you can't live that way forever. Frankly, I'm surprised it's lasted this long."

My father and I had shared a heartfelt conversation after he'd watched us perform in Las Vegas, but he understood very little of what my life was actually like. Nothing in his experience could have allowed him to imagine the world I inhabited. I'm sure I gained some respect in his eyes that night, and that was fantastic, but in many, if not most ways, we remained far apart. I was confident that in his own way, he loved me. I didn't doubt that, and I loved him, but I would always be the enigmatic eldest child who'd failed to graduate from college or, if nothing else, taken an honest job in the insurance business. At least I hadn't become a burden, I seemed to read behind his eyes. Not yet anyway.

Against all the odds, our makeshift band had grasped a shaky toehold in the Bay Area and made a precarious living playing music. We kept struggling, always working to get better, jostling our way to prominence in top San

Francisco and Southern California clubs and, astonishingly, Las Vegas nightspots and an internationally acclaimed resort hotel. We'd become a cottage industry for agents, personal and business managers—our recording career in the hands of a famous producer. The first record from our sessions in a top Hollywood studio had done relatively well in the East, and our second, and latest one, had been slated to be a big national hit. Though *Look Back In Love* wasn't panning out, studio time was already being booked. We'd be back recording again soon. At each milestone reached, my self-confidence had grown.

"I don't think you realize how much I've changed. I'm not the same beaten-down guy who got on that plane three years ago, you know." Dad swept the papers together and smoothed them out before putting them down. He moved on to the *Parade Magazine* section. "Being labeled a loser, a dreamer, had become ingrained in me. I didn't understand how much until I left home. The way things were going, I don't think that would have changed if I hadn't."

What was the use of explaining? It wasn't as if my dad wasn't listening as much as it was he couldn't comprehend what I meant. I swam in a sea of creative people where I lived now: musicians, composers, producers; respected people who openly considered themselves screenwriters, actors, sound engineers, television personalities. We met and performed for people making their living on film and TV crews as electricians, lighting professionals, grips. Checkers in stores, teachers, and wait staff in restaurants doubled as poets, stuntmen, composers, and backup singers. Everybody had a dream, and it was okay.

Here, questionable vocational choices like those labeled you an impractical romantic—guilty of poor judgment at best, cautionary tales to children at worst. From the first minute I'd set foot in California, I'd known I was more like everyone around me than in all my years in Indiana.

We were playing to record-breaking crowds; Dave, Les, and Mac exulted in our hometown success. Leonard and Mickey, on the other hand, were openly miserable. White Castle and Steak and Shake hamburgers, even a riding tour around the Speedway track hadn't brought them around. After months in Hawaii and long weeks, they were anxious to be home with their families in sunny Southern California. Though Mickey had seemed to adopt my family as his, he and Leonard hardly knew what to do with themselves off stage. Especially Leonard. He needed to get back to where everything stayed open all night and Sundays.

When a second letter full of intoxicating promises arrived from Theresa, I joined them in a subversive troika, eager to leave for LA. By living with my parents here, I'd almost saved enough money to pay for her ticket. I wrote back describing the places I wanted to show her and assuring her of how I longed to feel her flesh against mine, too. Dreaming wasn't a character flaw in California.

22 THERESA

May you have Grace in your Step, Song in your Hand and Aloha in your Heart.
    –Hula Blessing

July 8, 1968
North Hollywood, California

I DROPPED HER luggage, and Theresa tossed her bag and flower lei on the table, as the door slammed behind us. We embraced with a passionate kiss as though we meant to meld our bodies together. Before we got too far, she pushed me into one of the kitchen chairs.

"I have been dreaming of when we would be alone in California." She slipped out of her shoes with a provocative shy smile and demurely slid panties from beneath her cotton dress and kicked them away. Her body rocked seductively in front of me.

"Do you remember my *haole* man, the dancers at Kapiolani Park, how you wanted me to dance the hula for you?" Her deep, cocoa-brown eyes crinkled at the open-mouthed attention I was paying to her swaying body. "How you said that would be the best day ever? Do you remember?"

"Uh-huh, I do. And sweetheart, this is by far, the best day ever, but—"

"I have been practicing in front of a mirror for you." She turned to her left and rolled a hip toward me rotating in a circle to show me how things looked from the back before facing me again, hips never stopping, naked feet stepping.

She raised her arms gesturing sensually, fingers waving in tempo to the silent rhythm she danced to. "I'm telling you an ancient Polynesian story of love with my hands." She tipped her head in a teasing glance. "But I don't think you are paying any attention to them. Ah," she chuffed, "perhaps you do not think I am good-looking when I dance for you?" I hadn't seen her in weeks, and here she was, hips swaying, barefoot in front of me, wearing only a thin flowered sundress that clung to the curves of her sumptuous body. In my wildest fantasies, she couldn't have been more breathtaking.

"You are the most incredible vision I have ever seen." My voice husked with arousal. "I'm having trouble concentrating, though . . ." I frowned in pretend concern. "I remember someone telling me, historically, hula girls didn't wear tops. That might be what's throwing me off."

"Oh," she said with feigned surprise. "So, you think I am not an authentic Hawaiian girl then?" Theresa turned her back to me, gazing over her shoulder with parted lips as she kept her rear end swaying from side to side. She swept her torrent of hair aside and tilted her head so she could loosen the top of her dress. As it dropped, she retrieved the lei perfuming the mini-apartment and draped the garland around her neck. Arranging her soft, dark tresses over the flowers, she rolled her hips until she faced me again. The pebbly aureoles of her honey-gold breasts peeked between strands of raven hair and Plumeria blooms.

"Is this more what you had in mind?"

"Jesus, Theresa, you are killing me," I groaned in exquisite agony. "You do know that don't you?"

"What I like to dance most though, is Tahitian style. I worked on this for you, too." The swinging and swaying of her lower body double-timed as she lifted her hands high and danced with ferocity. Her eyes gleamed with anticipation, knowing we'd soon be doing everything we'd promised to each other in our passionate letters. She almost got the lei off before the floral sweetness of its soft blooms was crushed between us on the bed.

"Wait, wait," she said with a giggle, "I haven't finished all the moves I practiced yet." My girl was here, in my room, with me, at the Mid-Valley Motel; the weeks that had separated us evaporated as if they'd never been.

After a short nap with me beside her, Theresa woke in the late afternoon, reenergized from her long plane ride and the time difference. When I suggested a tour through Tinseltown, she eagerly agreed. I took the 101 across the Cahuenga Pass out of the Valley, turning south on the Hollywood Freeway in my trusty Ford Falcon. Dave and Mac had Cadillac convertibles, but my payments went toward a Hammond B3. We exited at Hollywood Boulevard. Being tourists, we stopped to gawk at the concrete footprints at Grauman's Chinese Theater before backtracking to La Brea and down to Sunset for a short ride through my history here.

The Travelodge at La Brea conjured bittersweet memories. I described the four ironic weeks we'd spent penniless here, before making a grand appearance at Caesars Palace two years ago. I told her how we'd only been able to pay for one room for one person; how most of us had to sneak in at night to sleep.

I took us west on Sunset to the psychedelically-embellished Aquarius Theater; when it was called the Hullabaloo, we'd played there with a slew of famous bands, musicians, vocalists, and even comedians in weekend marathons that ran until dawn. It had been our first full taste of fame after arriving from San Francisco. I pointed out the Red Velvet, where we'd replaced Ike and Tina Turner for a few weeks last year, so we'd be closer to the studio where we recorded. Within a few minutes, we passed the simple, one-story building housing that studio, Producer's Workshop, where we would soon be to work on our next releases.

Crescent Heights Boulevard marked the border between the city of Los Angeles and an unincorporated area sometimes called hippy heaven—or better known as the Sunset Strip. I told her about Pandora's Box, the nightclub Jimmy O'Neill had owned before becoming our manager. Though it was gone now, it had been here on the northeast corner of Crescent Heights. He'd wanted a venue where kids as young as fifteen and a half could see popular recording acts they couldn't have otherwise seen unless they were twenty-one. This corner had gotten so thick with teens on weekends, residents called for a police crackdown that sparked the Sunset Strip Riots of 1966. Last year, before we met Jimmy, the city fathers had forced him to sell the club so they could demolish it.

We cruised past the Whiskey A Go-Go, pimped out in Paris Red like a French disco. Next was the Galaxy nightclub. Between here and Gazzarri's, where we'd played for a few nights during those four weeks of starvation, midnight rovers brazenly bought, sold, and consumed grass, acid, heroin, and each other, along with who knew what else. Around the curve at Tower Records, we cruised by our manager's offices before abruptly exiting into the Beverly Hills flats. I stayed on Sunset through Jan and Dean's Dead Man's Curve, behind UCLA to Sepulveda until I could turn on Santa Monica. We followed it as it rambled toward a blazing Southern California sun beginning its nightly dive into the sea.

Fascinated, Theresa watched the beach come into view as we pulled into the parking lot by the Santa Monica Pier. The July evening breezes swept her hair out behind her as we walked on the sand, so she piled it into a tousled bun with provocative wisps twirling across her face in playful gusts. The early moon's spell moved shadows over the expansive beach and gentle surf. I thought I felt a distant presence.

"This is what your ocean looks like from this side," I said, smiling at her.

She was elated. "Oh, how I love this, Larry. All of it. And I love you. I cannot find words to tell you how filled I am with love for you right now. I hope someday you can care for me as much as I do for you this very minute."

She slipped off her sandals and walked along the water's edge, dipping her hand in the docile surge. "The water is cooler here. But I feel the way it touches my island. It tells me all is well in my home." She smiled at me, sliding her feet in the watery sand. "My island is happy I am here with you. It says you are the one for me. I'm glad because even if you weren't, I'm afraid I wouldn't be able to help myself. I would love you anyway." My heart melted.

We stopped for In-N-Out burgers and backtracked the same way we'd come until at Beverly Glen I turned up into the Hollywood Hills to Mulholland Drive near the same overlook Dave and I had gone to the night we'd ditched playing at Gazzarri's. Where I'd gazed across a sea of lights stretching to Santa Catalina Island, and tried to explain my crisis of faith in the band's musical integrity.

This night, Theresa and I made tender, awkward love in the front seat while overlooking this city, my home, that had gained one more angel this week. She fell asleep with her head on my thigh as we wound along the backbone of the Hollywood Hills, through Coldwater Canyon, and into the San Fernando Valley and home.

23 HOME ON THE ROAD

Home isn't a place, it's a feeling.
—Cecelia Ahern

July 9, 1968
North Hollywood, California

HER GENTLE PALM on my shoulder woke me to sweet reality the next morning. She'd already begun to change my world. We'd slept together in my bed—now it was ours. Though there'd been room to spare, we'd drifted into sleep entwined, skin to skin, as we had in the single bed at the Surfboard Hotel; no other touch could rival the encompassing peace it brought me. Theresa smiled as I rubbed my face into awareness, the aroma of fresh coffee filling what I could now call our cozy home.

"I need some things, honey," she said. "I have money from working in my mom's restaurant before I came here, so you won't have to pay. But would you take me shopping, yes?" She lay beside me, head propped up, face inches from mine.

"Sure sweetheart, but don't use your money. What do you need?" She sat cross-legged in front of me wearing one of my Tee shirts, making it difficult to concentrate on her words.

"We have to get rice so I can cook it here. The Mexican rice is sticky and gooey; ugh, I can't eat it. My rice looks and tastes very different. Poi is probably impossible to find, but I have to find my kind of rice." She looked so solemn I had to smile.

"Shouldn't be difficult. Rice in every grocery store around here, I imagine. Anything else?"

She hesitated before slipping off the bed. "We don't have to get it right away, but I would like a new dress to wear when we go to your nightclub. So you will be proud of me. A dress like the girls in California wear."

I smiled in reassurance. "Let's go get the rice and see if we can find some poi somewhere. I'm sure there's plenty of places selling dresses you'd like."

"Yes, we will go." She slipped under the covers beside me. "After we celebrate waking together."

After searching through groceries near us in the Valley, our expedition was running into a crisis. We couldn't find the right rice and Theresa was getting a little panicky. The grocers I asked shook their head in ignorance until one told us, "Maybe you're looking for something like Basmati or some kind of Asian rice. Try a Japanese or Indian food store." I'd had no idea there were so many different varieties of this stuff. After checking the yellow pages, we were soon on our way into the more ethnic neighborhoods over in the city. It was well into the afternoon when we returned with a twenty-five-pound cloth bag of her special rice. And we'd found a small package of powdered taro root we'd been promised would turn into poi when mixed with boiled water. Theresa eyed it with suspicion but decided to try it. It made no difference to me. I couldn't bring myself to eat it anyway. We bought fresh pineapple—though she hardly considered it fresh compared to the fruit available to her in Hawaii; pork cutlets, fish fillets, hamburger, peas, and sea salt among other assorted items filled the bags.

"Now I can cook for us," she said, blissfully unpacking groceries into the shelves of our mini kitchen. "And we will have many happy meals together."

Immediately after returning from Indianapolis, the band had held a group meeting at the Mid-Valley Motel. We'd been so caught up in "Hawaiian time" in Honolulu, we hadn't learned many new tunes. Some of it might have been in believing too much in how a hit record would change our lives. We were human, and it wasn't beyond us to get lazy, and the audiences there hadn't wanted new tunes anyway. In Indianapolis, we'd been distracted from rehearsing by friends and family and hadn't changed our playlist. Playing the same old tunes had gotten boring, and it showed. We agreed: we were tired of being mediocre. Our pride required us to dedicate ourselves to three afternoons of full rehearsals to add four new numbers a week while we were at the Rag Doll. Those of us with leads or difficult instrumental parts would work on our own so we could assemble our assignments at rehearsal. It was an exhausting schedule, but I'd welcomed the distraction from the growing anxiety I felt in reuniting with Theresa.

Les kicked things off these new additions with a song written by Jimmy Webb he'd begun learning in Indiana—Glen Campbell's *By the Time I Get to Phoenix*. It suited him perfectly. We learned some quick dance numbers for Mac, including an easy medley of Blue Cheer's psychedelic version of an Eddie Cochran's original '50s hit, *Summertime Blues*, and Creedence Clearwater's *Susie Q*.

But once Theresa arrived, I agonized through rehearsals. After the scorching disappointment of my homecoming in Indianapolis, I treasured every moment with her. As we re-familiarized ourselves, we grew closer in every way, reassuringly touching and stroking whenever we were together. But we still needed new songs. I took on Tommy James and the Shondells' *Kind of a Drag*, concentrating on getting comfortable singing while nailing the necessary organ riffs, eagerly anticipating who and what waited for me at home. Dave easily slipped into The Union Gap's latest, *Young Girl*—everything Gary Puckett sang was perfect for him—and the Young Rascals' *A Beautiful Morning*.

Most nights, Theresa came to the club with me, and her eyes drew me to her at every break. The Rag Doll never looked better than with her there. The guys seemed glad to see her. She reminded them of our dreamy days in the islands, I think. But not me—my Hawaiian fantasy had become a California reality. We were together here without a time limit. Her sweet scent permeated my clothes, skin, and our very room.

On our next night off, we felt our efforts deserved a break, and some of us gathered to imbibe a little herb and hang out in Mac and Joan's room. It was close quarters. Theresa and I practically sat on top of each other struggling to keep our hands from embarrassing each other.

Joan Brown, Mac's wife, pulled me aside. "You know you've got to give yourself some space from that girl."

"What?" Joan rarely gave me advice on girlfriends. In fact, I couldn't remember her giving me advice of any kind at all. She seemed to choose her words with care.

"If I hadn't had so much wine, I doubt I would be saying this, but she needs more than just you, and you need more than just her. You can't fill up her whole life, it's not going to be enough." Joan noted my awestruck surprise and obvious lack of comprehension.

"Listen, do the rest of us girls, even Les's new heartthrob Susie, follow our guys to work every night? I know Stark Naked's a great band, but every single night?"

Susie, a cute, daring-eyed blonde with a full and easy smile had walked into our guitar player's life at the Rag Doll before Theresa joined me in California. She seemed to capture his heart instantly. He learned the Buckingham's tune *Susan*, and when he sang it, he'd caught hers. His dark good looks and her delicate pale features, with a sprinkle of freckles across her nose, made them a striking couple. Theresa, a little intimidated by the older wives, had been drawn to Susie who was a little closer to her age. She would have liked to be better friends with her, given the opportunity; Les tended to keep his love interests apart from the rest of the girls. To her, Susie was the epitome of a California girl.

Joan's eyes rolled to where Theresa sat laughing with Leonard's wife, Paula, on the couch. "Your Hawaiian girl is so young. How old is she?"

"I thought she was nineteen, almost twenty when I asked her to come here, but she admitted at the last minute she was eighteen." I shrugged.

"So young," she repeated. "Eighteen." I thought I read disapproval on her face.

"What was I going to do, Joan? We were already in love. I'd bought the plane tickets; I made sure it was okay with her parents before she left." I spread my hands in helplessness. "I was already a goner."

"Well, who am I to say? Anyway, this was Lora and Paula's idea; you need to let her come and hang out with us some nights. Your girl needs her own gal pals, Larry. As a friend to you, we'll try to make her feel at home."

What a sweet gesture. Joan could seem rough and tough until reality occasionally broke through the aloof exterior protecting the kindhearted girl inside. There was something I wondered about though. She and Marie had been close once.

"What about Marie?"

"Well, what about her?" she countered, steel-eyed.

"You two were close before we went to Hawaii, weren't you? Is it possible for you to be friends with Theresa?"

"Like you said, you were with Marie." In a rare moment of frankness, she said, "Look, we don't get to choose who you guys go out with, or shack up with, or even marry. Marie was my friend while you were doing—whatever it was you two were doing. She's gone, and Theresa's here. It's that simple."

"Thanks, Joan, I didn't understand before, I didn't realize . . . but I get it now." After a short pause, I said, "Theresa told me she wished Susie could help her pick out a dress or two, something more appropriate for nightlife in California. Would you talk to her about helping Theresa find something like that? I'm not a good judge, I like everything she wears—or doesn't wear even more."

Joan's laugh came out a hoarse caw. "When I first saw Susie, I told Mac I thought she dressed like a hooker; told him I wasn't sure we could be friends." She dragged on her cigarette and shook her head. "And now your sweet, young girlfriend wants to dress like her." She paused for a moment, exhaling smoke. "We'll ask Theresa to hang out with us tomorrow night. She'll probably come and tell you. Why don't you encourage her?" She smiled, and I recognized the young girl in Joan, and a big sister instinct I'd never seen before. She added, "I've gotten to know Susie, and I like her well enough now. I'll talk to her."

Later, back in our room, Theresa told me she'd been asked to watch TV and play cards with the other girls tomorrow night while I went to work. "Do you think I should go? I guess I probably should get to know them better, but I always thought I would go with you to the Rag Doll at night. What do you think I should do?"

Turning to her as I shucked out of my jeans, I said, "Truth is I want us to be together every second of every day. You make me feel incredible like there's a wall around us and nothing bad can get through it if we don't want it to. But maybe it's better if you don't come with me every night, though I'll always want you to. Spend some time with the girls. They don't easily offer their friendship to girlfriends, not unless they think they're going to be around for a while."

"Is that what you think? Am I going to be around for a while, sweet man? Do you love me and want to hold me and touch me?" Grinning shamelessly she reached out. "Do you want me to touch you, and hold you in my hands like this, and then take you into me?" She rubbed her body against me and whispered into my ear, "I think you would find it extremely hard to send me away unless you send this with me."

For one of the rare times in my life, I was unable to get one smartass remark out before reality superseded imagination. Our easy intimacy continued to bring us closer together.

Mary Jo, the girl who had caught Dave's eye in Indianapolis, came to visit him. He wanted to show her old Mexico, so he organized an overnight trip to Papas and Beer, a famous bar and restaurant in Ensenada. He invited Theresa and me and Leonard and his wife, Paula. Dave and Mary Jo were in his car while we rode with Leonard and Paula. We hit the road early afternoon on Monday, our day off. Near San Juan Capistrano, about halfway to the Mexican border, Theresa became quiet and seemed queasy.

"Leonard," I called from the backseat. "Can you turn off the freeway at the next off ramp? Theresa needs some air," I reached across to open Theresa's window while she tried to keep her stomach down.

Paula turned to see, and quickly grasped the situation. "Leonard, Theresa's going to be sick. You've got to pull off on the shoulder right now."

As the car slowed, I jumped from the backseat and ran around to help Theresa out of the car. She wobbled a couple of steps and vomited. I held her hair out of the way until the heaves stopped and she looked at me with liquid puppy-dog eyes. Paula spread a beach towel, and Theresa sank to the ground gratefully wiping her mouth with a tissue.

"Are you okay, Treese?" I'd already started calling her a pet name. She nodded.

"What happened?" Leonard asked. "She get a bad burrito or something?"

Theresa shook her head, gulping. "I've never been in a car this long." She tried to smile. "Carsick, I guess." We laughed in relief.

She'd lived her whole life on an island you could drive around in about an hour and a half. This was the longest she'd ever been in a car, let alone on a high-speed freeway. When she felt better, we continued on to San Diego, crossed at Tijuana, and drove another hour down the Baja peninsula. I kept an eye on her, but she seemed to have gotten her highway legs and was fine through the rest of the trip. We played on the beach in Ensenada in the late afternoon and, after browsing souvenir shops, I chose chicken drowned in a fiery mole sauce in the picturesque Mexican restaurant we'd come to experience. Theresa stuck with black beans, vegetables, and fresh fish from the local bay accompanied by a flavorful salsa.

She'd looked forward to getting to know Paula and Mary Jo better on this trip, but something had come between Dave and Mary Jo that left her troubled and Dave moody. I was sorry to see that happen; she seemed like a sweet girl, and I'd hoped she'd stick. It wasn't a surprise when she flew back to Indiana soon afterward. I'd hoped for Dave's sake she would be coming with us to the Pussycat A' Go Go in Las Vegas.

Reinvigorated by our new songs, we settled into our regular rehearsal schedule. At the end of the week, we packed up and drove away, our vehicles arranged in a caravan for our trip across the Mojave Desert

24 A TRIP TO THE DESERT

> Las Vegas in the summer is that feeling when you open the oven to check the cookies and it burns your face . . . but there are no cookies, and you can't escape.
> —A Nony Mouse (someone who bakes cookies)

July 22, 1968
Las Vegas, Nevada

AFTER BLUE DIAMOND ROAD, Interstate 15 unwound into a broad shallow valley. I nodded ahead. "We're almost there, honey."

Her fingers swept her dark hair back as she leaned forward hoping for a glimpse of the famous gambling resorts.

"Can't see anything yet."

"Strip is still about twenty minutes away, but I'm going to turn off in about ten."

"This is so exciting. I've always wanted to see Las Vegas. One of my uncles came here and couldn't stop talking about it when he came home."

The lowering sun cast long, pre-dusk shadows from the Spring Mountains as our little caravan cruised along the gentle slope. Ahead of us, Leonard led in the equipment van with Paula and their young son Lenny, following behind. The rest of the band spread out along the highway behind us.

We'd gotten away from North Hollywood later than planned. Even though we'd gone the back way, taking the Pearblossom Highway behind the San Gabriel Mountains to meet the I-15 at Victorville, it had taken nearly five hours to get here. Fortunately, none of us had broken down. Traveling across the incandescent Mojave Desert in the middle of summer was a trip through Hades for older vehicles. The roadside had been scattered with overheated cars. We'd planned to leave after closing last night to miss the torrid daytime temperatures, but everybody was too exhausted. This was Theresa's longest car trip so far. Her interest in seeing a real desert had quickly waned. Before long she'd curled up on the front seat to rest her head on my thigh, face in the blast from the air conditioner. I'd waited to wake her until we crossed into Nevada at Stateline.

She'd woken with a big yawn followed by a huge smile. She lolled back next to me peering all around. "Are we there yet?" I had to tell her we still had another hour or more to go.

I left the interstate at the Las Vegas Boulevard exit, where it was still a two-lane country road paralleling the Interstate, north. Paula and Leonard led everyone else on to Sahara, a quicker route to our destination. I wanted Theresa to see Las Vegas the way I'd seen it the first time.

We traveled through open, scraggly desert brush until we caught a glimpse of the Hacienda Hotel's tower rising between us and the highway. Next, came the Tropicana's golf course on the right still as incongruous here as it would have been on the moon. Thick spumes of water drifted over the fairways and greens, evaporating into mist before they hit the turf. Then the Tropicana showed itself, followed by the Aladdin. The road widened into a four-lane highway as we approached the Dunes and Flamingo Road. We'd reached the heart of the Strip, and I enjoyed each of her oohs and aahs as we passed each hotel.

"Caesars Palace!" She grabbed my arm and squeezed, gazing past me to the huge fountains and glamorous grounds of the giant casino at the intersection of Las Vegas Boulevard and Flamingo Road. "You guys played there? Didn't it make you nervous? It's so huge and grand."

"I was scared to death every night," I admitted. "We can sightsee later tonight, or we'll find some time before setup tomorrow."

Past the Flamingo, I pointed further along Las Vegas Boulevard to a tall sign over a racebook wedged among a car rental agency, a liquor store, and a gas station, on the right. "Speaking of the Pussycat, it's dead ahead." High above us on the right, a black cat's face grinned down on us with a mischievous smile. As we drove, the marquee showed Stark Naked and the Car Thieves; below it was

Sly and the Family Stone. "Well, here's news. Our early band is amazing. Wait until you hear them."

We drove past the Cat toward the Desert Inn. "I have to turn here for the motel. The Sands and Sahara and a bunch more hotels are farther up the street. And look"—I pointed at a construction site on the west side of the street—"they're building a casino that looks like a giant circus tent. We'll have a lot of chances to look around later."

We were staying at a motel behind the Desert Inn's golf resort. As regular commuters, we'd discovered reasonably clean economical rent-by-the-week rooms with good showers, small kitchenettes, and a decent pool.

It was still sizzling hot as we hauled our luggage to our second-floor room. We put the basics away and considered quick showers before christening the accommodations, but our hunger for each other won out. Afterward, lying there bonded together felt wonderful. It was the perfect way to unwind after a long drive.

"When I was writing letters to you, you know—from my bedroom," Theresa giggled and turned to lay her hand on the side of my face, "I tried to imagine what being here with you would be like. I knew it would be great. I knew we would be so happy, and we would love each other and love being together. But sharing all this with you is so much more than I ever dreamed it would be."

She rolled over to kiss me, and we were considering another round of lovemaking when someone pounded on the door.

"Larry, it's Leonard," he yelled as if I wouldn't recognize his voice. "Too late for any of the buffets, so we're going to the Silver Slipper for dinner. See you guys downstairs in fifteen minutes, okay?"

"Okay, but make it twenty." We'd have to hurry, but there'd be time enough if we combined our urges with a quick shower.

Knowing Sly Stone was playing the early sets, most of us made it in to see their last set before we went on. Earlier, I'd found a little time to drive Theresa around town including a stop where she'd discovered the teal, off-the-shoulder print dress she was wearing tonight. She looked gorgeous, and I told her so as she delicately sipped a margarita and gazed around the darkened room. I tried to see the Pussycat through her eyes.

"This place probably doesn't seem very fancy after driving by all the big hotels on the Strip."

The Cat didn't even have a street entrance. It was hidden, tucked behind a racebook where anyone could walk in off the street and place a bet on a horserace anywhere in the country. Patrons had to drive through an alleyway next to the club to the parking lot and its main entrance. An unimpressive door led into a short corridor past a bar stretched along the north wall. Loose black drapes on the opposite side hid three blackjack tables and a few slot machines. Inside the showroom were two stages: one was large and curtained, where the headliner performed; the other smaller one, hugged the opposite wall with a large dance floor between them. The place wasn't dirty enough to be disreputable, but it was far from pristine. The one thing different since last time we'd been here: the small stage was empty. Both bands would be playing on the main stage.

"I think this place is perfect," Theresa responded. "It's got a great atmosphere, and it's going to be packed when you guys go on." She smiled in satisfaction. I felt her possessive palm, warm on my thigh, and reveled in the excitement and love shining in her dark-brown eyes. The room was almost full. The locals must be happy to have us back for the Cat to be this jammed on a Tuesday night.

"Some amazing things have happened to us here," I told her. "We were asked to audition at Caesars Palace when we became the main act. It may not look it, but all kinds of celebrities come in to let their hair down. A lot of great bands have played at the Cat. Tom Chase, Paul Revere and the Raiders, and the Checkmates, Ltd. played here, and some fantastic groups we're friends with play here regularly, like Orange Colored Sky and Sixth Cavalry. Last time in, we followed Gary Puckett and the Union Gap."

Dave pulled out a chair. "Hey, what's going on with the stage?"

"We're alternating the first two sets with Sly Stone," I told him. "Jack Turner says they're starting to book big national acts now and they aren't willing to play on the small stage. He says Sly Stone's band has been kicking ass, so he wants them to share the main stage with us. Guess they have a record getting some action, too."

"Dammit, wish we could get back in the studio. Wish Eddie would find us some decent songs."

I grinned at Dave. "He also said, 'You boys are still the headliners, you're still the big draw. Could change anytime so don't let it go to your heads.'"

Mac dropped into a chair swirling a rocks glass. "Hell yes, we're still the big draw. Read it in the paper."

Theresa, elbows resting on the table, had propped her head in her hands, listening intently. I put an affectionate hand on her arm. She leaned into me and put her hand on mine.

"I was about to tell Theresa that Sly had been our early act a couple of months before we went to Hawaii." I gestured toward the small, darkened stage. "They started out in the Bay Area, same as us. So, they had to start out on the little stage the way we did."

"Sly used to be on the radio. Used to listen to him goin across the Bay Bridge on my way to the Galaxie," Mac said. "Maybe one of us shoulda been a deejay."

"Getting onto the big stage at the Cat isn't easy," Dave said, "We'd been pretty well-known in San Francisco and made some noise in LA, but nobody knew us when we came here. Was like starting all over. Jack told us new bands had to play the regular bands' two off-nights as an audition, and, if you passed that, he might book you on the small stage, if he had an opening. If you did well enough there, you might get a shot at the main stage."

"I glanced at Dave and Mac remembering how we'd barely survived those rough days. "Learned that lesson the hard way."

"We was still wet behind the ears when it came to agents," Mac said. "This particular asshole agent booked us here for two nights, letting us believe it was for four weeks, like a normal gig. Had to hang out here for a month playin off-nights before we got on the small stage. The last week, Honest John's Casino paid us in all we could eat at the goddamned salad bar, and we needed it to keep from starvin."

"Was a hard time." I nodded. "Next time in, though, we made it on to the main stage. Played there ever since."

"'Scuse me," Dave stood, "gotta get some hot tea, start warming up my throat." He headed toward the bar.

Dave got back just as the curtain opened and the lights came up. Sly and the Family Stone hit, and held, the opening chord of James Brown's *Papa's Got a Brand New Bag*. Even on the big stage, they'd stuffed it with equipment; Sly had his Hammond B3 front and center, with his brother Freddy to his right. To the left, Larry Graham's amazing bass licks rumbled in perfect synch with the drums as they slipped into their own smooth groove of James Brown's instant classic. He pointed toward a table over on the far side. And there was James Brown himself, hopping and popping in the middle of his entourage.

Near the end of the tune, Sly lifted a hand from the keys of his keyboard to make a fist and then shake out fingers, one at a time, in an entirely new tempo. Without transition, the band instantly dropped into the pocket of *Dance to the Music*, with clever lyrics introducing each player and the instrument they played, in a party-funk style I'd never heard before. Without pause, Sly abruptly shook the band into another time-change with *Underdog*, a different kind of funk, before quickening the pace with *Turn Me Loose*, followed by a brilliant non-stop cascade of uniquely styled songs, most, but not all, originals. They closed with *Let Me Take You Higher*, and everybody came to their feet yelling before the stage lights went down.

Only one word described them—breathtaking. Instead of matching outfits, they wore crazy, colorful, San Francisco-pimp-fancy, Gypsy clothes. No patter, no front man, nothing but wall-to-wall music from beginning to end. Still couldn't get over how he could play in one tempo and count off a new cadence with his hand.

I hadn't said a word to Theresa, letting her soak them in as I had when I first saw them. "So, what do you think?" I said with satisfaction. "Fantastic, right?"

25 THE CAT AND THE FAMILY STONE

My school colors were unclear. We used to say, "I'm not naked, I'm in the band."
—Steven Wright

July 23, 1968
Las Vegas, Nevada

THE DESERT HEAT made summer the off-season for tourists in Las Vegas. Some nights, temperatures exceeding a hundred degrees still cooked the pavements outside when we ended at five in the morning. But Stark Naked and the Car Thieves, back-to-back with Sly and the Family Stone, burned even hotter inside than the air outside, lifting and inspiring each other until dawn. Lines of club-goers waited to get in, the crowd within thick with celebrities.

When Bill Cosby, who'd often came over between shows at the New Frontier to hang with us, told me he thought we were the best band he'd ever seen, he was being kind. After he'd seen Sly's band, I thought he'd change his mind, but he didn't. He said he liked us better. He thought we were "easy on stage"; like he could come to see us "in his pajamas." I told him he must have been as Irish as I was spouting so much malarkey. I knew better, and it was okay—even though we were the headline act, and we both played on the larger stage, it was clear to me who the best band was, and if anybody thought different it might be because Sly was inventing a new genre of music people hadn't caught on to yet. I didn't mind us being runner-up to such a spectacular and musically unique band as Sly and the Family Stone.

On a night when Theresa hadn't come with me, I spent my breaks at a table right smack in front of Sly's bassist, Larry Graham, so I could see his fingers up close. Through the night I watched and listened to his fingers, and a thumb, the fleshy end part longer than my longest digit, slap and pluck the strings. In an instant, he could deliver a sharp crack followed by a tender touch in perfect synchronicity. He reinvented playing bass for me. And then I heard him sing *Let Me Hear It From You*, a soulful ballad I hadn't heard them play before. Before he'd half finished, tears streamed down my face. It wasn't the lyrics that hit me so hard, it was the wrenching emotion and range of his incredible gospel voice delivering that message.

Between shows one night when I was sweaty, and the club's air-conditioning was really cranked, I slipped away from a table where Theresa and I were sitting to grab a sweater from the dressing room. Freddy and Gregg, Sly's drummer, waved as they climbed the stage stairs; they looked pretty beat. I hadn't gotten to know anyone in their band well; Sly himself seemed standoffish, but to be fair, each band was on stage while the other wasn't, we didn't have a lot of time to socialize. But I did make a point of making sure they knew how much I thought of their band. As I turned to leave, I noticed Cynthia, the trumpet player, slumped against the wall on the wooden steps to the stage.

"Cynthia, you okay?" She waved and nodded, but she choked, trying to hold her stomach down. She put her hands on her knees and dipped her head for a moment and gave me a sickly smile. The music on stage began without her.

"Oh man, do I feel bad. Only don't see how I can be. Puked everything already; ain't nothin' left to make me sick. Gotta go to LA tomorrow, be in the studio all day and night, right up until we come back here." She panted, gulping air. "Would you mind getting' me some water? Think if I rest a little, got some water, I could do the set."

"Sure, of course. Just sit here and take it easy." I helped her onto the built-in bench along the dressing-room wall.

Cynthia held her head in her arms when I got back. She took the glass and drained it, gave me a wan but grateful smile, and dragged herself out onto the stage.

I got it. We'd learned the same discipline from Eddie Pru, the gun-toting mobster at the Galaxie in North Beach who'd taught us stagecraft and reinforced the "show must go on" mentality. I remembered when the Asian Flu was running wild in San Francisco, and all the singers got ill the same night; Eddie wouldn't let us come off the stage. We took turns puking behind the curtain between songs. No matter the circumstances, you go on, you perform, sick or not.

While we were busy with rehearsals learning Cream's *Sunshine of Your Love*, and Dave adding another Gary Puckett tune, *Lady Willpower,* and other band business, Theresa found more chances to hang out with the girls. Though there was a pool at our motel, it was a short walk to three or four major hotels on the Strip. The veteran wives showed her and Susie how if you showed up in your bathing suit with shorts on, you could walk right through the hotel lobbies to the pool areas where you would be given towels and be pampered and catered to as if you were a hotel guest. The pool attendants figured out they were connected to Stark Naked and the Car Thieves, playing at the notorious Cat, but since the girls tipped generously, nobody seemed to mind.

I'd wanted to show Theresa the Valley of Fire, one of my favorite places, while we were here. About an hour northeast of town were acres and acres of brilliant red rock frozen into striped walls, arches, and wavy rock fields from when this had been the bottom of the sea and had risen in pre-historic times. But the temperatures were far too extreme to go there this trip. Instead, the band organized an expedition, including wives, girlfriends, and friends from the club as well, to trek up to a state park north of the city on Mount Charleston. We brought picnic supplies, plenty of grass, and Styrofoam chests of cold beer. The mountain meadows, vista points, and nature hikes in the Spring Mountains were high enough to provide welcome relief from the heat.

Before our last week, as the incredible engagement the two bands shared wound down, we got a harsh reminder that Vegas could still be a small-minded country town despite the sophistication of the big hotels.

One night, after we'd moved our equipment and left the stage after our first set, Sly and his band failed to begin playing. Not a real big deal; while the Pussycat liked to have as close to continuous live entertainment as possible, it was a considerable job to change equipment between sets. But somebody would probably catch a little hell.

The minutes stretched out until the curtain of the small stage opened to a plain stage light, and Sly stepped to a microphone stand, alone. He held his hands out asking for silence from an audience already loudly murmuring in response to his dramatic entrance.

"I've been threatened by the owner of this club," he said into the microphone, his voice booming through the room, "because my girlfriend, who happens to be white, can't sit at a table with me here. So rather than do what they tell us, we are going to leave. We are going to pack up and leave because we are being racially persecuted."

The curtain closed and recorded music returned to the house speakers. After a stunned silence, the packed room filled with angry applause. In a few minutes, some semblance of normalcy was restored, but we weren't sure what to do. We could hear noises of equipment moving behind the curtains.

Everybody but Mac and Mickey gravitated to the front of the stage where we waited around for somebody to come tell us something, but no one did. When it was the usual time to go on, we went back up to the stage. Sly's equipment was gone.

"Fuck man," Mac said, appearing as we got ready for our next set. "Mickey will be here in a minute. He says Bob Hirsch took Sly outta here with a gun to his head. Told him to pack up his band and get ready to ride." His face wrinkled in disgust. "I knew the guy was a red-neck son of a bitch, but I never thought he'd do nothing like this shit. He's got a whole flock of Vegas cop cars out back ready to escort Sly's band outta town, and make sure they don't stop nowhere short of the California line."

During our first song, we heard sirens wind up out back and fade away in the sultry desert night. Tonight, was a low moment in the life of this legendary club. I awakened Theresa when I got home to tell her about it. It wasn't only the racism that shocked and saddened me. In our country, you are allowed to have whatever opinion you wanted about people, even if it's ugly. But I didn't see how anybody, even an employer, could think they had the right to tell someone who they could be with. We finished out the gig with a local band hired to fill in on the small stage. The incident took most of the sheen off what had been an unbelievable engagement.

The next evening, near dusk, Theresa and I were hanging out around the motel pool. We'd be heading back to LA soon. I was lying at the side on a lounger thinking about going in to shower and get ready for work. Theresa was in the water, resting her head on her arms at the pool's edge. We'd been comfortably quiet for several minutes.

"I sent a letter to you a few days before I came to California. Do you remember it?" Theresa murmured.

"I remember every letter you sent. I read them over and over before you got here."

"I put a photo in the envelope—the one of me surfing."

I laughed gently. "I thought you looked cute balancing on the surfboard, but it must have been near the end of the ride, wasn't much of a wave you were on."

"When I got out there, you know . . . well, I was scared to get on the board. I hadn't been surfing for over a year. It took about an hour to get up the nerve to try to catch a wave. My cousin Linda was trying to take a picture of me but missed the shot whenever I finally did catch one. Anyway, that was the best one she got."

I smiled in her direction.

"Right after she took it, I tried to ride another wave so we could get a better photo." She didn't speak for a moment. "I fell off the board, and it conked me in the head; knocked me unconscious."

"What?"

"A guy next to me on the line pulled me out of the water, but I didn't wake up until I was lying on the beach." Her dark-brown eyes were huge and moist as she peered over the lip of the pool. "Larry, if he hadn't brought me in I would've drowned. I decided my surfing days were over."

She hid her head below the pool's edge. I could barely make out her words. "I can't help thinking if I'd drowned that day I wouldn't be here doing all the things we're doing together. I wouldn't have been here for you to tell me how bad you felt about what happened last night. I wouldn't be here to love and care for you. It makes me want to cry."

I slipped into the pool next to her and pulled her against me. "But you didn't drown, and honey, I'm so glad you didn't." I brushed a damp wave of silky hair from her face. "You're safe here with me now. You'll always be safe with me."

She pulled me close and put her head on my shoulder. "I am glad, too."

"Do you remember me telling you about Sandy Beach?" I whispered. "How I almost drowned?" I could feel her head nod yes. "A few nights later when we made love for the first time, I remember thinking about how glad I was I didn't die and miss out on that incredible night."

She lifted her head and studied me for a moment. "I don't want the way we feel about each other to ever end. I want you to know, you don't ever have to worry about me, I'll always be yours."

At our last rehearsal, we learned Glen Campbell's *Wichita Lineman* for Les. At the end of our last night, we packed the van to begin our nomadic migration back to the Rag Doll. Theresa was now a full-time, card-carrying member of the Stark Naked and the Car Thieves Traveling Roadshow.

26 THREE DOG NIGHT

Study the past if you would define the future.
—Confucius

August 13, 1968
North Hollywood, California

TONY FERRA MADE it clear he wanted us at the Rag Doll as often as possible, but he insisted on no more than four weeks at a time, so we'd always be fresh. He negotiated a standard price at top dollar for us with Howard King, even signing contracts for dates well into the future.

Howard had no problem working around this stipulation. In fact he used it as leverage to fill the open dates in our schedule with clubs around Southern California who were willing to match Tony's price. It gave us a circuit of clubs close to the music and entertainment industry, our manager's offices, and the best recording studios in LA, and included our regular visits to the Pussycat in Las Vegas.

When we'd returned from Vegas this time, Tony had hired an excellent little group called Heat Wave, a trio backing a female singer, to play our Monday off-nights at the Doll. Their drummer, Floyd Sneed, liked us enough to regularly come in to see us during the rest of the week. He often sat in with us, and he and Leonard soon became good friends. After Heat Wave's contract ended, Floyd still dropped in to hang out with Leonard and pound on his drums during late sets. One night, Floyd told us he'd quit Heat Wave; he'd been recruited to join a new supergroup Reb Foster, a well-known deejay on KRLA radio, was forming. Foster and his partner, Bill Utley, had begun managing bands. Their best-known one was a Manhattan Beach surf-rock band called the Crossfires who they'd renamed the Turtles. We played one of their songs, *Happy Together*, and I liked their music.

"Crazy thing about it," Floyd told us in his hoarse voice, "couple of weeks before we closed here, Reb Foster and one of the singers from the new group came in here looking to check you guys out. Being Monday, your off-night, of course, they missed you. But they stayed to watch Heat Wave, and I guess they liked the way I drummed."

"You mean the way you hold your sticks like hammers?" Leonard teased him with a grin.

"You got it, baby, that African lightning." He laughed uproariously. "They ask me if I'd be interested in drummin' in this band they're gettin' together." He shuffled his feet and leaned in conspiratorially.

"See, one of the singers originally got the idea for this new band from seeing you guys; he thought a rock act with three lead singers like you guys would be smokin' hot. Same as I do. You guys know how much I've want to play in a band like yours, and now look what's happened?" Floyd had a big personality and made no bones about how much he wanted to be in a band like Stark Naked and the Car Thieves. He'd playfully warn Leonard he should watch out for his Wheaties being poisoned so he could score his job. Floyd's rugged face beamed with pleasure. "I have learned wishin' shit can apparently make it come true."

"Floyd," Leonard said, "you're saying this guy Reb Foster's going to build a group like us when he could've just talked with us?" He realized what he'd said and added, "Well, we could have two drummers. After all, we got three lead singers." He grinned sheepishly, but his point was clear.

"Nah. You guys would never have made this deal. Can't exactly say what the cut is but management gets a huge piece, at least 25 percent, probably more, and that don't include agents, promoters, and other whatnots. Gotta expect that since they are fronting the dough for everything and we've already signed record contracts. And guess what? Guy named Burt Jacobs has joined Reb Foster and Associates. Soon as we get enough tunes in the can for an album, band's going out on tour with his band, Steppenwolf."

Steppenwolf! They were hot as hell with two huge hits on the charts, *Born to Be Wild* and the newly released *Magic Carpet Ride*. We hadn't known that Burt Jacobs managed Steppenwolf. Burt was the little guy with the terrible toupee Jimmy O'Neill had introduced as his partner at Seymour Heller's office, the same day we signed management contracts with him. The first business card Jimmy had given me had "B. J. Enterprises" printed on it. Burt must have left Jimmy behind to team up with Foster and Utley. Now they had Steppenwolf, with two current hits they could use to promote their brand-new act to a national audience. I had to shake my head—clever but ruthless.

"It's a sweet deal, everything all locked in, but"—Floyd smiled and brushed his thick, dark hand across the table— "that's why these guys get such a big percentage. Course I'm just a sideman, but brother it ain't bad, players get a piece of the pie even if it's only a taste compared to the singers, but at least it's something. And I get a good chunk of change as a musician, even for rehearsal, and a chance to ride with the big dogs. I like 'em, too. Great musicians, always a plus."

"Who are the singers, Floyd?" Dave asked. "Anybody we might know? What's the name of your new band?"

"Well, there's Cory Wells—he was the lead singer in the Enemies." He counted them off on his fingers. "Danny Hutton, who had a record of his own a while ago, and Chuck Negron, who's been singing in bands around LA."

"*Roses and Rainbows*?" Les asked. "Danny Hutton's record, right?"

"I remember that song," I said, flipping out a cigarette pack. "Good record. And I've heard of the Enemies. I think there's a photo of them on the wall at the Pussycat in Las Vegas."

"Cory says the Enemies played here at the Rag Doll," Floyd said. I shrugged.

"Since you asked," Floyd had an odd expression on his rugged face, "the new band's name is Three Dog Night, for God's sake."

"Three Dog Night?" Leonard mulled that over. "What's that?"

"I dunno. Danny's girlfriend, Jane, read in National Geographic or some such place about how many dogs you gotta sleep with to stay warm on a freezing night in Australia." Floyd grinned and leaned back in his chair. "But how can guys in a band called Stark Naked and the Car Thieves question anybody else's wacky name?" He showed us his big grin, and we laughed along with him.

"Anyway, we be woodsheddin' in an empty house on Hollywood Boulevard, working our asses off. Supposed to be ready to gig in four or five weeks."

After the Doll, we were booked in Cucamonga, a little town on the eastern edge of the Pomona Valley on the way to Las Vegas. Club 66 was named for its location on Route 66, a national highway so famous it had spawned a weekly TV show of the same name. The series featured stories in picturesque towns the road passed through from its beginning at Pacific Palisades, running through Hollywood's Sunset Strip, out to Cucamonga, and meandering east to its final destination in Chicago. Despite its romantic association, neither the city of Cucamonga nor the club could be considered charming. Club 66 was a huge, warehouse-like room with a big platform stage crammed with enthusiastic club-goers every night we were there. Howard King had charged a substantial premium for our appearance so far from our usual stomping grounds. While the extra money was welcome, it was a logistical nightmare. Even with carpooling, it meant a brutal, hundred-plus-miles-a-night round trip to Cucamonga and back if we kept our rooms at the Mid-Valley Motel—which led to a significant decision. Our business manager suggested it could be cheaper, in the long run, to rent apartments rather than move our entourage for each engagement, and he helped us figure out how our personal budgets could manage it.

Theresa and I found it difficult to be separated during these nightly excursions, so I was grateful she could spend her evenings with the girls from the band. When I got home at 3 AM or later and woke her, she was full of the things they'd seen on television or talked about. It was surprising to find out how developed this adjunct society of our band was. It was interesting to hear what they thought about their lives with us. While they watched shows, played cards, and planned group cookouts, the current excitement was about looking for furnished apartments. For the guys with families or committed relationships, their significant others were elated with the possibility of actual homes our rootless existence hadn't allowed. Joan, their de facto leader, had already started organizing expeditions to look for furnished houses or apartments in the better residential areas around North Hollywood.

Around this time, I'd begun to take seriously the idea that Theresa could, in actual fact, love me. Not only because of her daily pronouncements of affection, not even her need to be touching me whenever possible, but the pure joy she radiated when I came home exhausted from our nightly excursions and her growing excitement in setting up housekeeping. It was a big step, one I'd never been able to take with Marie. For the first time, the ties that bound my hidden heart, iron-clad since the agonizing end of my marriage, loosened a little in simultaneous pangs of rapture and anguish.

One night, after deep and satisfying love-making, Theresa made a request I should have realized would come up eventually, though it shocked me to the core. She sank across my chest and into my arms and reached to brush damp hair off my forehead.

"Larry, I love my life with you." She searched my eyes. "And it seems like you want me to stay with you for a long time." Theresa and I hadn't discussed what was next. I guess I thought we would continue on like this into some hazy, wonderful future.

"I can't imagine being apart from you, Treese." I wanted to say more. I wanted to express somehow the joy I felt surrounded by since she'd come to stay with me, but I'd been unable to put all I felt into words.

"I know, darling. I feel the same way, but when I came here, I couldn't be sure how long you would want me to stay." She scrunched a pillow behind her back. "I loved you when I came here, and though I didn't think it could be possible, I love you even more now." Her smile was bittersweet. "I want this life with you to go on forever, but can you understand when I say I miss my home in Hawaii, too?"

I froze in shock. "You want to go back to Hawaii?"

"Do you think I could go for a short visit?"

"Jeez, yes. Of course." *What an idiot I am. I should have realized she'd get homesick.* "I've been going along without thinking, assuming . . ."

She took my face in her two hands as her liquid eyes dived deep into mine. "I have to make you understand how much I love you, Larry. With all my heart.

I am yours forever, for as long as you want me." She dropped her hands to my chest. "I am a Hawaiian person. I think we Hawaiians are connected in some way to our little islands. I need to see my home, my family, and friends. I didn't have a chance to say goodbye to anyone. I didn't know if you would want to keep me with you or not. If it's possible, I need to do that."

"Honey, you are always free to come and go, you don't have to ask permission. I completely understand." Except I didn't. I hated the idea of her going anywhere, but I'd always accepted the possibility and responsibility of making sure she could return to Hawaii whenever she wanted to, whatever the reason, for a visit—or if it came to it, forever.

"I can make your reservations on the American Express card tomorrow. Might take a couple of paychecks and we'll eat rice and beans for a while, but I should have enough money to pay off your ticket by the time the bill comes."

"Oh, my darling man, I love you so. Do you think I could go home in time for my birthday?" *Gulp.*

I watched Theresa's plane disappear out over the Pacific. I'd been empty inside from the moment she'd told me she wanted to go, and desperately miserable now. As I looked into my little plastic viewer at the two of us again when we'd seemed so happy, a secret part of me read her smile differently and wondered if she'd come back. What about her life before me? Had she left someone there behind? Within days I was relieved to receive sweet and sexy heartsick letters filled with how much she loved and missed me, and how she couldn't wait to come back to me. She'd written that it had been a mistake to leave, even for ten days. I felt the same way.

27 OKRA AND THE WINGNUTS

> *That was the thing about the world: it wasn't that things were harder than you thought they were going to be, it was that they were hard in ways that you didn't expect.*
> —Lev Grossman

September 25, 1968
Hollywood, California

THERE HAD BEEN some difficulty in coordinating our appearance on *The Steve Allen Show* since we'd returned to Southern California. A few days after Theresa's flight to Hawaii, I was mooning around about not being with her on her birthday when Eve called: a slot had opened up on short notice—the following afternoon. The next day, the six of us met in a studio parking lot between Sunset and Hollywood Boulevard near the busy 101 freeway, excited to be doing our first live television performance. With less than a day's warning, we'd be doing a guest appearance on Steve Allen's new daytime show here in Hollywood. Probably good there wasn't much time to get nervous. I thought Steve Allen was one of the funniest, most intelligent, and talented people in entertainment; I'd loved staying up late to watch his wild skits on the original *Tonight Starring Steve Allen* from New York City as a kid.

Mac had Larry Grey with him. Larry had evolved from a fan to a great friend of the band. He worked regularly as a grip and best boy on various lighting and electrical crews for film and video shoots across the city. He often snuck us onto studio backlots when we had free afternoons. He was a big-time loadie and knew all the best sneak places to get high in the exterior stage sets. Colonial Street, a winding residential lane of house skeletons on the sprawling Universal lot, home to Beaver Cleaver, the Munsters, and Don Knotts in *The Ghost and Mr. Chicken*, was a favorite spot for sharing a couple of blunts before exploring the soundstages. There was something wickedly surreal about smoking weed in the Beav's house as I'd seen it on TV in Indiana, even though it was a simple raw frame inside. *How weird is this?* I thought, visualizing myself here in the circularity of time, getting high in my own history.

Larry took us onto working sets like *Gunsmoke*, where we spied on scenes being shot and met some of the actors who spent most of the time bored out of their skulls (some of whom didn't mind toking a hit or two when they weren't on camera). We learned we could go almost anywhere on the stage sets as long as we acted as though we belonged, were respectful, and followed the directions of the green and red lights.

Inside, on *The Steve Allen Show*'s television stage, we did a few quick runthroughs of *Cara Mia* in our street clothes. The mics and speakers sounded decent, though dry; there was no added ambiance at all. Afterward, we were directed to a smallish dressing room where we clambered into our freshly-pressed, dark-gold suits before being shown to the green room, which was actually painted gray, highlighted with a dull shade of blue.

It was currently occupied by a grey-haired, disheveled old fellow in a well-worn, old-fashioned tuxedo poking through a bowl of hard candies. He glanced at us with a snaggle-toothed grin.

"I know you," Leonard said in shock. "You're that professor guy. I saw you on *Laugh-In*, no wait, the *Smothers Brothers*. Professor Irwin Corey, yeah, that's you."

"I admit it. That's me." The professor nodded with confidence. "The World's Most Foremost Authority." He took another look at Leonard. "I know you, too. Now I understand why they keep you around; you make these other guys look almost handsome." Leonard appeared to be unsure if he should be offended or not.

"Of what?" Mickey said, taking the bait.

"Right." The professor nodded complacently before sticking and violently twisting a finger into his ear.

"No, I mean what are you the foremost authority of?"

"Why, I know you did. And I am." He picked out a purple candy and popped it into his mouth. "I only like the grape ones. I tried the other colors, didn't care for 'em and put 'em back. Not much here, but there are some soft drinks in the refrigerator I haven't opened yet.

Mickey looked at the old guy in surprise.

"Mick," Les told him trying to keep a straight face. "Professor Irwin Corey's act is being the World's Foremost Authority."

"Okay. So, of what. Foremost authority of what?" Mickey remained puzzled, not yet grasping the Professor's comedic satire.

"What do you need to know?" asked the quizzical Professor Corey. "Since we're all guests here, I won't charge you for an answer."

Mickey thought for a moment. "Hell, I don't know." He looked around in confusion.

Professor Corey nodded. "Oh well, that one's easy. Wet birds never fly at night." He pushed sticky fingers back into the bowl in search of an oval grape candy.

"Huh?" Mickey laughed out loud at the outrageous answer to a question he hadn't asked. "What's that supposed to mean—wet birds never fly at night?"

Professor Corey's rummage through the candy dish paused. He looked up in shocked surprise. "You mean they do?" He dropped the candies he'd been sorting through, wiped his fingers on his wrinkled coat and searched his pockets for a piece of paper and what turned out to be an actual piece of pencil. "I have to write this down. Maybe it's they always fly at night." He poked out the tip of his tongue to touch the lead, wrinkled up his face, and scribbled unintelligibly on the dog-eared paper.

Our nervousness was being laughed away when a lady came to drag Les and Mickey off to makeup; the rest of us would follow, two by two. Leonard chose not to be offended, I guess, he sat next to Professor Corey interrogating him about his act, comedy in general, and how he liked doing television shows, which seemed to interest them both.

When the test pattern on the television set in the corner switched to display the studio down the hall, we listened to Steve Allen, Jayne Meadows, and the director banter casually with the audience as it filled the room. They responded with occasional laughter and light applause. A girl poked her head in the room, "Okay you Stark Naked guys, time to go."

"Well, you boys break a leg." Professor Corey said. "I'll be out there soon, so warm 'em up for me." He stood and started yodeling like a cat with a bag of marbles caught in its throat.

Filing out to the stage, the director asked which one of us was Stark Naked, and everyone pointed at me. He told me Steve would be expecting me to go sit with him at his desk after the performance.

The inspiration for our name, Stark Naked and the Car Thieves, had resulted from a brief conversation with a trio of guys who were kidding around with Dave and I while we'd been promoting *In the Still of the Night* years ago in Chicago. I'd never known where they'd heard it from, but it had stuck with us, or possibly, on us. I'd been told Steve Allen once had an old routine involving two hats: one filled with singular nouns and the other plural. He would take a slip of paper from each hat and announce them together as a funny name for a new band, like "Okra" and the "Wingnuts." He might have wanted me to publicly admit he'd been the one to come up with the name. That was fine by me.

The frenetic director shushed us as we slipped into our places behind the closed curtain. He pulled Dave aside to place him out in front of the curtain with a hand mic. I could tell how nervous that made Dave by the stiff-legged way he walked out of our view. The house musicians stopped abruptly as the show returned from a commercial break. Across the open area to our right, Steve had recreated the hats routine with a couple of bowls, as though he planned to create a new batch of crazy rock-and-roll band names. Nobody had warned us of this, but all of a sudden he pulled out one slip of paper and said, "Stark Naked . . ." and then another continuing, ". . . and the Car Thieves?" He gave the audience a sly grin. "Who'd believe a name like that? Well, guess what folks, that's who we have here today. Welcome, Stark Naked and the Car Thieves."

The applause came, and the floor director signaled us to begin. We hesitated—the curtain wasn't open, and we hadn't rehearsed with Dave in front of the curtain. The director helicoptered his arms around in manic desperation, so before he blew a heart valve, Les shrugged and strummed the opening guitar chord. We heard Dave's disembodied voice begin singing the operatic intro through our monitors until Leonard's drum fill rattled us into the tune as the curtain rose to a studio audience giving us fervent applause, God bless 'em, even though they were being prompted. The sudden bright lights that hadn't been lit during sound check were so intense it was difficult to find our mics as we walked toward them. There'd been no distracting red-eyed camera swinging around us during the sound check either, but what killed the singers was we couldn't hear a note we were singing. The vocal monitors that had seemed decent earlier were either turned off or so low as to make no difference. Dave described it later like "singing into a wet rag." Leonard had unfortunately interpreted the director's request to play *softer* at the sound check to mean play *slower*, so the song limped through to the end. Vocally and instrumentally, we sounded horribly thin, and I was sure our background harmony was way off key. Later, I heard we'd gotten a standing ovation as the show went to another commercial, but I'd thought we'd sounded atrocious. I wanted to crawl in a hole and hide. As soon as the curtain closed I rushed off the stage without a word to anyone to grab my street clothes from the dressing room locker and leave the building in my stage suit. I was embarrassed; our first opportunity to perform on national television and we'd sounded like crap. I was told Steve Allen was upset that I hadn't gone to talk with him after we'd finished singing, but I hadn't meant any disrespect to him. I was so devastated about our performance the stage manager's request had flown right out of my mind. We'd been so bad, I don't know how I could have faced him anyway.

Mac told me later he and Larry Grey had been sitting in Larry's car in the parking lot finishing off a doob before driving home when the soundstage door flew open. Professor Irwin Corey appeared leading most of Steve's studio audience out in a conga line. Steve Allen loved bits that took the cameras outside the studio. Mac said he and Larry about pooped their pants when they realized the bobbing and weaving procession was headed right at them. Mac, stoned to the gills, said he played it cool and went with it, nodding in time with the Professor as he capered by at the head of the line, marijuana fumes reeking from the car's open window. Apparently, Larry's eyes popped, getting bigger and bigger as the studio audience frolicked past, certain he was being busted in front of a television audience of millions. When he was sure he could leave without running over anyone, he squealed out of the lot, and sped back to the Valley, sure an all-points bulletin had been issued for him.

As unhappy as I was without Theresa, I was glad she hadn't seen what a wimp I'd been. I took some solace in putting a deposit on a one-bedroom furnished apartment in a building we'd been looking at on Vanowen Street not far from the Rag Doll. Though it was a typical San Fernando Valley stucco apartment building with a central swimming pool, it was near everyone else, and a gigantic step up from the Surfboard Hotel in Honolulu and the Mid-Valley Motel in Studio City. When my girl returned, I would welcome her into a real home. It was good timing.

When I picked up Theresa at the Burbank airport on Sunday, her friend Charlene was with her. Apparently, she had decided at the last minute to fly with her to the mainland to visit relatives in Long Beach, on the other side of LA. The two of them oohed and aahed over the new apartment while I grinned at the pleasure and affection Theresa showed me in her new home. Charlene stayed overnight with us, and we chauffeured her to her family the next day.

I'd burned for Theresa from the moment she'd returned but tried to restrain myself while Charlene was with us. As soon as we returned from dropping off Charlene, we gave in to our instincts and were in each other's arms every moment we could, swearing never to allow anything to separate us again.

A few days later, I took Theresa to the new Universal City theme park in Studio City to celebrate the birthday I'd missed with her. Universal Pictures had attracted a Hilton Hotel and a couple of excellent restaurants in an attempt to turn a hill in their mammoth backlot into Universal City, an amusement attraction based around an entertainment mall and a studio tram tour to actual live productions. We stood together on Ben Hur's chariot for a photo, and I took her picture in a faux rain forest near the lake where *M*A*S*H* had been shot.

Theresa continually demonstrated how glad she was to be home in California with me, though she might have questioned it when we drove north in late fall of 1968 for a month in Nevada. We were making good on a promise we'd made to Ron Stevens to return to his Lemon Tree, in return for his recommending us to Stan Alapa's namesake last year. His Lemon Tree was located in the little town of Sparks, a mile or two outside of Reno. He'd done a ton of advertising, including a massive billboard on the road to Reno.

We had great crowds until a sharp cold snap changed the weather in northern Nevada to arctic. The first time Theresa got bundled up to go out in the snow, she giggled with wonder as snowflakes melted on her tongue, enthralled as it spread a glistening white blanket over the trees and ground. Though Ron and the entire staff treated Theresa like a rock star because she was from the Hawaiian club of the same name, she found it hard to endure the bleak weather and barren moonscape. She'd lived her whole life in a tropical island paradise.

To make things worse, a particularly virulent strain of Hong Kong flu ran rampant through the area. A couple of the guys caught the bug, but Les had been hammered by it. Knowing we couldn't go on without him, and none of us would get paid if he didn't, he manfully sat white-faced on a chair for a couple of nights until he could stand enough to lean on my B3 and limp through the end of the engagement. He demonstrated again the kind of professionalism we'd gained and the kind of dedication and care we showed to each other.

Though Theresa and I missed the flu, it was a tough gig, and she spent much of it in our hotel room wrapped in blankets. When we returned to the Rag Doll and decent Southern California weather again, I promised her I'd never take her back there again.

28 IT'S A GIRL

The hopes and fears of all our years are here with us tonight.
—Kurt Vonnegut

November 26, 1968
North Hollywood, California

WHEN WE PULLED into the Rag Doll's parking lot, I was relieved to be back in Southern California where we were no longer freezing our butts off. And I had every reason to expect a warm welcome home. The owner, Tony Ferra, had shown us his appreciation for our success at his club the previous weekend. Although we weren't there, his lovely daughter, Sandy, presented a trophy naming us "the best band to ever play at the Rag Doll" to Jimmy O'Neill in front of a packed house. We would have accepted it ourselves if a minor scheduling snafu hadn't resulted in us being here a week later than expected.

As a much more practical reward, Tony had promised us a week's paid vacation, a practically unheard-of gift from notoriously low-paying nightclub owners, though he'd always been generous with us. This one-week paycheck and a potential open week at the end of the gig, would allow us to let Mickey take his promised deer-hunting trip. He'd made us agree to time off for hunting during Oregon's deer season when he joined the band. The year would not be complete, he said, if he didn't get to kill his buck. Like it had his name on it or something.

Had Howard King been working directly with Tony on the scheduling blip, I'm sure they would have reached a quick compromise, though it might have taken a little bluster on both sides. Instead, Howard found himself dealing with a hardheaded nutball we knew as Big Mike, formerly the Rag Doll's head bartender. Apparently, there had been bitter words and hard feelings we hadn't known about, but I wouldn't have expected it to affect us since we no longer involved ourselves in booking negotiations.

"Come on, man." Mickey gave me a not-so-gentle push on the shoulder. We were out in the Doll's parking lot emptying equipment out of the van. "You gotta go ask him."

"Ow! Jesus, Mickey, quit shoving. Crap man, you don't know your own strength. I'll ask him, all right? But let's get everything on stage first. Use some of those muscles to help me get the B3 on the stage, and I'll go talk to Big Mike."

Agreeing to check on our paid week got me a lot of helping hands hoisting the organ, cradled in its heavy wooden dolly, and the two Leslie amplifiers up onto, and in place, on the stage. I ripped through a couple of runs and sat there for a moment. Dealing with Big Mike, often known as Filthy McNasty, hadn't been a breath of fresh air when he'd run the bar and managed the waitresses. I didn't expect his new authority would make him any easier.

"Hey, Mike," I said conversationally, strolling to where he thumbed through receipts at the end of the bar. "So, how you doing?"

"I'm okay. Whatta you want?" *Not big on small talk.*

"Where's Tony?"

His mouth carved an evil, gap-toothed grin into his unshaven face. Mike's body looked like a six-foot-four bowling pin with thinning hair and a bad complexion.

"Tony? Could you possibly be asking me about Tony Ferra?"

"Yeah, Mike," I said, sarcasm dripping. "Tony Ferra, the guy who owns this joint."

"Oh, *that* Tony Ferra, you mean the ex-owner of the Rag Doll." I couldn't help being startled. *The Doll without Tony?*

"Somebody else owns it? Who, you?"

He wiped moisture off the bar with a crusty-looking towel. "Nah, not me. But I'm general manager, though, so what I say goes." *No way this could be good.*

I tried a placating smile. "Well, here's the thing, Mike. Tony promised us a paid vacation-week next time we played here. So, we're here now. We could either play three weeks and get paid for four, or go all four, and collect an extra check at the end. We're about finished getting set up. Wanna sit down and figure this out?"

Mike's pimply face went rosy with outrage. "What the fuck? You want the club to pay you not to play? Though, that's not such a bad idea. Maybe you'd sound better that way."

"Mike, we helped Tony build this place into the hottest nightclub in the Valley, maybe all of LA County. Anyway, he offered us the paid week, we didn't ask for it."

He sneered. "Up to me, you guys wouldn't ever play here for the kind of money you get. Already payin' you twice what bands around here make."

Bands working in Southern California nightclubs generally got paid in proportion to how close or far they were to Hollywood. Every player in every band wanted to be where there was a chance they might get heard, be discovered, and somehow score a record contract. To do that, they were willing to take less. Truth was, A&R guys from the labels could rarely be pried out of the Hollywood bars to drive over the hill to the San Fernando Valley, but—every once in a while—they did.

"Clubs over the hill in Hollywood pay a quarter what we're paying you assholes. You oughta be fucking glad you got a job here at all." *Well, no sense arguing with someone who's not the owner.*

"Look, who can I talk to? Who's the new proprietor?"

His rubbery face twisted into a snarky grin. Not only was he gap-toothed, but the yellow teeth remaining were tinged brown with nicotine.

"Eddie Nash." He sneered at me in bright expectation.

"Where do I find Mr. Nash? Is he around here somewhere?" His cheeks puffed out like a crazed chipmunk, and he giggled like a little girl.

"Here? Eddie Nash, here? Nah. No fucking way you are gonna find him here. Don't know if he ever leaves his place in Hollywood. He's at the Seven Seas Supper Club if you're stupid enough to go get in the face of the most dangerous guy on the West Coast. Good luck with that, fucker."

I tried to fend off the band's questions, we couldn't afford to go crazy. We were making top dollar here, setting a record for local nightclubs at the time.

"Guys," I said, huddling everyone together in the parking lot. I didn't want to take too long discussing this. We needed to get home, settle in and get ready for work. I'd dropped Theresa off on the way so she could get us unpacked. "Listen, a lot's changed here. Apparently, Tony Ferra doesn't own this place anymore and—"

"Wait. Stop," Leonard broke in. "You said Tony doesn't own the Doll anymore?"

"That's what Big Mike told me." Leonard got his sorrowful face on. "As for our vacation plans," I continued, "Mike says a paid week is out of the question, implied he'd like to change our contract to a thousand bucks a week or less."

"What the hell? This is some serious bullshit." Mickey could get steamed up instantly, but he was especially touchy about this. "I got family plans. We were promised a paid week. Actually, I'm supposed to get two weeks." He was right, we had agreed he could take two weeks off each year, but we needed this bonus to make his request realistic. He stomped around for a minute before he stuck out his jaw. "So. How about if I beat that chubby fucker's face in? Think he'd give us our vacation money then?"

"While I'm sure you'd convince him, and I enjoy visualizing it, getting arrested for assault would cut into your hunting trip. It would be better if we tried to work it out." All eyes were on me. "Mike doesn't own the place, he's not the final word. Says the new owner is Eddie Nash, owns a place called the Seven Seas in Hollywood. Mick, I know it's messed up, but Tony's always been fair with us. He probably made an arrangement with the new owner for our paid week. We'll figure it out."

"Heard of that place." Mac rubbed his chin. "On Hollywood Boulevard, ain't it?"

"I'm going to call Tony," Leonard said. "Man, he would have told me if he was going to sell this place. This isn't like him." Leonard and Tony had become close, Leonard often stayed with the Ferras when he visited LA. Everybody not named Mickey shrugged or nodded. Wasn't turning out to be the homecoming we'd expected.

When I got to our apartment, Theresa had comfortably settled us in. Our unit was in front, on the ground floor opening out onto the street, not the most desirable location in the apartment building, but the furniture and rooms were reasonably clean and comfortable. Seeing her in this domestic setting, instantly warmed my heart—and other places. She gave me a big hug as I came in the door and it took all our restraint to stop there.

"Mmmm," she murmured, fingertips caressing the tightened front of my jeans. "Nice idea, but you'll have to calm that down until you've talked to Seymour. His office called and left a message. He wants you to call no matter what time we get in. Slip off your shoes, honey, and take a minute before you call."

It was still within office hours when Bette, his secretary, put him on the phone.

"Larry," Seymour said, "glad you're back in town. Talked to Bill Miller at the Flamingo this afternoon. Listen, they're building a new room that's going to stretch right out over the hotel's driveway; floor to ceiling glass windows all around looking out over the Strip. The place will be amazing. They're calling it the Sky Room.

"It will be the talk of the town, and the job is going to be yours for as long as we want. Bill holds out hope I'll put Liberace in the main room and he wants the Treniers in the lounge so he won't back out. Haven't got the contract back yet, but for our purposes, you can consider it done."

"Sounds fantastic, Seymour." After the worrying news at the Rag Doll, it soothed my scorched ego to hear the most legendary hotel in Las Vegas wanted us to star in a spectacular new room. Also, good to hear he was willing to use a little of Liberace's leverage to secure this opportunity for us. I wondered what Seymour's personal touch meant. We hadn't been hearing much from Jimmy O'Neill lately.

"You're going to love it. It's got a dance floor, and it's a showroom, too. Perfect for you guys, built for you, in fact. Here's what I want you to do. Take down this number and call John Lieu tomorrow. He's Lee's tailor, he's absolutely fantastic, I'm putting you boys in his hands. I want you to look amazing for this engagement. He'll design spectacular suits for the band to wear on stage. With your next record coming out soon, I'm expecting your career to take off from here."

Opening night at the Doll, teeming with fans and friends, was fun, and significantly improved by zero interaction with Mike Foley who had his hands full with the standing-room-only crowd. Somewhere around midnight, Leonard, banging a cowbell with a drumstick and capering out on the dance floor, got another one of his conga lines going until half the club's audience, hands on the hips of the person in front of them, spilled out into the parking lot, the crowd snaking along after him. After circling around outside, the line so long he had to cut through it, he suddenly decided—the way Leonard generally decided things—to lead them, laughing and shouting, across Lankershim at the corner. Then he took them across to Victory Boulevard, and corner-to-corner, back to Lankershim as the overlapping crocodile line blocked the intersection. His merry band of revelers romped back into the club before the tail end of the line had cleared the last corner. Fortunately, the drivers of the cars stuck at the intersection didn't seem too upset, and nobody called the police.

In our dressing room before the first set, I told everybody about the new engagement at the Flamingo Hotel and that Seymour had arranged to have custom-designed outfits made for us by John Lieu. Mac loved the idea of new stage clothes, but Mickey had questions. "Suits like that sound expensive, what are they gonna cost? Did you think to ask him that?" I could tell from his tone and body language Mickey was still stewing about his share of the bonus money and his hunting trip.

"Mickey, this is Liberace's tailor, not some guy in the yellow pages. Seymour will take care of it at first. We'll be making a lot more money in Vegas, so we'll set some aside to pay him back. It's going to cost us some money to look like we belong there. Appointment for fittings is a week from today, so plan for it.

"And don't forget, we're at Continental Sound Saturday and Sunday." Les took a moment to confirm this week's rehearsal schedule where we'd refresh our vocals for the upcoming recording sessions.

Like most nights, the band's girlfriends and wives congregated at their own table. It was group protocol to meet at least three new people each break, so I picked a table with three people where I could quickly say hi and thank them for coming in before I pulled Theresa away to sit with me.

"Crazy week, Treese. Lots of stuff happening." She smiled and snuggled closer.

"It's so exciting. The new Sky Room sounds amazing. Now you are recording again, getting new clothes, playing at a big hotel in Las Vegas. I love you so much, I'm glad I'm getting to be part of this with you." It was the only quiet moment we had together in the crush of an opening night on our home turf.

When I walked in the next evening, Ginny, the skinny head waitress with an edgy attitude, handed me a crumpled bar napkin.

"Somebody called for you earlier. When I told him you guys didn't go on till nine, he asked could I take a message. I said, 'What the fuck do I sound like—some kinda secretary?' Anyway, here's the number." I glanced at the phone number and the name Mariano on the napkin. *Who is this? Do I know anyone named Mariano?*

If Tony had been there, I would've asked to use the office phone, but I didn't want to ask Mike; he'd probably say no anyway. I took change I'd gotten from one of the bartenders to the public phone booth next to the cigarette machine by the restrooms. I closed the louvered door to muffle the nightclub's tumult as much as possible before dialing.

"Fourth floor, maternity." Once I got past that shock, I asked for Mariano and told them I didn't know the last name.

"Larry?"

"Yeah, it's me. Is this Mariano?"

"Yes, this is Nano." *Where had I heard that quiet voice before?* I racked my brain. *It couldn't be, could it?*

"Nano? Is this about Marie? Is she okay? What's going on?"

"For having a baby, she's okay I guess." I was stunned. Marie's younger brother couldn't have been more than nine or ten. He sounded so mature. "Are you still there?"

"Yeah, yeah, of course. I'm here."

"She wanted me to call you. She had a baby. A girl. She named her Lori. Lori Rene. Six pounds, four ounces, she said to call and tell you."

"Nano, I didn't even know she was pregnant." Now it was his turn to be silent. The thousand-pound elephant in the room spoke. "I guess you're calling me because she thinks I'm the father?"

"Alls I know is she told me to call and tell you what I just did."

"Is that all?"

"Yup, that's it."

"I'm not sure what I should say."

"You don't have to say nothin'. I don't think she expected you to say nothin'."

Being forced to concentrate on playing and singing got me through the early set, but by the first break, I'd made a decision. Before I could change my mind, I got a handful of quarters at the bar. This time I went to the phone booth outside the club. There was an abnormal sense of movement in the world around me, I could hear traffic in the distance from Victory and along Lankershim over the dull roar from the Hollywood Freeway.

"Larry, what a surprise. Yes, your father and I are still up. How wonderful to hear from you."

"Listen. I've got something to tell you guys." I gathered my breath. "You guys have a granddaughter. Her name is Lori Rene, I've been told. I can't tell you much else about her."

"What? What are you talking about?" Mom's voice sounded shrill and thin.

"Mom, I know, I know. I just found out myself. I'm only slightly less surprised than you are. I'm on a break so I can't speak long, but I wanted you to know right away. The baby's mother is Marie, a girl I was going out with for a long time, but we broke up months ago." *Nine months, to be exact.* "Before we went to Hawaii. Her little brother called me a few minutes ago to tell me." There was a lengthy pause.

"I don't know what to say."

"I know, Mom. Not sure what to say either. I phoned before I figured that out. I wanted to call right away and tell you because . . . well, hopefully, you'll worry less about me if I tell you about things that happen right away. You'll always know you'll hear it from me first." I shuffled around trying to manipulate a lighter and cigarette pack with one hand. "Anyway, I don't know what this means yet. Thought you should know and . . . well, I love you guys."

"We love you too, Larry, but . . . I don't know what else . . . Call us when you find out more. Please?"

"Yeah, sure, Mom. Gotta go back to work. You guys say hi to Cheryl for me."

Dave spotted me walking back into the club. "Hey man, what's the matter? Your dog run away from home?"

I walked to a deserted table, and we sat. "Marie's little brother Nano called me this afternoon. She's in the hospital. She had a baby girl."

"What? You haven't seen Marie since we left for Hawaii."

"If you work it out, that's about the right timing."

"You sure you're the father?"

I slumped back in the chair. "I can't say one way or the other. Called my folks on the pay phone outside before I tried to think about it. Though the more I do think about it, the more pissed off it makes me. Marie always took birth control pills. She must have stopped on purpose the last few weeks we were together. There's a good chance she was trying to get pregnant because we were breaking up. Dammit, a kid's not a souvenir."

"Probably should tell you . . . I have a daughter, too. With Helen, when we were at the Town Club." He pulled back from the table, and we sat quietly until an admirer came to the table to talk to Dave.

29 LIBERACE'S TAILOR

I always say: To be well dressed you must be well naked.
—Oscar de la Renta

December 7, 1968
Studio City, California

WE HAD TWO sessions scheduled at Continental Sound to record vocals we'd had ready for months. Recording on Saturday and Sunday meant we'd have tired voices after singing five hours a night since Tuesday and every night of the weekend. Didn't help my attitude. The quality of the songs we were going to record seemed questionable, and Les's arrangements not particularly inspired. Hard to blame him. He probably felt like I did: whatever we did would get changed later anyway. Of the four songs we had ready, including one written by Mac Davis, my only real hope was for *The Merry-Go-Round Is Slowing You Down*. I was worried at how disengaged Eddie seemed to be getting from us. We had to figure out what to change, what we needed to do to become the stellar vocal recording group I knew we should be. But I couldn't put my finger on how or what to do about it.

At the studio, Leonard told us he'd tried to reach Tony Ferra. "I called the house, but he's not there. The maid didn't speak much English, but I think she said the whole family was traveling in Europe, in Italy."

"Not good news."

Mickey made his conclusions clear: "You've got to go see the fucker in Hollywood, Larry, or I will. I gotta have answers." Reluctantly, I promised I'd go on Monday, our day off.

Tuesday at noon, the band straggled into John Lieu's tailor shop, a long, narrow storefront in downtown LA on Melrose making no attempt to attract walk-in customers. The dry, pleasant smells of new cloth filled the waiting room. Inside, bolts of fabric stood neatly stacked on tall shelves with three workstations strategically centered in front of winged full-length mirrors so multiple patrons could be fitted. Today we would be the only ones. Mickey arrived last, still in pursuit of his deer hunting holiday.

"Did you see that Eddie Nash guy? I got family waiting to hear if I'm going home to hunt or not."

I returned Mickey's pugnacious stare, but in my mind, I was seeing the Seven Seas Supper Club in Hollywood yesterday afternoon and realizing again why I was the bandleader.

Filthy curtained windows drabbed the brilliant California sunshine attempting to illuminate the club's dusty interior. *Here I am taking my only day off to do this crazy crap.* Floor-to-ceiling gauzy drapes separated the Polynesian-themed bar from the dim rumor of a showroom with an extended runway. Maybe after dark the place magically became Waikiki, but in the daytime, it stank of cigarettes and ancient sin; more like one of the dangerous places we'd been warned away from on King Street in Honolulu's Chinatown. Strange, considering it was across the street from a major tourist landmark like Grauman's Chinese Theater and a few doors from the famous Roosevelt Hotel on Hollywood Boulevard. But Hollywood was sliding downhill these days. A few blocks west was "Needle Palace," an abandoned Georgian-styled building known for the addicts who haunted it.

After a year at a topless club in San Francisco, I thought of myself as fairly urbane and sophisticated, but the practiced naughtiness of the Galaxie's topless girls always came with a giggle. This club felt wrong in some indefinable way. The skittish bartender and the young waitress with a faded face who told me

Eddie Nash was expecting me seemed like lost souls. At her listless signal, I stood and walked through the door next to the bar wishing I was anywhere else.

Offices in nightclubs, when they exist, are small and tight, this one was no exception. The room was jammed with papers, file drawers, and storage cabinets, leaving barely enough room for a desk and a sideways turn to get past it. There was a thick, musty incense smell I didn't recognize. A desk light glared, cutting through the cheerless daylight leaking from the room's high windows. A cadaverous, pale-skinned man with dark, bottlebrush hair and mask-like skin stretched across his facial structure sat hunched over the desk. He motioned me to the single chair with a jerk. Meetings here would be more like inquisitions.

Nash's jet-black, lifeless eyes pinned me like a bug on a display board. The bottomless depth of his ebony pupils made me think of Charles Crozier's piercing eyes, the attorney who'd dealt with my induction into the Army, but with less recognition of my humanity and none of his dark humor. I couldn't help swallowing as my mouth went dry. When he didn't speak, I felt forced to say something.

"Um, Mr. Nash?" Not an actual nod, but some slight acknowledgment in his glazed expression signaled I should continue. "My name is Larry Dunlap. My band is Stark Naked and the Car Thieves, and we're playing at the Rag Doll out in the Valley. Mike Foley told us Tony Ferra sold the club to you." Still no response, though something about his unnatural stillness made it seem his skeleton was ready to leap out of his skin, like his bones were on speed or something.

"Mr. Nash, Tony promised us a week's vacation for helping make his nightclub a huge success—as he put it. It was supposed to take effect when we returned for this engagement." I'd thought about this before coming in and attempted to finesse the issue. "I thought you could help me work out a schedule that would work best for both of us."

Nothing moved on Eddie Nash's taught face except a slight wriggle from his night-crawler lips. "No."

I paused, not sure how to reply. "Do you mean no, you don't want to work out a schedule, or are you saying no to the vacation week?"

If possible, his stare turned icier as his expression darkened. I was getting pretty pessimistic about how this would turn out. "No," he said louder.

"Just to be certain I understand, you're saying you don't want to honor Tony's commitment?" It was tough getting this out, but I knew I had to get this money we'd been promised or have a better answer than I had so far. "Tony . . . he did tell you about this bonus, this paid week, didn't he?"

"I said, NO!" I recoiled from his frozen, waxy face as he slammed a palm on the desk and leaned toward me exuding real malice. He hadn't spoken that much louder, but the sizzling intensity in his voice had ratcheted up to the ceiling.

My eyes refocused on Mickey in the tailor shop's waiting area. He was getting irritated because I hadn't answered him. Mickey could be a badass, even dangerous; I'd seen him use his fists in fights at the Pussycat where he felt it was his civic duty to bounce someone. But he was a pure spirit compared to the man I'd met yesterday. If it ever came to it, I'd rather square off against him than Eddie Nash. I'd lose either way, but I'd be more likely to survive if it was Mickey.

"Look. I asked the guy about the paid vacation week. He said no."

Everyone waited for me to say something else, but I didn't. I didn't know how to make them understand.

Mac said what they were thinking. "Come on, man. Got to be more to it. You musta had more conversation with the man than that."

"I'm only going to say this. I made our case to the guy. He said maybe four or five words, and three of them were no." I turned to Dave. "You remember me telling you about Crozier's eyes?"

Dave shrugged. "I think you said, 'Fucking scary as hell. Like two pee holes in the snow.'"

"This guy's eyes were worse, way worse. I was like a cockroach to him." I looked at each of them, daring someone to argue. "I told him politely, 'Thank you for your time, Mr. Nash,' and got my ass out of that skanky joint as fast as my wobbly legs could take me."

"Goddamn it," Mickey said, frustrated.

"I'm genuinely sorry Mickey, but we don't have any proof of what Tony promised, and we can't reach him. I'm not going to confront that son of a bitch without anything to show him. And I would be highly opposed to any of us trying to talk to him. This guy's dangerous, we do not want to be on his radar.

"Look. We'll finish at the Doll in a couple of weeks, and I'm sure we won't be coming back, even if we wanted to." I tried to catch everybody's eyes. "Which we don't. We have to move beyond this neighborhood kind of bar anyway.

"Let's concentrate on this long-term contract we're getting at the Flamingo. Every time we've gotten into a major hotel in Las Vegas, something's screwed it up. I wasn't sure we'd ever get another shot. The Sky Room sounds perfect. Let's have these outfits made, move on, and make sure what happened in Vegas in the past doesn't happen again."

John Lieu turned out to be a youngish Chinese man, though his age seemed indeterminate and he, mature beyond his looks. A big oak table, the kind I remembered from my local library in grade school, anchored the center of the shop. We sat with John while he asked questions and made sketches. His quick grasp and eye-popping ability became obvious as he rapidly roughed out the ideas materializing in our design session.

The first thing we wanted was a different kind of suit. Though we weren't sure in what way, we agreed we didn't like standard lapels. John suggested a tall collar like on dress shirts, à la Elvis. He sketched a swooping collar flaring up and out at the neck, suit coat edges descending cleanly in front.

"See, I put two buttons in front, this way. Now, coat no sag when you move." He pointed at his drawing. "No pockets," he insisted. "No, not even inside coat. Except for breast. How you like this?" He drew in a V-shaped breast pocket. "See, I make cut so hanky show more." The silhouette remained lean as he completed the suit coat detail.

"You want vest? Could be short waistcoat, small points, like this?" His pencil flashed across the large pad. Mac nodded vigorously, eyes gleaming. I joined in our murmured appreciation.

"Now pants. How you like pants?"

"No fly in front," Mac said. "I seen pants clean all the way across the front. Can you do that?"

"I do very quiet zipper on side. Clean front then. No pockets here either." His pencil swiftly drew in legs. "Now pants bottom. How cut? What kind of shoes you wear with suits? I say boots, yes?" We agreed, boots. "Maybe vee cut here, too, so leg drape over boot." The general design was there. If the sketches he was drafting could be brought to reality, these outfits would be spectacular.

"I have colors for you to see now, and we can match to boots. Come." He pulled bolts of material from the wall shelves throwing them onto the table, so long swaths rolled out. We chose a glowing burgundy, an electric blue he said would work, along with a rich gold fabric that changed tone in the light. They were brighter and flashier than anything I would have chosen, but the material felt expensive and classy. Definitely Liberace's tailor.

"You don't wear these suits on street. No, never. These are for stage only." He smiled. "These will be very fine. Now we fit. Take off all clothes but underwears and socks, please."

Three Chinese men came out from the back, yellow measuring tapes strung around their shoulders, and took us three at a time to workstations for a session lasting most of two hours. We were measured in every direction imaginable, starting at the forehead and extending to fingertips, heels, and toes. The tailors approached the fitting like engineers, noting everything in their small notebooks.

"Which way you dress, mister?" asked the man crouching below me. I wasn't sure what he meant. "Um, right handed?"

"No, no, what way you dress?" He scowled, gesturing at my genitals.

I cringed a little, uncomfortable with a man kneeling in front of me giving my crotch his full attention. He glared at me in frustration and spoke sharply in Chinese.

John Lieu stepped over to explain. "He want to know what side your stuff, your privates, hang on when you put on pants." He stared down at me. "Right now, I think you dress left. You comfortable that way?"

"Oh." I was aware for the first time of an organizing principle I dealt with every day without thought. "Okay, I see. Yeah. I dress left, definitely."

John spoke to his assistant who nodded in grim satisfaction. Without warning he reached out to cradle my family jewels in his palm, giving them a quick, professional heft before I could flinch away. He scratched squiggly Chinese characters into his little book.

"He need to know how much room to leave for 'resting' genitals," John reassured me. "We want pants form-fit, but not crowd, you know, not show too much."

Before I'd gotten over that shock, *my* tailor, as I possessively thought of him now, whipped off his yellow tape again and moved behind me to measure my buttocks from every conceivable angle. It was strange to see a Chinese man writing down more about my body than anyone other than Theresa knew.

Before our appointment ended at a little before five, John showed us the white-on-white dress shirts with French cuffs he recommended. "I make six shirts for you each. You will have neckties, handkerchiefs, cuff links, suede boots, everything match, you will see; you will have whole outfits. Look like million bucks, fit like two million." He gave me a wide and confident smile. "John Lieu make sure."

"John, thanks for an amazing experience, though I admit," I told him with a deadpan grin, "I felt like smoking a cigarette after your guy finished with me." His brow wrinkled in question. I waved away his concern beaming. "When do you think all this will be ready?"

He thought for a moment. "I go Hong Kong on Sunday, take plans. I think we have suits and shirts for you, everything, I think six to eight weeks."

I dropped into Jerry's Deli in Studio City to grab corned beef sandwiches to bring home. I had time for a few quick bites before jumping into the shower to get ready for work. "Honey, the fitting I got this afternoon was amazing," I said, stripping out of my clothes. "This tailor guy would make you jealous. He went over my whole body, head to toe. Took him more than two hours."

"Interesting," Theresa said, stroking long, gentle fingers and palms across my chest, and then heading south. "Even here?"

"Well, yes, especially there."

"How about this part?"

"Uh, well, kind of, but not like that of course. And he didn't get a rise out of me like you are," I groaned.

"That's a relief." She grinned a big wolfish grin. "How about lips? He didn't measure you with lips like I'm going to do, did he?"

I was late to work after all.

30 DEER PARK

Life can only be understood backwards; but it must be lived forwards.
—Søren Kierkegaard

December 13, 1968
Buena Park, California

MY BAND OF BROTHERS and I, with our wives and girlfriends, celebrated my twenty-seventh birthday a week later in Martoni's VIP room, our favorite restaurant in Hollywood. As I got toasted, in more ways than one, I figured I'd had a pretty incredible year.

As had happened before, I'd proved to myself that having your birthday fall on Friday the 13th occasionally had never turned out bad. I'd found this terrific girl next to me and was as happy and contented as I'd ever been.

We laughed and enjoyed ourselves, drank too much, and speculated about what the new room at the Flamingo would look like. But we also commiserated over the end of our era at the Rag Doll. It had been more than a nightclub where we played; we were losing the closest place we'd had to home. We lived in rented apartments close to the Doll and had established friendships extending beyond the club scene. Regulars like Larry Gray and members from the various dance groups seemed like close cousins. Les, in particular, had gathered an entourage. It starred Susie, of course, but it included several other followers, male and female.

The following Friday we woke to scorching Santa Ana winds that had scraped the sky so clean of dust and smog, it seemed you could reach out and touch the Hollywood Hills or cool your fingers in the glistening snowcaps of the San Gabriel Mountains. Magnificent. But the skin-crawling breezes with heat headed toward triple digits made us too restless to hang out at the pool. Remembering December snow as a youngster, it was weird to feel weather like this so near my birthday.

If we left soon, I told Theresa, we'd have time to spend an afternoon at Deer Park in Orange County, a trip I'd secretly planned for her birthday before she decided to visit Hawaii. Though we still weren't sure what a Deer Park was, it was out of the Valley where it was cooler, and it seemed to be a relaxing way to spend part of such a spectacular day.

When we realized we were out of weed for the tedious trip across the city through mind-bending traffic, we stopped by the Mid-Valley to see if Dave would loan us some of his stash. All he had was a baggy half-full of nasty-looking dried stems and seeds in it. We could have it, he said, if we'd take him with us away from the hot, nerve-jangling winds. We readily agreed.

Once into Orange County, I kept an eye out for the Buena Park Boulevard off-ramp, not far from the park according to the map.

"You guys, this shit is so harsh—'scuse the French, Theresa—killing my throat," Dave grunted. He slipped the peace pipe up front to Theresa in the passenger seat. We'd stuffed some of his withered-up looking seeds and stems into the bowl of a beat-up corncob pipe with little hope they'd provide much of a buzz. "Gotta get something to drink."

Theresa agreed. "Besides, we need munchies. I'm starving." She sipped in a hit that exploded a seed with a pop like a tiny firecracker before handing me the funky old pipe.

We piled into the first convenience store we found, laughing, and split up on little quests for snacking treasures. I felt pretty light headed all of a sudden. *Didn't realize seeds and stems could get you this high*, I thought happily. *Guess smoking that junk was worth it after all.*

I found Theresa, excited, arms full, surveying a board clipped with little plastic bags. "Look, look honey—salted plums. They sell salted plums here." Sure enough; this neighborhood must harbor some wayward Hawaiians.

She bubbled on about some of the things she'd found as we worked our way to where Dave waited in line at the register with soft drinks, chips, and gum. We bumped elbows and laughed, which seemed to irritate some of the people in front of us, or so we thought. "What?" Dave said loudly. "It's not cool to be happy or what?"

I whispered to my cohorts, "Do we look high? I mean these people are acting so weird. I bet they can tell we're loaded."

"I think you definitely look high, man," Dave spoke with exaggerated sincerity.

"Oh, stop it, you don't look high, Larry," Theresa said. "You're being paranoid."

"Treese, I hate to say this," I said peering into her eyes. "But I'm pretty sure you look high. I'm worried people can tell you're tripping."

The surprise on her face made Dave and I laugh, and her snicker. I noticed the people in line had disappeared. There were only us, and the counterman who glared at us. We must have irritated or scared him or something. His disapproving frowns were too hilarious for us to take seriously; we burst out laughing. I laughed so hard I couldn't speak, and the more I couldn't talk, the more I broke up. Theresa and Dave couldn't stop either. When I got so convulsed I thought I might fall over, I chucked my stuff onto the counter and staggered out unable to utter a word. I fled giggling to the car, trying to catch my breath before I passed out. Dave arrived right behind me, his hands empty, too, and we cracked up all over again. In a couple of minutes, Theresa strolled up to the car with a big smirk on her face; she hadn't been willing to give up her salted plums and other snacks. At least she'd bought us the drinks we'd wanted.

After rolling along for about ten minutes on Buena Park Boulevard, a squad car with lights flashing and siren screaming pulled us to the curb. Theresa scrambled to stuff our pipe and baggie into the glove box as if that would help if they decided to search the car. The patrolmen were cordial, but they knew what they were looking for. One glanced at the other. "Say, do you smell something funny in this car? Like marijuana for instance?"

"Yes, officer, I believe you are correct," the other one said, playing out the script. "I'm certain I detect the distinct odor of marijuana in the vicinity of this car. I think we should investigate further." The clerk from the convenience store must have called us in.

They emptied the glove box first, of course, which led to the three of us standing embarrassed at the curb while the policemen did a rough but thorough search of the car's interior and trunk. There was nothing more to find. Our highs quickly dissipated under these circumstances.

As we talked with the two arresting officers, we explained Dave and I performed at a nightclub over in the Valley; then we had to explain we meant the San Fernando Valley, not the Pomona Valley, and that my girlfriend Theresa had recently moved here from Hawaii. Once we became people to them, things went easier, and they took a moment to reassure Theresa they would make every effort to move us through the process quickly. Which wasn't really all that quick.

At the clean, little police station, Theresa offered me a brave smile as a female officer led her to another part of the jail. Dave and I emptied all our possessions into plastic bins, gave up our clothes except for underwear and socks, and pulled on bright-yellow coveralls marked with the large stenciled initials BPPD on the back. We were escorted into a tan, cement room with bars on one end that smelled of new paint and old disinfectant with only our cigarettes and lighters. Crime must be slow in Buena Park on Friday afternoons; we were the only inhabitants.

Good as their word, the officers who'd taken us into custody passed along to the desk officer that we were cooperative, good guys and our phone call came quickly. I almost believed they were embarrassed to have us in custody on such an inconsequential charge.

When I got back, Dave looked up from examining the turned-up sleeves and pants of his yellow prison uniform in dismay. "These things must come in only two sizes: fucking huge and extra-fucking huge." His face held a twisted grin. "Fortunately, I got the fucking huge size. Only room for me and two other equally-sized persons in here." I grinned back, trying to maintain a similar nonchalance.

"I called the office and got Eve instead of Jimmy. She said she couldn't reach him. Got the feeling he's somewhere tipping back a few. Asked her to call Charles Crozier." I felt Jimmy had let us down, let me down—not only regarding this but overall. I'd wanted him to be our Dick Clark, or at least our Reb Foster, but being a famous deejay hadn't necessarily made him a great personal manager. I liked him, he was a great guy, but when things went wrong, and I had to defend him to the group, they tended to take their frustration out on me.

"She'll do better anyway; she can be a bulldog," I said, rationalizing Jimmy's absence. I sat on the bench and leaned back against the concrete wall next to Dave.

After a few minutes, Dave changed positions, trying to get comfortable. "You knew Crozier handled my problem with the Army, didn't you?"

"About not reporting to summer camp?" Dave had joined the Army Reserve back in Indianapolis after dropping out of Murray State. Those days seemed forever ago now. "I remember when you got back from basic training. You came over to our house the same day. Man, you were some kinda fit."

"Yeah, they kicked my ass for six weeks. Got me in great shape, though. I only went in to keep out of the draft, you know. After basic, had to do another four months active duty, and agree to two weeks of summer training every year for ten years. Did two weeks the next summer, but the summer after that we were in California; no way I could leave for two weeks then."

I remembered how freaked out we'd been when Dave told us he had to go to Army summer camp just as we were catching a foothold at our first real job at a biker bar in the San Francisco Bay Area. "About the same time Les and his guys joined the band," I said. "Yeah, woulda been a disaster all right. So was the Army pretty pissed?"

He shook his head. "No, they gave me a work exclusion, it worked out okay. But the next summer, when we were at the Galaxie, I tried to get another exclusion. That didn't fly, but they let me extend my camp until September, about the time we'd come to LA to play the Pink Carousel."

I cocked my head at him. "You being the lead singer and all, I probably would have noticed if you were absent. I do remember Leonard being off for two weeks, he had the mumps, but not you."

Dave wrinkled his nose. "Glad you were paying attention. No, I didn't go. Never called 'em either. Ever."

"Must have crushed the generals at the Pentagon who'd been counting on you to win the war."

"My mom started forwarding the letters from the Army," Dave said. "Didn't open them. About a year ago, I open one and there's a letter in it looks a lot like the induction notice you got. It said I had two weeks to report for active duty or be listed as AWOL." He gave me a sheepish grin. "That date flew away a long time ago."

"Are you telling me you're AWOL right now? They think you're a deserter?"

"I try not to think about the possibility." Dave crossed one leg over the other. "Wondered if they'd send the MP's to get me. Catch me at a gig somewhere. After I saw the miracle Chuck Crozier pulled off for you, I called him—thanks for the number, by the way. You made a good impression on him. Didn't charge me a bent nickel."

I remembered giving Dave the attorney's phone number, but he either hadn't told me, or I'd been too distracted to notice what had happened.

"Told me he'd been a captain in the Air Force, stationed in the Pentagon for a while in whatever they call personnel, so he understood all the ins and outs. Said he'd send for a copy of my records and figure out what to do. Said not to worry, the Army wouldn't take any action soon as he notified them he's handling the case." Dave paused to light a smoke, so I joined him, and he lit us both. We leaned back and inhaled.

"About a month later, Crozier called to say he's got my records. Just sit tight, he says, don't do anything until you hear from me. For three months, maybe a little more, nothing, and then someone from Crozier's office calls me. Somehow he's worked his weird magic again; the case had been dropped, and I'm entirely exonerated. Not only that, no more summer camp either."

I had to chuckle. "The man is twisted as they come, but he's crafty. Did he tell you how he did it?"

"Way he explained it, he sent copies of my file with cover letters to various people in various departments in the Army who could have been, but weren't, involved in my case. He requested information or actions from them in the letters. When these people got this package, they would have to figure out why they got this big, complicated file and what they had to do about it. They'd stick it on the end of their desk and write 'what the hell?' letters to everybody mentioned in the file, including carbon copies to all of them. 'If they write back asking for clarification,' he said, 'I add their letter to the stack and forward the whole file on to some other wrong person.'"

I nodded. "I get it. Brilliant. Pretty soon the paper trail is snafued so bad no one can unravel what's going on." We crushed out our smokes in a coffee can filled with sand.

I paced behind our bars like a zoo animal as the minute hand on the caged clock outside moved closer to five. We'd been here for hours already, why hadn't we heard anything? Time seemed to crawl as we waited to hear if we would be stuck here for the weekend, while out in the world, time flew toward the close of the business day. I worried about Theresa. The parallel between being in jail with her here, and when Pat and I were jailed in Indianapolis for an even stupider reason, was too obvious to miss. That had happened on a Friday night, too. It had been a flashpoint for everything afterward. Christ, I didn't want us to spend the weekend in here. Theresa hated being away from me even while I was at work.

What if Eve hadn't been able to reach Crozier in time?

31 THINGS CHANGE

Everything comes to pass, nothing comes to stay.
—Matthew Flickstein

December 15, 1968
Buena Park, California

THE DESK OFFICER stuck his head into our room. "Hey, you guys. Bail is posted, you're out on your own recognizance. We gotta do the paperwork so probably another hour."

More like two, but pretty speedy considering the grinding gears of government. Theresa was waiting in front of the booking cage. She looked happy to see me, and incredibly cute swallowed up in her more stylish, but still neon-yellow, two-piece jumpsuit. I rushed to her.

"Honey, are you okay? I'm sorry about this, sweetheart. What a mess."

She smiled and snuggled into me. "Wasn't so bad. One of the matrons and I talked for a while. She was nice. She has a sister-in-law from Maui."

"Hey, don't you want your jail uniforms back?" I asked the desk officer, realizing we were standing there in our lemon-colored clown suits.

"Gotta keep what you were wearing for evidence. Usually, you wouldn't be out until morning, and we'd ask someone to bring you clothes. You got a good attorney, got quick bail, so you're out, but"—he shrugged— "no clothes."

"Apropos for a band called Stark Naked and the Car Thieves," I replied.

"Ha ha. Well, that's why we're sending you home in those coveralls unless you want to go in your skivvies. You got a week to send 'em back, or the city will bill you for them.

"Out of curiosity, how much."

"I dunno. Fifty bucks?"

At eight o'clock, or a little before, a squad car dropped us off where they'd let me park my car, an unusual courtesy. An angry sun had almost burned itself out of the lurid sky as we got on the freeway to North Hollywood.

"Better lead-foot it if we're going to have any chance of being on time," Dave said. I did my best, but when we turned off the 101 Freeway at Lankershim and headed east toward Victory, the dashboard clock read nine forty.

"So much for the first set." After a minute, I added, "Let's go in. Least we'll make the second set."

"Like this? In prison coveralls?" Dave said. "Are you nuts?"

"Come on, man. It'll be fun. We'll crack people up. Everybody in there is a friend anyway. We'll give 'em something to talk about."

Dave finally agreed but Theresa thought otherwise. "Nuh-uh, not me. I've got to get cleaned up. I feel all filthy from that place. If you guys want to go in, go ahead, but give me the car so I can go shower."

The rest of the band was milling around on the shadowy stage when Mickey caught sight of us strolling toward the stage. Mac spoke over the guffaws.

"What the fuck? What the hell kinda clothes you boys got on?"

We swung around so the big BPPD initials across our back couldn't be missed. "Buena Park Police Department." I slipped into my best convict shtick. "We got ratted out on a narcotic beef by a snitch on our way to Deer Park. Did some hard time over there this afternoon. We were supposed to get out in two hours on good behavior, but I attacked Dave with a shiv made out of a stale French fry, so they kept us longer. It's changed me, man. I went in an innocent young man; I've come out a hardened criminal." Everybody was laughing, and chuckles were breaking out along the ringside tables where people were figuring out what our overalls meant.

"Deer Park? Shoulda invited me," Mickey said. "What's the bag limit on 'em there?" I frowned at him.

"What's a Deer Park anyway," Mac asked.

"Can't say," I told him, and Dave nodded sagely. "We never got there."

Eve had thoughtfully left a message for the band and the club about our troubles behind the Orange Curtain, the imaginary barrier between LA, and the more conservative southern reaches of Orange County. It had given Mac and Les time to plan how to cover for the first set.

"Thought you guys was pulling a 'Gazzarri's' for a while," Mac said, referring to the night Dave and I had skived off from work in Hollywood.

The guys must have done a great job. Nobody, not even Big Mike, had a word to say about us being late. When the lights went on, Dave and I cavorted around the stage in our bright yellow jumpsuits as Les vamped a little of "we fought the law and the law won." Jail overalls might be good for a few laughs, but once the set ended, we rushed home for quick showers and a change of clothes.

Theresa was now a regular part of the group's female constellation, joining Lora Borden, Joan Brown, Paula Souza, and Les's girlfriend, Susie. Every once in a while, Dave stuck with a girl long enough to meet the girls the way a comet flies through the solar system and out again. Susie and Theresa were especially close. They were nearer in age, entered the band's orbit about the same time, and while the other girls were wives, they were significant others. Most of the time, the girls sat together at the club when they came in, but on our breaks, Theresa wanted to be with me, and it was the same for Susie and Les. I spent every moment I could with her. We breathed the same air and touched at every opportunity. Our appetite for each other's presence seemed insatiable. Most afternoons when I wasn't rehearsing, we spent long hours lying comfortably in each other's arms between hazy, languorous lovemaking. When we were alone, clothes had become optional, although nudity was favored. Theresa was curious about everything and a good listener, our conversations ranged far and wide in these intimate hours. Her constant assurances of her love for me in word and touch was slowly healing the encysted anguish I'd kept bottled-up after the disastrous end of my marriage to Pat. The guards I'd built over the years continued to loosen. Tentatively, I found myself sharing my deepest thoughts with her and started to trust my feelings again.

With our run at the Doll over, I hoped the Sky Room would replace it as our new home. But my confidence was shaken when Seymour called to inform me we wouldn't be christening what we'd already considered "our nightclub." At the last minute, Bill Miller had decided to hire Spiral Starecase for the first two weeks because he thought their name on the marquee would promote the staircase curving up to the Sky Room from the casino's front door. We were forced to swap with Spiral Starecase; we'd have to play at their home club in El Monte, the Forty Niner, for New Year's Eve, and a couple of weeks more before we could take our rightful place in Las Vegas. It meant a fairly subdued New Year's for us. I fervently hoped there would be no more surprises.

We'd put the best face on it we could and begun our gig at the Forty Niner where the owner and audiences couldn't have been more receptive. After an especially productive afternoon rehearsal where we'd put the finishing touches on a tremendous new set opener for Mac at the Sky Room, Otis Redding's *Hard to Handle*, I came home from El Monte to find Theresa basking by the pool in the late-winter sun with several of the ladies. When she saw me, she stood and ran to give me a kiss. I started back to the pool with her, but she turned me back toward our apartment. Well, that was a good idea, too. She glanced back at the girls to wave goodbye.

I'd begun getting comfortable when it dawned on me how anxious she seemed to be. I wondered what could be bothering her. We'd talked about another short visit home so she could see her family again. Was that it? We'd agreed if the Vegas gig turned out to be as good as promised, once things had gotten things stabilized, we would arrange it for her then.

I sat next to her and took her hands, studying her troubled eyes, waiting. Her head dipped for a moment and then lifted as if she was coming up for air after a dive in the pool.

"The girls said I should come right out and tell you. That would be the best way."

"The girls are usually right." I smiled at her. "They know the guys in the band better than we know ourselves." I hoped there would be something I could do to make her smile. Hopefully, it would end with an excuse to hop in the sack, though we never needed an excuse.

"Larry, I . . . I'm pregnant." A terrific, echoing, banging sound started from somewhere near the back of my head, and it seemed like certain parts of the room had suddenly gone black.

Part II images

Larry's Parents' home in Indianapolis

Larry & Theresa Universal City

Carrollton House

Theresa's Lei

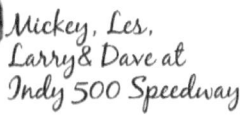

Mickey, Les, Larry & Dave at Indy 500 Speedway

PART III

The muse doesn't come without being called.

—P<small>YOTR</small> I<small>LYICH</small> T<small>CHAIKOVSKY</small>

32 THE SKY ROOM

> *By all means marry; if you get a good wife, you'll be happy; if you get a bad one, you'll become a philosopher.*
> —Socrates

January 14, 1969
Las Vegas, Nevada

A YOUTHFUL FIGURE in a shirt and tie stood at the top of the staircase smiling in open enthusiasm as he watched us climb the spiraling steps.

"You guys have to be Stark Naked and the Car Thieves. Welcome to the Sky Room!" I was glad to hear the warmth in Jim Seagrave's voice as he introduced himself. Maybe we'd get to stay here for a while this time. He pulled aside thick velvet curtains to usher us into a sleek, modern lounge manifesting an aura of the golden days of nightclubs.

A river of deep-pile carmine carpet rolled through the spacious lounge. Floor-to-ceiling windows enclosed the Sky Room on three sides, conveying a sense of floating above the casino entrance. Inside, ruby-red, faux-leather chairs arranged themselves companionably around burnished cocktail tables. Though the nightclub had already been open two weeks, I could still smell its newness. To our left, the undraped, half-moon stage faced a sunken dance floor—railed, to keep over-oiled patrons from accidentally tumbling onto its polished parquet. The most striking feature was the panoramic view we'd see every night through the windows in front of us. Below, at street level, chaotic traffic and pedestrian casino-goers flowed along the streets and corners of the busiest intersection on the Las Vegas Strip. Across the boulevard, a football-field-long driveway penetrated past numerous powerful fountains to a traffic circle in front of Caesars Palace's massive entrance. Encircled by the roundabout, stood a graphically erotic and violent sculpture from Roman history: a full-scale replica of the Rape of the Sabine Women. Las Vegas wasn't famous for subtlety.

"The term of your contract," Jim continued, weaving between tables, "is four-weeks indefinite—as close to permanent as you can get in this town. Better make yourselves comfortable fellas, looks like we'll be working together for a long time."

I'd had a hard time believing Seymour when he told me we could write our own ticket if we did well here. Though I liked Jim already and I'd nodded politely, past experiences at Caesars and the Thunderbird had taught us some harsh lessons. Contracts could suddenly disappear if you somehow honked off the wrong somebody. I tamped down my concerns, knowing things were different with Seymour representing us. He wielded the heavy leverage of representing Liberace, arguably the biggest star in Las Vegas.

"Technically, Bill Miller is your boss," Jim said. "He's the entertainment director, but you probably won't see much of him. He's busy night and day with the main showroom, lounges, and a ton of other responsibilities." We followed him behind a long, ebony bar glistening in the angled sunlight. "He's asked me to watch over you guys along with my day job as head of publicity for the Flamingo."

He opened a door on the interior wall. "In here is your dressing room." We wedged ourselves into a windowless sliver of a room shaped like a thin piece of lopsided pie. With the seven of us and four chairs, we stood elbow to elbow staring at each other.

"Um, it's a little snug." My mouth twisted into a wry smile. "Unless we change clothes one at a time in here, I don't think this will work as a dressing room."

His brow wrinkled, and he frowned. "No, no, you're right. Of course not. Don't know why we didn't realize this. It's more of a break room, isn't it? Look, don't worry about this. Bill and I will figure something out. We want you guys to be happy."

32 THE SKY ROOM

After Jim Seagrave left, we were supposed to begin bringing in our equipment. But I slid into one of the red upholstered side chairs at a window table. My eyes took in Las Vegas Boulevard sweeping north toward downtown as my thoughts turned inward wondering how soon I could bring my new fiancée home.

We hadn't played a note, but I already knew this place would be perfect. My first impression of Jim Seagrave, and what it would be like working for him, sealed the deal. I could send for Theresa weeks earlier than I'd planned. God, how I missed her. I'd tried to distract myself. I'd discovered a used bookstore and let a variety of new-to-me paperbacks follow me home. It wasn't enough. I lit up with a match torn from a new Flamingo-logoed matchbook in a similarly logoed cut-glass ashtray.

A lot had changed since Theresa's surprise announcement just before Christmas. *The main thing*, I'd told myself at the time, *don't say anything, nothing, not until you figure out what in the hell is the right thing to say.* I'd paced back and forth bumping between bed and chair in our motel room's cramped space. *Saying the wrong thing could ruin everything.*

"Well, you can't be pregnant," I'd blurted out. A perfect example of what I meant not to say. "Uh, no. Not what I meant. Of course, you can be. What I mean is . . . ah, you're sure . . . you are sure, aren't you?" I glanced into her amber-flecked irises on the verge of drowning in tears. Damn! I'd already begun badly, but I did need to be absolutely sure of what we were dealing with, didn't I? After all, I'd been here before. This was a crucial moment. Everything had to be handled exactly right, right from the beginning. *Stop! Take a breath. Think! Hysteria will not help.*

Theresa nodded and breathed out. "Susie took me to the doctor. Yes, honey. I'm sure." She looked at me helplessly, palm on her tummy. "Did I mess everything up? I mean we're so happy, does this mean it's the end for us? That you don't love me anymore?" Her eyes searched mine.

I reached for her hand. "No, it does not mean any of those things. I love you desperately. But things have happened—with me—before. I know what we're facing, what's ahead if we don't do this right."

"Do this right?" she said, puzzled. "I don't understand."

"I know, I know. That's the point. But see, I do. I hadn't considered it possible . . ." The shock and surprise must have still shown on my face, I couldn't seem to wipe it off. *What an incredible idiot I am.* I glanced at her. "I guess you weren't using any . . . I'd assumed you were taking birth control pills . . ." *What difference does that make now, lamebrain? Pregnancy is a door once opened, never closed.*

"No. I never have actually." Her face fell into her hands as she melted into misery. This wasn't going right.

Where was my head? Why hadn't I foreseen this? Was I doomed to repeat the same dumb mistakes over and over? At least this time I knew better, I was going to get it right. I would make sure of it. I loved this girl; I didn't question that. *But pregnancy pushes things to a different level. Do we have the kind of love that can last a lifetime?* I needed to think.

"Look, I need a little time to work out what's best for us. Give me a chance to figure this out. I know I can find the right way to get everything back on track." She was trying to deal with the emotions of this moment, I understood that, but I worried about damaging our futures. I'd hugged her long and tight, hoping to reassure her, before bolting wordlessly out the door.

Leonard's shout from the elevators broke into my thoughts. "Hey, Larry, bringing the van around front. Meet us downstairs in ten. Wanna pull the B3 out first. Okay?"

"Got it, ten minutes," I answered, mulling over Theresa's distress when I'd explained why I wanted her to go to Hawaii.

"If everything is okay," she'd asked, "why are you sending me away?" I could see the hurt behind Theresa's eyes, I wanted to ease her concerns, but we couldn't risk handling the situation wrong. I tried again.

"Treese, honey, I'm not sending you away—not away, away. I love you more than anything. But I've been working through this . . . situation. I told you about Pat, and how things ended so badly between us. But I've never told you the details. Because of the decisions her parents made without consulting us—and mine along with them—we were set up to fail. Before we even got started. I can't let that happen to us."

"But my parents think you are wonderful. I sent them pictures, and my mother and father think you are great, and my brothers say you look like a very good person. They are anxious to meet you. They wouldn't be like those awful people you're talking about."

How can I get through to her about something only I have experienced?

"This isn't about Pat's parents specifically. I never imagined I could get so close to anyone again; too much danger of . . . too much . . . I never thought someone like you would come into my life. It changes everything." I stopped spouting nonsense and tried to get back to the point.

"It's important that whenever you look back on this day, that you are rock-solid certain that I chose to marry you because you are the love of my life. Not for any other reason. Though you might not realize how important that is right now, I need this for you. And for me, too. I need to move beyond my own past and commit to you with everything in my soul."

"Couldn't you possibly just tell me how much you love me?" Her eyes beat between mine like the wings of a trapped butterfly, pleading for answers she could make sense of. "I would believe you. Wouldn't that be enough?"

"Maybe for now, maybe for a while. But if there comes a day when you wonder about my commitment to you, Treese, I don't want you ever to doubt why I chose to share my life with you."

"So, you are going to show me this by sending me to Hawaii?" She spoke slowly, trying to make sense of my reasoning.

I grimaced in frustration. "Yes, sort of. I mean it's the only way I can think of to make sure we're both sure. It gives us both a little time to think. If either of us changes our minds, this would be the time to do it. You did say you wanted to go home to Waipahu for a visit once we were settled in Vegas, right?"

"Yes," Theresa agreed grudgingly.

"This way you can go now. Listen, honey, the band's heading into new territory at the Flamingo. Always possible for something unexpected to happen in these Las Vegas hotels, it's happened before. You'll be safe in Hawaii while I make sure everything is secure there. You can see that makes sense, can't you?"

"Yes." Tiny, tiny voice.

"And last, but most important, you have to trust our love. You'll be going to Hawaii as my girlfriend, and if we love each other the way we say we do, you'll be coming back to be my wife, the mother of our child, and the one and only person I promise to love and cherish forever. Please, Treese. If I'm lying about this, you wouldn't want to marry me anyway."

"You know I will do whatever you want me to. But I will miss you every day and worry until I see you again. Right now, I don't want anything but to be with you, to love you in every way possible. What you are asking will be extremely difficult."

Pulling myself back to the Sky Room, I realized now what I hadn't then—she would never understand why this painful separation was necessary. She didn't have my memories. Her first letter she wrote to me following the phone call I'd made to her parents to ask for their blessing, was filled with excitement but also included long, desperate passages worrying if she'd done something wrong and if it would cost us our relationship.

> *I was so happy when you called me. I really blew everything didn't I? I keep worrying and thinking that I'm going to lose you, Larry. I pray you'll still love me the way you did before.*
>
> *I told my parents how much I love you and what a wonderful person you are. My mom told me that after talking to you it made her feel a lot better. She also said that you are a good person and she can't wait to meet you. They've got all kinds of plans for the wedding and I just can't wait. It will be the biggest and most beautiful Hawaiian wedding you would ever dream of. My parents and brothers are all so excited and happy for the both of us.*

Jesus wept, if she knew how I burned for her, she wouldn't worry. I was tortured by the need to fill my eyes with her, to hear her voice, to touch her skin, and taste and inhale her essence.

33 TRYING TO GET IT RIGHT

A man's wife is his compromise with the illusion of his first sweetheart.
—James A. Garfield

January 14, 1969
Las Vegas, Nevada

IN THE HOURS after Theresa's life-changing news, I'd drifted through the darkened streets of North Hollywood weighing our options. She was so much younger—I had to be responsible for both of us. My first impulse was marriage, of course. But I'd lived through the disaster of a marriage gone wrong. I couldn't let Theresa be hurt the way Pat had been—or me. I had to know with every molecule of my being that nothing short of the end of my existence could shake my commitment to her. It would crush her if I couldn't, she wouldn't understand. But it would be a pinprick compared to the agony we risked if we made the wrong decision. I wished we'd had more time for this outcome to happen naturally; I felt confident it would have.

The option of not having this child was never a part of my reasoning. Though she hadn't said so, I didn't think Theresa could conceive of it either. I wouldn't mention it to her, never make her have to choose. I had no moral objections and would defer to her, of course. It's just—a baby born from our love—it seemed miraculous, though it scared the holy crap out of me. A child would change us.

If we didn't marry, what would happen? I couldn't imagine us apart. I'd tried to turn off my feelings when I left Hawaii. That hadn't worked. When we were away from each other, even for a short time, the sun refused to shine. Could we go on living together as unmarried parents? A child would connect us forever. Would it end the romantic part of our relationship? Wouldn't it be worse to lose her affection and passion and yet be reminded of it every day?

I searched my deepest feelings about our relationship, the ones I would never share with anyone else, feelings I'd hidden even from myself. It was hard to penetrate the illusion of who we really were. So much stereotypical fantasy surrounded us: me an entertainer from the mainland, her an exquisite island girl. I'd been attracted to her from the moment I saw her. I'd thought her so overwhelmingly attractive I almost didn't dare meet her at the Lemon Tree. When we made love the first time, fireworks should have alerted the whole island. The intensity continued to grow, our physical intimacy so tender at times touch was more in our minds than our bodies, while in others we fucked like wild creatures trying to break the bounds of physicality and embed ourselves within each other. While I didn't know how I could live without that part, I knew it wouldn't be enough by itself. A fire that burns too hot can be too fierce to last forever. *What else did I feel?*

We communicated in verbal and non-verbal ways. I thought about the way she constantly touched and stroked me, continuously establishing and reinforcing our connection, a reminder of her ownership of me and my custodianship of her. Sometimes I thought we must have known and lost each other in a previous lifetime and could not consume enough of each other in this one to make up for it. I'd experienced something similar in my love affair with Pat—the bond we'd believed would hold us together forever.

Pat! I froze in my tracks. How could I commit to Theresa without resolving what had happened between us? I hadn't realized how deeply I'd buried my feelings until the raw emotions I'd never suspected surfaced in Indianapolis. I hadn't grasped how emotionally stuck I was—my feelings frozen from the moment Pat had walked away from me without a backward glance at the Oakland airport. I'd never meant for things to so disastrously.

Maybe it was guilt holding me like an insect pinned to a board—the realization of how my words and decisions had crushed her, the last person I'd ever wanted to hurt. I'd never intended the consequences to be so terrible. The choices had been horrifying. Give up the woman I'd loved since we were children, or return to Indiana to die in spirit and she sickened at the sight of me and I lost her anyway? Her actions after the divorce were swift. One unexpected domino after another toppled. In helpless shock and surprise, I'd witnessed rippling waves of devastation alter the lives of our boys, our families, our friends. I'd replayed the series of events leading to the decision I'd tried hard not to make. Though I'd never seen how I could've chosen differently, in my heart of hearts I'd always known I should have found a way. I'd failed my commitment to her when I couldn't.

I continued my aimless wandering. Dusk had fallen, but I barely noticed. Pat had found a way to move on, to move past me, for the boys' sake if for no other reason. I thought I was past it, too, but I was wrong. Instead, I'd cradled the pain inside me, created an encrusted tolerance for it the way an oyster hugs a pearl. *If I give up that treasured pain and guilt, expose my blighted soul to reason, it will sever the last precious threads that bind me to Pat.*

Could my relationship with Theresa overcome such a deep wound? Did her unexpected pregnancy disguise a fateful opportunity? A second chance to find and this time keep, happiness from slipping through my clumsy fingers? Raise a child? Make up in some way for how I'd failed David and Danny? God in heaven, I'd never expected it.

I stopped again, alone in the seemingly deserted neighborhood streets. Subdued lights from shadowed bungalow windows barely hinted at human existence. I needed her to understand. If I could talk to my wife, my ex-wife . . . but that was impossible. In desperation I found myself trying to conjure up the vivacious blonde teenager who'd rescued me in high school, the young and amazing wife and mother who I'd always thought would be my life partner. Inexplicably, I sensed her in the shadows cast by the streetlight through the limbs of a tree in the greenway between the street and sidewalk. I steadied myself against the rough bark of its trunk. Was this nothing more than an illusion created by my need? I didn't know but spoke anyway.

"Pat, I'm sorry for everything," I whispered, "for all the ways I failed you." I let myself believe she could hear me. I paused, trying to gauge my sincerity. *Was speaking to some projection of my mind and expecting something to come from it anything but a fantasy?* It didn't make any difference. I was sincere, and all I could do.

"I told you there would never be a day in this life when I didn't love you. It's true and always will be. But I finally get it. I understand now. You have another life, and I wish nothing but happiness for you and our boys in it." My eyes dropped to the sidewalk.

"I have to. . . I have to pack my love for you away so I can go on too. I'm saying goodbye at last, but I will always keep a special place in my heart for you whether we ever see or speak to each other again." In my waking dream, a light breeze moved through shadowed leaves, now empty of life.

Somewhere, in the plan taking shape, I would have to find time to grieve this loss. My decision made, I needed to set the stage for a new life with Theresa carefully; to make sure it unfolded in the right way.

34 STARRY VEGAS NIGHTS

Las Vegas looks the way you'd imagine heaven must look at night.
—Chuck Palahniuk

January 14, 1969
Las Vegas, Nevada

WE INTRODUCED OURSELVES to the standing-room-only Sky Room crowd with The Vogues' *Five O'clock World*. Though Dave sang lead, it featured all our voices and established our emphasis on vocals. The place had been jammed from the first note, and my nerves jangled as they usually did on critical nights. A long line of people waiting for tables snaked along outside the velvet ropes, corkscrewed around the landing, and extended halfway down the stairs. The room sparkled with the reflected blaze from the Strip and the fairy lights from Caesars Palace. Inside, table lights haloed in cigarette smoke and ankle-level illumination from the dance floor heightened the atmosphere.

Les and I, on guitar and organ, synched together to emulate the horn intro to Otis Redding's fabulous *Hard to Handle*, and Mickey and Leonard settled into the super-funky beat, our drummer popping off his seat with each crack of the snare. Mac ripped into the lyric while dancers rushed to the dance floor. Dave followed with Gary Puckett and the Union Gap's slightly-pedophilic hit, *Young Girl*, and as usual, he knocked it out of the park. My anxiety vanished in the wake of the audience's enthusiastic acclaim.

Since our performances began at the height of the evening, we featured our production numbers in our first two sets, presenting them more as shows than dance music. We sprinkled in larger percentages of dance numbers as the night advanced into the small hours of morning. Dave and Mac gave their best Sam and Dave impression next with *I Thank You,* and Les crooned *By the Time I Get to Phoenix.* Les's voice had the same timbre as Glen Campbell's, and the crowd loved him. We wanted a power ballad for Dave in the next slot, so we reached back in time for Dave's dramatic interpretation of *Unchained Melody.* It was a perfect choice, and the response pushed against us like a pressure wave.

Mac worked the stage with a boisterous delivery of *Who's Making Love (to your old lady, while you were out making love)* with a lot of audience participation. Next, we let loose our harmony on the Five Americans' *Western Union,* a song that used all our voices in its tricky staccato harmony. The song was just the right tempo for its spot in the show and tonight, and it sounded fresh and bright. Rounding things out, I put my heart into the Buckinghams' *Kind of a Drag* and didn't screw up the keyboard highlights too badly. After jumping back and forth between the front line and back to the organ a half-dozen times, I pulled my mic stand out to flank Dave, with Mac on his opposite side for the final tunes. We didn't often do our own records, but it felt right to sing *Look Back In Love* in our new home before closing with the Four Seasons' epic arrangement of *I've Got You Under My Skin,* a huge winner in Vegas ever since we'd performed it at Caesars Palace.

Our first standing ovation at the Sky Room made the hair on my arms stand up. Applause rolled over us from people coming to their feet at the tables, patrons at the bar, and standees along the back windows. Bartenders, wait-staff, and the maître d's joined in. People waiting in line behind the velvet ropes added hoots and hollers.

Before we scattered out into the room, excited and flushed, ready to greet and meet people before our early band, the Deltas, took over, we agreed to meet downstairs in the Flamingo coffee shop. Since none of the wives had chosen to brave the crush of opening night and Dave had yet to meet his new girlfriend-du-jour, there was an unspoken desire to stick together. I'd felt the tension in us before we'd begun, and though we might not admit it, we needed to share our relief and extend the high that came from an excellent performance.

We were seated in a big booth in the coffee shop's far reaches where we could spread out and relax. Leonard, our salad guy, ordered the Flamingo Salad Bowl, while the rest of us convinced the server to bring us the menu's grilled ground sirloin slapped between hamburger buns or at least bread slices.

While we waited for our orders, Mac told us about a regular from the Cat who'd stopped him after our set. He'd come in, Mac said, to thank the band for saving his life last year. After being fired from his job, he hadn't known how to break it to his wife. He'd hit rock bottom, even considered taking his life. He'd come into the Cat trying to soak up enough liquid courage to choose one path or the other.

"Told me it was us that lifted him up," Mac said. "Damndest thing. Said the joyful party atmosphere we'd created that night turned his head around. Got him to thinkin everything would be okay, long as he kept his head up. Went home, told his wife, and she and the kid stuck with him. Now he's got himself a better job, and he and his family are happier than ever. Bout broke my damn heart, man, guy was so thankful for us and our music." Mac's voice broke for a moment, and he gathered us up in his emotion.

"That's us, you know, that's what we do, touchin people's lives like that." He leaned in, patting his chest. "This is where it's at for me, boys. This is what I always wanna be doin with my life."

I thought about how I'd only wanted to sing alone with my vocal group buddies in a room with great echo so I could hear how cool our harmony sounded back in Indianapolis. Did not wanting to share our music make me selfish? I'd never thought of it that way. I hadn't chosen the life of a performer, even resisted it. Singing publicly often gave me the wobblies. But witnessing the potency of our music to generate powerful reactions from people in our audiences never failed to amaze me.

When Theresa stepped off the plane at McCarran Airport into the wintery sunlight of a desert-bright afternoon, she ran toward me and stopped short. Her eyes crinkled, seeming to drink me in; smiling, but tears ready to break. I thrilled to the almost supernatural allure drawing me to her as she burrowed into my arms.

"Oh, Larry, I love you, oh my God, how I love you. I worried so much. I don't want you ever to make me go away again. We have to stay together. I love you so much. I can't wait to be alone with my own darling fiancé."

Another little part of my heart melted. "Never, honey. We won't ever have to be apart again." My nostrils dilated as I buried my face in her hair, filling my lungs with her aroma.

"I've got a motel room near the Tropicana. It's not far from the airport," I told her as we loaded her luggage into the car. "But I've already found us an apartment. Only if you like it, though, we can stop and see it if you want to."

She gazed at me with a sexy grin. "Do you mind if we go after?" I drew a harsh breath; I could hardly exhale. I didn't need to ask what "after" meant.

With the edge off of our greedy hunger, I didn't feel like going anywhere, but Theresa poked and prodded until I agreed to show her our new home. I pretended to groan and complain as I dressed until she lost herself in laughter. I turned north on Las Vegas Boulevard out of the motel's parking lot and into an inconspicuous little street next to the Shell station north of Caesars Palace. The street ended in a nest of luxurious apartment buildings screened from Caesar's front parking lot and the Las Vegas Strip by a stand of beeches. The manager showed us to a second-floor furnished unit on Dauphin Way, and Theresa's enthusiastic approval confirmed my choice.

"Jim Seagrave at the Flamingo told me about these apartments. You'll meet him soon, Treese. He's taking care of us at the hotel and a great guy. Another thing you'll like, Susie and Les are living in the building next door."

"Oh my God, that's so perfect. I can hardly wait to see her and the other girls." She wandered through the long living room in wonder, fingers brushing the furniture, the counter separating the open kitchen.

"This is all ours? The rooms are huge. I love how I can see into our dining room and front room while I am making meals." The extra-large bedroom, dominated by a king-sized bed and super-sized TV, was off a corridor next to the kitchen. Theresa gave me a secret smile indicating she liked the looks of this, too, but she might just have been mirroring my lascivious leer. Whoever furnished and decorated our new apartment seemed to know exactly what we'd want.

"When can we move in, honey?"

I glanced at the manager.

"Don't see no reason I can't let you two have a key now." She looked back and forth between us; she seemed charmed by our happiness. "All we need is for us to go downstairs and finish the paperwork. Believe I can find you kids some basic essentials for the night, too."

"Oh, Larry, can we? Can we please?" Theresa begged. "I can settle us in, you know. I always put everything away when we moved before. We can get takeout for our first dinner here while we are out. When you come back in the morning, your fiancée," she said proudly, "will be here waiting in our new home." I couldn't have asked for more.

We settled into our new residence by consuming our first meal and consecrating our freshly made king-sized bed, more or less simultaneously, lazing around afterward watching the gigantic bedroom television. The Sky Room was a great place to perform, but I wasn't anxious to leave home tonight. Theresa tried to hide a couple of yawns, exhausted after her long trip. She asked me to tell the guys she'd see them and her girlfriends in the Sky Room tomorrow night.

My island girl followed me to the door barefoot, posing wantonly inside. "Wake me when you get home, honey. Your Kanaka girl wants more homecoming loving."

I hiked along the quiet road into the Strip's sudden tumult, the noise and bustle animating me for the night ahead. I strolled by the faux Roman Empire on my right to the corner of Flamingo, where the lights from the casino marquees around the intersection made it more like noon than the approaching witching hour. Crossing with a flock of tourists, I scooted under the porte-cochere where porters and valets hustled at their jobs, ushering people in and out of vehicles. Inside the casino entrance, I two-stepped up the stairs to join my friends for a nonstop night of entertaining.

A couple of weeks later, Jim Seagrave dropped in at rehearsal. "Now that you're settled in, I want to discuss something with you. The hotel wants to run an advertising campaign promoting the Sky Room featuring you guys and your name." He tossed our current publicity photo onto the table. Of the many promotional shots done for Stark Naked and the Car Thieves, this particular photo had become our trademark image. It was a black and white, head-on portrait of the band in two bare-skinned and brooding rows—implying nakedness without revealing anything below the waist. The enigmatic expressions on our faces didn't reflect our true nature—we were generally pretty happy—but I thought it gave us a kind of cool, edgy, bad-guy look.

"I want shots of you like this." He flicked his fingers toward the photo. "Well . . . unclothed."

"Naked?" Les said in surprise. I noticed several questioning expressions about where our new boss was going with this.

"Makes sense," I said. "Our sexy male bods are bound to bring in the ladies." That got the expected laugh, but I couldn't help wondering, too.

"No, of course not naked, naked," Jim said, with a mischievous grin. "At least not totally. Like your publicity picture, these shots will be strategic, only we'll shoot you individually. The plan is for each of you to be in some sort of action pose. We'll let the photo director figure that part out." He may have sensed a few misgivings, but before anybody could say anything, he said, "Tell you what, you can approve them, help pick out the shots we should use. Turns out you don't like them, we won't do it."

I arrived for my photo shoot a few days later at a second-floor studio. A stepladder and various props were laid out on a table next to a rounded-off corner of the room painted white. The photographer had chosen a straw hat for me, the flat kind known as a "skimmer" in the forties, and an actual stage light. I found myself surprisingly self-conscious stripped to my boxer briefs and socks holding the stage light high over my head in my right hand while flourishing the hat in the other.

"Jim says you're the band's leader." He grinned as he snapped shots from above me on the stepladder. "Was considering going full frontal nudity since you're obviously Stark Naked himself. But Jim worried you might scare the tourists and nixed the concept, so I came up with some other ideas." The laughs helped. The light fixture was heavy, I could only hold it up for a few seconds, but after a few takes and more jokes with the photographer and his assistant, I got into the spirit of the thing, even though it was killing my arm.

A few weeks later, a note on my Hammond B3, which was becoming my mailbox, notified us of a package from Seymour Heller's office. It was waiting in our new dressing rooms. The Flamingo's entertainment office's response to our need for a roomier place to dress and store our stage clothes had come almost immediately. Jim took us to two poolside cabana rooms next to an empty swimming pool in an older part of the hotel undergoing renovation. One of the rooms had been stripped of contents and fixtures and equipped with two makeup stations, a couple of full-length mirrors, and some random seating. With the bed pushed against the wall and extra chairs, the connecting room became our makeshift lounge. We stored our equipment cases in the first room closet and under the bed of the second, while Leonard managed our wardrobe from the second room's dresser and closet.

It wasn't glamorous, and it was inconvenient to schlep across the entire casino, out of the hotel, past two swimming pools and various buildings, to get to our dressing room. But with no guests in this part of the resort, we had plenty of privacy and space.

We rushed through practice wondering what our management office had sent. The "package" turned out to be several boxes of thick cardboard. The tallest and biggest three contained the custom-made creations we'd helped design last year in collaboration with Liberace's tailor, John Lieu.

Inside, two to a box, hung six personalized, protective holders encasing three sets of suits in deep shimmering burgundy, electric blue, and lustrous dark gold. Our names were stitched inside the suitcoats' white-silk linings, themselves embellished with fat pink and purple polka dots. A separate box held similarly polka-dotted neckties and handkerchiefs made from the same silk material as the suit lining. A pouch attached to each hanger cradled cufflink sets with extravagantly-sized stones color-matched to each outfit. Another box held three sets of suede boots in colors perfectly matching our ensembles. The final box held six sets of custom-fitted, French-cuff, ruffled, white-on-white dress shirts.

Each set of six shirts was personally monogrammed and neatly folded in a box with our names on them.

Giddy as a bunch of little girls, we tried on clothes that fit us like nothing we'd ever worn before. The shimmering blue pants of the suit we chose for that night fit flat across my stomach and zipped up the side, sheathing me from the waist down like an extra layer of skin. They were cut perfectly to my short, stocky legs, the fabric flexible and easy to move in. A hemmed notch at the front of each pant leg accommodated our new side-zippered boots that fit like high-heeled slippers. The tailored shirt hugged every part of my chest and arms in comfort no matter which way I stretched. And the coat—the coat was exactly what John Lieu had sketched from Mac's vision. The signature drape of the "Elvis" collar was perfectly accentuated, unmistakably unique, but not overbearing.

Done wrong, we would have looked like clowns. Instead, these clothes, without a pocket bulge anywhere, were sleek and professional. Stark Naked and the Car Thieves would put the ultimate twist on our name. We would be sartorial wonders.

The Sky Room was quickly becoming home. The shiny new furniture and fixtures, the elegant decor, and maître d's manning scarlet ropes, and velvet curtains screamed first class. But the hours and entertainment schedule of this hybrid showroom/dance club were unlike any other hotel's venue on the Las Vegas Strip. They were, however, strikingly similar to those of the Pussycat A' Go Go, the somewhat disreputable purveyor of rock, show, and dance music up the street where we'd found so much success.

It pointed to the Flamingo's objective in creating this room. As expected, our performances of upscale rock, gritty funk, R&B, and production ballads attracted our following—the late-night rounders and insiders, the Strip performers and renowned musicians—from the Pussycat.

The Flamingo's main room and lounges brought in world famous entertainers and the tourists who followed them. Our stylish stage appearance and showmanship coupled with the ironic contradiction of our playfully naughty name was the perfect act to bring these audiences together and keep them in the hotel. This vibrant crowd of people at the top of the spiral stairs kept the place energized deep into the morning. Though we were there to entertain them, interacting with these audiences was a constant source of surprise and wonder to me.

When Theresa was there to watch me on stage, my existence was complete. Whether the songs were my lead or not, I sang them to her, and when she wasn't watching, I sang them for her. Now she was home, all reservations lifted, and our commitments made, I was enveloped in contented happiness, unlike anything I'd experienced before. The aura of *us* sheltered me from the slights and brushes of everyday life in the band.

The brakes were off as we relaxed into our luxurious apartment and private lifestyle. We were inseparable, spending our private time together *au naturel* as much as possible, every part of our bodies accessible and familiar to one another. Though we augmented our sensations under the influence of cannabis, marijuana was not the source of our intimacy, simply an amplifier of it. I felt free to express myself in unfiltered streams of consciousness, and she joined me in exploring woven imaginings that appeared and disappeared like smoke rings in the air. She might not have had broad experience or formal education—but she was bright and imaginative and opened herself to me. We smiled and laughed and loved whenever we were together.

35 RING DAY

When you realize you want to spend the rest of your life with somebody, you want the rest of your life to start as soon as possible.
—Nora Ephron, *When Harry Met Sally*

February 10, 1969
Las Vegas, Nevada

ON A THURSDAY morning that for most people, was early afternoon, Theresa lay curled beside me following the gentle, loving encounter we'd woken to.

"We have to get up." She moved languidly against me like a cat. She threw a smug grin over her honey-tanned shoulder. "We have something special planned for today, you know."

"Really?" I pulled her closer looking puzzled. "Something besides loving on each other?" Her grin grew into a broad smile. It warmed my soul like it always did.

"Ahhhh." I groaned into a stretch I couldn't stop. "I know. You must be referring to breakfast."

"Well, no. But afterward." She playfully pummeled me with a pillow. "Stop it! You know what I mean!"

"You sound kind of excited about it." I fended off another wimpy blow.

"I cannot wait. I am so happy." She giggled like a child.

"Then let's fix a couple of fried egg sandwiches and get going." I jumped to my feet. "First one in the shower gets to soap the other one down."

Last week we'd been given some hints on where we could find a wedding ring Theresa would like, and I could afford, which turned out to be in downtown Las Vegas. The ring-sizing should be finished today, so we'd planned to pick it up.

There was something on Theresa's mind as we dressed after our shower. We seemed unable to keep our thoughts secret from one another.

"Is there something wrong, honey?"

"I can't help thinking about how much my family wanted us to come to Hawaii. They had such big plans for our wedding."

I nodded. I was disappointed too. "I know. It would have been incredible. I wish we could go."

They'd promised us an authentic Hawaiian blowout of a party with all the extended family coming, and a feast featuring a luau pig. Because of the way our relationship had flowered, I'd never met any of the members of her family in person. This could have made up for that in a big way. I felt terrible about not being able to give her this.

She stepped into panties and wrinkled her nose at me. "I know you can't leave right now. I understand. The band has only been at the Flamingo a few weeks, and you must be careful not to mess that up. You guys are becoming the hottest thing in Las Vegas." Almost every day, quarter- and eighth-page ads ran in the local papers and entertainment giveaways featuring us in the Flamingo's new entertainment spot. She pulled a new sundress over her head and gave me a satisfied smile. "It's not the right time."

That's the excuse I'd given, and it was true. We did need to make the best impression we could in these first weeks at the Sky Room. What I couldn't find a way to explain was how taking time off to go to Hawaii would set a precedent I didn't think I could afford. The most important of the band's unspoken commitments was for each of us to be on stage, every night, no matter how sick or important the demands of our personal lives. It was logical. If Dave or Les couldn't make it to the stage, we couldn't play, and if Mickey or Leonard weren't available, it would be difficult even with a fill-in. If we couldn't play, we wouldn't get paid, and could potentially be fired. We could probably work around Mac's leads if we had to, but it was me who could be most easily missed, and it had always made me feel vulnerable. I couldn't think of any reason they couldn't find a better singer and keyboard player to replace me—one of the main reasons I worked hard to be irreplaceable as a bandleader. I always had to set the best example.

"The important thing is we're going to get married, and I'm going to have your baby, a little Larry Dunlap." Her moisture-filled eyes found one of mine, and then the other. "Oh darling, I am so excited and happy. I am so much in love. Truly, everything is perfect. Going to Hawaii for the wedding would be fantastic, but honestly, I might explode if anything got more perfect."

We walked out of the courthouse to a bench facing the street. Theresa reached into the plastic bag to pull out a small velour pouch containing a ring box. She held the ring's stone to the sunlight while I admired the light shining in her eyes. This incredible young woman was already my wife as far as I was concerned; I'd already made my commitment to her, to us, to our new family. Marriage vows wouldn't make them any stronger. My heart swelled to see her happiness. I basked in being the one—me—who could bring her such joy and delight.

"Is it okay if I put it on? Please? I want to see it on my finger again. The jeweler only let me try it on for one tiny minute."

"I don't know. Not sure you're supposed to put on a wedding ring until the ceremony," I said, baiting her. "Maybe you better let me keep it until then."

Her face fell. She reluctantly slipped the ring back into its box, nestling it gently into the pouch. "When do you think we will get married? We haven't even begun planning yet." She handed the little bag back. I held it in my hand, fingers absently measuring the corners of the little box inside.

"I'm not sure. It's crazy, a lot going on right now. I can't complain, mostly good things, like us getting hitched. Our new record will be out in a couple of weeks, and we'll probably go to LA for more recording, hopefully, to work on an album. Plus, the Flamingo's planning some promotional stuff." Theresa's eyes followed the little bundle of cloth in my hands as I flicked it around by its drawstrings. "With everything that's happening, I don't know how to schedule our wedding so everybody who wants to come has enough time to get here. No matter what, we're going to offend somebody."

I glanced at the pouch in my palm. I hadn't told her I'd only been teasing. A crazy idea crossed my mind and my gaze shifted.

"Honey, would you like to wear your ring today?"

"Yes, but you said I couldn't." The tip of her tongue slipped out as she concentrated for a moment. "Not until . . ." Her eyes widened, and she clapped a palm across her mouth. "What are you thinking?"

"I'm thinking that planning and organizing a wedding would probably take another month. I'm also thinking everyone close to us already knows we're married, even if it's not official. And the clock is ticking . . ."

Her eyes followed mine to the courthouse across the street. "If we ran over there right this minute, we might get your ring on your finger today. There's no rush to have a reception; we can throw a party anytime. We could get our vows and the paperwork, what's important to us, over and done with." I grasped her shoulders and met her eyes. "I don't want to wait a minute longer for you to be my wife. What do you say?"

Startled, she grinned wide in astonishment.

"I say I love you, Larry J. Dunlap. I will always love you, and yes, I will marry you today. Since we're not going to Hawaii, today is a perfect day for us to get married. Yes, if they will let us, please put my ring on my finger today."

Minutes later, we walked into a small chapel, arms entwined, and I could feel her body trembling against mine. I gave a clerk $25 as an organist sat to play the wedding march on a miniature organ while her husband and the clerk presented themselves to stand beside us. A man in a white smock with one shirt-collar point hanging out stood in front of a small nondenominational altar to ask us the two essential questions, to which we answered, "I do." A few simple words followed before the standard permission: "You may kiss the bride." I looked at my glowing wife with my ring on her finger and collected my kiss with interest. Afterward, he assured us Justice of the Peace Roy Woofter and the State of Nevada would certify our union and pronounced us man and wife.

I didn't think marriage would make any difference; I believed Theresa and I already loved each other as much as two people could and a marriage certificate would only document it. But as I looked at her, radiant in our new relationship, any last reservations I might have had disappeared. I'd never asked her to make any commitments before this moment. In this simple ceremony, she'd changed everything. Of her own free will, officially, in front of witnesses, she'd chosen to give herself to me, only me, and tied our lives together forever. We walked out into a new life, linked together in a way we'd never been before.

We mostly waited to get home before celebrating in the time-honored fashion that was always new and perfect for us. I couldn't stop staring at her, my wife, my Theresa, my love—for all the days to come. During the next week, my wife and I let our families and friends know it was a busy time, and we loved each other too much to wait any longer to make our love official. Our spur-of-the-moment marriage hadn't surprised my band mates; they'd known we'd been as good as married already.

The following week, Jim Seagrave practically skipped into our rehearsal lugging a thick manila envelope.

"Well, here they are guys, the Naked Car Thieves in the flesh." He dealt out the proofs from our photo sessions onto a Sky Room table. We hadn't told each other what our poses had been, thinking it would be more fun to view them for the first time together.

Our laughter filled the place as we giggled at each other's photos. Leonard gripped one of his cracked crash cymbals under his arm with a crazed look in his eyes. *Pretty well captured how he presented himself to people*, I thought with a smile. Les, displaying his shit-eating-grin face while playing his sunburst Les Paul guitar, wore a railroad conductor's hat. He said the photographer put the cap on him because he was our conductor/arranger. Sounded right until I saw Dave's shot. He'd been posed in the same conductor hat wielding a conductor's wand. So much for that theory. Mickey scraped a violin bow across his bass guitar as he cocked it off his shoulder. The exaggerated perspective of the instrument's head and neck extended toward the camera created a cool, dramatic effect.

"Looks like you know how to hold a violin bow," I said to Mickey.

He made a face. "Why wouldn't I? Started playing violin when I was growing up, and our family was traveling and performing."

Les glanced at Mac's picture. "Since when did you become a guitar picker, Mac?"

"That's how I'd always pictured myself, rockin out on some screamin guitar solo. Never had no time to actually learn how to play the damn thing, but I look pretty damn good fakin though, don't I?"

"What do you think, guys? I have other shots here, but these are my favorites." We responded with a chorus of approval and enthusiasm. I thought the ones Jim had picked were perfect, revealing lots of personality from everyone. He nodded and pulled the six photos together in front of him at the table. "I want to use these in six different ads featuring each of you in all the local papers, magazines, and street handouts, every day for six weeks."

Soon, our individual ads were appearing in the Las Vegas newspapers, street flyers, and entertainment magazines. People mentioned them at the club. Who would've believed pictures of a bunch of naked guys would bring in crowds in this town? They might have been disappointed though when they found us turned out in our flashy new stage rags.

In the middle of April, Les and Susie revealed their marriage plans, both of them glowing with the news. I hadn't realized how serious those two had gotten until their surprise announcement. Theresa was thrilled, and soon she and Susie immersed themselves in wedding planning. The two girls were the first to join the band as new wives. Soon all of us, except our perennial bachelor, Dave, would be married.

I was happy for them. They made a great-looking couple and seemed thrilled with each other. I hoped they were as ecstatic as Theresa and I were. I was elated with the band's success in headlining our own room at the Flamingo and the life I shared with my cherished bride in our luxurious apartment next to Caesars Palace. The days of scuffling at the Town Club four years ago were long gone. Life at the top of the spiral stairs was exceedingly good.

36 MIXED EMOTIONS

The truth will set you free, but first it will piss you off.
—Gloria Steinem

February 25, 1969
Las Vegas, Nevada

ONE AFTERNOON AS the band was running through a final rehearsal of a fun, new party song by Crazy Elephant, *Gimme, Gimme Good Lovin'*, four figures hauling amps and instruments appeared next to the stage. One of them, a lanky guy, with bed-headed dark curls and wearing belled jeans, grinned.

"Hi, I'm Tommy Reynolds. We're Shango." His gesture took in the other three. "We're your new early band. You know, I've seen you guys at the Rag Doll many times. Big fan. Love your name, your vibe with the way you dress, your whole deal. You guys are seriously kickin' that tune, man."

"Cool." Mac stuck his hand out with a grin. "I'm Mac—these other guys—I let 'em back me up."

As we introduced ourselves, Tommy noticed Leonard looking over their steel drum. *Uh oh, new toy for Leonard.*

"We play a mix of Calypso and popular music. Pretty different from what you boys do. But we'll have fun playing with you, mon." Arranging equipment for set changes wouldn't be a problem. Their rhythm instruments sat on wheels leaving only two small amps to drag out of the way.

"Do I hear an accent, Tommy?" I asked.

He laughed easily. "I'm originally from the Virgin Islands, though I've been living in the San Fernando Valley for a while now. Haven't entirely mastered the Valley-boy accent yet."

Weeks before they'd come to the Flamingo, A&M Records had released, *Day After Day*, their Afro-Caribbean tune with a satirical, ear-catching melody about Los Angeles slipping away into the ocean after the "Big One." That was referring, of course, to the big earthquake right around the corner that's supposed to turn most of Southern California into beachfront property. Soon, their run-away record had climbed into LA radio's top ten, was rising on the national charts, and on the local airwaves here. Shango was on the verge of upstaging us as a recording act! They were going to have a hit record before us.

I was happy for Shango's success, and it helped publicize the Sky Room, but it still stung. I couldn't help thinking, when was it going to be our time? A lot of artists around us were getting hits, often they were in our audiences. Only a matter of time, our friends and managers assured us. *Time? How much time?*

Ray Harris, Eddie Cobb's partner who worked in our management office, notified me our third single, *Remember When*, the Mac Davis tune we'd recorded in November, was out on Sunburst Records and catching airplay on the East Coast and had strong support at an important station in Nashville. Maybe we'd get onto the charts. But there were no more reports. Never a whisper of it being on the radio anywhere. Though it got some airplay here on a station in Henderson, Nevada, this release had fared worse than all the others. It was depressing.

Our bedrock problem: we didn't like our recorded songs well enough to play them in our live sets. Our records weren't reflecting who we actually were. Plus, I wasn't pleased with the material Eddie selected for us or with our final mixes. Though Les had clearly demonstrated his ability to create fantastic vocal signatures, a limit remained as to how much brown you could polish off a piece of crap. It was especially infuriating to work hard on these songs and hear them changed for the worse in the final mix.

Eddie wasn't happy with us either; though he hadn't said it, I knew it. Despite his early enthusiasm, he hadn't been able to unlock our potential in the studio, and I'm sure it frustrated him. He was going through the motions with us now. He seemed more interested in recruiting other bands for AVI. Something had to change.

But before anything could, we received a letter from Eddie warning us to be ready for a trip to LA on a moment's notice. We'd been chosen to record *Mixed Emotions*, a theme song for a movie so secret we only knew the working title, *The Martyr*. It apparently involved hippies, protests, and going to jail. Everyone in the office in Hollywood seemed excited and energized. With both Capitol Records VP of Promotion Al Coury and the movie's PR people promoting the picture, we were being offered another tremendous opportunity to capture national attention.

"This is only the demo," Eddie wrote in the note packaged with a reel of quarter-inch tape. "They're working on the final tracks now, and it sounds fantastic. I'll be sending you a copy as soon as it's done." By they, he meant Capitol Records, who was picking up the tab, and it was expensive: they'd chosen a highly-regarded Australian arranger named Julian Lee, to produce the instrumental tracks. The production would use top-tier strings, horns, and percussionists and first-call studio players, from what is often referred to as the Wrecking Crew, to replace Mickey and Leonard—and me, of course, on keyboards. On the other hand, Les would be adding his own guitar solo when we arrived for the vocals.

Eddie also noted he wanted us to learn covers of several other popular songs for the film. One of them was *Crystal Blue Persuasion*, a tune I already sang; maybe I was going to sing in a movie!

Eddie was right about one thing. The instrumental tracks for *Mixed Emotions* were phenomenal, a lavish symphonic production reminding me of Jimmy Webb's *MacArthur Park*, featuring actor Richard Harris. Early Monday afternoon, the four of us took a commuter flight into Burbank and picked up a rental car to drive to American Sound in Studio City. We'd be working in the studio where most of Three Dog Night's hits were being recorded. Ritchie Podlar, not only the owner of the studio and an excellent producer, was first and best known around town as a premier audio engineer. He took command of the recording console with Emory Gordy, our usual engineer, sitting alongside to assist.

Eddie didn't make an appearance, leaving the vocal production to Julian, a tall, imposing figure with thick, white hair. He was blind, but only through his eyes. His ears detected the slightest waver in pitch or tone, or as Dave so aptly put it, "The man could hear a flea fart."

Mixed Emotions was going to be part of the picture's soundtrack as well as play behind the screen credits, there was a tight schedule to get the master to post-production for film editing. Nevertheless, the actual process of recording involves a lot of waiting for engineers to set things up, to get sounds out of the microphones the producer wants to hear, and all the other myriad details requiring attention before the tape recorders are turned on. Once we got rolling, Les would get his guitar solo on tape first, and we'd record the vocal tracks next.

Without much to do at first, I found a phone in a vacant office and called Theresa, collect. We acted like the newly married young lovers we were and whispered the things we wished we could be doing to and with each other. We commiserated over being forced to sleep apart tonight. Afterward, I discovered and read a dog-eared Ross MacDonald paperback, *The Far Side of the Dollar*, someone had left behind, before awkwardly dozing in a chair. I think Mac napped too, but Dave, a poor sleeper anyway, got little rest.

We were professionals who worked six nights a week, tired voices wasn't news, but the height of the allergy season created an extra scratchiness in the back of our throats. Dave laid down a quick reference vocal so the background singers would have a rough idea of how the lead would sound. I thought he sounded a little ragged already. When we gathered in the studio around two shock-mounted Sennheiser microphones suspended between us, I was shocked and kind of irritated to find three studio vocalists, two girls and a guy, had been added to augment our voices. They were studio-skilled sight readers who sang like angels. It would be hard to complain about them, but we certainly weren't going to sound like Stark Naked and the Car Thieves with our voices mixed together. The seven of us, including Dave, slipped on and adjusted our headphones.

As we began laying tracks, I slid one side of my headphones off my ear so I could hear our voices in their natural ambiance. Mac stood crouched directly across from me. He closed his eyes and made squinty faces when he sang. I was having a hard time not howling with laughter as I watched him. Dave and Les stared across at each other, cracking each other up, which got the other three going, too. Finally, after overcoming a couple of these laughing jags, Les directed us, and we got back to business, and then we waited, and waited, between playbacks from the control room booth until Julian eventually thought we'd done well enough to come in and listen.

The song was a heavy-duty power ballad, and it should have fit right into Dave's wheelhouse, and we'd thoroughly rehearsed it before getting here. It was ten o'clock before he was recording the lead vocal in earnest. And he was having trouble with it.

The first problem was timing, the way some of the lyrics worked against the melody. Dave's dilemma was fitting the five-beat hook line into the four-beat time segment allowed by the music, and there were a few other lyric-vs-time spots in the piece as well. The written lyrics were more suited to being spoken than sung in certain spots, similar to how Richard Harris voice-acted the lines in *MacArthur Park*. It wasn't a natural style for Dave.

As our primary lead singer, he carried the heaviest workload for five hours or more, six nights a week. Between allergies and the dry Vegas winds, his vocal cords were shot. But he was an experienced pro and did his best to work around it—which was passable—for a while.

As Dave's voice tired, he tended to lose notes in the crack between his natural full-voice and his falsetto. *Mixed Emotions* required a lot of the lead vocal to be sung right in that space, at the top of his full-voice. I cringed listening to him as Julian demanded that he do it over and over again. He became increasingly frustrated with his loss of control as he forced himself through those difficult passages, singing them exactly the same each time, without any direction or suggestion for change.

Meanwhile, Julian and Ritchie were engaged in tense discussions between takes behind the control-room glass. Sometimes Ritchie or Emory would pop into the studio to make minuscule changes to the mic, though each effort seemed indistinguishable from the previous one.

Probably, they were constantly tweaking the console's dials, knobs, sliders, and mic settings in search of some sound or tone they never found. Julian, despite his auditory acuity, didn't seem to notice Dave's distress and how these unceasing run-throughs were taking a brutal toll on his voice. And they never talked to him to tell what was going on, or what he could do to make them happy.

Oddly enough, I actually liked several of the earlier flawed takes. When Dave was rested, or at least in reasonable condition, his voice flowed seamlessly between falsetto and full-voice. With his voice overworked, sort of like an over-driven guitar amp, he battled to hit notes, resulting in natural cracks that created an emotional, exhausted performance portraying a tormented lover better than the lyric itself.

But as the night wore on, the magic moment passed, and his voice turned to shit. He could hardly talk. Again, we faced the limitations of a working band in the studio. There was no coming back tomorrow. All we had was this one night squeezed in between nights of demanding performances to get this right. Groups who made recording their first priority might take weeks or more to get each element right. The Beach Boys' *Good Vibrations*—that one song alone—took six months to complete. Finally, it was over, and the production team kept the best take Dave had left in him.

We straggled out of the studio around three in the morning and stopped in at Jerry's Deli on Ventura for a subdued breakfast of healing chicken soup before hitting our motel beds for a few hours and catching the early-bird flight back to Vegas.

We waited anxiously to hear when the movie would be released. I hoped the final mix of *Mixed Emotions* would turn out to be good enough, but nobody in Hollywood gave us any indication. When we were recording, time could stretch out endlessly in a world shrunk to the size of the studio.

Back in the real world of the Flamingo Sky Room, Stark Naked and the Car Thieves had become the talk of Las Vegas. Our individual ads appeared in every publication, nearly every day we were mentioned in newspaper columns. I saw a feature magazine article about the band in one of the ubiquitous Las Vegas giveaway magazines given to every passenger arriving at the airport. Jim Seagrave was blitzing the media—earning his salary. I thought we looked incredible in our new suits and our performances inspired. Live, in person at the Sky Room, we were rocking every set, sizzling all night long.

37 LATE NIGHT WITH LENNY

> *Genius has its limitations. Insanity . . . not so much.*
> —Darynda Jones

March 16, 1969
Las Vegas, Nevada

MOST LAS VEGANS learned later that Howard Hughes had arrived here under cover of darkness in his private two-car train for Thanksgiving in 1966. He'd squirreled himself and his entourage at the Desert Inn in the penthouse about the same time we were auditioning for Caesars Palace. But few locals had ever met or seen the reclusive billionaire in person. He'd liked the place. A lot. His visit extended longer than the hotel expected.

When the DI, the local acronym for the Desert Inn, wanted to refurbish the penthouse suite and make it available to other guests, Hughes declined to vacate it. The mob-family owners attempted to evict him, so he made them an offer they couldn't refuse, and it became his permanent headquarters.

In the years since, he'd added the Sands, the Frontier, and our favorite breakfast spot, the Silver Slipper, including all their land and a lot more, now valued at around $200 million, to his holdings. Just another entertaining Vegas story until a message from Seymour sent me to Jim Seagrave. His office door was open, I knocked on the doorjamb.

"Larry! Glad you're here." Jim zipped around his desk to sit with me, his enthusiasm contagious. "I've got some exciting news for you. You probably know Channel 8 is the only twenty-four-hour television station in Vegas, right?" I nodded. I knew there was a late night channel the girls often tuned in to, but I was usually here.

"Do you know who Howard Hughes is?"

My eyes rolled off to the side, thinking. "Um, big director or producer in Hollywood or something? And rich, owned some huge business with government contracts. Airplanes, I think." Most of what I could recall about Howard Hughes came from a dim memory of his exploits fictionalized in Harold Robbins's *The Carpetbaggers*, and some controversy about a gigantic airplane that could barely get off the ground.

"That's him," Jim nodded. "He lives on the top floor of the DI. He bought the station last year so they could broadcast his old movies, he likes to watch them when he can't sleep. Either they've run out of old movies, or more people are tuning in. They're starting a local late-night talk show between films and would like to interview some of our entertainers. Bill wants you guys to go over to the station and promote the Sky Room—and your band, of course."

"Well, sure, sounds like a great idea."

"Okay. I've arranged for you to go to their studio Thursday night between your second and third set." Jim handed me a handwritten note with the television station's address. "It'll give you an opportunity to promote your record, too."

Thursday, or more accurately, early Friday morning, we found ourselves east of Las Vegas Boulevard in an unimpressive single-story building reached by dirt road. We spread out on a couch and a couple of chairs hastily pushed next to a desk. Instead of a backdrop behind us, lights were artfully pooled around us in the dark. Vacated sets for news, weather, and sports—temporarily pushed out of the way—crouched around us in the gloom. A television camera focused on Bob, the show's anchor, sitting at the desk. When the camera's red light came on, he looked into it and spoke.

"And now, ladies and gentlemen, welcome to the *Swinging Shift*—programming until dawn for your late,"—Bob beamed blearily into the camera— "late entertainment." Being a TV talk show host in these wee hours was no doubt new to him.

"Hi fellas," Bob said, turning his attention our way. "Why don't you tell the folks the name of your band and what hotel you're playing in?"

Mac piped up. "We're called Stark Naked and the Car Thieves, and we play every night at the hottest dance and showroom in town, the Flamingo Sky Room." He glanced around for approval, which we freely gave.

Bob perked up. "Where in heaven's name did you ever get such a moniker?"

Les gave him our stock answer. "Some people think Steve Allen made up the name on his show when he had a comedy routine where he picked slips of paper from two hats to make up random names of rock bands. One of us meant to ask him when we were on his show but"—he gave me a roguish grin— "somebody's signals got crossed, and we never found out for sure."

"See," I added, setting the record straight, "we used to be known as the Checkmates, which became a problem since another group, I assume you're familiar with, has that name."

"Of course, the Checkmates Ltd. I've seen them many times."

"They're from Indiana, too; we'd never heard of them until we were booked in a club in Fort Wayne, their hometown. We were fired halfway through the first night because we weren't them. A few months later we came to the West Coast, and they were here too, they've continued to haunt us ever since. Even here in Las Vegas; they played the Pussycat A' Go-Go before we did, but we caught up with them when we played on the same bill at Caesars Palace for Nero's Nook opening."

I didn't go into why our Vegas trajectories had gone in such different directions. They were making a big name for themselves in hotel lounges and showrooms while we were bouncing around rock dance clubs on the Strip. Maybe a long run at the Flamingo would even things out between us a little.

"So obviously," I concluded, "we wanted a unique name."

"Mission accomplished, I would guess." Bob referred to some notes. "Now, which one of you is Leonard?"

Leonard plastered on one of his loopy grins.

"I understand you play quite an exciting drum solo. How did that come about?" Leonard jumped to his feet.

"Well, there's not much room here, but I could try to show you . . ." He pulled out a couple of his huge drumsticks to paradiddle all around us on the couch, chairs, and desk. He couldn't seem to find the surface he was looking for. The camera pulled back when he got a little outside the floor area designated for this show. "If I could find something more like drums. Maybe . . ." He moved toward the news set.

I saw the cameraman glance in surprise at the director, who grinned and motioned him to follow. Somebody got a light on Leonard, now firmly on the news set. He pretended not to know where he was until he tripped and fell into the news anchor seat. He glanced up in apparent surprise.

Assuming a newsman's clipped tone, he said, "There was a freak accident on Boulder Highway today when two hippies' cars ran into each other." Despite the rip-off from George Carlin's Hippy Dippy Weatherman routine, it was genius for off-the-cuff, and we all laughed. He gave us his stock-in-trade gaze, the same one in his individual Flamingo Sky Room ad that was running in the local papers. It always made me think of a stunned mongoose. He leaped from one chair to another, tapping and rapping, his drumsticks searching for a deeper rhythm.

Leonard's spontaneous hijinks always entertained us. We laughed uproariously, along with Bob and his skeleton production crew. There was no live audience, but we created an impromptu laugh track.

Leonard stumbled into another set. Someone thought to keep the lights and camera following him adding another lit area on the production floor. Leonard feigned bewilderment in finding himself on the weather set and pretended that's where he'd meant to be all along.

He wielded his drumstick as a pointer as though he was preparing to do a weather report. He examined a local weather map suspended from above by nearly-invisible wires, and then rested his drumstick on a random spot somewhere in Clark County before turning to the camera with a big grin on his face. As he opened his mouth to speak, he leaned into the drumstick causing him to awkwardly tumble behind the weather map, which spun wildly on its wire supports.

Leonard popped back into view with his mad mongoose expression again, snapping his head left and right as if hoping to spot whoever had moved the map, and our hilarity became uncontrollable. He horsed around for another couple of minutes, tripping and falling all through the weather set until tangled in all sorts of furniture and cables, he frowned in frustration and spoke into the camera in a serious tone. "And now, Bob, back to you for a message from our sponsors."

The director, playing along with the gag, had a second camera running and switched to Bob struggling to maintain his composure.

"You can catch Stark Naked and the Car Thieves starring at the Flamingo Sky Room from late evening till dawn, Tuesday through Sunday. And as Leonard says—back in a moment."

We got back to the Flamingo with plenty of time before our next set, laughing with Leonard about his hilarious improvisational sketch. It was hard to know if anyone had actually seen our guest spot on KLAS, but we'd had a hoot even if no one was watching.

About a week later, a note from Jim Seagrave appeared on my organ. The TV station wanted Leonard to come back for his own segment of the show, same time as before—this time, alone. For the next few weeks, Leonard was a feature on the *Swinging Shift*. Howard Hughes must have thought he was funny. Other people noticed too. "Leaping Lenny" Souza was developing his own fans from his TV appearances before they knew he drummed for Stark Naked and the Car Thieves.

38 COPY 'CATS

The menu is not the meal.
—Alan W. Watts

April 28, 1969
Las Vegas, Nevada

THOUGH I COULDN'T have been happier in my personal life, and the Sky Room was turning out to be the perfect job for Stark Naked in most ways, I couldn't help worrying about our future as recording artists. We'd received bad news from LA. *The Martyr*, the movie we'd recorded *Mixed Emotions* for, had been canceled without explanation. The master would be shelved in a can until somebody figured out what to do with it. There were no further sessions planned. We weren't making any headway in our recording career. Instead, we were going backward.

I'd been thinking about the state of the band for a while. Forming a nightclub band had been a matter of survival when the four of us from the Midwest found ourselves pulled back together as if magnetized four years ago in California. But the band had always been based on the vocal group I'd started in Indianapolis and the way we learned music then.

My journey in music began in high school when I'd been captivated by a song on the radio. I was sixteen. The following day I'd convinced two neighborhood brothers, the Baldwins, to try singing it with me. I'd figured we needed a record of the song so we could learn it, but I didn't have the foggiest idea of where to go from there. None of us knew how to sing.

Fortunately, Perry, the youngest of the Baldwins, knew Hastings Smith, Jr., a kid in his class who sang in all the choirs at Shortridge. I hadn't heard of him, but I wouldn't have. After all, I was a junior and he a lowly freshman in a school of 2200 kids. Perry asked him if he could help, and he agreed to try if we would come to his house late in the afternoon the following Saturday.

I'd biked east on 34th from my house several blocks to Fairfax Avenue angling northeast to Watson Road. As I pedaled north, everything changed. I'd thought I knew every neighborhood around Shortridge, but this street was different. Instead of square blocks, it wove through a park-like suburb of big brick and stone houses set in huge lawns with towering oaks and maples and no sidewalks. The grass everywhere had been neatly cut and trimmed, and though the leaves had begun to turn, most yards had been freshly raked. It seemed to smell fresher here and was a great place to ride a bike. I arrived at the Smith's home early, even Hasty wasn't there yet, but his mother showed me where to park my English racer, took my jacket, and welcomed me in.

I was sitting at the breakfast bar warming my hands on a steaming mug of cocoa with marshmallows bobbing around in it when I heard someone behind me say hi. My first impression of Hasty was his full, ivory-toothed smile in a suntanned face—*after a long winter in Indianapolis?* I marveled—under his perfect, flat-top haircut. He was slight, and a little shorter than me. He wore a lightweight, slightly rumpled, navy-blue sweater with thin red piping at the sleeves and vee-collar, with a little red logo on the breast. It was pulled over a crisp white dress shirt, open at the neck with French cuffs showing at the sleeves. He wore khakis, white buck shoes. What kid dresses like that on a Saturday, I wondered. He looked damp like he'd recently walked out of a shower.

"Sorry I wasn't here to meet you," he said strolling over to shake my hand. "Our family plays golf at Meridian Hills almost every weekend, and my dad tries to get in thirty-six holes every Saturday and Sunday if he can. He likes it when I try to keep up with him."

I wanted to find a flaw in his perfect, preppy appearance and easy poise, but his lack of conceit caught me off balance. To avoid looking too stupid, I nodded and only said, "Hi."

He hopped on a stool and rested his chin in his hand, gazing at me. "Perry Baldwin says you want to get a singing group going with him and his brother."

"I'm not sure about starting a singing group," I said, trying to clarify the situation. "It's mostly about singing this song I heard on the radio. But since it needs a group of guys to sing it . . ." I shrugged my shoulders. "Yeah, I guess a singing group. Perry said we'd probably need four guys, one to sing the words and three to sing the background."

"Well, most modern songs tend to have three-part harmony behind a lead vocal," Hasty explained. *Wow, that sounded so smart and right.* There was a lot I didn't know about what I wanted to do.

"Where did you learn all this stuff?"

"My brother and I have been taking private singing lessons since we were little kids. I play a little piano, too. My mom thinks it's important to know stuff like this."

"Yeah, I get that," I agreed. "I had to take piano for six months before my mom gave in. I hated the stupid music my teacher made me play. Worse, my mother made me learn ballroom dancing at summer-school manners classes last year at School 66." I pointed a finger down my throat and made gagging noises.

"At 66? I went to grade school there last year," Hasty sat up. "I didn't like ballroom dancing much either. I had to take private classes at the Meridian Hills country club. What a bunch of snooty girls there. Even if some of them were kinda cute." He grinned.

We were both laughing when Hasty's mom came from some other part of the kitchen and poured him a hot mug of cocoa from a big silver pitcher. It wouldn't be possible at my house for my mom to come from some other part of the kitchen—our kitchen didn't have rooms.

"I'm glad you boys are getting along. Do you want me to freshen your mug, Larry?" I hadn't even tried it yet. I dipped my face into the warm chocolatey goodness and sipped the best cocoa I'd ever tasted. My face must have shown it because Hasty's mom added more cocoa to my cup and walked away smiling. She treated me like I was an old friend of Hasty's even though we'd never met until today.

"Wow, this is great cocoa," I said, and Hasty grinned. "Do you mind if I ask how you got the name, Hasty? I've never heard a name like that before."

"Hastings Alexander Smith, Junior," he grinned. "You might say it's a family heirloom I inherited. But everybody usually calls me Hasty." I nodded and greedily sipped more cocoa.

"What song do you want to sing?" he asked. "Did you bring the record with you?"

"Oh yeah, sure, right here," I said, pulling the brand new 45-rpm disk out of an old *Indianapolis Times* delivery bag I'd brought in from my bike.

"*Silhouettes?*" he read out loud, taking it from me and reading the label, "by the Rays."

I nodded, "Yeah, silhouettes, like shadows."

"Well, while we're waiting for Perry and Ginko, what do you say we give this thing a spin? Follow me." He grabbed his mug and hopped down from his stool.

Pictures of athletes—mostly golfers, posters for musicals, and a Purdue University banner decorated the dark-green walls of my new friend's bedroom. There was a putting matt with golf balls on it along one wall, and a large, very professional-looking golf bag lay tipped against a long, mirrored dresser. A double bed, nicely made up with a thick brown comforter, was set into an alcove. A row of golf trophies stood on top of a low bookcase next to a desk under a dormer window. Hasty opened a drawer to retrieve a plastic spindle adapter that let 45-rpm records play on 78-rpm record players. He popped it in place and gently set my record on the turntable of an expensive looking portable record player on his desk.

He listened to *Silhouettes*, tapping his foot and humming every once in a while. "Nice key change," he said over the music as the song reached the crescendo of "ahhs" near the end. After the record stopped, he sat in the chair at the desk, motioned me to an easy chair. "I like the lyrics. Neat story. Great song!"

"Yeah." I smiled. "I like it, too."

Hasty grinned back. "That's what I hear." We heard footsteps on the hardwood outside his bedroom door. Perry and Ginko walked in carrying hot mugs of cocoa. After we'd sorted out all the hellos and unneeded introductions,

Hasty said, "Find a spot on the bed or a piece of rug." We all got comfortable. "Well, I've listened to this song, *Silhouettes*. I think it's great. It should be fun to sing."

Perry and Ginko Baldwin and I shook our heads enthusiastically.

"How do we do this?" I asked. "How do we figure out how to sing it?"

"Well," Hasty said to me, "I assume you started this because you want to sing the words, the lead vocal part, right?"

"I just want to be part of singing the song. I didn't think about which part. Maybe the words part—uh, the lead vocal."

"You should sing the words, man," Ginko said, sipping on his chocolate. His brother nodded in agreement.

"Okay, that's settled. Do you know the words to the song yet? The lyrics?" I must have looked unsure. "You probably know more than you realize," he continued. He handed me a lined pad and an automatic pencil. "You can write down the words you remember now and when we need to play the record, try to catch some more, while we work out the harmony."

Hasty pulled out a round harmonica thing he called a pitch pipe and blew a single note or two. He started the record player for a moment and let it run to where the singing started, he blew a couple more notes and lifted the record arm. "Okay, this song starts off in the key of F, so let's start by making an F major chord. This should be familiar to you from your piano lessons, Larry." I shrugged my shoulders—it seemed doubtful.

"It will take three voices. I'll go first. I'm a natural baritone, so I'll take the low note, the root of the chord, which," he grinned, "is not surprisingly an F." He blew a note and sang a crystal-clear tone. He made it seem natural to sing right out loud in front of everybody, and it set the stage for the other guys and me to sing out without worrying if we'd get laughed at.

"Now you, Ginko, you're going to sing the second note of the chord, an A. It's up a third." He blew another higher note. Ginko looked bewildered but manfully struggled to find the tone and gave us all a chagrinned grimace when he couldn't. He did better when Hasty sang the note with him to help him find it. Hasty then told Ginko to try singing his note alone. Ginko wiped his palms on his pants and concentrated with all his might. It took several tries, but when he could, Hasty joined in with his note to make a simple harmony.

It was kind of funny at first because as soon as Hasty started to sing, Ginko would drop his voice down to the same note Hasty was singing. Perry and I started to laugh, but we stopped as soon as we saw how uncomfortable it made him. After a few more tries it improved a little. We all encouraged Ginko, and it seemed to make him feel better.

"Okay, I've got the root of the chord, and you're singing the third, Ginko. Now Perry will take the fifth." We all laughed about taking the fifth, but after we settled down, Hasty sounded the next note, a C. Perry looked a little uncertain, but not as panicked as Ginko, and got it right on the second try. Perry's voice was kind of thin and breathy compared to Hasty's, but it sounded okay. Ginko and I gave each other grins and nodded.

Hasty built the harmony again starting with Ginko, then him, and then Perry. Ginko struggled with holding his note, and beads of perspiration stood out on his forehead as he concentrated. But Hasty's quiet confidence that they were going to be able to sing their notes assured them everything was going to be okay if they kept at it.

For a moment, the way the sun breaks through on a cloudy day, there was a three-part chord. It held for an instant and then crashed, but Perry and Ginko and I had heard it. We had the first inkling of what we could create and a growing awareness of what it was going to require. I was a little bit jealous not to have been a part of it.

Hasty joined us in congratulating ourselves for a moment before continuing what was a music lesson as much as showing us what to sing. We didn't grasp everything he was saying, but it helped to have labels for things we were singing and doing. Some of it was starting to filter through to those hated hours of practice on the piano. I was beginning to visualize the fingers of my right hand making the F-chord Hasty talked about on a piano keyboard. Ginko gave Hasty his rapt attention, knowing he was being trusted with an important role and not wanting to let anyone down.

"There are three main notes to this major chord in F," Hasty explained, "and now we've sung them—F, A, and C—but we will have to learn three more chords in this key to make the song work. Most rock-and-roll ballads use the same three or four chord structure.

"Let's try the second chord change, a D minor. This is easy." Hasty turned to Ginko.

"Gink, you and I will sing exactly the same notes we've been singing. Perry, you're the only one who will sing a different note, a step higher. I'm going to show you your old note." Hasty blew on the pitch pipe. "And here's your new note." The pitch pipe produced a higher note. Perry nodded that he understood.

"Ginko, you and I have to hold steady on the notes we've already learned, okay?"

Hasty was amazing. I saw what he was doing. He was so patient with Perry and Ginko, just taking it step-by-step, no rush, no judgment. He didn't get upset when Ginko had trouble holding his notes or when Perry giggled in the middle of building a harmony. He smiled and laughed. He seemed to be one of us even though he was guiding the whole practice.

By the end of the day, the three guys were able to hold their notes fairly well and sing an F chord, and, with a lot of hits and misses, turn it into a D minor, then a G minor, and then a C seventh. As Hasty turned the record player on at times for reference, I began to understand how these chord changes worked in the song.

"I think we've done enough for today," Hasty said around five o'clock. He was right; the two brothers were tired, especially Ginko. Perry seemed to grasp the musical concepts Hasty was teaching us, but Ginko was finding it hard, hard work to hold those notes, and when he did they seemed to drift up and down a little.

"I think, if we work at it," Hasty told us, "we'll be able to sing this song in a few more practices, or at least most of it." I recognized how far we had come today. Singing this song was going to take a lot longer than I guessed. I'd wanted to be doing it by now. On the other hand, I felt a camaraderie building between us in the support we gave each other when we put ourselves out there trying to sing. I was beginning to picture how we could get there.

Hasty's mom cracked the door and stuck her head in. "Mr. Baldwin is downstairs to collect Perry and Ginko. I've brought you your coats, boys."

"When are we going to meet again and do this some more?" Perry asked as he and his older brother stood to leave. We looked at Hasty.

"Tuesday after school would be good for me if you guys can make it. Perry says you live close to school and we can rehearse at your house, Larry. If that's okay, let's meet there. You should have the lead vocal lyrics memorized by then, Larry. Try singing them along with the record."

We said goodbye to the Baldwins and gathered empty cocoa mugs to bring downstairs when Hasty stopped me for a moment.

"If you don't mind a piece of advice . . ."

"Sure." I nodded. "Anything."

"We made good progress today, considering, and that's exciting. Everyone is trying but trying alone isn't going to be enough. It should be fairly obvious that people who want to sing actually need to *learn* how to sing." He looked at me sideways as if watching to see if I was offended. "How serious are you about this?"

"I'll do whatever you think I should to learn more about the things you showed us today. That was amazing."

"I could see if Mr. Martin would be willing to take you into the Acappella Choir at school. If I can get him to agree, would you do it?" he asked. "You would get you some music theory along with singing techniques and the experience of singing in harmony with other voices."

"Yeah, sure. Sounds terrific! I'd love to do that."

Hasty nodded, "Getting you in this semester might be difficult. There is a waiting list to get into choir, and I don't think he usually lets anyone into his classes after the semester starts, but he likes me so maybe . . ."

"Tell him I'll do whatever it takes," I said as we left his room to go downstairs. "I want us to sound exactly like those Rays."

During the months and years ahead as the vocal group evolved from our beginnings as the Aristocats, and even after Hasty left us, to the Reflections, we would sit around a record player picking out our parts and trying them out until we sounded exactly like the artists we heard. There wasn't a recording studio or record company in our town; there were no well-known recording artists there to learn from. Our only models were the finished songs we heard on the radio and records. We never saw the sausage being made—the messy process of how a song was composed, arranged and came to life in a studio. We measured ourselves against the perfection of a finished recording when we learned songs by the artists we admired. We worked hard to copy every subtlety on the record. That hadn't changed until, as the Reflections, we were recorded for the first time—an experience so short, we barely registered what we were doing.

We made a slight change when we re-formed as a professional band in California. The process of learning vocals evolved as Les realized how much time it would save for him to pick out the vocal parts on the record while he was learning the chords and riffs he needed to play it on guitar. From then on, whoever sang lead, usually Dave, learned the song's lyrics ahead of time. At rehearsal, Les would show whoever was singing background parts the harmony and we'd put it all together and rehearse before we took it on stage. It was baked into our DNA to copy every nuance of the songs we learned, to do our best to sound exactly like the record. That's what we'd taught ourselves.

When Eddie Cobb started finding songs for us to record two years ago, Les had moved beyond showing us our parts into creating our vocal arrangements, which he would only reveal to us when he was ready to teach them to us. Though he didn't include the rest of us in the process—collaboration not being his strongest suit—we were usually pleased and often impressed with what he brought us. Though we got songs to the stage faster, it further removed the singers from the creative process and the composition of original songs.

We had to change that mindset. Much like those long ago days, before I met Hasty Smith, Jr., I wasn't exactly sure what steps would get us there, but I had a plan. At our next rehearsal, I was going to roll it out. I didn't want us to give up on our ultimate dream of recording success.

39 CHASING THE MUSE

Beware the lollipop of mediocrity. Lick it once and you'll suck forever.
—Brian Wilson

April 30, 1969
Las Vegas, Nevada

"WHAT IN HELL?" Mickey said, shoving his way into the lounging half of our dressing rooms. He'd spotted the six packages I'd stacked on an old, beat-up cocktail table.

"Wait a second, Leonard's almost here. I'll explain when everybody's in." As the guys settled down, I passed out the white cardboard cartons.

Mac got his open first. "This some kinda midget tape recorder or somethin?" He dropped his cigarette in a Flamingo ashtray so he could lift out the contents and examine it from every angle. "What're we supposed to do with these things?"

"Listen, guys," I said, a little nervous, "this is important. We're all disappointed in how badly our records are doing. From the beginning, we'd believed we'd get discovered somewhere, and somebody would find us hit songs, somebody else would take us into the studio to record them, and we'd become big stars. Well, Jimmy O'Neill did discover us, and it did seem like we were on our way.

Two years later and it still hasn't worked out. Now it seems like our producer is losing interest in us. If we want things to change, it's going to be up to us to do it. We know we have the talent; we can compete with any vocal group on the charts. But if we don't have great songs to show it, no one will know. We can't count on anyone, not even Eddie, to find us the right kind of songs.

Look, nobody knows us better than ourselves, we need to create our own songs. If we can, we'll have a lot more control over how we're recorded. The Beach Boys have Brian Wilson, the Four Seasons have Bob Gaudio, and the Beatles have John and Paul. Even the Stones have Jagger and Keith Richards. We need to create our own material the way they do."

"Nice speech. And these toy recorders are going to write them for us how?" Les said in the dismissive way he could when something wasn't his idea. It could've gone either way; I'd hoped after Les's wedding, where we'd worn our blue stage suits in a heartening sign of unity to celebrate his marriage to Susie, he'd be a little easier to approach about this issue. Apparently not.

"I got them because they're portable. They're not much bigger than a camera, and they come with a case and strap, so they're easy to carry. Whenever we come up with an idea, wherever we are, we can play, sing, or speak it, we can get it on tape." The silence was deafening. My bandmates were hiding their enthusiasm well.

Leonard broke the pause. "Seems kinda stupid if you ask me." He dropped his recorder back in the box. Recording wasn't high on his wish list. While his personality and emotional playing served him well in live performance, he tended to freeze in the studio. It wasn't as though he didn't have the chops. He was an excellent drummer; it was a mental thing.

"Come on guys, give this idea a chance. What we've been doing, waiting for Eddie to figure things out and letting him make all the recording decisions isn't working."

"Larry, you come up with some really idiotic ideas, but this is the stupidest one yet." Les shook his head in disdain. "Nobody is going to record anything decent on these Japanese pieces of shit—they probably sound like somebody banging trash cans together." He tossed his box with the mini-recorder onto a shelf and took off his shoes. "I'm not using this piece of garbage."

Embarrassed, I tried not to lose my cool. Up until now, the first principle of my leadership had been keeping us together. But now, at the Flamingo, we had security. What had given me the courage to change course, to actually step out and try to lead on an issue, was my relationship with Theresa. She was my safe haven, she believed me capable of anything, so I did too.

"Look, the quality of the recorder isn't what is important," I tried to explain. "That's not what they're for. They're personal recorders. They are for capturing ideas so we can brainstorm with you later. If we think we might have something good, we can bring it to you to help refine and combine these scraps together. Something like that might get us started."

Mickey snorted. "I ain't got time for more bullshit. We play music five hours a night, five nights a week, and seven hours on Sundays. And then we're supposed to get in three rehearsals. I got a family, buddy. I can't be here any more than I already am." I shrugged. While I hoped everyone would contribute, I wasn't surprised by his lack of interest.

"Not going to happen, Dunlap." Les shook his head, lips compressed in resolve. "Not if I have anything to say about it."

We considered Les our musical director, and for the most part, he was. He was our best musician, he showed us our vocal parts and arranged all our background vocals for the studio. It fell to him naturally. But he could get fiercely defensive with anything or anyone he felt challenged that status, and he was even more stubborn than me. Nobody would use these mini-recorders now that he'd dumped on them.

I hadn't meant it as a provocation. Based on Les's arrangements and musicianship, I'd always expected he'd become our Bob Gaudio someday. I'd subtly suggested it to him several times, but if he'd ever done anything about it, he'd never let me know. Then again, he was a perfectionist, so attuned to criticism and imagined slights, he probably wouldn't let me or any of us hear anything until it was flawless, which might as well be never.

Les didn't think any of us were capable of composing. He wouldn't find it easy to collaborate with any of us on songwriting. But if he didn't write songs for the band, he owed it to us, and himself, to encourage us to bring ideas to him in any way we could. If any of us could grab a bit of melody, a lyric idea or two, or if he and Leonard and Mickey came up with fresh, innovative rhythm tracks, perhaps these snippets could inspire and incubate compositions. Maybe one us had a hidden talent, or we could do it as a group, or maybe some combination of us would grow into a writing team. He'd proven he could create amazing vocal arrangements. If he could just bring himself to encourage us, inspire us to bring him pieces to work with, I believed in my heart he could make us stars.

I remembered how that kind of inventiveness had resulted in a near hit for the Reflections six years ago. That was before Dave and I had even met Les, of course, even before we'd begun recording in Indianapolis.

We hadn't intended to rearrange *In the Still of the Night*, we were just warming up our voices with some nonsense syllables in standard rock changes. While we were vamping, Dave spontaneously began singing the lyrics to the Five Satins' classic over the top of it. It seemed to work, so for fun, we took some time to arrange the song to the rhythmic vocal background we were playing with. Dave wasn't even sure he was singing the right words, but there was no reason to think it would matter. Never in our wildest dreams could we have guessed we'd record it. If we'd taken the next step of simply altering the melody and creating our own words—it would have been our first composition. We were that close to being songwriters.

After my mini-recorder plan fell flat, we hiked up to the hotel to finish B.J. Thomas's glorious *Hooked On a Feeling* for Les. We finished in time to begin work on the vocals for *The Worst That Could Happen*, a fabulous Jimmy Webb power ballad, perfectly suited for Dave. Johnny Maestro had recently recorded it with his new group, Brooklyn Bridge. *Man, if we could write songs like these, our problems would be over.*

After practice, three of the white cartons lay discarded in the dressing room. Didn't take long to figure out who'd left them. I had one, I saw Dave grab another, and I guessed Mac had the third. They'd quietly taken them. Maybe something would come of that. Disheartening as this defeat was, I wasn't about to let it go. There had to be a way to find our muse and develop our creativity.

Until now, I'd led by being the cushion between our various personalities, always trying to find a way forward by finding the lowest common denominators that bound us together. But that kind of leadership meant we were reacting to events rather than planning for them.

Now that I was attempting real leadership, I risked my position in the band. My opinion would be discredited by those who looked down on my musicianship. I accepted that, but musical ability wasn't the real issue here; creating a creative environment was. I wanted us to develop an atmosphere that would stimulate and encourage our imagination. We needed to believe first that we could do it—that we could create something unique from our combined musical tastes. It wasn't that I thought I was a composer, though I hoped I could contribute. I felt it was imperative to bring it out of ourselves.

We were locked into Eddie Cobb and Ray Harris's production contract with AVI, which now included Seymour. They would decide who produced us, or God forbid, if nobody did, for the next three years. If we could tap our own creativity and bring the right material to them, I believed we could convince them to give us studio time with Emory Gordy or Ron Hitchcock or one of the other engineers at Producer's Workshop. After all, he and Ray and Seymour were in business to make hit records, no matter who produced them. I believed Eddie was a good guy at heart; he might support a plan like this.

Eddie had been the bass singer in the Four Preps, famous for their incredibly tight harmonies and two Top Five hits in 1958. I'd expected him to be the perfect producer for us. He'd know how to refine our vocals for the studio. With his help and guidance, we would be able to compete with the best production rock artists.

I must have misread Eddie's self-deprecating attitude about being in the Preps. Maybe he felt they were a "lollipop" band and his actual preferences were grittier. It was not what I'd expected his style as a producer to be. I hadn't realized then that he'd written and produced *Dirty Water*, a bitter tribute to the city of Boston, and the Stones-like *Sometimes Good Guys Don't Wear White*, for our stable-mates, the Standells, three years ago. Both productions were edgy, verging on punk rock, productions. I hadn't known he'd composed the moody *Tainted Love*, recorded by Gloria Jones, and the R&B classic-sounding *Every Little Bit Hurts* for Brenda Holloway. If I'd realized he wanted to produce hard-edged R&B or punk, I would've instantly known he was the wrong producer for us.

Eddie had expended remarkably little effort in finding out who we were or what we wanted to be. I couldn't remember him ever coming to see us play. Instead, he'd tried to remake us into what he wanted. After two years of recording us, he must have been disappointed to discover he couldn't mold us into that kind of act. I'd grown frustrated, too; we weren't getting the vocal creativity, leadership, or production style I'd wanted and expected. I knew what I was asking of us was no easy task, but I believed we had to take control of our recording future if we wanted to have one.

My next suggestion—that we get together some afternoons to jam in pursuit of a riff, a rhythm, or scrap of melody—resulted in a frustrating waste of time. Working six nights a week made trying to be creative and original together difficult. Playing so often fatigued our relationship with music, and to some degree, each other.

We needed a new approach, and there was a proven solution right in front of us. It was openly endorsed by the most successful and creative recording artists in the world—the Beatles, the Rolling Stones, the Doors, the Beach Boys, the Mamas and Papas, and many, many, if not most, others. We needed a chemical reaction, an expansion of our minds. An acid lucidity that would bring us together, connect us to our muse, and give birth to our creativity.

40 A FOOT ON THE BRIDGE

How bold one gets when one is sure of being loved.
—Sigmund Freud

June 5, 1969
Las Vegas, Nevada

I CAREFULLY FLOATED the idea of an Electric Kool-Aid acid trip with my bandmates and gotten everything from an enthusiastic "Hell, yeah" from Mac to Leonard's half-hearted agreement. I took the surprising lack of resistance to mean everybody realized we needed to do something to change our path. It seemed promising enough that I'd begun considering where we could find a trustworthy source for LSD and a reliable guide to make sure we had a good and safe trip. About then, Leonard brought me a reasonable concern.

He didn't want to do LSD, even if it was the right thing for the group, he admitted, which he doubted anyway. But there was another, more important reason.; he explained in painful detail a developing situation with his wife, Paula.

I'd considered their marriage rock solid, but he'd been keeping a secret from her, and from us. He'd met a girl who worked cocktails in the high-end gambling pit at the Sahara. He thought she was a dead ringer for Anne Margaret and fell hard for her. Agonizing over finding someone he didn't think he could live without, his integrity forced him to open his heart to Paula, raising the possibility of a messy divorce to follow. Considering custody of their son could be at stake, the potential repercussions of an acid trip might damage his chances. But he had a suggestion for me that would have far-reaching consequences.

"Sorry I changed my mind about this acid trip thing with you and the guys, but you do understand, don't you?" Leonard's anxiety leaked out of him in a cold sweat. "I just can't take the chance."

I had my own anxieties about LSD. I'd heard stories of people being mentally damaged by a bad trip. I feared losing control of my senses or imbibing anything that might injure my mind. I hadn't dared to try marijuana until I was twenty-five. That I was even suggesting this risk indicated my concern for our future.

"Sure, I get it," I reassured, Leonard. "Didn't realize you had this going on in your personal life. Not sure whether I should commiserate or congratulate you. I know what happens when you find your special person, so I'm no one to judge. We'll find a different answer, buddy." I couldn't help being relieved myself. "Something like this, we've got to do together or none of us should. We have to take the same trip at the same time and end in the same place together, nobody left behind."

"I know you're trying to do what's best for us, Larry. I do. I've heard about something you might want to check out. This girl I know has been trying to get me interested in this scientific philosophy thing she's into. Sounds like something we could try that wouldn't involve any drugs. She introduced me to a guy, and uh—," Leonard fidgeted for a moment. "I might have mentioned to him what we were planning, and well, I think you should meet him and talk about it before you do anything." He glanced at me with worried eyes. "Hope you're not upset I mentioned this to a stranger."

"No, no, that's cool. Do you know anything more about this science philosophy thing?"

"No man, don't really get it. Too deep for me."

"Okay, well sure, I'll meet him." I crossed my fingers hoping Leonard's friend knew what she was talking about. I had an open mind about anything that would help us find our unified voice.

When I was introduced to a roly-poly gnome with blond hair thinning around a tonsured pate, he reminded me of the seven brightly smiling pottery monks my mother used to set out as Christmas decorations. This incandescent cherub could have been the eighth one.

"Larry," Leonard said, "this is Charlie. He's with the science philosophy thing I told you about." Charlie transformed his daffy smile into a weird facial expression of unhinged concern.

"Leonard tells me you're looking for a way to improve your band's outlook and their ability to work better as a group." Thankfully, Charlie didn't sound as far out of his tree as he looked.

"Well, yes. I'm trying to find a way to bring us closer so we can be more creative. It's not happening right now."

"Tell me more about what you are trying to achieve. It sounds like good timing brought us together." As I articulated the thoughts swirling in my mind, Charlie's laser-like focus on the words I spoke made them the most important thing in his universe. I warmed to expressing to such a good listener what I hoped would happen if the band experienced some kind of mind-expansion.

To the background of Shango's steel drums, I explained we were succeeding as performers, but not at our main ambition of becoming successful recording artists. We had different personalities, musical tastes, and aspirations. I thought there should be some way we could meld them together, turn them into strengths, use our differences to create our own original music, but I wasn't having much success.

After our next set ended, I pulled him into another earlock. I spelled out how I wanted our harmony to be featured and our musical differences reconciled. I described myself as the most pop-oriented of us, which intersected with Dave's love of power ballads. Though Les liked all kinds of music, I thought he leaned toward pop, like me, except more to single artists, while my preference was for groups who featured harmony. Sometimes, he seemed so distant I questioned whether he wanted to be in a band at all.

Mac oozed R&B to the tip of his toes and would like to be backed by a horn section like James Brown or Otis Redding. Mickey, an impressive bassist live, had a heavy style not well-suited to the studio, though I doubted he would admit it. I thought he treated playing in Stark Naked and the Car Thieves as a decent-enough job working with some guys he liked more than others.

As for Leonard, he was our comic star, a rock-and-roll caveman who was most effective in person. I wondered if his secret ambition was to be miraculously discovered by a Hollywood television producer who would cast us, or at least him, in a comedy TV series. This wide variety of musical disparity might be an advantage for a nightclub band who needed to satisfy a broad audience, but it wasn't for recording.

"We need to break ourselves down," I spewed without restraint, "view each other's musical vision in a way that gets us to our creative center, where a unique style could emerge, a fusion expressing the totality of who we are." Charlie had let me run my mouth without interruption for an hour or more.

"You know, a lot of Scientology books are about the give and take of people in groups the way you're talking about." *Books.* I nodded. *Perfect.*

"What's the first book about Scientology?" I asked.

"Ron's first book is *The Original Thesis,* but I recommend reading this book first." Charlie hauled out a large, hardbound volume titled *Dianetics: The Modern Science of Mental Health.*

"Ron's?"

"L. Ron Hubbard. He likes us to call him Ron. He writes all the books about Scientology and Dianetics. He wants you to know everything you read about it is direct from him." He extended the Dianetics book. "Here. It's a gift."

"Thanks," I said, flipped through the pages before handing it back. "But I like to begin at the beginning. I don't mind buying the *Original Thesis.*"

"I don't advise starting there. It's pure theory, not easy reading."

"Perfect, that's what I need."

Charlie returned the following night with the slim volume for me. I swallowed it in a day, intrigued by the way Ron Hubbard came to his conclusions. It contained information about marriage and children and causes of conflict—honesty and ethics—interesting concepts to contemplate. I talked with Theresa about how some of these ideas might apply to our own, soon to expand, little family. I decided to read more.

After browsing the publications at the new Scientology Celebrity Centre downtown, I asked for the first eight books by publication date so I could buy them in the order they'd been written.

I flew through them and quickly grasped what the fairly Einsteinian MEST Universe referred to, and the life continuum, the fascinating Chart of Attitudes and the Tone Scale. Much of it was interesting, food for thought, but what I wanted was clear-cut answers. Like a squirrel scratching for a nut, I dug through the pages searching for some specific technique or nugget of information that could help us.

In *The Fundamentals of Thought*, I read about the conscious mind and its animal counterpart, the reactive mind; that might be a place to start. I asked Charlie one afternoon while he sipped iced tea at our apartment if our reactive minds could be at the root of the band's dilemma. He put his glass on the coffee table and stopped me.

"It's great, the way you're going through all these books. Incredible actually."

I nodded. "Yup, reading all the propaganda." I laughed. "I'm on a mission, you know."

"You have to understand there's more to this than reading alone. You must have come across the ARC triangle, which describes the three flows, what you take in, what you give to someone else, and what you get from observing the give and take between others. You're doing fine on the first part, you're gathering a lot of information from your reading—but you need to experience the other flows to achieve comprehension. You need to participate in an auditing session, where there is a flow between yourself and an auditor."

"I saw the prices; auditing is not something I can afford." I'd had no intention of being audited. Charging money for helping people was one of my main issues with this applied philosophy thing. If it had something to help us, I meant to find it in the books.

"Not for you, you're a celebrity. I'm authorized to offer everyone in the band free Dianetics processing."

"Really? You think we're celebrities?" I tried to think of myself as a famous person. It failed to fit.

"Of course, you are. You guys are influencers. Look around the Sky Room tonight." He lifted his glass in salute, wearing his cherubic grin. Well, free is free, I was willing to reconsider if it would speed up finding what I was looking for.

"Well, why start with Dianetics?" I asked him. "Why not Scientology processing? If there's an answer, I think that's where it would be." Theresa brought fresh iced tea into the living room and sat on the couch with me. I considered lighting a joint but lit a cigarette instead. I'd smoked dope around Charlie before to gauge his reaction. I got a charge out of tweaking what I considered other's pretensions, but he hadn't reacted. I still couldn't decide how I felt about Scientology beyond what I had read, but Charlie was graciously spending a lot of time and effort in helping me search for the answers I needed. No need to be rude.

"Think of Dianetics as a way to prepare your MEST—Matter, Energy, Space, and Time—body for the more spiritual processing of Scientology OT levels. We like you to get as close to Clear as you can before starting OT auditing."

OT stood for Operating Thetan, what Scientology referred to as "the being who's driving the body." The idea of not being your body had always seemed logical, it was a concept I could readily accept.

After talking more about the auditing process, I accepted the Dianetics book he'd offered. He scheduled training sessions for anyone in the band, including Theresa, to learn about Auditor Training Routines, numbered 0 through 4, before auditing.

The most important thing about this applied philosophy to me, as Charlie described it, was its results-based technology. "It's not an ideology," he assured me. "Ron Hubbard approached his theories like an engineer. When you cross a bridge, faith isn't required to get to the other side. You count on the science, engineering, and construction skills of trained professionals to be sure you'll arrive safely on the other side. Scientology uses the analogy of a bridge to describe progress to higher levels of self-control for the same reason. As long as you apply the principles of this philosophy," he said, "the results are guaranteed, whether you believe in them or not."

41 AN APPLIED PHILOSOPHY

It is the mark of an educated mind to be able to entertain a thought without accepting it.
—Aristotle

May 23, 1969
Las Vegas, Nevada

THE SO-CALLED "Soul Concert" with Dobie Gray felt strange from the beginning. Jim Seagrave had called me into his office a few days earlier to tell me Bill Miller had blessed Seymour Heller's request for us to perform in a local concert with Dobie Gray. Dobie Gray had been primarily known as a songwriter until a sizeable hit with *The 'In' Crowd,* apparently convinced him he liked being a recording star, too. He was on a swing through Las Vegas promoting his new release, *I Never Promised You a Rose Garden.*

"We're excited to be part of it." I scratched at my mustache; it needed trimming. "This is our first concert. Wish we had a better idea of what to expect." All we'd been told was to be prepared to play four songs: our recent release, *Remember When,* our most successful record, *Look Back In Love,* and two more. Due to their success with *Day After Day,* Shango was on the bill too. Along with somebody called the Mod Squad.

"Don't worry," Jim reassured me. "You guys will be fantastic."

The Las Vegas Convention Center's Rotunda was large enough to hold a small, concert-sized crowd, but it was more than half empty at show time. Young kids—the oldest high school age—scrambled around in the seats playing games and yelling as if they were on a playground. Groups of tolerant parents supervised their hijinks.

Mod Squad, a five-man act, went on first. They were a lounge act appearing at a small Strip casino called the Castaways. They opened with a Gershwin standard, *Someone to Watch Over Me*, they'd apparently released as a cover. Surprising, since about everybody who's anybody in jazz had already covered it since Ella Fitzgerald had made it famous in the fifties. I had to stop for a moment and listen though; the lead singer, Lee Greenwood, was doing a solid performance on the song. It was entirely lost on the kids in the seats. We didn't catch much of their act as we were changing for our show, but I heard another ballad with excellent vocals through the walls, but they were out of their depth on this stage.

Shango came out next. It was surprising to see our name higher on the bill than Shango's; their hit record was soaring up the national charts and still sizzling in the local top ten and Southern California radio. Probably, it was because we were better known in Las Vegas, or they needed to get to the Sky Room before we did. But I bet it was Seymour's influence behind the scenes.

I slipped through a side door to watch Tommy and his guys perform. They sounded great, the same as every night, but the soft steel drum reggae beat completely missed here. The kids in the crowd hardly acknowledged there were performers on stage, though they seemed to be having a fun cavorting around on the makeshift dance floor.

When it was our turn, a couple of inexperienced volunteers attempted to help us ready our equipment. Despite their well-intended efforts, we had to find and do everything ourselves while fully dressed for our show. It didn't take long to become a disastrous, embarrassing mess—re-running cables and attempting an incomplete sound and microphone check. Behind us, Leonard thumped around arranging his kit on the drum stand. What were the promoters thinking in not having scheduled a sound check hours before the performance?

Before the curtain rose, I stood in front of my microphone next to Dave and Mac, perspiring a river from effort and anxiety. We'd taken so long to get going and appeared so unprofessional, that any semblance of a rock-concert aura had fled. The powerful sound system blared our vocals to *Look Back In Love* throughout the rotunda, but Les and Mickey's amps were massively inadequate for this size venue. Leonard slammed away at his drums as though he was John Bonham in Led Zeppelin. We couldn't hear ourselves sing in the stage monitors. The sound balance was absolutely terrible.

We glanced at each other in alarm as our worst fears materialized. We'd received little response from the kids out front after our first song. Next, Mac worked the stage hard on *Summertime Blues*, but our discomfort was palpable. Spacing our microphones so far apart made responding to each other or an audience awkward; we'd put no thought into presenting ourselves on an expansive stage like this.

As Mac attempted his emcee patter between songs, another bad choice in this kind of setting, I was horrified. We were being exposed as a nightclub band masquerading as a concert act. The agony continued as *Remember When* died in its tepid juices, and we closed our four-song set with exactly the wrong song for these kids, the operatic rock ballad, *Cara Mia*.

In a daze, we packed our stuff and skulked away while Dobie Gray, the headliner, prepared to go on. I didn't envy him.

Our wives had come to see us perform, and they chattered with each other as if they hadn't even noticed how badly things had gone. I didn't have much to say until we were on our way back to the Flamingo. "Oh my God, we were terrible!" exploded out of me.

"I don't think anyone was particularly good," Dave said from the backseat.

"What went wrong?" Theresa asked, stroking my shoulder. I clenched the steering wheel as we wound through traffic on Paradise Road. "I didn't think you guys sounded so bad."

"Thanks, honey, but we were awful. We're not ready to perform on a concert stage, not that there was anything professional about this whole disaster. We looked like what we are, a club act pretending to be concert artists." The car went silent for a minute.

"Felt bad for Mac," Dave said. "Those kids out there didn't want to hear him talk. We should have played the songs back-to-back."

"It's not like we don't have the talent and potential to put on a great rock show," I said. "But we have to learn how to do it."

When, and if, we ever got to tour, we needed roadies to wrangle the equipment, audio people to get our sound right, and the right amplification gear. We, the band, had to learn, or be taught, stagecraft techniques for this kind of environment. *Most of all, we had to record songs that would get us to a concert stage.*

Charlie told us our Dianetics auditing would be more effective if we were familiar with the skills an auditor needed. We'd learn best by getting a taste of their training. The first and most important skill was the TR-0, short for Training Routine Zero. It appeared to be a Zen-like meditative state, but he explained it was simply a way to become fully receptive to any kind of communication without reacting to it. Leonard and Mickey dropped out the moment these exercises were offered. I don't think they'd intended to participate anyway. But Theresa, the dearest thing in my life, accompanied me to the downtown Scientology Celebrity Centre for most of the training sessions.

Once we could maintain this state of "being," we took part in a curious training exercise called "bull-baiting." Two people took on the roles of prospective auditor and coach. The coach attempted to break the new auditor's TR-0 state with verbal or physical no-touching harassment. He could startle, mimic, curse, or tell them a joke—virtually anything except touch them. Mac, Dave, Les, Theresa, and I spent a few hilarious evenings before work trying to break each other's composure. Our efforts at self-control weren't highly successful, primarily because of Les. None of us could withstand his sharp taunts and witticisms for long. It wasn't a problem. While an auditor-in-training had to maintain a constant TR-0 demeanor for two hours under duress to pass, we didn't. We weren't going to become auditors.

An outcome of the next training routine, TR-1, turned out to be something we could immediately use. It was defined as: "Communication is intention across space to duplicate information." By concentrating on making eye contact with our audiences while thinking about the meaning of the lyrics, the song's message had more effect on an audience. Mac, Les, and I jumped all over the idea. But Dave, whose shyness could make it difficult to connect with an audience, had the most dramatic results. He received increased applause after, before, and during his songs when he did this.

This was a killer performance technique ideally suited to Mac's brashness, and he was seeing incredible results until, for some reason, he abandoned us. I'd missed it at the time, but he'd joined Mickey and Leonard in secretly resenting the time the others of us were spending on Scientology—particularly the influence they believed it held over me.

42 SMOKELESS

Each of us thinks we know what's real, but reality has more sides than a disco ball.
—Fredrick Zackel

June 1, 1969
Las Vegas, Nevada

I WAS SO annoyed with Charlie I wanted to scream. I would've phoned him if he'd given me his number. When he finally came to the Sky Room, I pulled him aside, not hiding my displeasure.

"There's a big story about Scientology in the *Las Vegas Sun*, Charlie, claiming it's a religion. And that bugs me—a lot. I agreed to go on this ride because you assured me this applied philosophy stuff is as reliable as a bridge. Something that works whether I have faith in it or not."

"It is. It still is," he said, trying to appease me. "Ron considers Scientology to be philosophical engineering, just the way I told you. You don't have to have faith in anything. Everything you've learned works 100 percent as long as the tech is followed 100 percent."

I resisted saying something spiteful that would wipe the earnest, used-car-salesman smirk off his face.

"Larry," he went on, kneading his hands, stinking of sincerity. "We're being forced to become a religion to avoid paying unfairly high taxes. Ron has been battling the IRS for a long time about this. We need all our resources to clear the entire planet, you know."

"You better be right," I groused. "I'm not trying to save the damned planet. Just want to know if Scientology can help us write songs."

I'd put a lot of effort into studying, without finding a clear-cut remedy for us. I didn't want to waste any more time on it. I was willing to try auditing, and if it worked, fine. If not, I was done. To know for sure, I had to do everything right, give it a fair chance.

I followed every pre-audit requirement for my auditing session to the letter. I needed to be well rested: my session had been set for two in the afternoon allowing me to catch a solid eight hours of sleep. No alcohol for twenty-four hours or smoking marijuana for at least a week. I rarely drank, even beer, so skipping booze was easy, but not getting high for seven long days and nights had been a significant sacrifice. Theresa and I tended to be daytime loadies. Because of my working hours, we were inclined to be affectionate during the afternoon and early evenings, and we'd grown accustomed to letting the love-weed heighten our erotically-charged lovemaking. But I endured the temporary loss of our enhancer for the sake of research.

When I arrived at the Celebrity Center, they tucked me into a small cube of a room with no windows. Indirect lighting disclosed a card table in the middle divided by a cardboard partition on top, with two folding chairs on either side. Before sitting, I caught sight of an E-meter connected to two empty unlabeled metal cans and a pad and pen on the other side of the cardboard barrier. I'd seen an E-meter and the cans before and had gotten some idea of how it worked. A box of tissues perched on my side; no pictures hung on the wall. *Nothing to distract the PC*, I remembered. My mind wandered while I waited.

As the date for auditing had drawn near, Les had backed out, leaving Dave and I to continue on. The other guys not only refused auditing, some of them were unhappy about me going ahead. Their response was frustrating. Couldn't they get it through their heads—I was doing this for the band? But maybe it was best for Dave and me, or at least me, to be the guinea pigs. I was the one pushing for change, I accepted it was my responsibility to find out if it would help. And what's the big deal, anyway? How could it hurt, sitting in a room talking to someone for a few minutes? Why all the drama?

Theresa hadn't shown interest in being audited, and I'd never suggested she should. She was curious and interested in the concepts Charlie and I discussed, but she understood I wasn't doing this for personal reasons. We were perfectly happy in our life together. She'd been sticking with me through all this so we could be together, and that was perfect.

Eventually, a young man made his way to the table and sat behind the cardboard panel across from me. He fiddled behind the partition for a moment before he gazed at me, smiling at me the way acquaintances do, and though I didn't know him, I returned his smile. He asked how I felt, and I said fine.

"Have you had a full night's sleep?" he asked. "And have you avoided marijuana and alcohol for the proscribed time limits?" I told him yes, I'd been a good boy, and he said, "Okay, pick up the cans, and we can proceed. The next few questions are mainly to set the meter." I grabbed a can in each hand; they were nothing special. They might have contained frozen orange juice before their labels had been removed. Alligator clips, fastened to the cans, connected to wires running under the cardboard to the E-meter.

With his eyes on the E-meter, he asked my name, address, what city we were in, questions like that. His expression showed that his TR-1 routine was nicely in place, and I was comfortable and receptive.

"Okay, this begins the auditing session."

What happened next wasn't particularly exciting: simple queries that began with "Can you remember a time when . . ." followed by phrases like "you felt sad," or "you didn't have enough to eat," or "you thought you'd gotten lost," or "you felt happy," and so on down a checklist he was obviously ticking off. I let myself answer without thinking much about it. As I listened to my replies, I realized I'd slipped into a serene zone where a verbal stream of consciousness flowed without effort from mind to mouth. I didn't try to monitor anything. I was totally into the spirit of things.

I remembered trying to describe something to the auditor when things changed, though it didn't seem significant at the time. He'd asked me when the incident I was describing had happened, and I realized I couldn't place a time or date for it. I rummaged around in my mind, searching, like shuffling through long-discarded items in the back of an attic. I couldn't decide whether I was recounting something I'd been doing, or if I was witnessing someone else doing something, but in trying to connect to when it happened, something odd took place. I'd felt as though I was recalling someone else's memories, though I knew they were mine. I paused all other thought to peer deeper into this narrow crack between reality and imagining. The concentration must've been apparent on my face, but my auditor waited quietly.

"Is it possible," I asked, musing, "and I know this will sound weird, but could I be remembering something from before I was born, like in a previous lifetime? Something like that?" I'd read science fiction since adolescence; the concept of past lives wasn't inconceivable.

The young man, who'd been writing, glanced at me in a futile attempt to keep his TR-0 neutrality from slipping. I sensed something had changed, but nothing that disturbed me.

"Tell me what you see," he said. This is the only kind of a response an auditor can make to someone being audited. It was considered vital not to add content to a communication originating with the PC.

I couldn't summon anything more about the experience than I'd already described. Though it had been vivid, it had been entirely commonplace—nothing earth-shattering, no big dramatic event. Something to do with a barn, and harnessing a farm animal, possibly a horse. After a few minutes of repeating what I remembered, the auditor, trembling, excused himself and left the room. I'd never been audited before, but I'd read that an auditor should never leave this way—it was called "blowing out of a session."

I drifted along happily, though, remarkably comfortable, not thinking about much of anything until my auditor returned, trying to pretend nothing unusual had happened. He might've needed a bathroom break, I suppose, but the way I'd understood what I'd read, auditors are almost required to wet their pants rather than desert a PC in session. He asked if there was anything more I wanted to tell him, but after sifting through what I'd already mentioned, I didn't.

"I'd like to indicate you have a floating needle." He observed me. "How do you feel?"

"I'm fine. Actually, I'm extremely relaxed." Peaceful would also be the right word to describe my state of mind, but wide awake as I'd ever been was correct, too.

"Please wait a moment. Another auditor will be here shortly." He stood to leave, and a man a little older entered with a similar friendly smile to the one I'd gotten earlier and took his seat. I smiled back.

He checked the meter, and after a moment, he glanced at me. "I'd like to indicate your needle is still floating," he said and made a notation on the pad.

"Is there anything you'd like to say?" When I said no, he responded with, "Then, that's it." "That's it" always signals the end of a session or process in Scientology. I stood and followed him out of the room.

Out in the brilliant Las Vegas afternoon, I noticed how the drifting particles in the desert air seemed to intensify the pastel colors around me. By the time Theresa arrived, I was euphoric with the clarity of my senses to see, hear, and even taste things in the air I couldn't explain. Maybe this was like an acid trip. The closest thing I could even slightly relate to it was how I felt after amazing sex or a scorching hot jam on stage, wrung out but curiously invigorated.

Amused by my demeanor, Theresa examined me from the driver's seat. "Based on the loopy grin on your face, I'd say something must have happened in there."

"Yeah, I guess so. But I can't tell you what exactly."

"Oh." Her glance questioned me. "Is it secret?"

"What? No, no, I don't mean like that. I meant there actually isn't anything to tell. A guy asked me some questions about things I remembered, and I tried to answer them. Nothing breathtaking, although I remember I saw something from my own two eyes, but I wasn't the one thinking about what I was seeing." Uh oh, I wasn't making any sense. I stopped trying to explain until I could get it straight myself and decided to definitely not say anything about remembering something from a past life. That sounded way too far out. Not relevant anyway. I didn't believe it myself.

"Well, what do you want to do now?" She broke into my thoughts. "It's after six. You were in there a long time."

I gazed at the clock on the dashboard with disbelief.

"I don't understand . . . I couldn't have been in there more than an hour at most." I gazed out the window as buildings passed by in a scene only vaguely familiar.

"Well," I leaned back with a deep sigh, "unless you brought some loco weed with you, we should go home. I promised myself a thick joint, and there's not much time left before work. Can't go into the Sky Room stoned, you know." She turned right on to Las Vegas Boulevard, heading north. I was noticing things along the street I'd never seen before.

She grinned at me. "Don't worry, honey, I've got something waiting on the coffee table for you."

Theresa walked into the kitchen to pour glasses of fruit juice while I simultaneously switched on the TV and lit the perfect cylinder she'd rolled for me. She'd perfected rolling while I'd gotten sloppier, still not impressed by style points. The smoke I drew in was bitter and sour. *Jeez, it's only been seven days, and I'm not used to getting high anymore?* I forced in the fumes and sipped more air. When I exhaled, there was no rush. I tried a few more caustic hits until a headache started coming on. Pinching out the joint, I dropped it half-smoked in the ashtray.

Theresa came back into the room. "Everything okay in here? You tripping yet, honey?"

"I'm not sure. Flying high for sure, but not from smoking. Some kind of natural high from the auditing, I guess. I know it sounds strange. Don't understand it myself." I gestured toward the ashtray. "Is this the same grass we had last week? It's not something new, is it? Smells terrible, like dog vomit, or the dog did something worse."

She shrugged. "Not unless you bought some somewhere. I haven't gotten stoned since the last time we did, there should be a lot in the baggie."

I nodded, deciding not to worry about it.

"Maybe you're oversensitive right now," she said, taking my hand. "Let's go lay down. You should get some rest before tonight."

Even after the sweetest, most laid-back but hyper-aware lovemaking brought me another glimpse of heaven, I couldn't fall asleep as Theresa drifted into slumber. I wanted more than anything to stay in this safe place with her as night deepened, but once I hit the street, I found myself eager to make music in the Sky Room. I floated through the hours, experiencing every song as though I was singing or playing it for the first time. I found myself understanding and appreciating the lyrics and chord progressions in a way I never had before. I wanted to welcome everybody in the room personally.

Dave and Leonard wanted to know how the auditing had gone, but I deflected questions saying everything had been routine, which wasn't a lie, at least in one sense. I didn't understand what had happened well enough to describe it, and I wanted to protect whatever made me feel the way I did from skepticism.

When Charlie came in to ask what I thought of my first auditing experience, I told him about feeling high afterward, and he beamed like a headlight. "You had a steady floating needle," he said with a knowing smile. Charlie failed to share my concern about not being able to get stoned but thought the effect would wear off in a few hours or at most, days. Nothing to worry about, he assured me.

Instead of curling next to Theresa when I got home, I left her to sleep undisturbed. Television was too distracting and so was reading. I tried to examine why I felt so stimulated, my mind so active. I considered going out to walk along the Strip in the early light of dawn but didn't. Theresa woke, surprised to find I hadn't slept. We went through a typical day with the expectation I'd probably want a nap, but I didn't. I worked happily through six sets on Sunday, our longest night of the week, when Shango was off, before finally crashing into sleep.

Over the following days, I tried smoking at home with Theresa, always with the same result. I tried getting high with Dave and Mac several times. I told them about what I thought had happened but didn't make a big deal of it. They didn't believe me, of course. It was beyond their reality. Mine too.

Dave's auditing extended over several sessions. He reported a sense of euphoria at one point, though not as strong as mine, but he was still able to get high. When he'd been told he'd reached Level 4 as a pre-Clear, somebody at the Celebrity Centre chose to tell him Jesus Christ had been a Level 4. Dave had been raised as a bible-thumping Baptist, and when he heard that, which had been meant to motivate him, he was so pissed off he immediately quit auditing and refused to go back. I could only shake my head at the arrogance of some of the people at the Celebrity Center.

Charlie eventually brought me an answer to what had happened or at least part of one. While he couldn't access my records, he knew someone who'd seen them. The auditor had apparently reported me as going Clear during a standard Dianetics rundown. Not impossible, but relatively rare—rare enough that the notes from my session had been sent to LA for verification.

I understood what the state of being Clear signified in Scientology. I'd read about it. It meant I was no longer driven or affected by my reactive mind. Apparently whatever hidden pain the herb had been shielding me from had gotten zapped during auditing. The largish unintended and unwanted consequence: no longer could I share love-leaf with my wife or head-change sessions with my friends and bandmates—a basic tenet of our communal connection. Marijuana only gave me headaches now. And though I'd lost the ability to get high, I hadn't lost the desire. Not Charlie or anyone at the Celebrity Centre could tell me if I'd ever be able to get high again. Not what I'd intended. Not at all.

43 THE TWENTY-FIVE YEAR PHONE CALL

The axe forgets what the tree remembers.
—African proverb

May 15, 1969
Las Vegas, Nevada

"I DON'T GET IT, and I don't like it." Mickey eyed me like I was responsible for whatever was biting him. "We're doing all the work, while Seymour and Howard are getting paid for doing nothin'." Mac nodded, his frown making it clear he agreed. Though we were making more money and had more security than ever, there was grumbling in the ranks, especially from Mickey, with Mac egging him on. The six of us were scattered around a booth and table at rehearsal in the Sky Room. We were casually attired, from Leonard in shorts and muscle tee to Dave's belled jeans and a collared shirt with rolled up sleeves, and the rest of us somewhere in between.

"We've been working our asses off for months while they're gettin' a commission they ain't doing nothin' to deserve," Mickey complained. Like a tennis match, the rest of the band's attention turned my way.

I shrugged. "Seems simple enough, and let me remind you I didn't invent how the entertainment industry works, so don't take it out on me. Howard is our agent; he takes ten percent of the gigs he books like every other agent. Not ten percent for part of the gig, ten percent of the whole job. Seymour, who usually gets twenty percent of everything his clients earn, though he's cut his commission in half for us, manages our career every day, so he gets his cut every day."

"Don't you talk down to me you little shit." Mickey had a way with words. "I traveled with my parents playin' music while you were dickin' around in grade school. What I do know is they ain't doing crap for us right now, and we're still payin' them." He stared me down. The attention switched back toward me.

"What do you want me to do? Go ask Seymour what he's doing for us today?"

"First right thing you've said in a month." He leaned back with a smirk. I could see other guys agreeing with him.

I understood why Mickey and Mac were pushing hard on this; they needed more money. Getting paid here worked about the same as in the other Vegas hotels we'd played: I received a "chit," a note with a dollar amount for the week, authorized by the entertainment director. I took the chit to the casino cage and exchanged it for cash before separating the bills into individual pay envelopes, including one for band expenses. When Mac discovered I could draw out advances from the cage, most of his check would be depleted when it came time to fill his envelope. Mickey hadn't reached the same level of need, but I knew the two of them frequented the Pussycat in the early hours after the Sky Room closed. God knew, and so did we—those blackjack games there weren't right. After a drink or two when we'd been at the Cat, and despite friendly dealers warning glances, I'd wasted a few dollars on them myself. I had a feeling they were bending the elbow there and letting their money get slippery on those twisted tables.

"You guys are seriously considering making me fly to LA to cross-examine Seymour?" I stared at them incredulously.

Somehow, I'd failed to play this thing right. Theresa had laughed when I'd told her over dinner her how I'd let myself get talked into a corner and would have to fly to LA in the morning. That's why I found myself waiting in front of Bette Rosenthal's desk outside Seymour's office in West Hollywood the next day.

Bette told me she'd give me a longer than usual spot in his schedule only because it was me, but for her, please, make an effort to keep my meeting to fifteen minutes, she had so much work for him. That's what she always said, but not a problem today. I didn't expect to be here long.

A while later, Seymour opened his door looking like a grandfatherly gnome in a dark, pinstriped suit and open-collared dress shirt. He welcomed me with a smile as I followed him across the length of his office. He gestured me to a leather chair and seated himself behind an impressive desk, created from the case of a grand piano, Liberace had given him. After a little small talk, he asked why I'd come. I rubbed my mustache with a thumb and finger before speaking.

"This isn't something I would normally bring to you Seymour, but the guys wanted me to ask you a question. As the band's leader, I felt obligated."

"And? What's the question?"

"Some of us—" He had to notice my reluctance as I shifted around in the chair and started over. "Some of *them* are wondering why, after working at the Flamingo for several months, we continue to pay agency and management commissions for a job that doesn't seem to require any effort to maintain."

Seymour's smile spread his curly white muttonchops out from the sides of his face, and his eyes crinkled beneath the square cut of his black-rimmed glasses. He rearranged the single paper on his desktop. "I get questions like this every once in a while, and I have a good answer. I heard it long ago from my partner Dick Gabbe in New York. The fact is, it's such a good answer it's as true today as it was then."

I leaned in, knowing this would be good.

"You know Howard King is the agent of record on your contract at the Flamingo for a reason?"

Rhetorical question, but I nodded, and he went on.

"Personal managers aren't licensed to procure employment for artists. In fact, they are strictly prohibited from doing so." He snugged back into his chair crossing his hands over his belly. "However, you are at the Flamingo through my long-standing relationship with Bill Miller after many, many years of booking artists in Las Vegas." He gestured at his Rolodex as he continued. "Like Liberace and the Treniers, not to mention Billy Joe Royal, Joe South, and many more.

"So, here's my answer: You and your band are right, it probably didn't take me more than fifteen minutes to finalize our agreement with Bill Miller. Bill and I had been talking about this since Kirk Kerkorian bought the Flamingo and decided to redesign the casino's entrance to face Las Vegas Boulevard. They planned the new entryway around a covered driveway, a porte-cochere, with a room above overlooking Las Vegas Boulevard.

Lot of people expected the room to become a restaurant, but Bill and I want entertainment in it. I believed it would be an ideal place for Stark Naked and the Car Thieves and helped him plan it with you in mind. But I wouldn't have been in the position to work Bill on this if I hadn't earned his confidence over twenty-five years of making deals with him."

He glanced at me to confirm my comprehension. "So, you see, a fifteen-minute conversation goes back to the relationships I've made and the trust I've earned over my years in personal management."

I got it. Actually, I loved it. It was entirely logical, and I would never forget it. Seymour wasn't getting a fee for a single booking, we were paying him for applying the expertise and connections he'd acquired over his long career on our behalf. *Good enough for me.* I stood to leave. "Thanks, Seymour, that was brilliant—"

"Hold on a minute, Larry, wait a minute." He motioned me back into my chair. "I've got some news for you since you're here. Kerkorian is planning on opening the International Hotel soon. Claims it will be the largest resort hotel in the world."

I nodded. "The place is gigantic, it's been under construction for longer than we've been at the Flamingo."

Seymour dipped his head in a half nod. "The success of the Sky Room has them planning a similar nightspot called the Crown Room on the penthouse floor. Bill wants Stark Naked and the Car Thieves to go over to the new hotel and kick the place off." I sat up straight.

"That would be fantastic. The Sky Room is outta sight, perfect for us. It's the only late-night combination showroom and dance room in a Strip hotel. It fits us to a T, but it makes me a little uneasy, too. Knowing there's another place for the band to work in Vegas would ease that worry."

Seymour gave me a paternal smile hinting of a surprise to come.

"You're probably aware, along with everyone else in Vegas, Elvis Presley is going to the new International Hotel."

I nodded. The Las Vegas news outlets had been falling all over themselves ever since Colonel Tom Parker, Elvis's personal manager, had publicly agreed to Elvis's appearance at a groundbreaking ceremony at the new hotel's construction site. It wouldn't be the first time Elvis played Vegas. During the years of the Rat Pack, when Frank Sinatra was king, Elvis's appearance at the Frontier Hotel hadn't gone particularly well. That was a long time ago, and though his name was generating a lot of excitement, it wasn't guaranteed he'd be successful at Kerkorian's dream hotel.

"Bill tells me Elvis will be performing in the Showroom Internationale the night the hotel opens. He hasn't got Tom Parker signed on the dotted line quite yet, but he assures me there won't be a problem. So," his eyes twinkled, "wouldn't it be sensational if Stark Naked and the Car Thieves was there to open the new Crown Room at the top of the largest resort hotel in the world while Elvis opens the showroom downstairs?"

I smiled ear to ear. As far as I knew, who would star at the grand opening hadn't been announced. Now apparently, I did.

Seymour earned his money this afternoon, I thought, as he called in Bette to put me on the next flight home and paged his private cab to give me a quick ride to the airport. He had all the travel arrangements back and forth to Vegas grooved. When Liberace, Lee to his friends, played in Vegas, which happened often, Seymour flew there every night, seven nights a week, to catch his shows, hopping the redeye home to be in his office at eight the next morning.

When the band came to work that night, I called them together before we left for the stage. "Okay guys, here's the answer to your burning question, along with news hot off the press."

"Well ain't you the cat that ate the cream?" Mickey said taken aback.

"This is what Seymour told me. It was simple. Could have saved the plane fare. He said we were right, it only took him a few minutes to make the call that got us into the Sky Room, but he pointed out that it took him twenty-five years to earn the trust and relationship to make the call and to know the person who answered would listen to him."

I pulled out an official Flamingo Hotel memo with a copied newspaper column attached. "And this was waiting for me when I got back." Jim Seagrave had sent me a copy of a great review of Stark Naked and the Car Thieves from the *Daily Variety Magazine* in New York. "I'd say things are going pretty well. Look, Seymour's connections and knowledge are what we're paying for, and those are ongoing. Don't you think it's time we stop trying to bite the hand that's feeding us? Can anybody really argue with that?"

After waiting for any rebuttal, I went on. "Didn't think so. I didn't have anything more to say to him either. Now here's some real news. When the International Hotel opens in six weeks or so, there's going to be a room like the Sky Room over there. They're calling it the Crown Room—and Bill Miller wants us to open the place." Most of the guys reacted with varying degrees of pleased surprise.

"Might not be such a great deal," Les cautioned. "It's not on the Strip. No major hotel has ever survived away from Las Vegas Boulevard." He shook his head in skepticism.

"They didn't have anyone with the star power of who Bill Miller's got booked to open the International, Bear. When they raise the curtain in the showroom, Elvis Presley will be onstage. And they want us to get things rolling in the Crown Room at the same time." Les's eyes lit up. Elvis was his biggest idol. He'd want this event in his scrapbook.

Since we'd begun at the Sky Room, there'd been constant rumors of Elvis sightings around town. Celebrities of all kinds peppered out audiences, some of us thought he'd come in to see us soon. It wasn't a stretch. We'd gotten to know Tom Jones, who regularly starred in the Flamingo's Showroom. It wasn't unusual, pardon the pun, to find him in our audience before, between, and after his shows. He was always friendly and complimentary, but it's safe to say the scores of alluring women enticed him more than the musical artistry of Stark Naked and the Car Thieves. Big Jim Sullivan, Tom's guitar player and close friend, hung out in the Sky Room even more than Tom. He and Leonard became instant best pals, as like souls will do. Once Lenny realized how close

Tom and Big Jim were to Elvis, he badgered them to bring the brightest current star in the Las Vegas firmament to the Sky Room. Several times, Tom mentioned he'd invited him, but so far it hadn't happened.

I wasn't as star-struck by Elvis as my bandmates. His immense popularity had always been a mystery to me. I would have been a lot more interested in meeting Brian Wilson, Paul McCartney, or Bob Gaudio from the Four Seasons.

44 VEGAS BLUES

The night is the hardest time to be alive and 4 AM knows all my secrets.
—Poppy Z. Brite

June 9, 1969
Las Vegas, Nevada

"YOUR NAME LOOKS GIGANTIC up on that sign." Theresa's reverential whisper was almost lost in the roar of our Javelin's ineffectual battle with triple-digit heat. We gazed in awe at the road-side marquee on Paradise Road in front of the soon-to-open International Hotel. STARK NAKED AND THE CAR THIEVES was spread across one of the sign's two huge wings on two lines. A third, smaller line underneath read: "Appearing Soon in the Crown Room. Dancing till five AM."

Les had told us the previous night he'd seen our name in six-foot red letters here, so Theresa and I came to see. Very temporary, I knew, but damn! Still impressive. In one of those rare moments when I thought about taking a photo, I wished I had a camera to capture the moment. It confirmed what Seymour had said. We'd be going to the International soon.

Behind the sign, the resort's lawn was only half sodded, the landscaping unfinished; much of the resort casino was still in the final throes of construction. But inside, some shops and restaurants in the vast shopping arcades were already serving customers next to gaping wood-framed holes where other vendors hadn't begun their buildouts yet. Meanwhile, guests were checking into a few of the finished rooms available.

I glanced at Theresa and grinned. "That's pretty amazing, our name up there where Elvis Presley's will be. Wonder why his name's not there already?"

"This is going to be big for you guys." She turned to face me. "Speaking of big," she patted her stomach, "I'm getting kind of big, too." She took my hand, and, with moisture starting in the corners of her eyes, tentatively placed it on her gently rounded belly. With a month to go, her pregnancy barely showed. She seemed more radiant than ever, especially at night before we turned out the light and she curled into a tight embrace in my arms to sleep.

"Yes, with our baby." We sat looking into each other's eyes for a minute. I thought in quiet desperation about how terror-stricken I would be in a few hours after I put her on an evening flight so she could sleep through the night from LA to Honolulu. A tear started and hung from one of her long dark lashes. I reached to catch it on my finger.

"This is going to be so fucking difficult. We've never been apart this long."

"I know, my darling, I know it will, but I need to be with my mom when the baby comes." Much as I'd wanted to, I couldn't deny her request. She'd seemed desperate to go. I'd taken her from her home in Hawaii without meeting anyone in her family and still hadn't met any of them face-to-face. I hadn't even been able to let them give Theresa to me in an authentic Hawaiian wedding ceremony as they'd asked. Undoubtedly, it would be better for her to have her mother and family and friends to help care for her and our new child. But for me, it would be agony.

"Even after you have the baby, it will be six more weeks until you can fly. You're going to be gone two and a half months." I tried not to whimper like a puppy. "They're planning to send people to the moon and back in two weeks, way sooner than it's going to take you to have our baby and come home."

"I must go, honey, but I promise I will come back with our son as soon as I can. I love you forever. I'm more worried you might forget me and how much I adore you."

"Too late, I could never forget you. I'm addicted. I don't see how I could take another breath without you."

"Charlie says our baby will arrive on the twenty-fourth," she said with a tight smile. "If he's right, I can be home a few days earlier than we'd planned."

Charlie, the miracle worker, I thought sourly. I hadn't expressed my reservations about Scientology to her yet. I couldn't deny something powerful had happened to me, but the unexpected results, the way it changed me in whatever the hell way it wanted, without my permission, creeped me out. And auditing had failed to produce a way to kick the band's creativity into gear.

We traded kisses and bittersweet smiles before we turned for home, her head on my shoulder.

When I came back from the airport, the rooms of our apartment seemed dismal and vacant. Loneliness was already rising like a deadly fever as the reality of the many solitary days and nights ahead sunk in.

A few nights later, as we prepared for our next-to-last set, I still struggled to overcome my despondency. With two hours to go, this was about the time the room usually wound down. Instead, a sudden rush of people arrived to fill empty tables in the club. People around the bar were suddenly three-deep, and standees were jammed along the inside wall and in front of the tall windows. Stepping on the stage, I caught sight of a line forming outside the entrance ropes spiraling to the first floor. What was going on?

Vince, the head maître d, walked over to whisper in Mickey's ear. There was a rumor Tom Jones and Elvis Presley were on their way to the Sky Room. We immediately reassessed our playlist. A twinge of disappointment struck me—if it was true, Theresa wouldn't be here to see it.

We'd begun leaning into *Five O'clock World*, as the set opener, when Elvis Presley, Tom Jones, and Big Jim Sullivan arrived trailing followers like a mass of droning bees swarming their queen. The maître ds efficiently interceded and escorted them to a cordoned-off table about halfway back near ringside. Las Vegas royalty had deigned to visit the Sky Room. After our set, we joined the parade of supplicants lined up at their table. Tom and Big Jim had twinkles in their eyes as I greeted them. When it was my turn, I gave Elvis a quick handshake. He mumbled something polite, smooth and southern as sweet potato pie, in an accent I remembered from my college years in Murray, Kentucky. I nodded, keeping my reply short so the other guys could have more time with him.

My aversion to the ingratiating fervor the man aroused probably materialized from my rotten mood, but I'd always been perplexed by Elvis hysteria. I mean, gimme a break. *Hound Dog* was the first record of his I'd ever heard. What's never having caught a rabbit have to do with friendship, for God's sake? And a song about a hound crocking all the time? What in the hell does that even mean? And who would care anyway? How could a song about a dog become a smash hit? When Elvis covered Carl Perkins's *Blue Suede Shoes*, how was his version any better?

As his career went on to scale the heights of rock-and-roll legend, I didn't hear many songs I cared for. I know, I know—he had a good voice, lots of control, and pretty good range, but his technique seemed artificial, too melodramatic for me. His style seemed more hillbilly than rock, and I didn't get the big commotion over his hip movements. I didn't begrudge him his notoriety just because I didn't get it. I mean, everybody's got a right to like what they like, right? But I thought it was demeaning for us to stand in line to pay homage to the Godfather of Rockabilly music. We'd never done that for anybody else. If he was any kind of human being, I imagined he was pretty damned tired of people treating him like God's second son. But then I was in a crappy mood and hated standing in line for pretty much anything.

Theresa's letters declaring everlasting love began arriving. She must have started writing the moment she got off the plane. She enclosed photos, one showed her in a pregnancy sunsuit at the beach. She was radiant. She always made it a point to remind me of the pleasures in store for me when we held each other again. I matched her feelings and eroticism in my shorter, but descriptive replies, wild with the physical need to feel, smell, and taste her. I couldn't wait to rip the envelopes open, even though their content was like a heroin addiction—each time a letter eased my loneliness, my distress rose to barely-restrained panic by the time I finished it.

Charlie pressured me to become a minister—in name only—he assured me so I could continue auditing for free, which he insisted was doubly important now. Clear meant no longer being troubled by unresolved engrams—

unprocessed pain—for now. But, he hinted, this condition left me undefended from some more significant, unspecified threat.

Using scare tactics as motivation immediately put me off. Religions, in my opinion, too often wield their version of faith—by definition, a belief in something unprovable—to use the fear of death and the unknown in this life by offering believers a backstage pass into an unlikely fairyland in the next. I quietly decided to separate myself from Scientology and anyone involved with it. I didn't try to deny what had happened, how could I? I still couldn't smoke grass without a disorienting headache. But it hadn't done a damn thing to help the band with what we needed.

A couple of weeks after Theresa's departure, I received notice that our lease on Dauphin Way wouldn't be renewed. Not surprising, Caesars was expanding, and the land these apartments were on to was too valuable for rental housing. I needed to find somewhere else for us to live. I wasn't comfortable here with Theresa gone, anyway, so I began looking and almost immediately found a lovely three-bedroom, nicely furnished, tract home with a pool in a neighborhood fifteen minutes northwest of the Flamingo. I wasn't sure we could afford the rent, but it would be a perfect home for our expanding little family.

Before I could begin moving, I got a message at work: opening the Crown Room had been put on hold.

"The way I heard it from Seymour," I said after I'd corralled everybody at rehearsal, "the problem started when Colonel Tom Parker, Elvis's manager, walked the hotel last week with Alex Shoofey—"

"Shoofey? Who's Alex Shoofey?" Mac wanted to know, putting an ashtray on my B3. He saw my frown and took it off.

"He's the big boss at the International," Leonard said. Leonard loved Las Vegas; he was embedded here now. He always seemed to know what was going on here in his realm.

"Yeah," I confirmed. "He's the new GM. Anyway, Colonel Tom was looking things over with him at the International, checking how the construction's going and everything, when they came to the showroom—they're calling it the Showroom Internationale—Colonel Tom looks around and says the room looks half-finished. Like it won't be done in time."

"Whole place does," Les agreed, "including the Crown Room. I poked around up there a few days ago. Except for the drywall, the club doesn't look like anybody's worked on it since we went up there last month."

I nodded; that added up. "Well, Colonel Tom tells Shoofey, and I love this line: 'I don't think this place is going to be finished in time for my guy. Let the girl open the place,' the girl being Barbra Streisand, of course."

"Figured something was going on," Leonard said. "Streisand's name is all over town announcing she's going to the International. But I don't get what that's got to do with us? Why aren't we going over there when the hotel opens?"

"Jeez, Leonard, I don't know. Probably the room isn't going be ready in time. All I can tell you is what I've been told." I moved to the end of the bench, my hand drifting across the keys. We planned to learn a song by Traffic this afternoon. *Feelin' Alright* was an up-tempo dance tune that would give Mac another chance to move around and work the crowd. "All I can tell you is everybody's schedule went haywire when Elvis changed his mind. For all I know, we could hear it's all back on again."

"Did Seymour tell you what Elvis plans to do?" Les asked. "Maybe he and his manager know something we don't."

"My impression is Colonel Parker's pushing Elvis's slot back four weeks, following Streisand." I shrugged. "If I had to guess, I'd say they want us to start over there the same time Elvis does. Like a second opening, you know? Who can say, though. Hopefully, somebody will come around and tell us something soon."

But nobody called or came to tell us anything. At the beginning of July, Barbara Streisand opened at the International Hotel to worldwide publicity and enormous fanfare, though the reviews complained of trouble with sound and other glitches in the main showroom during the first shows. Other than missing the opportunity to be part of the excitement, I wasn't disappointed. I liked the Sky Room. If only my soulmate were with me, I'd be ecstatic.

45 FUN DAYS

The best way out is always through.
—Robert Frost

June 29, 1969
Las Vegas, Nevada

"CRAP, ANOTHER MEETING. Hate meetings," Les stalked around a cocktail table in the Sky Room giving me the "stink eye," as Theresa's friend Charlene called it. The Sky Room's floor-to-ceiling windows shattered the sun's brilliant rays across the dance floor next to the tables where we'd gathered. "We've got a song to relearn," he grumbled. "Or should I just say learn since it sounded so damned horrible last night."

"We'll get to it," I said. Les wasn't the only grouch today. "First there are some important problems we need to talk about." Leonard wandered to the drum stand and fiddled with the nut on a cymbal stand. Everyone's posture conveyed the sour mood we'd wrapped ourselves in too often recently.

"The band is getting stale," I continued.

"Sure the fuck got that right. We ain't had a new song in two weeks," Mac agreed to a murmured chorus of assent. "Ain't had a new tune myself since Moby Dick was a fuckin minnow."

"If you'd pay attention to the finger I give you in rehearsal," Les held up his left hand and pointed to his ring finger, "you'd get more songs because we'd get more done." When we worked on vocal arrangements, he often referred us to our individual harmony parts by where he fingered a string on his guitar's fretboard.

"Yeah, I got a finger for you too, Bear, and you don't have to sing it neither."

While this might seem like harmless zinging, I didn't like the nastiness I heard behind the jabs. We'd begun to develop individual relationships outside of the band. Mine, of course, was Theresa; we were like binary stars, rotating around one another, complete within ourselves. And though I had nothing to do with it anymore, my recent foray into Scientology had put space between me and everyone except Dave. This fracturing worried me. The comfortable, carbon-copy days in the Sky Room were settling us onto a rocky plateau, accentuating our inherent differences in personality, temperament, and culture. Sniping at each other only pushed us further apart.

"Look," I started again. "At the end of the night, we all go our separate ways. When we leave, we don't see each other again until we meet in the dressing room the next night or for rehearsal."

"So?" Mickey's tousled blond hair and shadowed eyes gave evidence of a lack of sleep and a likely hangover. Mick and I often rubbed each other the wrong way—somehow we'd managed to find another bass player who didn't like the way I did things.

"Not a bad thing on the surface, of course . . ." I paused trying to find the best way to explain my thinking. "Until the Flamingo, we were always on the road, and we shared everything we cared about with each other. For years we've been like brothers, we've always been each other's best friends. When times were tough, we learned to count on one another. We cared about each other. It's different now, we're feeling secure. All of us except Dave, who never had one, gave up our apartments back in the Valley and found homes here. That's all good, but I'm afraid we're letting too much distance grow between us." I stood and got a smoke going. The gaudy, daytime glitz outside the tall windows shimmered in the blazing sun. I could almost smell the heat radiating from sidewalks. I tried to catch everybody's eyes as I went on.

"We're comfortable here, got a smooth gig. Place is packed nearly every night. We're coasting, and we all know it. We're getting sloppy, and it's because we're not turning our song list over fast enough and getting bored. Some songs suck so bad my stomach turns over when I hear Leonard call 'em out." I gestured in disgust. "Some nights I feel less like performing than I ever have." Dave and Mac and Leonard nodded, even Les, a bit. "It shouldn't be like that. And setting aside our need to write original material, Eddie is pissed that we're slow to work on the tunes he's given us to arrange for the studio."

Mickey realized he was on an island. "Yeah? So, what do we do?" he asked with a touch of civility. "Lora is real happy having a house to live in. She likes living a normal life, much as that's possible with our hours anyway. We work all night. I got a family, Larry. I don't have a lot of time to dick around with you guys." That rang a little hollow. Most of Mickey's Las Vegas friends were local hunters and outdoorsmen he'd befriended while we were at the Cat—he seemed to find enough time for them.

"Would help if you actually went home after we're done here at four in the morning instead of drinking and fighting till noon at the Pussycat," Les snapped at Mickey. Might've been where Mickey had been last night, out on one of his famous Crown Royal and Heineken binges. Recently I'd dropped into our old stomping grounds to see Orange Colored Sky and noticed a three-high pyramid of green beer cans and rocks glasses on top of the table he and Mac shared, both of them barely able to sit astride a chair.

I chain-lit another cigarette wishing Les could've picked another time for this, though. Les's friends and camp followers concerned me even more. He'd attracted an entourage who idolized and fawned over him as the underappreciated star of the band, a perspective he appeared to encourage. There were a few guys, some couples, and a girl named Crickett, who'd attached themselves to him during our last months at the Rag Doll. They organized trips from California to see him at the Sky Room, and he joined them for afternoon and evening lakeside parties at Lake Mead on our off-nights. I wasn't sure how his new wife dealt with them. I'd barely seen Susie since Theresa's departure. Approving of his friends wasn't part of my job, but I couldn't help wishing they were bigger fans of the whole band. I wasn't comfortable with the way they specifically singled him out. Couldn't be good for us—or Les's ego.

"Now, see, that's how things can get troublesome, big boy," Mickey responded to Les's cut. He eased himself out of his chair. "You don't get to comment on my personal life."

"Hold on, just hold on, you guys," I held out my palms. "This is not helpful. It's the situation we're in, and we have to adjust to it. We're not the scuffling traveling band we used to be. It's probably normal to have individual differences and interests, and friends we don't share in common."

Here came the "sell" point: "But it's a big mistake to think we don't still need and depend on each other. I'm suggesting we spend some hang time together, away from work, to keep our connections fresh."

"I don't see how I can do that," Leonard said, walking to the front of the stage. We'd seen a lot less of him lately. He'd begun developing new friends, too, ones that came along with his new girlfriend, Marie. Those he and Paula shared left with her when they'd split up.

"Me neither," Mac cut in. "I got a family needs time with me, waste enough time with you turkeys already." He laughed his throaty laugh. Mac had the uncanny ability to make a friend out of a barstool and knew more people than any of us put together—including mutual friends he and Mickey knew from the Cat. The trouble was most of them were drinkers.

"Let me finish, please. Will you let me get the idea out on the table before you shoot it down? Okay?" I stood, glaring at each of them, catching their eyes one by one. "I mean, damn it, we can hardly have a conversation without everyone getting all edgy. Quit yapping for a minute. You know I can't make any of you do anything you don't want to. Give me a fair listen and afterward, if somebody thinks they've got a better idea, we can do something different." The silence brimmed with restless movement.

I breathed deep, knowing this would be the hard part. "You remember the Fun Days thing we started when we were in North Hollywood? I think we need them again."

"What in the the hell is a Fun Day?" Mickey demanded. His expression darkened when he realized he was the only one who didn't know.

I strolled past a table to tap ash off my cigarette. "Before you joined the band, we used one rehearsal day a month for a group activity. A day when each guy chooses something he wants to do, something he'd like to share with the rest of us. And, like rehearsal—you have to show up, and you have to be on time."

"So, you figure you'll increase us getting more songs on the list by cutting a rehearsal day? Did you flunk math?" The Bear had his edge on today.

I stifled a retort but sighed when I realized my pause would probably piss him off anyway. "Look, we need good chemistry between us to maintain the band, and we're losing ours. Yes, it's urgent we work on fresh material, but I'm worried if we don't find more to like about each other, maybe we're not too far from not wanting to play and sing with each other."

The dead air and downcast glances told me I'd struck a nerve. They realized the truth in this, at least. It took another hour of wrangling before we could agree on various conditions and rules about how Fun Days would work. I was happy to let the discussion take its course. The final step was picking who would choose first. We agreed to draw straws, and Leonard hustled to the bar for plastic cocktail stirrers. I broke one in half and held them out at the same length so everyone could grab one.

"If I win, I'm not sharing what I like to do best," Dave said with a twinkle in his eye. "You saw the little fox I was with last night. Ain't had so much fun since the hogs ate my little brother. Not sharing her with any of you horndogs." That lightened the mood.

Mac pulled the short straw.

"First goddamn thing I won in a long while and I waste it on a damn drink stirrer." But he grinned. "Well, I know what I want to do. Been plannin on doin it anyways, guess this is good a time as any. I want to go shootin in the desert."

"What? You want to do what?" Leonard lurched half out of his chair.

"Now there's a damn fine idea," Mickey said, a grin splitting his face. "Varmint hunting."

"I'm not hunting anything." Leonard wasn't buying this. "That's a stupid idea, Mac."

"You didn't mean hunting, did you, Mac?" I said, hoping he noticed my eyes.

"Well no, wasn't my first thought, Mick. Been thinkin I'd go do me a little target shootin, keep my eye sharp, you know. I'd like to take my rifle and my pistol out there somewhere, set up some targets, and shoot some."

"That's within the rules I guess. But I don't have a gun, and others don't either." I glanced around.

Les paused for a second. "I bought a double fast-draw rig with six-shooters a few weeks ago." There was something I hadn't known. "I'd like to try 'em out."

"I'd be willing to get a gun—buy a gun," I said. I wanted this to work. "That might be okay."

Dave nodded. "Guess I'd buy a gun, too. Always wanted to get one someday."

Leonard looked uncertain, but Mac turned to him, "Look here Lenny, got me a pistol and a long gun, got a shotgun, too. You can use 'em. You can shoot one while I'm shootin one of the others. You could do that, couldn't you?"

Leonard noticed us all looking at him. He'd always been a group-oriented guy and gave us a reluctant nod. We were going shooting in the desert.

Mickey asked how we were going to pick who'd choose the activity for the next Fun Day. A good question, so we pulled straws again, and he won the Fun Day that would follow. He smiled and said he'd tell us what we'd be doing when he figured it out.

Over the next ten days, the group's attitude improved markedly as everybody prepared for our first Fun Day in more than two years. Les and Mac took Dave and me to a gun shop on Industrial Road, enthusiastically showing us around while they bought shells. I hadn't realized Les was a firearm enthusiast, he explained the difference between automatics and single and double-action revolvers. I decided on a James Bond pistol, a Beretta 9-millimeter semi-automatic with three 15-bullet magazines, a holster, and a cleaning kit to maintain it. Les added an impressive, silver-plated Ruger to his arsenal. Dave mentioned he'd always wanted a shotgun, so he and Mac picked out a double-barreled one with a walnut stock he admired.

We took dozens of glass, soda and beer, bottles and all the mayonnaise and jelly jars we could find with us to Mount Charleston for our Fun Day. It was a wonderful day among the trees, noticeably cooler and the air fresher than in the city. The smell of gunpowder hung over us for the next hour and a half. Leonard didn't enjoy the shooting as much as he did hanging out together, the way we used to do. He was a lot like me, locked up with his new girlfriend, Marie, though I pined for my distant wife; I wouldn't see for many more weeks.

I liked my pistol, admired it for its precision craftsmanship and enjoyed target practice. I learned how to clean it and found the smell of gun oil strangely fascinating. I never wanted to shoot at anything other than a coke bottle with it, though.

46 KEOKI

The name of a man is a numbing blow from which he never recovers.
—Marshall McLuhan

July 25, 1969
Las Vegas, Nevada

I HOPED FOLLOWING the Apollo 11 expedition would help distract me from worrying about Theresa. I'd received a letter from her a few days earlier.

She always mentioned how much she wished she were home, but she seemed especially dispirited in this letter, writing over and over how sad and lonely she was. Her words seemed steeped in remorse and fear for some reason. Everything will be okay, she promised, "as soon as I'm back in your arms again." She grieved over leaving me and begged me to believe she never would again, that she loved me forever. She wanted to call, she wrote, but knew she'd cry so hard she wouldn't be able to talk. The weight of her sadness dogged me at every step.

Was this normal? I didn't remember Pat experiencing this kind of depression before David or Dan's birth. I wanted to call and comfort her, but I hadn't yet.

For someone who'd loved science fiction from adolescence, the most astonishing aspect of sending men to the moon was watching it on television. Cruising to Mother Earth's satellite was no big deal in the books and stories I read—but actually watching Buzz Aldrin and Neil Armstrong step on another celestial body, live, from my couch, on TV, even in shaky black and white, set my brain on fire. None of my favorite science fiction authors had imagined that possibility.

I'd followed the mission's progress since the Saturn V launch rocket had lifted these intrepid heroes from the Kennedy Space Center in Florida as closely as I could. I'd snapped on the television early Thursday morning after work, forcing myself awake to witness Columbia's splashdown. Once the Navy helicopters had safely airlifted the astronauts to the aircraft carrier Hornet, I'd fallen asleep on the couch like a ton of bricks.

The next morning, a phone call from Theresa's mom, Wilhelmina, woke me. Every other thought in my head vanished. Mama Willi sounded tired but elated.

"Larry, your Theresa girl, she has given us a new baby boy last night. He weigh six pounds, eight ounces." A boy. Another son. *Why was a baby's weight so important when there were so many other important things to consider?*

"Is he healthy, Willi? That's the important thing."

"Oh, yes," her island-tinged accent whispered through the line. "He is fine. Especially his lungs. As for Theresa, she is doing fine now, too."

What? "Say that again, Willi, sounded like you said fine—now."

"There were some problems. She lost more blood than they expected. But she is well now, Larry. And you have one beautiful addition to your family." Had Theresa been in critical danger?

"You're sure she's all right? I mean, wasn't anything serious, was it?"

"Just like I say, she is tired from the delivery, but she is fine. Don't you worry your head." Somewhat relieved, I tried to be okay with that. If Mama Willi isn't too concerned, I guess I shouldn't be.

"Does our baby boy have a name yet?"

Theresa and I'd talked about what to call a boy. I'd suggested Malcolm, after my dad. I felt obligated. When Pat and I named our first son David, after Dave Dunn and two years later our second, Daniel, for no better reason than alliteration, Dad hadn't said a word. I'd never mentioned how much I'd disliked my names, first or last, to anyone before. I thought Lawrence was pretentious and provoked taunting, and Larry, weird and wimpy. Even my middle name, John, was a nickname for a toilet.

Youthful tormentors from my school years generally agreed with me by referring to me by my last name, Dunlap, in scorn, or its clever equivalent, Dumbass, or close cousins Dumbfuck, Dumbshit, or several other colorful epithets. I'd always believed name-teasing led to my early low esteem. I didn't want my sons' names to make them an easy target for taunting.

But when Pat and I decided to call the dog we adopted for the kids, George Malcolm, even though we nicknamed him Georgie, I noticed the skin around Dad's eyes and mouth tighten. Theresa and I should probably make amends for that, I reasoned. Theresa hadn't shown any enthusiasm for Malcolm, however, which gave me the excuse I needed. Malcolm was ten times worse than Lawrence; I didn't think it would be fair to our kid either. We settled on George to honor her father before Theresa judiciously proposed Malcolm for his middle name, and though he would share the same name with Dave and Dan's pet dog, that would have to appease my dad.

"I think the birth certificate only says Baby Dunlap right now," Willi said in response to my question. "She wants to talk with you before they complete it, but I think she would like Keoki Malcolm Dunlap."

I loved the idea of our boy having a Hawaiian name; not only was his birthright half Hawaiian, but his birthplace was an island paradise. That was definitely cool. But, I wondered why she hadn't named him George as we'd agreed.

"Thank you for calling Willi. Such exciting news. You're a wonderful grandmother. When do you think I can talk to her?"

"She'll be home on Monday. Why don't you call her then? Not too early so she will be fresh."

When I called, Theresa was only able to speak with me for a few minutes. She sounded breathless and weak but thrilled to hear my voice, and anxious to swear how much she loved and missed me and wanted to be home. If I'd had a magic genie, I would have rubbed the skin off its bones to grant her wish.

"Treese, honey, I want you home more than anything in the world. I love you with everything in my being. I'm so excited about seeing you and meeting our new son."

"He's sleeping now, my darling. He's such a big boy already. You would not believe it, but he has wisps of blond hair and blue eyes. He looks all over you, I swear. Mom and Dad are so excited and proud. I'm so happy honey, except I want to be with you, you are my whole life." She stopped, gasping, out of breath. The tremor in her voice made me shiver.

"Honey, please, take it easy. Everything is perfect and ready for you here. I've found a wonderful new house you will love, we even have our own swimming pool. You don't need to worry about a thing—just rest and get strong."

"Did Mama tell you I would like his name to be Keoki Malcolm Dunlap?"

"She did. It's great that he'll have a Hawaiian first name, that's perfect, but I thought you wanted to name him after your dad?"

Though the timbre of her laugh was shallow, I reveled in the joy of it as always. "Keoki means George in Hawaiian. So he is still George."

Theresa's long airmailed letter arrived three days later explaining what I hadn't been able to ask her. Keoki's birth had been much harsher than her mother let on. Her brothers and father gave extra blood at the hospital to help cover the cost of the four transfusions she'd received. My eyes blurred with the thought of nearly losing her. Here I was, twenty-five hundred miles away. That's not where a husband and father should be. But how could I have been there? I missed her desperately. She asked me to say hi to Joan and Lora and wondered if Susie was still in LA. Whatever was going on between Susie and Les that had caused her to leave him looked bad. Les wouldn't say anything, of course. He was unapproachable about personal matters. If Susie had told Theresa about what was going on, she wouldn't admit it. I couldn't imagine why they'd separated. I'd been as surprised as anyone.

47 HOT VEGAS NIGHTS

People will forget you said, people will forget what you did, but people will never forget how you made them feel.
—Maya Angelou

July 31, 1969
Las Vegas, Nevada

IN THE DAYS following Barbara Streisand's opening at Kerkorian's International Hotel, before Elvis's off-again, on-again debut, the town went insane. Not even Frank Sinatra could have electrified the city more than Elvis Presley's upcoming appearance. As every day passed, I was sure at any moment we'd be asked to move to the Crown Room in concurrence with what would be history, even for Vegas: Elvis's legendary opening night.

But I couldn't get a confirmation from Seymour or Bill Miller's office. It was as if they didn't know or there was something secret about it. Construction had stalled at the new nightclub. Though the Sky Room felt like home and I wasn't anxious to leave, the silence was disconcerting.

After his opening night, Elvis frenzy continued to rise. We thought he might drop in to see us once the delirium settled a little. But the hysteria grew. I'm sure he found it difficult to go anywhere in public that August. Though he didn't come in then, most of his TCB—Taking Care of Business— band, as he'd named the musicians who backed him, dropped in at one time or another.

All of us in the band, especially Les, were thrilled when James Burton, Elvis's guitarist, strolled through the curtains into the Sky Room. We welcomed him, and he remembered us from when we'd played back to back together at the Hullabaloo Afterhours in Hollywood. We didn't encourage musicians to sit in with us the way we had at the Cat, but when spectacular players came in, it was exciting to have them come up and play with us, and it often created memorable experiences. One night, late, James brought his guitar case to the stage. It was an indelible musical moment to watch the great James Burton trade licks with our Bear, Les, who held his own with this guitar master.

A few minutes later, Leonard gave his drumsticks to a lanky guy with a boyish smile who'd stepped up to join us. I didn't know much about Jim Gordon at the time. He was considered the heir-apparent to Hal Blaine, a founding member of the Wrecking Crew and every producer on the West Coast's first-call drummer. He'd teamed with Eric Clapton in the Delaney and Bonnie band and would soon help form Derek and the Dominoes with Eric. The two of them would collaborate on Clapton's classic lament of hopeless love, *Layla*, inspired by Clapton's uncontrollable passion for Pattie Boyd, who was married to his friend George Harrison of the Beatles—one of the most famous and public love triangles in rock-and-roll history.

With Burton and Gordon on stage with us, though I was far from the greatest keyboard player on either coast, I played the Hammond B3 organ like I was possessed. The skills and talent of the players on stage were so rock solid, I was caught up in their sheer musicality and constrained emotion as we burned through lengthy jams extending far past our usual break.

Afterward, I was drained flat by the purity of the music that had flowed without volition from my fingers, not a note out of place. The unyielding rhythms had lifted and guided me through time without measure, synchronizing the flow of my heart's blood to the sublime players, who I now held as cherished companions who I'd shared an other-worldly experience with. I felt weirdly exposed and embarrassed when our public intimacy ended. I slouched quietly at my B3 letting the sensitivity recede. These musicians had taken me as a guest to the lodestone, to sip at the virginal source of music's great river of emotion true musicians can tap right out of the ether and transform into reality. I'd been gripped by euphoric moments while singing perfect harmonies at times, but though I'd sat at this keyboard for six out of seven nights for three years, I'd never experienced such powerful sense of unity as I had just now as a player. I'd caught a glimpse of something so fundamental that there were no words for it. It was the most memorable night of my life as a musician.

The Flamingo Sky Room, now the place to see and be seen in Las Vegas, attracted star power. It was never short of beautiful people, a natural outcome of its design. Having famous personalities, artists, and entertainers, some of them appearing on billboards, the sides of buses, and main room marquees, show up in our room any given night intimidated us at first. But over time, stars and dignitaries became a regular part of the scenery.

Out of respect, we made it a point to recognize celebs visiting the Sky Room. Though we were the headliner, we realized celebrity watching was a popular attraction for many. We knew much of our popularity was from the reflected glory of their presence. Many of the well-known, I've found, will say they wish to remain anonymous in public, but were as often incensed by not being acknowledged. Knowing when and when not to publicly notice someone famous is a gray line, not always perceptible, but we tried. I took it upon myself to make sure luminaries who came in never felt slighted and to offer hospitable welcomes to those we might have missed acknowledging from the stage. Most people were gracious, and some welcomed conversation, but I never presumed beyond providing a simple thanks for visiting.

Late one night, Johnny Carson came in and sat alone at a cocktail table near a floor-to-ceiling column between us and the bar. On my way off stage, I walked by to greet him.

"Hi, thank you for dropping by, Mr. Carson," I said with a smile. He glanced at me, a viciousness in his eyes, before enunciating with the slow, distinct clarity of the exceedingly intoxicated, "Get. The fuck. Away from me."

Surprised and chastened, I hid my shock and sidled away. He must have had a rough day.

As for our own celebrity, I never considered us that way at all, and I think most of my brethren agreed. We couldn't think of ourselves in that strata until we'd put a hit on top of the *Billboard* charts. I didn't feel any kind of special. I was simply a guy from Indiana who'd been miraculously whipped across the sky at hundreds of miles an hour to a magical land. Over the last few years, I'd followed the yellow brick road of music from San Francisco to Hollywood to Honolulu through many adventures to here in Oz. I'm not suggesting we hadn't worked hard to become a skilled and respected vocal group and performing band, but the memories of scuffling along the backside of life, a resident outsider in my own hometown, remained fresh.

The band developed warm relationships with favorite shared celebrities like Billy Joe Royal, Tom Jones, Herbie and Sonny from the Platters, and too many others to list. But my personal favorites were Don and Phil Everly, who could have been neighborhood pals from down the block in Indianapolis. Phil liked to kid around about having to get Don back to the hotel so he could plug him into an electrical outlet in their suite. He was referring to Phil's therapy after a tough recovery from some mind-bending painkillers. Then they'd laugh with each other like maniacs. They seemed to take everything in stride.

I'd listened to their hits narrate my teenage life and thought they got more harmony out of two voices than many groups did with four or more. In the days they played in Las Vegas and came in to see us, their hits were mostly behind them, but everybody in music knew their signature sound, and their string of successes. Their creativity made them rock-and-roll nobility forever.

Leonard was in his element in this environment. Without a way to take his crazy conga line outside the way he had at other nightclubs, he'd toyed with the idea of taking a long column of Sky Room patrons down the stairs to the casino until Jim Seagrave got wind of it and scotched that notion. Undeterred, he worked out other outrageous routines spun off from his nightly drum solo that made him a fan favorite.

Somewhere, he'd acquired a giant rubber ball with a handle he could bounce on from behind his drums out onto the dance floor, and even weave through the tables. When Big Jim Sullivan first brought Tom Jones in to see us, Leonard popped out from behind his drums to jump his spheroid vehicle into the crowd, where he proceeded to torment Tom with a plastic hammer that produced squeaky noises when he pummeled him with it. Tom thought it was hilarious and from that moment on, people in the audience tried to attract Leonard to bounce their way to them and wallop them with his squeaky hammer.

One night, a car crash at the intersection on the Strip below our window was so loud it penetrated the double-paned glass and brought everyone to the windows to see what had happened. One of Las Vegas's most beloved comics, Shecky Green, had piled his car against a streetlight in the median just before Flamingo Road. A few minutes later, after Mac had narrated his trip away from the accident, across Las Vegas Boulevard without getting hit, into the casino entrance, and up the stairs to the Sky Room, Shecky arrived at the bar laughing with everybody and trading friendly quips with Mac at the microphone.

I'd taken enormous pleasure in introducing Theresa to fascinating people we'd only seen on television, in movies, or heard on records. As the summer months passed, I missed not having her with me to meet more of the amazing people I was brushing shoulders with in our star-studded environment. As the months ran on, it became an example of how the most spectacular of times can eventually become commonplace.

48 REUNITED

Every person, all the events of your life are there because you have drawn them there.
       —Richard Bach

August 6, 1969
Las Vegas, Nevada

TIME FLOWED TOO slow—and too fast. While I could barely wait until Theresa and I could resume the threads of our interrupted life, my skin crawled with anxiety. After two and a half months of endless longing and the momentous change Keoki's birth presented, our realities had split. Things were different now; she was familiar with the reality of our new child. Did she wonder and worry how or if we could return to our fairytale life, as I did?

My mind was running through these concerns as we got a surprise when we came in to start a new week. There was a new band ending the second of their early sets. Shango had disappeared without warning. Too bad, they'd been easy guys to get along with and an excellent little band.

A few hours later, Mac came looking for me in the break room. Dave, Les, and I sat wedged around a table playing three-handed, cut-throat Euchre where they were beating my socks off-5. "Hey man, you ain't never gonna guess who's out there askin for you. Remember Mark Anthony, our bartender pal from the Pink Carousel?"

It had been two years since I'd seen or heard from Mark. He'd been bartending at a club in Downey, California, where we were while he waited for his big break as a standup comic. I would never forget his friendship and help after I'd received an induction notice and almost everyone, including me, was sure I'd be shipped to Vietnam. We clutched and hugged each other. I found us seats at the bar and ordered drinks. He had the same lopsided smile, but the playful sparkle in his eye was missing.

"Don't go by Mark Anthony anymore," he said when I asked how things were with him. "Not since the standup thing didn't pan out. Wanted a career in comedy, but turns out I needed to get paid, too. Those two things turned out to be mutually exclusive. I'm plain old Mark Pichnarcik now." He dipped his face into a bourbon and rocks.

"Had to get outta LA, man. Lucky to catch a ride to Vegas with friends. Now I'm seeing how far I can get before my shoes wear out."

I was surprised to see how badly his confidence had been blown but hesitated to ask. "What's going on in SoCal?"

"Weird you should ask. Something that made me think of you. You and some of the guys used to get your hair cut at Jay Sebring's in Bev Hills, didn't you?

"Yeah, but not Beverly Hills. We went to his salon on Fairfax. Been a while, though. Other than a quick overnighter for recording, haven't been to Hollywood since we opened the Sky Room. Still order Sebring shampoo and conditioner by mail, though. Love the stuff." I zipped open the cellophane on a pack of Tareyton 100's and peeled back the foil on top. I'd been pretty fickle about brands lately, smoking Viceroys, Raleighs, and Parliaments, too. If I couldn't find something I liked soon, I might have to give the damn things up.

"Then you haven't heard what happened to him?"

"What do you mean?" I pounded out a couple of smokes and offered one to Mark.

"All over the news there. Someone broke into a party in the Hollywood Hills and killed him—him and four other people including the director Roman Polanski's wife, Sharon Tate, and Abigail Folger, the Folger Coffee heiress."

"Jesus! That's horrible. I met Jay and saw him a few times, but he never cut my hair personally. He was either at the other salon or more often on a movie set. What kind of maniac would do something like that?"

"*LA Times* reported it as some kind of drug deal gone wrong at first, but the brutal way these people were tortured before they were murdered, they're starting to question that. The rumors are getting really creepy. Sharon Tate was nearly full-term pregnant, and brother, the way she and the baby were carved up . . ." He shook his head, deeply troubled. "Truthfully, it was the last straw. Too much sick shit in the news there had to book, man." I'd never seen him so low. "I'm telling you, man, scary shit—people talking about a possible race war. Took the first chance to pull up stakes and split."

I'd heard something about celebrity murders in LA, but my thoughts had been elsewhere; I wasn't paying much attention to current affairs. But even before we'd left, I'd noticed a growing tension in California. The unrest that had begun as a peace movement seemed to have taken a darker turn.

A light-bulb idea clicked on. I remembered how Mark's optimism had helped me through a dark time. His humor and persistent belief that things would work out kept my spirits up when I'd thought it would cost me my place in the band, not to mention the strong possibility of getting my ass shot off in some Southeast Asian jungle. Despite his shocking news, seeing him cheered me; maybe I could return the favor.

"Where are you staying?"

"Haven't figured it out yet. Got any inexpensive suggestions? Motel on the Strip, or downtown somewhere?"

"No. Have a better idea." I crushed out my cigarette. "Come stay with me."

"Don't know, man. I never intended to stay. On my way home eventually, just needed to get away for a while before I slink back to Arizona."

"Look, you won't be an imposition. In fact, you'll be helping me out. My wife, who you'll meet, gave birth to our new baby boy in Hawaii a few days ago. She's there with her family and can't fly home yet. I'm living in an empty house I hate going home to every night. If you haven't got anywhere you have to be, please keep me from going nuts until she gets here."

Mark was an upbeat, funny guy when he was his usual self, and there was plenty of room in the three-bedroom house I rattled around in. He'd help fill the lonely hours that dragged at me, and I welcomed the opportunity to repay his previous kindnesses. We'd lift each other out of our brown moods. He accepted my offer to stay for a night or two, but after a couple of days, he agreed to remain until Theresa came home if I accepted his offer to maintain the pool and grounds, and, he'd throw in being my personal bartender, too.

Mark and I stood on the McCarran Airport tarmac, made tacky by the raging July sun in a sky so brilliant it was almost white. We watched Theresa's Western Airlines jet rotate its front wheel toward us. The ground crew rushed the rolling stairs to the fuselage. I'd filled Mark's ears with how much I missed Theresa, how incredible and lovely she was, and how happy I was that he would be able to meet her. I tried to contain my nervous excitement. As her arrival with our new child had drawn near, I'd grown more and more jittery, even more anxious than when she'd first come from Hawaii.

Our letters were full of passion and promise, but sometimes hers seemed laced with insecurity and remorse for not staying home in Las Vegas. I attempted to ease her worries in my replies. A few days earlier, sensing the unease in her words, I'd called to suggest upgrading her to first class; I also offered to fly to Honolulu and ride back to assist her with the baby. I'd been surprised when I received an air-mailed letter from her yesterday. In it, she written that her best friend Charlene would be flying with her to help with Keoki for a few days.

Please don't upgrade my ticket, she'd written. If I did, Charlene wouldn't be able to help her with Keoki, and she'd be alone in the front cabin. *Why*, I wondered, *did she wait until the last minute to tell me this in a letter?* I'd been waiting for a phone call so I could change her reservation if she wanted to fly first class or to book one for myself. *Did she think I would disapprove?* I liked the idea of someone to help her, but I sensed something troubling in the panicky way she expressed her need for Charlene to come with her. *Did she want someone along for moral support, did she fear things might have changed between us?* I shoved the thought aside—that was crazy—nothing could change the way I felt about her. Any concerns she had would disappear as soon as we held each other again.

After the first rush of passenger unloading, Theresa, with Charlene close behind, slipped past the airplane's open door cradling a light-blue bundle. I shuffled forward, entranced, absorbing every moment of her descent. She knew I was there, but she wouldn't look my way. I guessed she was nervous, too. But when she stepped down from the last step, she lifted her eyes and my heart melted. Neither of us could stop the tears streaming down our faces. She swiped fingers across her eyes before she lifted the light blanket covering Keoki's face for me to see. He wrinkled his tiny face at me, and I smiled. I saw the elation on her face as she handed him off to Charlene and rushed into the big hug I'd been dying to give her.

"God," I whispered into her ear, the rich aroma of her hair beginning to untangle my soul. "I've missed holding you, sweetheart. I don't want to let go, not even long enough to get us home." She held me tight, laughing through her tears.

"Hold me, darling, forever long as you like. I don't want to let go either."

Eventually, it got embarrassing, so we reluctantly separated. Mark had gotten acquainted with Charlene, and I introduced him to Theresa. I'd written to her what a fantastic friend he'd been, and how he'd kept me sane during these last few days.

Theresa loved our new home, and it didn't take us long to get organized. Charlene agreed to bunk in with Keoki so Mark could stay in the second bedroom he occupied rather than moving to the couch before he set off for Phoenix in the next couple of days. While Charlene unpacked for the baby and herself, I finally had the chance to be alone with Theresa in the master bedroom where I'd brought her suitcases.

"Honey, I know you just got off the plane, and I haven't even shown you around our new home, but I'm not sure I can wait any longer," I said after a steamy round of passionate kisses. "If you're okay with it, I desperately want to make love to you."

"I've been fantasizing about this moment for so long," she whispered, dreamy-eyed. "I would be in my bedroom sometimes and think it wasn't real, that you weren't real. I need to feel you, all of you, so I'll know it's true. I need to know I'm really home with you again." She stopped for a moment to glance down apologetically. "Unless you think I'm too fat. I thought I could work off the weight I gained, but these last few pounds have been harder to lose than I expected."

"Let me show you what I think." My fingers trembled, fumbling with zippers and buttons as I removed her clothing. My wife and new mother of our son posed hesitantly, her eyes searching mine for approval. God help me, she was as stunning as ever. I tried not to tire her out, but I couldn't get enough of being close to her. I hoped Keoki would be okay without his mom for the next few hours. When Theresa and I eventually emerged, we were far more refreshed and relaxed. Leaving for work that night was difficult, but I forced myself out into the late-night air knowing my wife was finally home sleeping in our own bed.

49 WHISPERS IN THE WIND

Sometimes your heart needs more time to accept what your mind already knows.
—widely accepted relationship truism

August 28, 1969
Las Vegas, Nevada

THE FOLLOWING THURSDAY, as Les returned from a break, an energetic young guy bounced over to dump a guitar amplifier on the Sky Room stage. The amp was upholstered in a sparkly, turquoise-green, tuck-and-roll vinyl, a style more often seen in SoCal low-rider cars reupholstered in Tijuana. I got there in time to hear him tell Les, "Got a deal for you, man, if you want it."

Les turned away to take his guitar off its stand.

"Don't you even want to know what it is? Pretty sure you'll like it."

"Okay," Les said with little enthusiasm. "I'll probably be sorry, but I'll bite. What's your deal?"

"Simple. You try out this amplifier I manufacture. You like it, and promise to use it, it's yours." Les stopped fiddling with his guitar knobs to listen. "My name is Bud Ross. I own Kustom Electronics." He flopped a hand at his speaker. "We make amps. I'm here displaying them at the Music Dealer's show at the convention center this weekend. Asked around for who's the best band with the best guitar picker who hadn't been invited to Woodstock. Turned out to be you guys. If people from the show see you playing my Kustom amp when they come in here, and a lot of 'em will, cheap advertising for me, and lucky for you."

Les wouldn't promise anything, but he agreed to try it. At the end of the set, I couldn't hear any difference between the Kustom and his Fender speakers. He looked out at the table where Bud Ross sat with a couple of other guys and nodded. Some of us hung out at Bud's table during our breaks. He turned out to be a fast-talking, fun-loving guy hailing from Chanute, Kansas, with an accent as broad as the plains he lived on. But oh, how he loved Vegas and he adored hanging out with musicians. He thought of himself as more of a bass player than an amplifier manufacturer, he liked being one of the guys, he told us. And, oh yeah, the money was better in the selling amplifiers business.

A package with a tape in it from Eddie arrived the next day instructing us to learn and arrange the vocal lyrics of the instrumental theme *What Is a Youth*, from the four-Oscar-nominated movie *Romeo and Juliet*. The plan was to back it with *Mixed Emotions* and release them as a single. It would only be Dave, Les, and me on the vocals. To save time, more of the first-call Wrecking Crew session players, the same expert studio players who'd performed on *Mixed Emotions*, were already recording the basic tracks. Les would contribute his guitar work to the instrumental track while we were there.

Be ready, he wrote, *to fly to LA on short notice.* I hoped it wouldn't be too soon. I was getting used to a house full of family and friends.

Motherhood demanded Theresa arrange her hours around Keoki, not me, so it was generally Mark who kept me company as the evening hours dwindled before I got ready for work. He took his job as bartender seriously, concocting various drinks I would sample. He told me it helped keep his skills sharp, and he was currently working his way through differing Galliano-based recipes. Since the night he'd come to stay, I could tell he wasn't sure what to do with his life, and we talked about many things during those hours. I hoped I was helping him rebuild his confidence; I was sure he could be successful at whatever he chose. When I got the call telling us to be in LA the next Monday, I was happy he and Charlene would be there to watch over my little family. Maybe it would feed the little spark of something I thought I noticed between them.

On Saturday night, after the trade show ended, Bud dropped into the Sky Room again. We thought only Les had gotten lucky until he gathered us around him to make us another offer.

"Look, I think we can help each other out here. Les says you guys endorse Mosrite guitars, damn fine instruments. Got a Mosrite bass myself. What say Kustom sponsors you? I got a whole passel of matching Cascade Sparkle Naugahyde amps, teal ones like the one I already gave you. I mean speakers built for everywhere a band would ever play. Hell, you could work an arena with what-all I got for you. Be a damn sight cheaper to drop 'em off for you than truck 'em back to Kansas, I'll save money in the long run."

As he'd promised, a huge truck arrived late Sunday afternoon and left us a wide variety of amps of all sizes. He didn't have the paperwork with him, he said, but he would leave everything anyway. He intended to be back in Vegas soon, and we'd sign the endorsement agreement then. He'd outfitted us with little studio amplifiers, mid-size ones for nightclubs, even five-foot-high multi-speaker units for vocals and concert stages that I didn't see how we'd fit in our van. Bud included a funny little monster-doll made of the same stuff covering the amps—he called it a Nauga.

Dave, Les, and I piled into a rental car after we arrived at LAX Monday morning. Though worn from long hours over the last six nights, our voices were in decent shape. Our pal Emory Gordy, whose musical talent and studio skills we'd come to respect, had done the charts for the musical arrangement. I listened in pleasure to the final track, brilliant from the beginning with ringing piano lines, French horns, little rising string and woodwind themes that accentuated, supported, and framed the vocals without competing with them. Eddie was there for most of the session, but it was Emory's show.

With the tracks laid down, it didn't take long to get into the vocals. We hadn't had much time to rehearse it, but Les had decided we'd do *What Is a Youth* in a Letterman style. Dave's voice held out, and the recording went smoothly, Emory was a joy to work with. This was my favorite session since we'd come to California. I thought the three of us blended perfectly, and if we'd had a bit more time to polish it, I thought it could have been even better.

I corralled Eddie suggesting he find us some original ballads the three of us could sing, not in this chamber music style or this close to the Lettermen, but still emphasizing our harmony. "No," He'd said, "I miss Mac's voice in the mix. His voice is so textured, he sings on both sides of the note, mellows out the pure voices of you three."

I hadn't thought of it in that context, and while I got the point, I might have been more willing to concede it if Mac took better care of his voice. It was another clue I remembered when I reconsidered the way Eddie wanted to produce our voices.

We got back to Las Vegas late, so I was careful not to wake anyone. The next morning Mark abruptly announced he was leaving for Phoenix. He'd called home and found that his father was extremely ill. Within a day or two, Charlene continued on to California before returning to Hawaii. Once they were gone, our little nuclear family searched for a rhythm of life on our own.

Things had changed with the group's wives. While Theresa had been away, the surprise separation of Susie and Les had fractured their little society. Les had begun dating a nurse from Spring Valley Hospital named Vikki. She seemed nice, but she hadn't become a part of the girls' society, and since Les and Susie weren't divorced yet, that wouldn't change anytime soon. While Theresa found occasional opportunities to bring Keoki to evenings with Lora and Joan, Mickey and Mac's wives, they no longer got together regularly. The dynamics of the foursome were gone, and she missed her best friend, Susie. It left her disappointed and missing the camaraderie of her friends. Our normal routine wasn't the same as before she'd left, either. We were parents now, and far too often on the wrong side of the clock from each other.

50 ROOM WITH A VIEW

Fear of heights is fear of a desire to jump.
—Amruta Patil

September 19, 1969
Las Vegas, Nevada

ELEVEN WEEKS AND two days after the International Hotel's official opening, I finally trundled my B3 out of the elevator onto the spacious landing of the penthouse floor. The Crown Room was finally ready for us. Moving from the Sky Room felt somewhat anticlimactic, though. We'd missed being part of the International's worldwide launch and Barbara Streisand's gala performances in the two-thousand-seat supper club. I'd assumed we'd move to the Crown Room when Elvis followed her there, but the room still wasn't finished, and it seemed like nobody was working on it. It remained that way through the four weeks of Elvis's legendary fifty-eight sold-out appearances. When Nancy Sinatra took over the showroom from Elvis with an elaborate show that brought out the entire Sinatra clan, we were still at the Flamingo Sky Room. Now, she was in her last week.

In a short corridor on the right, I were a set of gleaming paneled doors—the Elvis suite. He could be in there now—it was his new Las Vegas home-away-from-Memphis. I wheeled my beast of an organ in the opposite direction toward the nightclub's curtained entrance. Inside, I gazed through the floor-to-ceiling windows into a late-afternoon western sky beyond the Las Vegas Strip. Herringbone cloud patterns stitched shadows from the valley up into the Spring

Mountain foothills. Overall, the room's layout was similar to the Sky Room's, though it seemed larger, extending farther beyond the bar. The stage was comparable, though higher here because the dance floor wasn't sunken.

We were scheduled for Friday night so we could open the weekend with a bang. The maître d's and the bar and wait staff, along with our early band, the Happy Medium, had begun working out the kinks in a "soft" opening three nights earlier. They combined to welcome us and made us feel at home.

The view through the Crown Room's windows at night when we kicked off our first set was as impressive as the Sky Room's, though for different reasons. At the Flamingo, we'd overlooked zooming traffic and the hustle and bustle of the busy intersection below us from the height of a single story. Here on the thirtieth floor, tucked below the roof's forty-foot-tall International sign, we had an eagle's eye view. The light show from the Strip ran south to the Flamingo Hotel and beyond as it bent to the southwest, and north toward the haloed sky above downtown Vegas.

We hadn't received the publicity I'd expected from the new hotel; our name didn't even appear on the marquee. Where it had once appeared on six-foot letters on the Paradise Road marquee, the mammoth sign at the hotel's entrance only mentioned "Dancing Nightly in the Crown Room;" as if we were an afterthought. Word-of-mouth must have been responsible for the full house when we stepped on stage—and a line that curlicued outside the velvet drapes—and the long, and unexpected queue waiting patiently in front of the express elevator on the first floor.

Of course, I considered with sardonic skepticism, *the highly publicized kinetic color wall might have been what packed the place.* The seventy-foot-long wall decoration embedded along the interior wall had received more national and local hype in newspapers and television than we had. Created by a local nuclear engineer, this ballyhooed attraction was supposed to produce colors and patterns in reaction to the music. Instead, it displayed turgid undulations generally unnoticed and ignored by the crowd. So, my guess, probably not.

We played our usual mix of music for much of the same audience who'd followed us from the Flamingo, though there were more hotel guests and tourists mixed in here. With numerous restaurants, shops, entertainment spots, and gambling venues inside the giant resort, many guests elected to stay here rather than hop a cab over to the Strip.

While our co-workers made us feel at home, the same could not be said for top management. There was no Jim Seagrave here, no go-to guy I could count on. Though I didn't know Jim's boss, Bill Miller well, he always seemed congenial and made us feel we were an essential part of the Flamingo's talent lineup. I'd thought Bill would manage the entertainment for both hotels. If so, he apparently didn't choose to interfere with the way the International's GM, Alex Shoofey, supervised our room. I remember meeting Mr. Shoofey early in our engagement. I felt I'd been excised from his memory in the time it took him to turn away. Maybe he didn't like rock and roll, or our name—that wouldn't be a first. My guess was he would have preferred a restaurant at the top of his hotel and had gotten stuck with us instead. But apparently, as long as the numbers for the room remained high enough, he left us alone. I never heard from him again. Not even when I needed help with the serious problem of not having a dressing room for the band. Not even a break room. The main reason the club was bigger than the Sky Room was the entertainers' break room had been eliminated, we didn't even have that tiny refuge. There was no place to keep our stage clothes or dress for the night, or to escape between the long sets without riding the elevator down to the casino level to look for somewhere in the crowds to hang out. No one seemed to care about our problems except us, though, which led to our forays out onto the roof.

A few weeks into the gig, Mac nudged me as we were going on break.

"Come on, bub." He gestured toward our singular view from the Crown Room windows. "Let's go smoke a doob and check out the scenery."

The band's resolve about smoking weed at work had weakened at the Flamingo after we'd been there for a while. Our dressing rooms were so isolated it wasn't uncommon for those of us who partook to sip a joint after the night was over. But there was no place like that here, so Mac, being Mac, had somehow charmed one of the maîtres d's to unlock the fire door to the roof.

I started to remind him that we'd agreed as a band not to get stoned at work but hesitated. It was difficult to take the moral high ground now that I no longer smoked.

"You do remember I can't get loaded, don't you?" I said, exasperated.

"Oh, sure. Right," he said in that off-handed way that let me know he hadn't. In his heart, Mac maintained a profound disbelief in my claim to be physically unable to get high from smoking marijuana. We'd had a short conversation between us shortly after I'd told him I was no longer affected by reefer madness.

"So assumin what you're sayin's true, explain to me how this thing is possible," he said, eye's squinted against the smoke from a joint's blazing cherry. "Use small words now, so I can comprehend it. Did that auditing deal mess with your mind some way? Make you not want to get high anymore?"

"You kidding me? Hell no. I would give anything to get stoned. With you and Dave, and Bear if he was willing. Especially with Theresa." Neither Mickey nor Leonard cared for loco weed. My sigh came out like a groan. "I haven't changed a lick, Mac. I just can't."

"Maybe you was hypnotized."

"No, I wasn't hypnotized. Guy asked me a bunch of simple questions and asked me to tell him what they made me think of. Nothing else." He thought it over.

"You ever think of just sittin down with a pile of joints and smokin til you like—broke through or somethin?"

"Won't work. I did say I can't get high. Didn't say I couldn't get sick. Grass gives me a headache and an upset stomach." Mac wasn't the only one. It went against my bandmates' sense of reality that holding a couple of empty frozen juice cans while talking to someone could cause me to lose my pathway to earthly bliss.

"You've got to know by now it's true. How many times have I tried to smoke with you and Dave?" It frustrated me; how could guys who knew me so well think I would, or even could, try to fool them about this? What would be the point? Did everybody think I snuck off and zoned out by myself? When I was feeling charitable, I had to admit it seemed impossible, too.

"Come out, anyway," Mac pushed out through the door to the roof. "We can still dig the vibe together, man."

At least, I thought, if he was going to smoke grass, there was less chance of getting caught here than sneaking around outside the hotel.

I cautiously put a foot out onto the International's roof. Being three hundred feet above the desert below scared the bejeezus out of me. A stiff breeze wafted in an acrid stink from the cooling roofing material. The bulk of the forty-foot International sign rose above me as I stepped out, still holding tight to the door. Since there was no public access, there were no safety railings or other precautions to keep anyone from falling off the edge.

"What's the matter, Larry?" Les grabbed my arm and tried to pull me away from the door; I hadn't realized he was out here. He knew heights terrified me and loved to torment me about it. He'd forced me onto a Wild Mouse roller coaster in Cincinnati in front of the rest of the band not so long ago. I'd swallowed my own puke halfway through the ride and crawled away afterward.

"The view is incredible out at the edge. You're not going to want to miss this." I white-knuckled my grip on the doorframe and hung on for dear life. "Don't worry." He grinned like the Joker in a Batman comic. "I won't let you fall."

My fear of heights wasn't a secret, and in general, if I kept a tight rein on my imagination, it didn't affect me too much when I was in a jetliner. A couple of weeks earlier that had been tested. Bud Ross, who owned Kustom Amplifiers had flown back to Vegas in his new Learjet. He'd arranged a time for us to meet and sign an endorsement contract and take publicity photos with him and the new equipment. When we met him at the airport, he told us his schedule had changed, and he needed to postpone our photo session until the next day.

"Look, I've got some business to do, but since you guys had to come here, got a special treat for you. My pilot wants to show off my plane to a buddy from Nellis he used to fly with in the Air Force. So, you guys get to go along for the ride." Nellis was a massive Air Force base not far north of Vegas.

I'd have chewed my arm off to the elbow to miss this particular honor but considering the thousands of dollars of equipment lavished on us, I felt obligated. I frantically reviewed excuses to avoid getting on the tiny jet about the size of a Lincoln Town Car with swept-back wings. I generally didn't mind flying—as long as it was in big jets, like the ones we flew to and from Hawaii. But this thing was ridiculous. It was like a toy. It was way too tiny and flimsy.

Bud cheerily herded me in last and lifted the step to close the door behind me. The only space left was a narrow seat tucked into the plane's tail. I'd barely gotten myself wedged in before the aircraft began to taxi. I thought we were approaching the runway for takeoff when our pilot suddenly accelerated and stuck the jet's nose straight up in a vertical climb toward outer space.

It took all my effort to literally keep my shit inside as the G-force hit us, and I'm sure I screamed into the roar the engines created. Within fifteen minutes, the pilot announced we'd arrived over the Grand Canyon before flipping a wing and zooming into a gut-clenching dive into the massive rip in the earth's crust. He seemed determined to pancake us into the Colorado River.

Windows, inches from my head to the left and right made it impossible to ignore the speed we traveled and how close we were flying to the canyon wall. Back where I was, the slipstream growled in a malignant whine, and violent vibrations shook my body. Before my insides could follow, the jet nosed up toward the sun again; the view from my windows would have been spectacular to anyone who didn't fear traveling where only angels flew.

When we finally dropped into an abrupt landing at McCarran Airport, I had to be pried out of the seat. I am sure I indented permanent claw marks into the armrests. Everybody but Leonard, who wasn't with us, told me I looked white as toothpaste. Les near laughed himself to death. He considered that kind of thing hysterical.

Eventually, Les gave up on the fun he'd anticipated in pulling me to the brink of the roof and joined the others in pretending to push one another off. Once I thought it was safe, I took a couple of half-crawling steps out on the roof. Open space spread out along the north wing of the hotel next to the club. I spotted a flat area with some bars or scaffolding, perhaps for some future structure. I held on to a metal bar and felt secure enough in the rippling desert breeze to let in the sights.

A quarter moon revealed streams of headlights moving below like tiny nocturnal insects along Paradise Road, mostly from the south, and on Sahara coming across from Las Vegas Boulevard. I could make out the moaning susurration of their motors in the chilly night. The International Hotel had become a destination; the perception of whether a major resort could exist away from the Strip was no longer in question. A shudder passed through me. *Enough adventure.* I scuttled back to the safety of the Crown Room.

Our little family celebrated Theresa's twentieth birthday quietly at home, though Keoki, at three months, napped through most of it. He was a studious infant, serenely examining his mom and me and everything around him as she opened presents in the cusp of our little family's glow. Celebrating her birthday with our little boy was a bonding moment for us to treasure.

It was a happy evening, but it reminded how much I'd missed her on her last birthday when she'd gone to Hawaii to visit friends and family. She'd spoken of how she hadn't had a chance to say goodbye and needed to return to her island home every now and again, so she could be comfortable away from it. I accepted that. She was a young girl and had never lived anywhere else in her life before she'd come to California. We hadn't formally committed to each other then. I'd believed that all we'd experienced with each other in Waikiki and our constant pledges of love and affection since, held us together. Still, while she was gone, I'd worried and wondered if she would come back.

Now, life had finally begun to settle into a routine. Keoki pretty much set his own hours and required a lot of attention, Theresa was usually asleep before I hit the shower to get ready for work. But tonight, after bedding down the baby, she stayed up with me to celebrate with lengthy lovemaking and shared bathing before I had to go. Locking the door behind me, knowing the center of my life slept in these darkened rooms, made leaving difficult. Never more so than this night.

51 THE INTERNATIONAL CROWN ROOM

> *Las Vegas is a city of kickbacks. A desert city of greased palms. A place where a $20 bill can buy approval, a $100 bill adulation and $1,000 canonization.*
>
> —Nicholas Pileggi

October 7, 1969
Las Vegas, Nevada

RED FOXX WAS headlining in the lounge, and I wanted to experience him live. Pat and I and our married friends had gotten a lot of laughs from his comedy albums back in Indiana. Red's humor was shockingly blue, but so funny we laughed ourselves into hiccups. At the Flamingo, professional courtesy would usually get us into any show; as long as there were empty back booths or tables, we'd be welcome to sit at them.

The same policy didn't apply at the International, but no one seemed to mind if I snuck into the lighting booths to savor performances by consummate entertainers. Watching Red Foxx work from high above the stage became a favorite way to spend long breaks; his spontaneity made every show hilariously different.

After a while, I realized that though he played off his audience's responses, his sketches weren't as off-the-cuff as they seemed; skill and planning were involved. Red had been playing nightclubs for more years than I'd been alive, and his stagecraft was so smooth, the mechanics were nearly invisible.

At first, I'd assumed he'd been doing his routines for so long he could walk out cold and wing it with a crowd solely relying on his vast repertoire of jokes and stories. After several consecutive shows, I noticed the way his act veered off in consistently specific directions no matter where he started or how an audience reacted. He even arranged help from co-conspirators. He prepped waiters and waitresses to respond to specific comments that let him switch to pre-determined topics during a performance. Most anecdotes he related spun a thread to another; Red navigated his show like a boat captain on a river. He sometimes extemporized, of course, but not for long. Soon, he'd work his way back to a well-worn path. Such quick-witted improvisation would have been virtually impossible for a comic performing two or more shows a night, every night. Especially considering his questionable sobriety from show to show. He'd worked out a clever illusion to make himself appear brilliantly spontaneous.

Mort Sahl's routine when we'd appeared with him at Caesars Palace had been different. He'd been one of my longtime favorite comedians, too, and I'd been astonished to see his name on the bill with ours at Caesars Palace. I slipped in repeatedly to enjoy his act from the back of the lounge. When he followed us, I often spotted him backstage paging through a newspaper and whispering to himself as we came off, working frantically on his presentation until the last possible moment.

Most of the time, he was hilarious, but his shows had a lot of dips and valleys, too. As astute as he was, using the New York Times as a script didn't always provide the fodder he needed to unleash his scathingly topical humor.

Red Foxx's strategy was ingenious, and a part of it triggered an idea I thought our band could use.

"Say again how this works?" Mac frowned as I explained my idea. I nodded and glanced at Les.

"Certain songs on our playlist," I said to him, "naturally follow other songs, right, Bear?"

"Even though I tweak the lineup every night, you guys pretty much know how the sets are gonna go. First two are strongest. I begin with something upbeat, usually the second-best song of the set so we can close with the best one. In between, I space things out, so we never get two ballads in a row, try to mix in Mac's tunes with Dave's and get a lead in from you, Mickey, or me."

"And me. Don't forget when I do *Spooky*." Leonard begged us to let him sing this Classics IV song seriously—at first. He desperately hoped to vocalize with us the way Ringo did with the Beatles, but the poor guy was tone deaf and treated melody like a vague suggestion. Eventually, he'd fallen into parodying the song. It was more in his wheelhouse, and our audiences more receptive.

Les cracked a grin and nodded. "Yeah, and the drum solo, have to get that in."

"Well, here's what I'm suggesting." I thought this might help the flow of our performance through a set. "How about we string two or three songs together in a row, the same way you'd fit them together anyway. When Leonard calls the first number, we automatically know what the next couple will be. I don't mean as medleys, he just clicks his sticks to set the tempo and bam, we're into the next one. It will save Leonard having to yell out what song's next every time, and Mac from having to announce it—we'll move the show along faster."

Mac was all elbows and angles, thinking. "Not sure yet, bro, but I think I like the idea. Gets tiresome trying to think of somethin to say besides 'be sure to tip your bartenders and waitresses,' or 'we'll be here till Thursday.' Or my personal favorite"—he grinned his mischievous grin— "'don't none of you people out there piss me off tonight! I still got plenty of good places to hide the bodies.'"

"Cuttin out some of them spots could be good."

"Right." I nodded with a grin. "Won't work for every song, wouldn't want it to, we still need to let our personalities show. But if we shoehorned a couple of these strings into each set, I think we'd improve the pacing of our shows."

Les scratched his head. "Think I could figure out some combinations right away. I mean some are almost automatic already. We could start with those. I'd add one thing—I think Leonard should keep singing out the song titles until we're sure we'll remember them. No false starts while we work on this."

"Cool, good idea. If this works, you can thank Red Foxx for the tip."

During the vacation we took so Mickey could hunt deer in Oregon, Theresa and I accepted Izzy Marion's invitation-only, soft opening for his new restaurant, Isadore's. My wife looked fantastic on our dinner date with her hair draped long over a three-quarter-sleeved, high necked, animal print shift emphasizing her long, tanned legs and dark-tan pumps. It was a straight, waistless dress that somehow managed to accentuate her curves. She was excited and animated as a young girl to be out for the evening, but as soon as we were in public, she slipped into her public cool and serene composure. It amazed me how open and expressive facial expressions became when we were alone or comfortable with close friends. Kind of cute, I thought.

We'd become friends with Izzy Marion and his brother after one of our shows at Nero's Nook a few years ago. They'd loved the band's performances and offered us free grooming in their salon in the Caesars mall. Some of us had continued to drop into his shop to get our ears widened when we were in town. Once we'd settled in at the Flamingo, Theresa joined the rest of us as a regular customer, too.

Though Izzy's new high-dollar restaurant with its Italian decor was elegant, only half the tables were occupied. When he noticed us, he came to our table.

"Great place, Izzy," I told him. "Fantastic décor."

"Thanks." I'd known him long enough to realize his Italian nature was volatile and emotional. He seemed to be a basket case tonight.

"Just what Vegas needs, huh? Another restaurant." His laugh was high and nervous. "It's all my own family's recipes. My mom's food."

"I'm sure it will be a big success," Theresa said; our twin smiles conveyed something between sympathy and hope.

After talking with us for a few minutes, he paused, staring at her. "Have an idea. Theresa, would you consider working here? You'd sure dress up the place." He glanced at me. "If that's okay with Larry."

"I think that would be pretty difficult. Theresa's a brand-new mom, doubt she's quite ready for this yet." *What a crazy idea.*

Theresa nodded. "I'm flattered, it would be a lot of fun, but I don't see how I could manage it." She glanced at me.

"Well, let me know if you change your mind. Better get back to the kitchen. Be sure to try Mama's Tiramisu before you go." He kissed his fingers. "Mwaa. Favoloso!" After he'd gone, Theresa seemed disappointed.

"Are you okay sweetheart? What? Would you really like working here?"

"Well, maybe. I've got experience from waitressing at my mom's restaurant . . . and I really need to get out sometimes. I can't go with you at night to the club anymore or do most daytime things. In Waipahu, I would always have someone around to watch Keoki." She put down her fork and leaned in. "What if Izzy would let me help part-time or something? Do you think that might be possible?"

"What will we do about Keoki?"

"Honey, I love Keoki to death, but I'm all alone with him most of the time. That was okay when Charlene was here, she would take care of him . . ." She looked into my eyes, and I could see this was important to her. "You know, if you would watch him sometimes, and we got a sitter . . . I'm sure this place could use someone during dinner when the rush is heavy. It would just be for a few hours, and if Izzy would agree, I'd be home long before you start getting ready for work." Her eyes pleaded. "Could we try to find a way?"

I didn't see how I could deny her. Maybe it would've been different if Susie and the other wives were still close, but she was all on her own with the hours I worked. I wondered what made me so uncomfortable with this. I felt a tiny undercurrent of fear. Something I hadn't felt for a very long time and never with Theresa, but I recognized it for what it was—a glancing, stomach-wrenching tinge of jealousy, though I couldn't explain why. Which is why we made it a point to find Izzy after dinner.

Within a week Theresa was waiting tables at Isadore's and seemed happy to have some time on her own four hours a day, four days a week. She didn't make a lot of money, but she worked hard and took pride in earning it.

52 BAD MICKEY

My buddy told me I was too drunk to drive. He encouraged me to take a bus home. Turned out he was right, there was a police checkpoint set up, and they waved the bus right on through. I was pleasantly surprised. I'd never driven a bus before.

—Unknown

October 22, 1968
Las Vegas, Nevada

MICKEY ENJOYED A bare-fisted bar fight the way most people like chicken dinner on Sunday. Last year, a few months after we'd returned from Hawaii, Mickey went off to Oregon for his annual deer-hunting trip. He invited Mac to come along with him for a week. Mac, who visualized himself a reborn frontiersman despite the fact he was born and raised in the middle of a big city, and I'd never known anyone more urban, jumped at the chance. After a week in the wild with Mickey, Mac returned to what we considered our home then, the Mid-Valley Motel in North Hollywood, full of stories. Most fairy tales start with "Once upon a time," but Mac's stories generally began with "You ain't' gonna believe this shit." One evening, when we'd gotten settled in one of our rooms sharing beers and companionable tokes, he was easily coaxed into telling us about his trip to Prineville, Oregon, Mickey's hometown. On the first night, he began . . .

"See, Mick—'cause of that long blond Viking hair of his—says to me, 'people in Prineville don't much like what they call long-haired hippie peace-queers, so we need to handle that, first thing. Don't have time to mess around with that. Can't let it get in the way of huntin'."

Mac relaxed into the tale with a joint in one hand and a vodka tonic within reach. His wife Joan, Dave and his girl du jour, Les and Susie back when their relationship was still in bloom, along with Theresa and I, smiled, knowing a cool story was about to begin.

"So, I ask, what are you gonna do about it, Mick? And he tells me, most of the bars in town are on both sides of this one long street." Mac sipped and grinned wide. "Now, you ain't gonna believe this shit, but he says we're going to one end of that street and cross back and forth into each of these establishments, one by one. 'We'll have us a drink,' he says, 'and then move on to the next. I'm giving anyone who wants to this one chance to say something about my hair, and if anybody does, I'll kick the shit out of 'em until we run outta bars.'"

"Shit-house mouse!" Dave choked out, exhaling smoke out of both sides of a laugh. We guffawed. You could never tell when Dave would pop up with one these Indiana-isms. "How'd that work out for you, man?"

"Just like he said it would." Mac smiled wider. "'Fore we got started, Mickey tells me, 'I won't be the one throwin' the second shot, Mac. Guy who connects first wins ninety percent of bar fights. You can call it a sucker punch if you want, but the rule is, put the bastard on the floor first and don't let him up. Removes his incentive to keep fighting. As for the other rules, there aren't any.'"

"In the first joint, we go to the bar, and Mickey flips his long hair around like a girl would, laughing real friendly-like, tryin to entice somebody to say somethin about it. Guy next to him asks some dumbass question like, did he use peroxide on his 'do'? And Mick puts him down 'fore he finishes his sentence. Felt like we was in the Old West. Mickey slapped some money on the bar, tippin real good, and we left before anything more could be said. Then we walked on to the next joint. Didn't have to do this too many times before nobody would say nothin to him about his hair, or much of anything else except 'Howdy, Mick.' Guess news was travelin up the street ahead of us."

Joan had heard the story before, but she posed a question. "You never mentioned whether you needed to go to all the bars on the street or not."

"Don't know if we needed to, but we did. We also switched from whiskey to beers in the bottle so we could carry between barrooms, but we hit 'em all, everyone. Mick said no one would bother us after that, and for as long as I was there, he was right. But he still figured he'd have to do it all over again next deer season."

Mickey was a hunter, even in civilization. The first time we played the Pussycat with him, he'd become friendly with the club's security guard, a Vegas ex-cop named Scottie. He admired Scottie's pugnacious, rough-and-tumble style of policing the Cat. He'd kept a watchful eye on Scottie, alert for a favorable opportunity to help him with a fractious incident. It wasn't long in coming, and, apparently, Scottie approved of his technique.

We played the Cat a few more times before Seymour got us into the Flamingo Sky Room. By then, Mickey had gained credibility with the Cat's management in assisting Scottie with unruly customers as long as he was under Scottie's supervision.

Once we'd settled into the Sky Room, Mickey and Mac often slipped out to the Cat during long breaks and sometimes after our night was over. Accounts of Scottie and our bass player's scrapes and scuffles reached me at times, but I laughed them off along with everybody else. *Scottie would keep Mickey in line, wouldn't he? And after all, he was on the side of the angels, helping to maintain the peace, wasn't he?*

Recently, since we'd moved to the Crown Room, the rumors had turned ugly as Mickey's most explosive escapade surfaced among the rounders. Mac tried to deflect my concern saying it was just Mickey's fun-loving way of blowing off steam. I was sure part of that was true. Brawling was how Mickey dealt with his frustrations, and I firmly believed some poor son of a bitch occasionally took an uppercut so Mickey could sublimate punching my lights out.

Mac's vivid description of this recent scuffle forced me to reconsider "fun-loving" as a reasonable explanation for Mickey's actions. He told me he'd been playing at the only single-deck blackjack table left at the Cat when everything got started that night. He'd described Mickey as being mired in a dark funk, using both hands to chase Crown Royal with Heineken. Mac even called Scottie over to warn him Mick had blood in his eye, but it didn't make any difference.

"Few minutes later, Scottie's having words with some asshole sittin at the bar," Mac said. "Mick gets there before Scottie can say jack-shit to him and steps in to confront the troublemaker, warnin him to take his bullshit walkin, or he'll stick his head so far up his ass, he'll have a permanent brown smile. Guy snaps back he's from New York fuckin City, and he has flushed scarier lookin turds than Mickey, and he don't take shit off nobody, 'specially some hillbilly pecker like him. Mickey promptly socks him in the face, and says, 'Well I'm from Prineville, Oregon, motherfucker—so fuck you!'

"Despite the punch, which is sayin somethin right there, the guy grabs Mickey in a bear hug, wrestlin and rollin with him right on the damn bar stool. The guy bites him on the chest, teeth going right into one of Mick's pecs. Turns out he is maybe five-foot-six, or thereabouts. When Mick pulls away, the guy's hangin off Mick's teat by his teeth like a badger or somethin while Mick is trying to punch away at his head with both fists. In a way, the funniest thing I ever saw in a fistfight. Finally, Scottie gets the two of 'em outside where Mick's rage does not subside. He wants to kill the guy, who's laid out in the parkin lot now that they got him detached from Mick's chest.

"Scottie can't calm him down. But by then, of course, the Vegas squad cars are showin up, and an ambulance they shuffle the little guy into. Medics want to give Mickey some shots or something for all the germs and bugs that come from gettin man-bit, but he rages on. Scottie tries to get Mick to go quietly in the squad car, but he's too far gone, can't get him back. Cops force him into the car, and he proceeds to try kickin the back window out of the police car as they're drivin away."

I wondered if Mickey's current incident had anything to do with our long-term contracts here. They made it difficult to give him as much time for deer hunting as we'd promised. We'd only been able to negotiate one week off, and that had been more than a year ago. Maybe that was frustrating him. I worried about Mickey's rage; it seemed pretty extreme. But I worried more about this kind of notoriety getting us booted out of the Kerkorian-owned hotels. I felt we were more vulnerable here at the International, and unsure of how to handle either worry.

Mickey wasn't the only one with issues, there were several troubling undercurrents in the band, his was just the most public. There was one thing we could try if it was possible, one thing that had helped in the past and it played into one of the fondest wishes those of us from the Midwest had expressed. I'd have to talk to Howard King, but maybe we could go out of town for a while.

A few weeks later, after Theresa and I had watched Butch Cassidy and the Sundance Kid battle it out in a losing cause at the movies, we took off our jackets and settled into a booth at a steakhouse on Charleston, a block west of the Strip. It had been an impressive film, and I wondered out loud if we should learn the theme song, *Raindrops Keep Fallin' On My Head*, thinking it would be a good tune for Les; he usually sang our B. J. Thomas songs. We sipped glasses of water, smoked cigarettes, and talked about it for a few minutes until I brought up something from a couple of nights ago.

"Honey, I'm sorry it didn't work out for you at Isadore's. I know you enjoyed being out." Izzy had been right to worry about how long his restaurant would last. It hadn't been long. His loss, though, was my gain; I had Theresa home with Keoki and me again.

"Well, it couldn't have gone on much longer anyway." She reached out and laced her long gentle fingers in mine. "I missed Keoki and having more time with you before work." I agreed. I was spoiled, I guess, and I'm sure Keoki preferred having his mom home, too.

"You remember me telling you how we helped Don Ho out of a jam, sweetie?"

"Yes." She pouted playfully. "The night I wanted you home keeping me warm."

"Um, yeah. Wished I could've too," I lost my place in the story for a second before resuming. "I told you he was having some kind of luau for his birthday and the band he'd hired was a no-show, and how we saved the day when we agreed to come to the main room and cover for them at his party?"

"I remember."

"Wasn't sure you were paying attention. You seemed distracted at the time."

"Not my fault." She reached for a menu and pretended to study the choices. "I was having such a sexy dream when you woke me." She grinned. "Oh, wait. What you were doing, that wasn't a dream, was it?"

"Now I'm the one getting distracted." We laughed. "I wanted to tell you what happened afterward. Don Ho sent his card with his phone number and a message to me in the Crown Room. Not only is Duke's his home club in Waikiki, but he's the entertainment manager for the Outrigger now. He wants me to have Seymour contact him about booking us in Honolulu."

She let the menu drop. "Oh, Larry, do you think it would be possible? That would be a fantastic place for the band to play. And you'd get to meet my family."

"Sure sounds like it. Have to see what Seymour can work out, but if Don Ho wants us there, seems like a good bet." I raised my water glass. "We need a break from Vegas. There's a lot of restlessness in the band. Maybe a trip to the islands would suit them, although some of the guys got rock fever pretty bad last time we were there." I ground out my smoke.

"Give me a day's notice, honey, and I will have us packed. Keoki wants to go see his Mama Willi."

After we'd ordered, I mentioned another possibility involving family.

"Howard called me this afternoon while you were out with the baby. He heard back from a club in Indianapolis, the top night spot in the city." I grinned and reached for her hand. "He thinks they're going to make an offer."

My wife, though I still thought of her as my girl, smiled tentatively and put her hand on my arm. "I would meet your family? Your mom and dad and your sister?" She was silent for a moment. "Would you want us to bring Keoki?"

"Sure. That's the main reason I want to go, I want to show off my wife and let them see their new grandson. But we shouldn't get ahead of ourselves; we need to wait to see what kind of offer they make. When I talked to Seymour about Don Ho, we discussed both possibilities. We decided if we had the option, Hawaii would be a better career move for the band."

I considered what else Seymour had said as our order arrived. Even over the phone, I could visualize him shaking his head. "I know how it works in Las Vegas," he'd said. "Out of sight, out of mind. You leave for a few weeks and they could find somebody they like better and forget your name. It's usually best if you stay as long as you can. The Treniers played Vegas for five years before they started taking outside dates."

I salted everything before picking up a knife. "Either way, Seymour's not thrilled about us leaving Vegas." I cut a bite out of the Porterhouse sizzling in front of me. "He's right, and I understand why. But despite everything I've tried to do to keep the band grounded, things keep spinning out of control. If one of these jobs is available, I think we have to risk going out of town for a while. But no matter where we go, we've got to be sure we have a solid booking back here before we accept anything."

Despite the hour, I'd ordered coffee. I took a sip and voiced my real hope to Theresa and the Universe:

"If we do go out of town, I hope we can arrange to come back to the Sky Room instead of the Crown Room."

53 DISTURBING ELVIS

Man, I really like Vegas.
—Elvis Presley

December 13, 1969
Las Vegas, Nevada

WHEN MY BIRTHDAY rolled around, the three of us celebrated with a pancake breakfast. Keoki probably wore more pancakes than he got into his tummy, but he seemed to enjoy them, inside or out. Later, in a quiet moment, I unwrapped a Blood, Sweat & Tears 8-track tape Theresa gave me. She slipped it from my hand into our new player and pressed play until some horn lines introduced, *You've Made Me So Very Happy.* She gazed over her shoulder at me as David Clayton Thomas's smoky voice rumbled into the lyrics.

"If I could sing, honey," she said, eyes gleaming, her smile beaming with affection, "I would sing this song to you. It says how I feel. You came along when I didn't expect it, and every day you make me so very, very happy. Sometimes I love you so much I can't contain it inside me, I'm afraid I'll explode."

I reached for her. All I asked of life was to bask in her joy, to witness her smile, and listen to her laugh. Her eyes gazed into mine before flicking hungrily at my mouth and back to my eyes again. She raised a palm to my cheek, lifting her face to mine. We kissed the way we'd kissed from the beginning, the way we always kissed, never a simple peck; our lips met in full-mouth passionate kisses—instant arousal.

Until Keoki woke, the rest of the afternoon was ours, and we made the most of it. I would never forget the enraptured expression on Theresa's face the first time we'd fused our bodies together on Kuhio Beach. I'd asked her once about the emotions I'd seen racing across her face, and she laughed it away saying she had no idea what I was talking about. As we joined ourselves together this dreamy afternoon, I saw those fleeting expressions again, and it brought tears to my eyes to think someone could react with such intensity to my affection and love. I could not begin to gauge the depth of my adoration for this woman.

Keoki slept late, and we lazed around in our temporary nudist camp, alternatively used as our living room. It turned chilly, and I went into the kitchen to pour glasses of orange juice while she rounded up jeans and sweatshirts from the bedroom. Once we'd dressed, something seemed to be on her mind.

"You look so serious. What is it? What's going on?"

"I want to tell you something, but I don't want it to make you mad."

"When have I ever been angry with you Treese? I can't even imagine it."

"I hope not, but maybe you will." She stood and paced a little, a tight hunch in her shoulders. "I'm worried about you and Keoki," she finally got out. She glanced at me, and I stared back in confusion.

"You don't seem to play with him or hold him very often. I . . . I'm wondering if you don't like him very much."

"I don't understand. You and I both played with him earlier, before his nap."

"Yes, when we're together. But you never pick him up or play with him on your own. Don't you realize that?"

I tried to meet her gaze. Could that be true? "If I don't, it's not on purpose. Of course, I love him. How could I not? He's our baby boy."

"Are you sure? Sometimes it seems like you ignore him. It worries me." Theresa sank down beside me, reaching for my hands. I strained to pull my thoughts together.

"You think I might not love our son?" I shook my hands loose and took my turn pacing through the living room. I didn't know how to respond. I tried to see myself objectively. *Maybe I don't spend as much time with him as I should*, I thought, struggling to be objective. *But I know I love him. I had too, didn't I?* I walked out the front door into wintery dusk without a thought of where I was headed. I dropped to the steps, sunk in despair, a chill creeping through me. Not only did I not want to disappoint Theresa, but something deeper and darker rose in my mind.

My last New Year's Eve in Indianapolis with Pat we'd hosted a party with close friends including the guys in my singing group. Late in the night, when we were both a little tipsy, she'd asked me to check on the boys.

They slept soundly in their night-lit bedroom, exhausted from the excitement of Danny's second birthday today. Dave had turned four two weeks earlier and had been as excited as Dan, though we'd had to diplomatically explain the gifts were for his younger brother this time. Asleep, they looked like little blond angels. I'd bent down to place hands on their diminutive bodies so I could feel them breathe together when I fell to a knee in despair. I was struck by how much they depended upon me, and how hopelessly unprepared I was. I was supposed to be the daddy, the husband, with all the answers. They counted on me to be strong, to be smart, to know what to do next, know what was going to happen. I didn't know how to be any of that, and most of Pat's family made sure I didn't forget it. It took Pat's confidence and the strength of our love to keep me going. I was overwhelmed, stuck; I couldn't put a foot forward, sideways, backward; no matter where I looked, the future was a gray cloud of reality hiding the edge of a cliff. These little guys were too young to understand now. *But for how much longer?* I'd wondered.

Not long, as it turned out; within months, I would fail them. I bit back waves of fear and hot regret. *Was I falling short again? Did I not have it in me to be a good father?*

I felt Theresa kneel behind me, arms encircling me, her cheek smooth against the nape of my neck. "I'm sorry, honey. I know you must love our baby boy."

I put a palm on her arm. "Theresa, sometimes my heart is so full of you, there's hardly room for anything else. I'll do better, I swear it. I don't want to disappoint you. I promise you, I'll never let anything bad happen to our little family."

I heard a choking sob behind me. I turned my head to a warm, salty kiss I wished would never end. I was twenty-eight years old.

The Las Vegas Christmas season was always a big tourist event, though to my Midwestern consciousness, staying in a casino seemed a strange way to celebrate such a home and family-oriented holiday. Crowds milled through every nook and cranny of the gigantic International Hotel, especially in the mall running through the center of the ground floor. Christmas Eve fell on a Wednesday night. Theresa and I spent a quiet evening in front of the tree opening presents and playing with Keoki and his new toys. After all the excitement, he dropped into an early and sound sleep. When I stepped out of the shower, Theresa had joined him in the arms of Morpheus. Getting ready to go out while everyone else slept felt more unnatural than usual on such a special holiday. I shaved, dressed, and, anointed for the night ahead, left them with light kisses.

Seymour told me he'd tried over and over again to reach Don Ho, but his letters and phone calls weren't being returned. I was embarrassed that Seymour was being snubbed after I'd brought him what I'd thought was a sincere offer to play at the Outrigger. It was the most famous resort hotel in Hawaii and would have been an enormous feather in our cap. I hoped it was a miscommunication and there would be a way to resurrect the offer someday. When Bill Miller decided in early January that he wanted Stark Naked and the Car Thieves back in the Sky Room, Seymour asked him to delay it four weeks so we could play in our hometown before returning to the Flamingo. He agreed, and we accepted the Holyoke's offer for early February.

 Elvis returned for his second engagement at the International about ten days before we would leave for Indianapolis. After he and his entourage moved into the Elvis Suite, I occasionally noticed him as we were entering or exiting the express elevator. Sometimes he'd nod, but I didn't sense he recognized any of us from the Flamingo.

 I knew the layout of his suite from when it had been under construction. We'd come up to the thirtieth floor to check out progress on the Crown Room. At the time, everything was mainly framing. The suite entrance was nothing more than cordoned-off rough openings in the wall instead of the double-doors securing the rooms now. We'd ignored the ropes and wandered through the structure, curious about what was being built on this side of the penthouse floor.

Floor-to-ceiling windows looked east to the Sunrise and Frenchman Mountains—a spectacular if bleak, panorama that probably hadn't looked much different ten thousand years ago. There were so many rooms I thought they were intended to become several luxury suites at first. But when we discovered a huge unfinished kitchen, dining room, and living room, we realized it was a mammoth penthouse suite. We reassessed and counted seventeen bedrooms and many more bathrooms. This five-thousand-square-foot collection of rooms, originally called the Imperial Suite, was now simply known as the Elvis Suite.

On Elvis's opening night, our bird's eye view from the roof revealed ropes of vehicles flowing through brilliant arteries along Paradise Road and over from the Strip along Desert Inn and Sahara Avenues. Emilio, head maître d' at the Showroom Internationale, told us a line for tickets had formed at 10 AM, and the phones rang off the hook all day. A hundred-dollar tip would've got you a ringside table for most nights at Elvis's first appearance last summer; over the next week it doubled and tripled. Though he didn't drop in to see us in the little time we had left, he did make one personal appearance.

Late one afternoon as we were running through Gary Puckett and the Union Gap's tune *This Girl Is a Woman Now*, a figure with dark rumpled hair and wrapped in a fluffy white bathrobe draped to his ankles appeared next to the stage. Even without the big, black cursive "E" on it, we would've known who it was. Elvis waved his arms energetically, like ground crew directing an airplane, to get our attention, and we crashed to a stop.

"Uh, you boys sound good, really great. But I'm trying to get some sleep over here. If y'all wouldn't mind playin' a little bit quieter, I'd truly appreciate it." He still didn't seem to remember seeing us at the Sky Room, but to be fair, he was probably sleepy.

We quickly agreed, and he acknowledged us with a quick nod before disappearing like the ghost of Christmas past.

"Did you see that?" Dave's eyes went wide. "That was Elvis."

We'd gotten ourselves fired from the Thunderbird for not being willing to turn down the volume, but for Elvis, Leonard willingly clicked his drumsticks together while Les and Mickey unplugged from their amps and we sang a cappella for the rest of rehearsal. We accidentally bothered him one more time, but a member of his Nashville Mafia politely requested us to turn it down.

With a confirmed date in Indianapolis, I called to alert Mom and Dad to our arrival. They were excited to hear we'd be there soon, and my own excitement was building toward the moment when the Hoosier Dunlaps could embrace our new California/Hawaii branch of the family. At the last minute, though, Theresa voiced concerns about bringing Keoki. We'd just returned home from buying new clothes for the trip when she asked me to sit with her. "I'm worried about taking our baby so far for so long, honey. He's only six months old, four weeks is too long for him."

I was shocked and knew my family would be, too.

"My mom and dad will be disappointed, Theresa."

"I hate to disappoint them, but we can go see them again soon. When you're not working, on a real vacation when we can both take care of Keoki. If we bring him, I will always be the one who would have to watch him. You'll be gone a lot of the time, or too busy." I told her his grandmother, and aunt Cheryl would be pleased and excited to look after their new little grandson and nephew, but she was adamant. Maybe she was right. He was still very young.

"I want to take him to stay with Mama Willi. Please let me. I'll fly right back to go with you, and we'll have a wonderful time." Two days before we were to leave for Indianapolis, Theresa flew round trip to Hawaii before returning to catch our flight to the Midwest.

Though my enthusiasm had been dented and our bank account deflated, I would not allow anything to detract from the thrill of bringing the love of my life home to my family. This time things would be different. I'd be bringing my new wife, who loved me. We'd make new memories and wipe out whatever demons might remain in the Circle City.

54 A HAWAIIAN IN HOOSIERVILLE

It's a Hoosier thing, you wouldn't understand.
—Bob Kevoian & Tom Griswold, Indianapolis Deejays

February 2, 1970
Indianapolis, Indiana

EVERY EYE HAD turned to her when she walked in behind Mom and Dad. My Hawaiian wife, resplendent in an exotic, harem-inspired dress, was a living fantasy out of *Arabian Nights*. Light caught in the jewels of the delicate netting cradling her hair. The sheer aquamarine pantaloons and long-sleeved bodice, though lightly veiled, revealed much more of Theresa's lush shape than I'd realized. The weather might be freezing outside, but inside, the temperature of every male had risen several degrees. I got to my feet, motioning her and my parents to the table where my sister, Cheryl, and I sat.

I'd seen this outfit on Theresa before we bought it. She'd modeled it for me in Las Vegas, and I'd thought it would be perfect. But this was the first time I'd seen this gauzy confection in public. The crowd at the Holyoke followed her progress dumbfounded. I'd expected to relish the dramatic impact she would make but seeing her through staid Hoosier eyes gave me second thoughts. Not only for how much of her physical beauty it exposed, that was bad enough, but because I realized it was a costume that hid her real allure. She liked being well-dressed where we worked, but more than anything she wanted to fit in; she wasn't flamboyant. I'd encouraged her to wear this garment imagining it would enhance her natural beauty. It was more likely to arouse lascivious fantasies than the admiration I'd anticipated. What was I thinking, asking her to display herself like this? I feared I knew; I was showing her off.

"Larry," she said in a worried whisper. "Everybody is staring at me. I don't think I like it." I stood to seat her and gave her a kiss trying to cover my regret with a comforting smile.

"Forget about them, honey. You're absolutely stunning." Nothing could be truer. I hoped the affection in my eyes reassured her.

I caught a glance of Cheryl gawking at Theresa.

"Close your mouth little sister, you're gonna let all the flies in." She clamped her jaw shut, chastened for a moment. But then she grinned. The days when I could intimidate her were long gone.

She put a hand on Theresa's arm, "You look magnificent, Theresa." My wife smiled gratefully.

Cheryl wore a pomegranate-red cardigan over a simple white blouse and a dark pencil skirt with ankle socks and penny loafers. A costume in its own way for Midwestern college students. She'd driven in from Bloomington where she was a sophomore at Indiana University. She was only a few months older than Theresa, and I counted heavily on them becoming the best of friends.

Compliments from the guys as they dropped by helped Theresa relax. She often displayed stress as disinterest or boredom, so I was relieved to see her chatting and smiling with Cheryl and Mom and Dad.

We'd arranged to skip Sunday at the Crown Room for an extra travel day but opening on Monday night still hadn't allowed us much spare time. We'd gotten Leonard and Mickey installed in their motel yesterday and rushed to get our equipment unpacked and ready today. Mac's wife, Joan, had arrived from Cincinnati for opening night. Mac planned on staying with local friends and commuting to her parents' home to be with her and his daughter on days off. Before Theresa's arrival, when we'd walked to the dressing room to get ready for the show, an early full house of excited friends and families greeted us with a scattered round of applause.

The Holyoke, well known on the Midwest circuit, often presented well-known R&B, pop, and rock artists: Little Richard, Jerry Lee Lewis, and Chuck Berry were among a long list of classic performers who'd appeared here. Though

I'd grown up in this city, I'd never been here before. I'd become a young parent at nineteen, bars and nightclubs were not and never had been a part of my lifestyle then. The first time I'd gone into a bar, Dave and I met Mac. And when we'd been putting together our first band, Pat and I, along with the guys in my singing group, went to a downtown dive called Susie's Twist Lounge. That night had ended with us in jail for most of the following weekend, and a made a tragic imprint on our marriage.

I would have liked seeing some of the acts who had played here in those early days, but the club was located out on East Washington Street, well known as a rough, blue-collar neighborhood especially for those of us from the north side, and especially during our frenzied high school basketball seasons. Being out of bounds gave the Holyoke a certain mystique in those days, but I hadn't noticed any vestiges of glamor or mystery when I dragged my B3 in this afternoon. Other than a decent-sized but plain stage, there wasn't anything remarkable about the room despite its hallowed past. Compared to the venues we played these days, it was a pit.

Opening night was fun for a while. Mom and Dad left before midnight, and soon afterward Cheryl took Theresa home, her harem dress hidden beneath a jacket my sister lent her. I think it's fair to say she was anxious to get out of those clothes.

As the nights went by, the room continued to draw big and responsive crowds. We were considered a huge success. But for me, we could've been at any of the nondescript clubs we'd played in our earlier years—except the weather was worse. I walked out to the frozen parking lot one break and was startled to remember Al Green's drive-in restaurant, not far from here, where delivery girls in thick coats and short skirts delivered foot-long, greasy pork tenderloin sandwiches to car windows on roller skates. Things like that, and the bitter wind cutting through my jacket, made me definitely realize I was in Indianapolis.

Many things didn't go as I'd expected. Theresa attached herself to me soon after we arrived. Her unease grew when my parents went out of their way to treat me like the returning prodigal son and her too deferentially, like a Hawaiian princess, emphasizing her differences more than welcoming her as a family member. I think my folks weren't sure what to make of her at first. When

I broke the news that we hadn't brought their grandson, Keoki Malcolm, with us, they'd struggled to hide their disappointment. I explained we'd been forced to make the decision at the last minute, and Theresa had flown to Hawaii and back in less than twenty-four hours before we'd flown to Indiana. Even so, there was no excuse. I should've called to warn them. Theresa took their dismay personally.

We'd been settled in the back two-room apartment plus bathroom with its own outdoor entry and a door separating us from the rest of the house. Most nights my mother prepared home-cooked meals. Hoosier style. Heavy on meat and potatoes, vegetables done to death. Not much like California home cooking, let alone Hawaiian. There was no Asian rice, no poi, and no what she would consider, fresh fish. I aggravated the problem by inflicting greasy burgers on her from White Castle, Steak 'n Shake, the Tee Pee, and other favorite foods from high school. Theresa's system did not tolerate the onslaught of Hoosier eats well.

I encouraged her to spend time with my folks, but she stared at me in panic when I left for rehearsal and begged to go with me every night. When she did stay home, my parents, nonplussed—to use their word—floundered in their attempts to entertain her. Pat, of course, had played bridge, any number of board and party games, and other kinds of activities house-bound Hoosiers shut in during cold weather, liked to do. But Theresa had been raised in an outdoor paradise and we'd never done those things together. The harder they tried, the more withdrawn and distracted she became. My mom wrung her hands in anxiety, tearfully explaining how my wife closed herself away in our section of the house, reluctant to appear until I returned.

It was our natural habit to touch, caress, kiss, and stroke, wordlessly expressing our affection. Here, in my parent's home, we tended to limit ourselves to discreet pats and occasional handholding in front of them. If she reached out to me, it was usually a panicky need for reassurance. When I was home, she wanted us to remain behind our closed door as much as possible. Her enticements were compelling, but I forced myself to resist when I thought we were too impolite. My parents must have thought we rutted like rabbits.

My wife missed Keoki terribly and couldn't stop thinking and worrying about him. She asked me if she could cut her visit short—to a week or two at most—

so she could fly to Honolulu early. I wanted her with me, I wanted to figure this out, but I also wanted her to be happy. I would have agreed, of course, but with all the travel, we were broke.

I took Theresa on a tour of my old haunts hoping to distract her: the schools I'd attended from elementary to college, the drive-in restaurants, my favorite drives around town. But nearly every place was a reminder of my past marriage. The rooms we slept in, where Pat and I had slept together as newlyweds before and after the birth of our first son, were drenched with memories.

It was not getting through my thick head what an impact my first marriage was having on Theresa. I'd tried to explain how much I'd loved my first wife. How I'd still lost her and our children. How I'd tried to confront and shed the past before I proposed to her. I'd thought I was describing these feelings to Theresa to explain why the depth of my commitment to her and our marriage was so vital to me. I might have done the opposite. I can't say for sure. Sometimes I can read the subtlest signs of how someone feels and at others be so blunderingly oblivious you'd wonder if I'd managed to misplace my senses.

Probably worst of all, Cheryl and Theresa turned out to be oil and water together. The college girl, ripe with ambition, and the island girl, a new mother from a distant, exotic island, misread each other's signs and struggled to find much in common.

As the month drew to an end, and though the local radio stations still weren't playing any of our records, the band was enjoying more success than we'd had our first time home, a year and a half earlier at the Rat Fink. Dave and Les seemed pleased to be home, and Mac received rave reviews from the stream of Ohio Buckeye friends and family who'd journeyed up from Cincinnati most nights. Leonard and Mickey had known from previous experience they'd be counting the days before we could return to Vegas, but I hadn't expected Theresa and I to be as fervently counting days as they were. By the end of the fourth week, I was as anxious and relieved as she was to climb aboard the big bird to fly home to Las Vegas.

We'd been celebrating being home in our king-size bed in the usual loving way we celebrated most things when the phone rang. It was our first night back and even for Vegas, the hour was late. I sprawled bonelessly across the bed under a bath towel damp from the shower. Theresa was curled next to me, exhausted and contented. As I'd felt us resume our usual connectedness, I realized how much tension we'd been under. Here, in this town that never sleeps, we were more relaxed than in my hometown. Finally, when the telephone's harsh ringing refused to quit, I rolled to the nightstand with a sigh.

"Larry, Larry," Leonard said, out of breath. "Man, we got trouble. Big trouble."

Crap, now what? My heartbeat accelerated. "Calm down, Leonard. Tell me what's happening."

"I'm here. At the Sky Room. I ran into Dickie Dodd over here." *That's Leonard, we're only back in town hours before he's checking things out at the club.*

Dick Dodd, who'd been better known as Dickie Dodd when he was one of Disney's original Mickey Mouse Club Mouseketeers, was also managed by Seymour Heller and produced by Eddie Cobb. Eddie had written and produced a big hit for Dick's old band, the Standells, *Dirty Water*. Now Dick had a new group, the Big Train, who had been filling in for us at the Sky Room while we were away.

"He should be closing tonight. Is there some kind of problem?"

"His band's closing all right, but we're not booked in here next. He doesn't know who is, but man, it ain't us. What's going on?" I didn't have a clue and wouldn't until I could contact someone tomorrow morning.

The news was bad. Our schedule had gotten badly screwed up, and nobody wanted to take responsibility for it. Seymour's office responded that as far as they knew, the dates were right, and wondered what we were doing back from Indianapolis so soon. Howard King swore he'd told everyone we would be in Indianapolis for only four weeks. I couldn't reach Bill Miller, but the Flamingo's entertainment office said they weren't expecting us back yet, either. Jim Seagrave didn't know what happened and promised to look into it. Everybody started scrambling. But no matter how we'd gotten into this mess, it was too late to find somewhere else to play this week. And for a bunch of guys who'd gotten complacent about living check-to-check, that meant pure panic.

"Larry," Theresa said in alarm. "I've got to go get Keoki, I've got to. I talked to my mom, and she loves her grandson, but she told me, 'Girl, get back here and get your boy.' Even if I have to catch the first flight back, I have to go get our son, now. My reservation is for Thursday, it's been made for a month. Larry, I have to be on that plane."

"I know, sweetheart, I know." I tried to soothe the desperation in her voice. "We should be able to straighten things out in a day or two, maybe even before you leave. We'll know better how to plan. If I don't know by then, I won't make a return reservation for you until I know where we'll be playing." *Or how to pay for it*, I worried. "I'm hoping Howard can find something here or not too far away in California."

Intimacy was usually the best antidote for our worries, but Theresa's anxiety clouded her usual bright and sunny attitude. Though things were better when we shared each other's love, things weren't likely to get back to normal until she returned home with our child.

55 BACK TO THE RAT

You know what the issue is with this world? Everyone wants a magical solution to their problem, and everyone refuses to believe in magic.
—Lewis Carroll, Alice in *Alice in Wonderland*

March 8, 1970
Las Vegas, Nevada

"HI. HOWARD KING here."

"Howard, it's Larry. Got a message says you have news."

"Yeah, I think you might love this. Hope so. I've been shaking the trees everywhere and, as you guys know, you are a high-rent property. Not a lot of gigs for an act like yours at the last minute." *Yada yada yada*, I thought, *you're telling me you can't find us work because we're too popular? Really? Because we're too good?*

"What've you got, Howard?"

"Got a call from some old friends of Mac's, I guess. They saw the band at the Holyoke and want you at their place. George Saliba, the Saliba brothers. They own the Rat Fink Lounge there in Indianapolis."

My heart sank. *Good news?* "Howard, have you lost your freaking mind? We just got back from Indianapolis. We played the Rat Fink two years ago, and it was a hell hole then. Are you seriously suggesting we fly back?"

"Okay, okay, let's not go blaming this snafu on me. We've been down this road. I warned you stuff like this could happen if you didn't make me your exclusive agent so I could keep everything all coordinated. But no, you guys figure you're too big for that. You want me when you need me but not when you got something else going on. You did it one time too many this time. I did my job, got you booked into Indianapolis like you asked. I'm not saying anything bad about Seymour, he's the salt of the earth, but where do you think you guys stand in the pecking order over there? Maybe more important than Liberace? More than the Treniers, who have been with him since his bris? You need somebody who's on the case for you all the time."

Everybody wants to yell at each other when the ship's sinking, but nobody wants to pick up a bucket and bail. I sighed out loud.

"Well," he went on, "you better make your mind up in a hurry or this opportunity goes away. I can put you in this club next Monday if you tell me in the next twenty-four hours. And, in case you hadn't noticed, I don't see anybody else offering you work starting next week."

I promised to call Howard no later than tomorrow afternoon. This would be a tough sell to the band. We met in the Flamingo coffee shop.

"Love your family, Larry. Fantastic folks. But, nope, ain't goin'. You can get yourself another picker 'cause this country boy ain't going back to your hometown. No way, no how." Mickey's opinion didn't surprise me.

Leonard was reluctant, too. He considered Las Vegas the Entertainment Capital of the World. He'd reached his dream destination, and now that we lived and worked here, he hated to leave. Despite the surprising number of fans he'd made in Indianapolis, he felt like a fish out of water there, actually anywhere else.

"Look, guys, we're back in the Sky Room four weeks from next Tuesday. I've already agreed to that; couldn't take a chance it might get away. But we're out of work this week and in danger of being unemployed until then. That's potentially four more weeks without a payday." I paced back and forth in front of them. Their expressions were grim.

"I don't want to go either," I continued. "Frankly, I've had enough of Indianapolis. I'm miserable every time we go there. But that's what's available immediately. I haven't been given any other options, and it should be obvious we can't play anywhere else in Vegas—not even if there was something available on such short notice." My glance took in Mickey and Mac's unasked question.

"No, not even the Cat." Once you're in the hotels, you can't go back to playing in nightclubs.

"But I have to tell you." Worry made my words come out scratchy. "With all the traveling and other expenses I've had, I'm looking at dead broke. I'm already late on the rent, I'm going to have to use every penny I can find for plane fare. No matter what we do, I have to let our house go and hope to hell I can find something cheaper when we get back. At least I'll save a month's rent." I glanced around trying to gauge their reaction. "Look, I'll stay and take the chance we'll find something if the five of you agree on what you want to do, but I'll have to bunk with one of you." I put on a wry grin. "It's gonna hurt like hell if we don't find work for the next four weeks." I paused to calculate. "Let's see, today's the third, be the . . . be close to the middle of next month before we see a paycheck, though I might be able to swing a draw a few days early. So, what do you think?"

"Sonofabitch!" Mac realized the odd irony. "Can't believe we'll be back in that goddamned club with them Saliba brothers again. Michele's one weird little creep. Joan will be glad to see her kin again so soon, but it's sure the fuck strange the way a guy's got to keep payin for his past sins. This'll be my fourth damn time playin there."

It hadn't been a foregone conclusion they would agree, but none of us had saved enough to go without work for five weeks; I'd gotten used to regular checks and cut it too close myself. We'd have to drain whatever money was in the group fund to travel and supplement it from our own pockets somehow.

Sunday morning, we rode the jet stream back to Indiana. Two days earlier I'd put Theresa on a five-hour flight going the opposite direction, and now she was halfway around the world from me. *Crap! This is so incredibly fucked up!*

Tough, ice-skinned snow, undaunted by the thin afternoon sun, hugged the ground outside as Dad helped me haul my luggage in from the car to the back bedroom. I tried to explain why I was back, but I doubt I made much sense, my mind was mush. Mom made soothing noises and gave me a note. I needed to phone somebody at the airport as soon as possible.

"Yeah, this is airfreight."

"I got a message to call. What's the problem?"

"You got a reference number on that message?" I found it and read it to him.

"Okay, gimme a second." The line went dead as I was put on hold. I dropped into the kitchen chair, my brain trying to catch up with my body. In a couple of minutes, the voice came back. "What we got here is a damaged shipping crate. Looks like the thing got banged up getting off the plane or something. You wanna come down here and make a claim on it or what?"

My heart fell. "What kind of package? Can you tell me about it?"

"Well, for one thing, got your name and this phone number on it. It's a big wooden crate, breakage all around, especially the top. Not sure what's in it, could be a desk maybe. Some sorta furniture?"

At the freight terminal in the morning, my fears were confirmed. My crated Hammond B3 organ must have been shoved off the plane while still in the air, or a brick building had been dropped on it. The wooden box had been crushed just below the top on all four corners. No one had attempted to touch it before I'd arrived. I could've pulled the fragmented lid off with my fingers.

The way I prepared my Hammond organ for shipping should have protected my instrument from all but the most catastrophic damage. I used a dolly system with wide, canvas belts clamped around the organ's cabinet to keep it secure. The dolly included pull-out handles and wheels that descended and locked on both sides for rolling. I left it strapped in the dolly and tied furniture-moving blankets over everything before having a custom shipping crate built around the whole bundle. My heart clenched when I pushed aside mangled pieces of wood to peer inside. The dolly remained attached, but through the padding, I could see the slumped body of the B3's cabinet. The organ was ruined. I felt like someone close to me had died.

The shipping clerk kept making tsk, tsk noises, which irritated the crap out of me. Yeah, I knew the damn thing looked like it had been bashed by a giant hammer.

He turned his washed-out green eyes on me. "So, guess you'll want a claims form, right? Unless you've got insurance, of course." I didn't have insurance.

"Yeah, guess I do, but I don't know what the hell I'm going to do tomorrow night." Obviously not his concern.

"You can fill the form out now or take it with you and mail it here." He pointed to an address on the back of the form he brandished at me like a magic cure. When I took it, he cocked his head toward the broken crate. "Whaddaya wanna do with this?"

I had polished and cared for this beast since the day I'd gotten it. There hadn't been a scratch on its hide, but now I thought about asking him to catapult the thing into the nearest trash bin.

"We got these other packages over here, should we bring this along with 'em to the delivery address?"

I nodded glumly, trying not to look at my poor, broken instrument.

I arrived first for setup at the Rat Fink Monday afternoon. The nightclub existed in the same time warp as the last time I'd been here. *Didn't anybody ever clean this joint?* I tried to prepare myself before walking into the showroom hoping the damage wasn't as severe as I remembered. My hapless Hammond B3 sat slumped in its mutilated crate on the stage with loose pieces of wood stacked on it. The undamaged wooden-crated Leslie speakers huddled next to it in dismal empathy. I pulled away the fractured wood, wondering numbly if I could find a B3 or a Lowry or some kind of electric organ to rent in time for tonight. Fully uncrated, without the dolly and blankets holding everything together, it was evident the organ's cabinet would probably disintegrate.

Leonard came in and began pulling shipping cases out on the dance floor while I surveyed my mangled baby. Our dressing area was too small to hold all our stage clothes, he'd planned to take most of them to his motel and bring the outfits we needed with him each night.

"Wait a minute, wait a minute," I heard him mumble. "Missing two trunks. Larry, were you here when these got delivered?" I shook my head. With no expectations I ran the power cord to a socket and surprisingly, the little light by the keyboard turned green. I uncrated one of the Leslies to check if the organ could produce sound.

"What's missing?" I asked as he cracked open the trunks. I listened to him rummaging around as I wedged the crate sides off of the speaker and pulled the cable to the organ.

"Oh my God. I can't believe this!" His voice rose in concern. "Can't find our burgundy or gold suits. I think all or most of the suede boots are missing, too. And the ties and cufflinks; and our custom-made shirts and stuff."

This keeps getting worse and worse. "Got a number for United Airfreight you can call. Maybe they just forgot to deliver them." Not likely though. Considering the state of my B3, I think we both knew they were another part of the disaster that had struck us.

I uncovered the top of the organ's cabinet; it seemed to be intact, but the long piece of wood running beneath the keys rested on the opposite ends of the dolly. Though the legs remained in place, they'd been crunched and weren't supporting anything. I would have to leave the organ cabinet strapped in place. It would be a miracle if it produced noise, let alone music. I held my breath and stroked a chord, throwing the switch to spin the speaker horns out of chorale into pulsating reverb. My broken and crippled B3 still played, though I couldn't guess why or for how long.

I used several strips of duct tape in hopes of protecting the organ from falling to pieces. I was finishing my rough patch as the rest of us filtered in. They listened to Leonard's news with mixed fury and dismay; they gazed in awe at my damaged B3, murmuring words of sympathy. United Airlines had taken an enormous fucking bite out of us. Mickey plugged his bass in and disappeared. He wasn't happy about waking up in Indiana again.

Les came to the table where I was sitting before the first set. "I've given you a lotta shit about that organ since the day you started with it, but I want to tell you, we'd sure as hell miss it if you weren't here banging on it."

I gave him a wan smile. I realized it was his way of saying he was sorry about what had happened; and also, a gentle reminder that everyone was on stage waiting for me. I climbed behind the poor damaged creature. Once on, I decided not to turn it off between sets. I wasn't confident it would revive again. I adjusted the slides for the first tune.

George Saliba hadn't had much time to arrange advertising, but he'd managed to get a small ad in the *Indianapolis Star*. He was pleased and excited by the turnout. It appeared the Salibas' club might manage a whale-sized splash before its last breath. The Rat Fink, along with several other buildings in the neighborhood, had been condemned by the city to construct an exit ramp from the new ring highway being built around the town. The building was scheduled for leveling the day after we closed. I suspected George's real source of happiness stemmed from the money he expected to receive from the city.

One night during the first week, Leonard's drum solo got so far out of hand, to the audience's delight, he knocked over a temporary wall hiding some of the demolition work. As his nature insisted, Leonard played it to the hilt. The crowd thought the carnage was part of the show and loved it. I thought George would be angry, but his reaction was the opposite: if the crowd loved it, then he did too. What difference did it make, he said, when they're going to knock the whole goddamn place down after we finish, anyway.

Leonard became a one-man wrecking crew during his solos, and later, at odd times on breaks, he would gouge a hole and pretend to break through openings. By the end of the gig, he'd rigged false walls to topple when he attacked them with his drumsticks or bounced into them riding on his big rubber ball. He was becoming legendary in Naptown.

56 TELEPATHY

There's good self-consciousness, and then there's toxic, paralyzing, raped-by-psychic-Bedouins self-consciousness.
—David Foster Wallace

March 29, 1970
Indianapolis, Indiana

EXCEPT FOR THE shattering effect of being apart from Theresa and our little son, who, with all our separations, I was beginning to feel I barely knew, the gig was going better than expected. Even Mickey had relented and resigned himself to our stay in Hoosierland. My parents had gotten re-accustomed to having me in the house, and we quickly adjusted to a semi-normal routine. I found time to contemplate and come to terms with a lot of my Indianapolis past. I'd left here in the midst of failure and disaster. No matter what I accomplished anywhere else, the remnants of my tattered life here would always haunt me. I was coming to the conclusion that outside of localized feelings for family and friends, even those I'd lost touch with, I could no longer consider Indianapolis home. It would never be just another city; the origin of who I am had taken root here. I couldn't change anything from my past, but I was anxious to get back to my real home and little family where I was accepted and respected for who I was: Las Vegas. Theresa's loving and encouraging letters that I answered with equal affection gave me the patience and inspiration to cope.

I hadn't discussed Theresa's visit with my family—not really our way to talk about these kinds of things. Mom wrote it off as a new mother being away from her child and told me she looked forward to when I could take some time off and bring Theresa and Keoki to Indiana again. Dad said he thought she was a beautiful and wonderful girl and didn't understand what all the fuss was about. They agreed it would be easier for everyone when we came back on vacation. I willingly let it go. Other than myself, I didn't see how anyone could be blamed for how poorly things had gone, but it was over and done with now.

Around 10:30 on the band's last night off, my parents had yawned off to bed while I sat at the kitchen table quietly reflecting on these thoughts. Earlier, they'd carved me up in a game of three-handed bridge. As usual, Mom won, she was a deceptive bidder and a ruthless card player who rarely made a mistake, while Dad and I played too recklessly. Her only equal had been Pat.

Restless, I decided on a snack before going to my room. The Kellogg Corn Flakes box I pulled out reminded me of living with my grandparents in Earlville, a tiny village in upstate New York. They'd taken care of me during my kindergarten year while Mom cared for Dad as he slowly recovered from a severe back injury in a New York City hospital. Grandma Marion and Grandpa Ray often allowed me a bowl of the giant golden flakes while listening to a radio serial before bed.

I'd put my dish and spoon into the sink, anticipating curling up to more adventures of international superspy Sam Durrell, this one in Karachi, Pakistan, before falling asleep. The house was inky-dark beyond the light spilling on to the captain's table. I took a few steps into the shadowed dining room to retrieve my paperback from where I'd left it. As I turned back to the kitchen, a bolt of darkness hammered me. I'd thought it might be a stroke or a heart attack, but there was no pain.

The resounding smack had felt like being hit in the brain with a baseball bat, once, hard. I staggered to the wall to keep from falling, shaking my head to clear it. But my mind wasn't foggy, the darkness was more of a sensation than a blackout. In fact, my thoughts were intensely focused, searching for something, something I couldn't define, something important—no, more, something momentous. Something was happening, had happened, I wasn't sure which. I wasn't sure where . . . here? No, somewhere else . . . in Las Vegas? California? Hawaii? I instantly knew this impalpable connection was tied to Hawaii as surely as I knew I existed. My heightened awareness darted in every direction like a minnow searching for safety. I stood engulfed in dread of . . . of what? I couldn't specifically say. Theresa? A new thought formed . . . I'm connected to her in a way I've never been connected to anyone else.

I glanced at the clock, 11:45, only 6:45 in Waipahu. It was crazy to call but how could it hurt to check? I used the phone in the room Dad kept as a part-time office next to the back bedroom so I wouldn't disturb my folks.

"Willi," I said when Theresa's mom answered. "It's Larry. I'm calling from Indianapolis. Is everything okay there?"

"Oh yes, everything is fine here, thank you for asking."

"Is Theresa home, can I speak to her?"

"I am so sorry Larry, she has gone out with friends. I can tell her you called."

"Willi, is the baby okay? Is Keoki okay?"

"Why yes, of course, he is. He is sleeping now."

"I know this will sound strange, but would you take a quick look at him while I'm on the line? I had the strangest feeling . . ."

"I will check for you right now. Don't you worry, I'll be right back."

I waited impatiently wondering where Theresa might be and if I could reach her. Still early there, I reminded myself; she could be anywhere. I heard a rustling sound, and Mama Willi's voice returned.

"Larry, your baby boy is fine, sleeping on his tummy and dreaming of going surfing soon." I heard the smile in her voice and grinned in relief.

"Thanks, Willi, I appreciate it. Sorry about acting so strange. Will you ask Theresa to call me, though? As soon as she can? Ask her to use our phone card or call collect, will you?"

"Of course, I will tell her, Larry. What time is it over there?"

"It's nearly midnight here."

"Okay, if she isn't back in one hour, you shouldn't expect to hear from her until tomorrow."

"All right Willi, thanks. Have a good evening and give my little guy a hug when he wakes up."

Sitting there at Dad's desk with my hand on the receiver, I realized I still quivered, the adrenaline still pumped. *What an odd feeling?* Whatever was going on didn't seem to involve my little family at least.

I tried to calm myself for sleep. Receiving mystical notifications of some unknown happening thousands of miles away defied sanity. I finally dozed off, leaving the door to my room open so I could hear if the phone rang. But she didn't call.

I didn't hear from Theresa Monday morning either, which made me nervous until, in the sober light of day, I got hold of myself. I had to stop acting so childish. There was nothing to be worried about. If anything terrible had happened to Theresa, she or somebody would have contacted me by now. Throughout the day, when I started to worry, I reminded myself I would be back in Las Vegas in days. I'd find us a new place to live, one more in line with our budget this time. I didn't expect it to take long. I ached for us to get back to normal. I would redouble my efforts to be a bigger part of Keoki's life. Everything had gone a little nuts with this side trip back to Indianapolis. It would be okay soon. What I should be concerned about is what to do about my battered B3. Would it survive the flight back? That was a real problem to worry about.

Leonard's act was epic during our last week at the Rat Fink. His storied drum solos were becoming famous around town, especially at nearby Butler University. Tables of unlikely drinking-aged students consumed buckets of beer. He continued his assault on the nightclub, with the Saliba Brothers roaring in laughter along with the crowd. Though he never uttered a word, his expressions of surprise and innocent malapropisms kept everyone in stitches. On our last night, Leonard broke through the wall into the parking lot outside, all planned ahead of time, of course. The weather cooperated, and those who stayed to the end, pretty much everyone, left satisfied knowing they'd witnessed the destruction of a nightclub. We'd had a much better time than expected, and we joked around with each other in our excitement and relief to be heading home to the Flamingo Sky Room where we belonged. And this time the booking was secure. I'd checked.

By the end of the week, I still hadn't heard from Theresa, but she knew money was tight, I consoled myself. She probably wanted to save the long-distance charges. I'd call her the minute I got off the plane in Vegas. As I finished packing my suitcase, the telephone rang in the other room, and my heart stopped for a second, hoping it was her. Mom called me to the phone. Before I could express my relief, she said, "Mama Willi told me you called. What do you want?"

Theresa! But she sounded so resentful and defensive, unlike I'd ever heard her before.

"Uh. I wanted to talk to you, make sure you were okay, and like always, to tell you I love you and can't wait to make love to you again."

Silence hissed on the other end of the line.

"Honey, I had this weird experience Sunday night. I've never felt anything like it. I had this sudden, powerful feeling that something had happened to you. Or Keoki. Crazy, I know. I had to be sure you were okay."

Still silence.

"Are . . . are you angry that I called?" I was nearly speechless at what I was hearing, or actually, what I was not hearing.

"No."

"Well, I'm glad you're okay," I stuttered in confusion. "You are, aren't you? Okay? Nothing bad happened last Sunday at oh . . . six or seven, did it?"

"No."

What was going on? I struggled to maintain our one-way conversation, searching for something I could say that would change her tone. "Okay, well, I'm about ready to leave for the airport. We'll be back in Vegas tonight. Are you excited about coming home soon, too? I'm sure I can have a new place ready for us in a few days. Do you have an idea of when you'd like me to make reservations?"

"I don't know yet. You need to be sure we've got a place to live first. Anyway, Keoki isn't feeling well right now. You'll have to call when you get to Las Vegas."

"What's wrong? Anything serious? When I talked to your mom Sunday, he seemed okay."

"Well, he's sick now. It's not a big deal, a bad cold or something. But I can't take him on an airplane sick."

"No. Of course not. I understand. When do you want me to call?"

"I don't know. I'm not sure. I'll call you when he's better." *What the hell?* She sounded exasperated with me.

"Theresa? Baby, what's wrong? I can hear it in your voice. Something's definitely wrong."

"Just stop. Nothing is wrong. Call me when you get to Vegas, okay?

Part III images

The Sky Room

Seymour Heller

Performing

PR photo at the bar

The View

Sky Room Ads

PART IV

Write clear and hard about what hurts.

—Earnest Hemmingway

57 A HAWAIIAN HEARTACHE

You can love someone so much . . . but you can never love people as much as you can miss them.
—John Green

April 7, 1970
Las Vegas, Nevada

I UNLOCKED THE furnished condo-apartment I'd rented on Stewart Avenue. The rooms were musty and needed airing out. I opened windows in the two bedrooms and the living room looking out over the tiny front yard. The furniture was more functional than aesthetically pleasing. I'd insisted on a king-sized bed for the master bedroom, the second bedroom had a double. We'd be replacing it with a crib and nursery things as soon as Theresa was home, and we could shop for them.

As performers at the Flamingo's Sky Room, our band made more money than we ever had, more than twice as much as we ever had, even after paying our agent and managers and setting aside money for band expenses. But renting the big house with a pool in a nicer neighborhood west of the interstate had been a mistake. We'd been living too near the edge of my income. One week out of work, one hiccup, and I'd had to let it go, especially after all the travel costs back and forth to Hawaii and Indianapolis. The rent here was much more reasonable, and closer to work. We were a couple blocks north of Charleston about half-way between the Las Vegas Strip and downtown. Nothing was endearing about this modest home at the moment, but once our little family filled these rooms, we'd make it our own. We'd made homes with a lot less.

The telephones were installed. I wondered if they were connected. I rummaged in a box for an ashtray, set it by the living room phone with my cigarette in it, and lifted the receiver. The dial tone's buzz made me think about calling, but it was only seven in the morning in Hawaii. Maybe I should get a few things done first. The boxes and television sets I moved in from storage yesterday could wait, but I wanted to get the clothes in my suitcases and steamer trunk put away and make the bed so I could sleep here tonight. I'd been bunking with Dave for the last couple of days while I located a new place for the Dunlaps to live. There would be plenty of time to call Theresa before I was due for setup at the Sky Room.

I puzzled over the confusing phone conversation I'd had with my wife before leaving Indianapolis. I'd never heard her voice like that before. Not even close. We rarely disagreed and never argued. The only exception was minor, and there'd been sadness, but no anger in it. We'd been upset for different reasons. On my birthday last December Theresa told me she was worried that I didn't love our son and thought I wasn't spending enough time with him. Her concern had troubled me and made me worry about being a good father. Within minutes she'd folded her arms around me, no words were needed—a simple warm and soothing hug that melted my heart. I'd made a commitment to be a more significant part of Keoki's life, and I thought I'd done that in the few months before we'd gone to Indiana. I was sure, now that he was older, it would be even easier to interact with him. Theresa's attitude in our last call had to have been a strange anomaly. I reminded myself that within a matter of days we would all be together, and we'd soon get back to normal. But I couldn't shake a sense of uneasiness as I dialed. Theresa's mother answered.

"No, Larry, she went out early this morning. Haven't you heard from her? She told me she called you. Did you miss a message or something?"

"We talked for a few minutes before I left for the airport in Indianapolis, but not since." I needed to hear my wife's voice as I remembered it, excited and full of love for me no matter what we talked about. "Please let her know I'm home in Las Vegas. I'm moving us into our new apartment. Ask her to call me collect here, at our new phone number. I'm anxious to hear from her." I gave Willi the number and paused for a moment. "How's Keoki doing? Is he feeling better?" I was sure he must be. Kids bounce back quickly from runny noses and sniffles.

"What do you mean?" Mama Willi laughed. "That boy, he is doing fine like always. He is eating well and sleeping well, and he laughs a lot. You have a wonderful son and we love him so much." My nerves went all jangly. Theresa had told me she'd delayed her return home because Keoki was ill.

At the Sky Room, my next worry was the condition of my damaged organ. It might have arrived as a jumble of keys, switches, and pieces of wood on the bottom of the crate. I'd stuffed every kind of cushioning I could find around the dolly before shipping it, hoping to keep the cabinet from completely detaching from the base. After levering off the wooden slats, my poor wounded beast appeared no worse than when I'd surrendered it to Sky Freight's tender mercies, though the visible damage still shocked me. I removed the crate slat by slat but left the B3 strapped tightly to the dolly. Thankfully, the on-switch light lit green and the Leslie horns revolved. After a couple of quick runs, I sat behind my keyboard gazing around the room and out the windows overlooking Caesars' busy parkway. It had been more than six months since we'd been on this stage, and the faint hint of stale cigarettes mixed with the Sky Room's own unique aroma of spilled drinks and dishwashing soap reminded me I was home. It was a start. I desperately wanted things to get back to our customary routine.

A few minutes before we kicked off the opening set, Mac came to the stage and put his drink on the organ. He started to lean on it, but I quickly lifted my hand in warning.

"This thing that fragile?"

"Yeah, think so. Not even sure you should put your glass on it."

He shrugged and held out a stack of mail. "Got this bunch of BS from Vince. Says there some stuff in there for you." Vince Gardiner was the head maître d', and he seemed excited about our return.

I rifled through union notifications, a couple of flyers about the band returning, and two envelopes, one from United Airlines. I ripped it open hoping for an answer to my insurance claim. I was anxious to get it repaired or replaced if necessary. A check dropped out of the letter as I unfolded and scanned it.

"Fuck. Fuckity fuck, fuck, fuck." I held up the check and laughed hopelessly. "I've been screwed six ways from Sunday."

"What is it, man?" Dave asked. He and Les craned their necks to see the letter.

"United Airlines. They approved my claim. Their investigators say the organ is damaged beyond repair."

"Don't sound like it's making you too happy," Mac said.

"I can't imagine why. This check is their compensation for a complete loss. They want me to junk my B3 and buy a brand new one. Assuming I can find somebody selling them for $150.31."

"What?" Mac said. "Man, I remember you sayin this organ set you back two grand or more."

"Not counting the Leslie speakers, they cost a bundle." I finished the letter and gazed through the Sky Room windows. "United says unless I paid extra for specific flight insurance, they pay by weight. Apparently, the damned thing isn't worth what it weighs."

I examined the other envelope. "Uh oh, here's something from Union Bank. Wonder what they have to say for themselves." I ripped it open. As the legal owner of the Hammond B3, they'd received a damage report from the airport in Indianapolis. They'd sent me an official letter reminding me I was still financially obligated to pay every penny I still owed on the organ unless I had private insurance elsewhere.

My brain wanted to overload with distress. With opening night moments away, I needed to set my worries aside and go to work. I stood next to Dave and Mac as we offered up an old favorite, the Buckinghams *Five O'clock World*. We were warmed by the enthusiastic response from our club and hotel co-workers and a massive pack of fans and friends. The room stayed busy until the small hours of the morning. I attempted to keep my spirits up for everyone, but in the back of my mind, I couldn't put aside the discrepancy between what Theresa had told me and her mother's assurances of Keoki's health—and what to do about my disintegrating B3.

I waited impatiently for Theresa to phone me over the next few days. The hunger to pick up the phone and call her became almost irresistible. My desire was tempered by what appeared to be a clumsy lie to avoid coming home. I couldn't imagine why she would do that. And I feared hearing the voice I'd only known as warm and loving sound as cold and uncaring as it had in our last conversation.

In the past, whenever we were apart, we wrote long, passionate letters to each other. Maybe I could unlock her heart if I could find the right words to send to her. When I knew my airmailed letter must have arrived and I still hadn't heard from her, I couldn't put it off any longer. She answered on the third ring.

"Theresa, honey, did you get my letter?"

An audible sigh before, "Yes."

I picked my words carefully, her voice sounded as sullen and troubled as it had on the phone in Indianapolis. "Did you understand what I wrote? I know there must have been something I've said or done that's causing you to feel the way you do. I understand that now and take full responsibility for it. I'm so sorry, honey."

A moment of silence and then, "Yes. I read what you wrote."

"All I need is a little help in figuring out what I can do or change to make it okay. If we could just talk about it, get everything straightened out between us—"

"I don't feel much like talking right now."

"You know if we were together, if you could come home, I'm sure we could work this out. We've always been happy when we're together, honey."

The oceanic winds of the Pacific howled between us in muted silence as I waited on the line. "I learned a new song yesterday—*Close to You*, by the Carpenters. Every time I hear it, I think of you. So now I can sing it for you."

Nothing.

"Can you give me an idea when you'd like me to make reservations for you?"

"I don't exactly know yet. There are some doctor appointments I have to go to."

"Treese, you have a doctor here, you know."

"Keoki's baby doctor is here," she said in a petulant tone. "And he has an appointment."

I wanted to push for some kind of timetable but sensed the same unwillingness as before and retreated. "Well, will you call me soon, in the next few days, so we can get the tickets?"

"Yeah. Sure. I need to go."

"Theresa, honey, I want you to know I love you. I don't exactly understand what's going on, but keep it safe in your heart that I love you."

"I know. Me too. Bye." And with that, she was gone.

"Larry, need to talk," Dave said during an early break at the height of the evening. He gestured to a bench off the path on the way to our dressing rooms. Outside, intoxicating night-blooming jasmine permeated the soft air around us. "I'm worried about Mac. He was drinking pretty heavy in Indianapolis, but I chalked it up to being around his old friends. Seems to be as bad or worse here. I've watched him order a couple of stiff jolts before we even begin to get himself going, and he doesn't let up all night."

He seemed to finally notice me sitting, steeped in gloom, staring at the grass between my feet. I watched a cigarette between my fingers burn into long, gray ash in front of me.

"What's troubling you, brother?"

"Been over two weeks and Theresa hasn't come home yet."

"Is something wrong? You told me Keoki was sick."

"No. Turns out he's actually not. If it was anything, it was sniffles or something. Got a feeling something's going on over there, something bad, but I don't know what it is." I pulled in both elbows trying to cut off a shudder.

He nodded and put a hand on my shoulder. "Don't worry, man, she'll get here. That woman adores you. Maybe you should give her a little more time."

"She's acting pretty weird, Dave." I turned toward him. "When I call, her folks have trouble getting her to come to the phone. She's not real communicative."

"Well hang in there, buddy. It'll work out." *From your mouth to her ears*, I thought, . . . *if she's even listening.*

"Yeah. Hope you're right. Hope it's soon." I looked at my cigarette; burned to the filter. I checked the pockets of my new safari jacket for the pack. We only had one set of our pocketless John Lieu suits left since the United Airlines disaster, and we weren't wearing them tonight. Our new replacement Safari suits weren't as nice, but they had plenty of pockets. And they were cheap. They had to be, considering how little United had given us for the lost wardrobe cases.

58 THE GREETER

Lead us not into temptation. Just tell us where it is; we'll find it for ourselves.

—Sam Levenson

May 21, 1970
Las Vegas, Nevada

"SO WHY DID YOU decide to enter a beauty contest in the first place?" I'd always been curious why pretty young women would be willing to subject themselves to public appraisal and judgment in beauty contests.

"I had a friend in high school who moved to Florida and entered a pageant there," Sheri leaned her elbow on the table, flicking her fingers as she answered my question. "She told me she had a blast, so I wanted to try."

Sheri Schruhl and I sat across from one another in the Flamingo coffee shop, comfortably sharing the space: me, half-sprawled across my side of the booth; her, describing one thing or another in her life. When the band's long breaks synched with her dinner hour, we'd begun keeping each other company in here, the way we were tonight. These interludes were a welcome break from my anxieties.

When we'd returned three weeks ago, this eye-popping girl in heels wearing a white bikini about the size of my pocket-handkerchief had been stationed outside the casino entrance at the bottom of the Sky Room. A Miss Nevada banner spanned her five-foot-seven body from shoulder to hip. She'd been hired as the Flamingo's official greeter. Las Vegas is full of dazzling girls, but Sheri was a homegrown stunner who'd taken home the Miss Nevada trophy last month and followed it by capturing second runner-up at the Miss USA pageant in Miami only days ago.

We'd become friends soon after I first noticed her. Though I'm not exactly certain how that happened, I remembered feeling embarrassed for her vulnerability and giving her friendly smiles and hellos, to which she responded. I was trying to reassure her that not every guy gawked at the spectacle of her near nakedness. We fell into the habit of looking for each other. After a little while, I walked down the Sky Room stairs to sit on the bottom steps during our short breaks. She'd steal some time to wander over and talk with me before returning to her official greeting duties, such as they were. In the bits of conversation we shared, her sunny attitude cheered me out of my malaise, and we eventually found opportunities to sit together in the hotel's coffee shop.

I had no worries about what I was doing; my heart knew my interest in her was entirely innocent. I was immune to Sheri's physical charms. Gazing at her centerfold body and angelic features only reminded me that I already belonged to the most wonderful girl in the world. Though Theresa's strange reluctance to come home had extended into weeks, for some reason I didn't question, when I was with Sheri, I felt closer to the day when my wife would be home, and we'd be happy again.

Sheri and Theresa shared many common attributes: both had long, lush, dark hair and lustrous, deep-brown eyes. They were both drop-dead gorgeous, and they liked hanging out with me. Conversing with this lovely girl helped ease some of my lonely hours. Besides, the thought of a Miss Any-State-in-the-Union having any interest beyond friendship was ridiculous.

"I sent away for the forms to enter a Miss Las Vegas pageant," Sheri continued, "and it turned out, I'd actually entered a state-wide contest. Too funny, huh?" I smiled, amused by the direct way she expressed herself. She lifted her left hand as she spoke, slender fingers grasping, patting, shaping—dancing to the rhythm of her earnest comments.

"When I made it to the top twelve hundred, they called me in for an IQ test and to hear me sing because, you know, you have to have an outside talent of some kind. When it got down to the final seven, my mom finally believed and got involved."

While listening to her, my mind's eye was drifting over the two of us alone in this quiet part of the restaurant, and how we might appear to some invisible observer. I'd taken a course in oil painting in college and drawing courses when I'd been dead set on becoming a cartoonist in high school. The malleability of light and texture in the medium of oil-based paint particularly fascinated me, and, though I was no prodigy, I believed my eye wasn't altogether terrible. I visualized a dreamy composition of the two of us sitting here together from a viewpoint across the room. *The Beauty Queen and the Rock Singer.* Me, disheveled in my shiny, old-gold suit, collar open, tie askew, rumpled from a recent performance; her, perched on the edge of her side of the booth in her white bikini, high heels, and Miss Nevada sash. I could see how to paint us; her expression animated and focused, me sprawled, listening and admiring; the over-bright light in the restaurant, saturating the colors and deepening shadows like an Edward Hopper composition, a sliver of smoke from the ashtray in front of me, no one but us in the picture.

"I believe in positive thinking. You can accomplish anything if you set your mind to it, you know." She dipped her head in solemn emphasis. "And when you do, then other good things will follow. Success breeds success." I bobbed my head in agreement with Sheri's simple formula for achievement.

"My mom found a mentor for me at our church. Her name is Joanie, and she'd been a Miss Nevada and second runner-up Miss USA in 1957. If she would coach me, I knew I'd definitely have a great chance to win. I had to go to her house for an audition, and afterward, she agreed to work with me. And I did have a great chance—I won."

Had she ever. She'd followed in the footsteps of her mentor in both state and national competition. The Flamingo, who'd sponsored her, decided she'd be the perfect ornament for the hotel during the off-season summer months. When I'd first seen her on display at the hotel's entrance, I'd thought her a little forlorn in nothing but her tiny bikini, banner, dazzling beauty, and her innocent smile. But she didn't see it that way at all. To her, she explained, it was an explicit validation of all she'd accomplished.

"What's next for you?" I asked.

"I'm planning on going to UNLV next year. I'm interested in marine biology. I love learning about stuff like that. I want to learn everything I can."

Once past Sheri's spectacular looks, she was a sweet, intelligent girl. I thought of her as a precocious little sister, her company going a long way toward keeping me out of the dark funks I tended to drop into at the end of the night. My empty apartment seemed to silently reproach me for my unfulfilled promises of a wife and little boy to fill its empty rooms. I loved knowing I could be friends with her without getting caught up in her beauty. And, she was eighteen, almost ten years younger than me. For a moment it crossed my mind that she wasn't much younger than Theresa, about the same age as she'd been when we met a year ago. I quickly set that thought aside. The point was, I could admire her without desiring her. Perfect.

I can't say exactly when things changed, but when they did, it was unmistakable. Subtlety wasn't Sheri's long suit; she didn't really need it to be.

"Larry, you've got a long break coming, don't you?" she'd said, smiling innocently. "Could you give me a ride home when I get off?"

Like a stag, comfortable and at home in his part of the woods, who suddenly feels the rifle's sights on him, I froze. We'd never been out of the hotel together. But I reconsidered. I had to be misreading the signals. *A beauty queen interested that way in me? Larry, please, get over yourself, however ego-stroking it might be to imagine.*

When we arrived at Sheri's north Vegas home, I met her mother who was getting ready for bed. We exchanged pleasantries until Sheri grabbed my hand and pulled me to her room. Apparently not a problem for her mother. She must not have realized what a hormonally-driven, sex-crazed danger I might have been to her nubile daughter if I'd been someone else. Sheri sat at a little table removing her makeup and chattering away about nothing I could absorb. I gazed around her room, seeing her Western High banner and movie posters on the wall, stuffed toys on her nicely made bed. Face scrubbed of masterful makeup, her clean features revealed her actual age, not so much the inaccessible pinup. But when she slipped into her bathroom to change, I caught glimpses of her astonishing and distinctly adult figure through the half-closed door. If possible, she had become even more alluring and decidedly more forbidden. I sat without thinking or moving on the bed. Her bed.

When she came back into the bedroom in a filmy shift, she glided to where I sat and leaned down to kiss me lightly. Without a word, she held out her hand, and when I stood, she kissed me as thoroughly as I've ever been kissed and pressed her award-winning body against me from lips to toes. I returned her affection with every bit of my being, my mind working overtime to convince myself the fire I was playing with could be contained.

"You know," she said, her voice warm and husky, "if you asked me, I'd go out with you." It was clear she knew what she wanted and was confident in getting it. She reached behind her to my arms and pushed my hands down until my palms were cradling the cheeks of her ass. *God help me because there's no one else here who can. There's nothing but warm flesh beneath my fingers.* Her arms moved around my neck as she ground herself against the part of me that was giving her its complete attention.

I looked over her shoulder at her bed longingly, the wrong part of my body insistent on taking over. Until now, it had been pretend. But we were no longer playing; I missed Theresa terribly, and Sheri was here . . .

"Sheri," I choked out. "I don't know what to say." Nothing had ever been truer.

"You don't have to say anything. Just do what comes naturally."

"I . . . I'd better get back to the hotel for our next set."

She kissed me again and I thought my head would explode. "I think there's enough time for what I have in mind." She knew my schedule as well as I did. Besides, if I was late, the guys would cover. Either way this turned out I was going to hate myself in the morning.

"Sheri, I'm flattered—no, way more—I am tempted beyond belief." I smiled the agonized smile of a starving man walking away from a gourmet meal. "But I can't. I can't do this right now." I left as quickly as I politely could.

My experience with Sheri the Greeter had frightened and confused me. I was married to my fantasy girl. I'd never been attracted to anyone else since I'd met her. Theresa fulfilled everything I'd ever dreamed of and many things I could never have imagined. Though I'd walked, no, ran from Sheri, how could I have let myself come so close to a fire that could threaten everything I had? I was shaken to the core because I hadn't thought it was possible. I must have missed Theresa so much, I'd given in to a moment of weakness.

I'd never mentioned Theresa to Sheri, I realized in a flash of revelation. Sheri had been a break from my loneliness; we'd existed in a different world from the one where I was alone all the time. Had I been hiding Theresa from her? Would the beauty queen have been as friendly if she'd known I was married?

I was determined to make it up to Theresa, though I hadn't done anything but give in to a few kisses and an incredibly intimate embrace. Was that so wrong? If so, on a scale of one to ten, how wrong? Maybe a two? No more than a three, right? I brushed the thought away and rededicated myself to thinking how to get our little family back together, and, only parenthetically, how unbearably horny I was.

59 FOUR SAFE WORDS

Some choices we live not only once, but a thousand times over, remembering them for the rest of our lives.
—Richard Bach

May 28, 1970
Las Vegas, Nevada

"DID YOU TALK to Mac?" Dave stopped me as I slipped away from the organ bench, anxious to get off the stage. "We've got to get him to cut back. He's already stewed, and we've got another set to go. Getting embarrassing to be on stage with him when he's like this."

"Didn't know I was supposed to."

Dave stared at me like I had two heads. "I told you about this days ago. Man, you're the leader. I've mentioned his drinking to him several times. If I say anything more, it'll mean a hassle." He twisted his grin into a wry smile. "And I'll be forced to kick his scrawny little ass."

"Oh. Well, yeah. Sure, sure. Sorry, had other things on my mind." Like a misplaced wife in Hawaii and a near miss with Miss Nevada. I saw Sheri every night as she strutted outside the casino downstairs. She still said hi and waved, but I didn't come down to sit on the steps anymore or join her in the coffee shop. She didn't seem offended; she was as friendly as ever. Why should she be? She could have her pick of lovers. One thing was obvious: I had to do something about Theresa before I got in big trouble.

Several days later, I sat staring at the telephone, trying to pull myself together before dialing Theresa's number in Waipahu. I lit a smoke and took a big drag, and dropped it in the ashtray when I noticed how badly my fingers were shaking.

"I wondered how long it would be before you called me back," she said listlessly after our hellos. I'd been calling every few days and getting her on the phone less than once a week. As she'd run out of excuses, she mostly cried when I asked when she was coming home. I listened helplessly; once she got to that place in our calls, there was almost nothing I could say that would coax her to speak.

"Theresa." My heart was in my throat hoping this time she would respond to what I had to say. Either way, she would have to listen. It was ultimatum time. "Are you trying to end our marriage?" I'd been too afraid to ask her before. "Is that what you want? Is that what you're trying to tell me with all these excuses for not coming home? You're like a stranger. I feel like I'm married to someone I used to know but don't anymore. Do you still love me, do you have any feelings for me?"

She wept quietly on the other end of the line.

"Treese honey, please, I need to know. I've been thinking about almost nothing but what's happening to us—or what's not—I guess. Listen, I have something I need to say." I paused before taking the plunge. "If you still love me, sweetheart, if you want our marriage to survive, then I'm here for you, all the way. I can't say I totally understand what's going on with us, but I swear to you, whatever it is, I'll go with you all the way to the end if that's what it will take to save us."

She still wept.

"If you want that from me, I only ask one thing. You have to tell me if you want me to stop. If you want me to walk away and never bother you again just say, 'I don't love you.' You say those four words, or write them, and I promise, I will walk away. Forever. Say them anytime. In fact, I'm pleading with you, begging you. Say them right now if you wish I'd stop calling and leave you alone because if you do, you'll be saving my life. Right now, Theresa, right now I'm dying every day. I'll do anything if it will bring us back together. But if there is no way back, please, don't leave me hanging. Just say it, tell me you don't love me."

Weeping.

"Are you still there, honey?"

"Yes." Choking.

"Do you understand? Do you agree?"

"Yes." A whisper.

"One other thing. I'm worried about us, about me, but mostly about you. You seem so depressed whenever we talk. Something's seriously wrong, honey. I think you need help, professional help. I want you to find a therapist. A professional who can help you find your way out of the dark place you seem to be in. Will you do that, please?"

A pause and a sigh. "My mother wants me to do that, too. Yes, I'll do that."

Though I'd hoped to get more from her, one way or the other, I figured I'd accomplished all I could for the moment. But before I ended the call, I'd give her another chance to end the uncertainty.

"Treese, I love you. Do you understand? I mean, you're the most important thing in the world to me. I'm telling you this now when things are tough when it really counts. This is the kind of crucible where you find out if someone truly loves you, Treese."

"Yes. I understand."

"So." I took a deep breath. "Do you want to tell me you don't love me? Right now? I promise it's alright for you to say it if you don't. You'll be doing me a favor if that's the way things are."

"No, I don't want to say that."

"Okay, darling." My mind and heart raced, one glad she hadn't said it, the other in despair at the yawning path through hell opening in front of me. "I'm going to say goodnight now, honey. Try to get some sleep. I hope you have sweet dreams tonight."

I hadn't been avoiding Dave on purpose. Maybe I would have if I'd remembered he'd be looking for me. "Well, did you talk to Mac?" Dave zipped up the side of his gold suit pants and reached for his jacket.

"What? Oh yeah. Sure, I did," I lied. "Why?"

"Because, if possible, he's been more drunk than usual." He checked his hair in the mirror, patting a couple of strands in place.

"Okay." I nodded, noncommittal.

"No, it's not okay," he said, still staring at his reflection.

I shrugged. "I'll see what I can do," I said, heading for the door. It wasn't likely that I would.

Before we could leave the room, Les stopped us. "Hey. Wait, Larry. You missed rehearsal this afternoon. First break, you two and Mac come back here to the dressing room so we can work on *Love Grows*. The harmony has slipped so bad it's off the setlist until it's fixed. Larry, you and Mac particularly sound like crap. I'm not sure you two are even singing the right words let alone the right notes."

I ducked past him and lit out for the stage. I was anxious to get the night started, anything to distract myself from the anxiety dominating my mind. For the first time in weeks, Theresa and I'd had something resembling a conversation in our last phone call. I couldn't decide if we'd somehow turned a corner or if I was being teased with a tenuous hope that would disappear when we talked again.

"Come on, Larry, sing your part, alone, watch this finger." Les tapped a digit on one of his guitar's strings.

"What? Oh, sure."

"Man! Where in the hell is your head?"

"Sorry, forgot."

"Well, get it together. Let me hear your part."

We went through the harmony, but I couldn't concentrate. I usually liked it when we sang our harmonies, accompanied by his unplugged guitar. Of course, we didn't sound as good as I would've liked. We didn't polish our vocals the way we used to when we were a vocal group. Like now, Mac had his eyes shut and sang with his teeth clenched. It didn't sound like a voice at all, more like a buzz that changed notes. It's no wonder his voice had such a different tone than the rest of us. But it didn't make any difference. My part was pretty half-assed, too.

All I cared about was getting this stupid exercise over with so Les would get off my case.

Four days later, I went looking for Mac. My situational memory had kicked in, and I remembered Dave's demand that I talk to him. It gave me a perfect excuse to ask him about something else I wanted to know.

"Jesus H. Christ, bub, what's goin on with you?" he asked when I found him where I knew I would, near the service bar nursing a drink. He held his rocks glass out a little and looked at me like he'd never seen me before. "Your damn suits are hangin on you, bro. Guess this shit I'm hearin about Theresa's not bein here's weighin on you some."

"Yeah, yeah, I know, lost some pounds. Can't seem to help it." I hung my head. *This is so goddamned embarrassing.* I didn't like people seeing me all fucked up like this. As controlled panic had given way to uncontrolled panic, had given way to high functioning catatonia, I couldn't seem to eat anything, couldn't stand to put solid food in my mouth. I'd been living on milk, a couple of quarts a day.

"Somethin you want to talk to me about?" Mac gave me a quizzical look as he sipped his usual Crown Royal.

"Yeah," I grimaced as my stomach growled from some odd pain and sidled up to him on the bar stool. "It's about that." I pointed at the glass he'd rested on the bar. "Dave wants me to talk to you about how hard you're hitting the booze. Looks like you gotta have two, three highballs before you even hit the stage."

Mac's expression told me he didn't like me talking to him like this. *What's wrong with how I'm talking to him?* I wondered. "And you don't slow down all night. It's amazing you're still standing by the last set."

Mac gave me a disgusted look and slipped off his stool to walk away. I put a hand out to stop him. He glared at me. "You got your hand on me, Larry."

"Yeah, I know." I dropped my hand, not because it bothered him, but because he'd stopped.

"So now I told you. Look, I can't make you stop drinking. Nobody can. You're over twenty-one. But Dave says I'm the leader, so I have to talk to you about it." I nodded my head, mostly for myself. "That's what he said."

He studied me for a minute. "You all right, bub? You don't sound like yourself."

"No, of course, I'm not all right. You don't lose thirty fucking pounds in three weeks if you're goddamned all right." I toned that down. But really, it should have been obvious. "That's not the point. Look, I've known you a long time—since I asked you to join the Reflections in Indianapolis. Been trying to be the best leader I can ever since you and Dave got me to California." Thinking about all those years of trying to be good at something made me sad for some reason. I pulled my act together and glared at him, got right in his face.

"I am so totally fucked up, man. Look, I need your help. I need you to cut down on your drinking on your own because I can't deal with it right now. You have to handle it on your own. I need you to pick up the leader slack for me." Mac glowered into his rocks glass.

"I ain't no leader, man." He shook his head. "Can't do that gig."

"No, not officially. I don't mean that. But can't you act like a leader somehow? Like by example? There's so much negative crap going on in this band . . . and I'm up to my ass in alligators right now. I don't have anything left to solve the group's problems. Will you help me out, Mac? Calling on you as a friend."

"I guess," he mumbled. "Much as I can anyway."

"One more thing."

He glanced at me. "I tried drinking like you do, you know, every day." I reached past him to the bar and grabbed a Camel out of his pack. I looked longingly across to the rows and rows of colorful labels, all promising sweet, deadening relief from the painful disease of memory. "I couldn't do it. I mean actually, could not fucking do it. I was able to get halfway drunk for three days this week, but after that, I couldn't make myself even look at anymore booze." I dipped my head to his lighter and got my smoke going. "Show me how you do it. I need to sleep at night, you know. I need to know how to stay drunk but still functional you know, the way you do."

"Hey, fuck you, man." He snapped the lighter shut.

"What?" I frowned a little. *He probably thought I was tweaking him, but I needed an answer.* "I'm serious, Mac. You're the fucking expert. I'm not kidding around. I need to know how to get some relief. Can't smoke dope anymore. Gotta find some way to turn my goddamn mind off."

"Ain't nobody can teach you to do that." He shook his head. "You'll find your way through this shit, man, and be glad you couldn't."

60 ENTURBULATED

> *Who knows what true loneliness is—not the conventional word but the naked terror?*
>
> —Joseph Conrad

June 10, 1970
Las Vegas, Nevada

I PROBABLY SHOULD have considered coming here earlier, I thought, bypassing the Celebrity Centre's sun-scorched door handle to shoulder my way in. Blistering bone-dry air instantly dried hot little snot knives in my nose as I'd gotten out of the car. Everything around me appeared glassy, colors supersaturated in their attempt to reflect back too much sunlight. It was the beginning of summer, but Vegas was getting an early taste of the high, triple-digit days to come.

I wasn't thinking about that, though. I was thinking how one day the girl of my dreams was mine and swore she'd love me forever, and then the next day—just gone. No warning, like a bolt of lightning out of a sunny sky, no building cumulus of issues. *What in hell had happened?* The girl who'd made me feel like the greatest man walking now made me feel like a creep, a stalker, for calling her from 2500 miles away. *What was I supposed to do?* I walked to the reception desk, hoping I could find some relief here.

"Can I help you?" The young woman at the front desk asked.

"Charlie Groff, is he here?" She flipped through a card file. I guessed she was a young pre-Clear working here to earn her auditing.

"Give me a minute." She walked away while I looked around. The place appeared less temporary than the last time I'd been here, more of a lived-in look.

"I'm sorry, but Charlie's in Hawaii right now. Is there anyone else you could speak with?"

I thought about that. Charlie knew Theresa and me. I'd feel a lot more comfortable talking to him than to some stranger. I considered leaving, but I was desperate. "Well, I'm not sure where to start." She gave me her best learning-to-be-an-auditor look.

"I've had like this major upset in my life and Charlie was, I dunno, my mentor, my minister? Whatever."

She cocked her head. "I understand. Sounds like you need an emergency assist. Let me find someone to help you. What's your name?"

I told her, and she ushered me into a small room, similar to the one I had been audited in. An impossibly young guy with a notebook and a folder came in and seated himself in front of an E-meter and cans on the table between us. He opened the folder and studied it for a minute or two.

He gazed at me with a hint of surprise. "I'm not sure if you know this, but your last session here was re-classified. The senior auditor determined that you went Clear in your Dianetics auditing. The next action we're supposed to take is to check that."

I wrinkled my brow. "Yeah, I blew off smoking marijuana. Turned out not to be such a great thing. Not why I'm here, though. I have a bigger problem, an intense grief issue, and I need help dealing with it."

"Yes, I understand. But the indicated action here is to complete the Clear result. We need a floating needle on that." He gave me the pleasant, standard auditor expression.

"If I agree to do whatever the hell that is, is there some kind of relief I can get for the grief?"

"Sure." He shuffled a couple of papers in the folder. "Have you had any liquor in the last twenty-four hours?"

"Unfortunately, no."

"Have you smoked any marijuana in the last week?"

"As you may have heard me say, I can't smoke grass anymore, so the answer would be no."

"Gotta ask." He gestured at his checklist. "Okay, your auditor will be right in."

I sat there, glumly waiting for something to happen. I guessed I might as well be waiting here as anywhere else.

An overweight woman a few years older than me came in and took a seat. She didn't say a word but indicated that I grasp the cans. She put her hand on the E-meter and gave me a gentle smile. "These next questions are simply for balancing the meter." She asked me simple things like what was my name, what the weather was like, and whether I'd had anything to eat recently.

After a few moments, she told me to put down the cans. "I'm sorry, but your needle is jumping all over the place. I can't get it settled enough to audit you. You mentioned you hadn't eaten today, that's probably the problem."

"Well, sure. But that's why I'm in here. I haven't been able to eat solid food. I need help with that."

"I understand. But we can't audit you until we get a floating needle. You're too enturbulated for me to help you at the moment." She smiled her gentle smile.

"You're telling me that I can't get the help I need because the thing I need help with is the thing that is keeping me from getting the help I need?" God, that pretzel logic didn't even make sense to me.

"You have to be able to apply your full attention to your upset. Right now, you don't have enough attention units free. Why don't you try to get something in your stomach and come back? Maybe tomorrow morning after a good night's sleep." Gentle smile.

I scraped my fingers across my scalp in frustration. I was beginning to shake, holding on with both hands trying not to totally lose it in front of her.

"Isn't it obvious?" Quiet desperation hissed out around my words. "That's the problem. I can't sleep, and I can't eat. That's why I'm here."

"According to this re-classification in your folder, you're a Clear. You are experiencing things now in a way you never did before. You haven't had any OT, Operating Thetan, training, so you don't have access to tools that might help you deal with certain things. It's unfortunate, but there's nothing I can do until some of this upset you're dealing with has run its course. Your mind must be rested for auditing. I'm sorry, but until then I can't help you."

"Jesus Christ!" I was getting sick and tired of her gentle smile. "I'm having a serious problem! Can't you at least fix it so I can get high again?"

My escort left me at the door, and I stumbled out into brilliant desert sunshine, my breath shortened in the scorched air.

Later in the week, Mac and Mickey were walking, laughing together as they sauntered past the first pool on the path to our dressing rooms.

"Hey," Dave called ahead to them, "heard you guys were tearing up the Cat last night."

"Oh yeah? You heard that from who?" Mickey asked, slowing his step.

"Actually, one of Leonard's friends told me. Said you knocked over tables, broke glasses and spilled drinks—practically started a riot. And Mac was with you. Said both of you were so wasted you could hardly stand."

"If you're referring to me giving Scottie some help with some guys who decided they wanted to bust up the place," Mickey said with a sarcastic grin and a dangerous glint in his eye, "then yeah, could've been me." He held his arms out in innocence. "Other than being a good Samaritan, don't see no problem."

Mac shook his head. "You know what? I don't like people talkin shit about me behind my back. If I want to go to the Cat and cut loose a little, then I want to do it without it bein a big deal to anybody else. Ain't none of their damn business."

Leonard tried to catch my eye, but I pretended not to notice. Usually, he steered clear of these issues, but when he couldn't get me to respond, he apparently felt compelled to say something. "The thing is, Mac, we're pretty well-known in town. When you guys do stuff that gets us the wrong kind of attention, people are going to talk. You and Mick are getting kinda famous for going over there and getting hammered. Personally, I think everyone's got a right to their privacy, but when you're in the limelight like we are, it's just reality."

I veered around everybody and took for the stage. In the past, I would've probably attempted to defuse the situation. Instead, I avoided it. I was what

Scientology would call "lacking attention units" for these squabbles. I flipped on the B3, no longer even giving thanks for the minor miracle when the pile of crap started. I no longer thought about what I would do when it didn't. I only wanted to hunch behind my keyboard and not notice anything. The rest of the guys reached the stage, everybody taking a bite out of everybody else. It was enough that none of the chomping was directed at me.

Nights at the club passed like a blur. The disagreements and unresolved problems made the group feel like greasy dynamite, unsettled and volatile. Mickey and Mac and their wives were spending more time together and isolating themselves from everybody else. We learned a slightly speeded up version of the Ronettes' *Walking in the Rain*. My God, Dave killed on that song. I loved singing it, but it filled me with desperate melancholy.

My life off stage remained difficult. The unendurable pain of separation from Theresa was only slightly alleviated by the few horrible conversations we had. As I mentally struck off the passing days, the way a prisoner carves them into his cell wall, one of them came when she called me. We made a little small talk for a minute or two. It was unusual—she'd called me, so I asked why.

"Oh. Well . . . I thought you'd want to hear what happened with the psychiatrist." She paused as if waiting for me to say something. But before I could, she said, "I stopped seeing him."

"Oh. Of course." That slim hope flew out the window to escape with the rest of the flock. "I'm not surprised, but I hoped it would help."

I heard her deep sigh. "I don't think you'll want to pay the bill when it comes, though."

"Why? What happened?"

"Because I slept with him." If I'd thought I was so numb she couldn't hurt me, I was wrong. I felt gut-punched. I choked trying to catch my breath. My lungs worked my chest like a bellows, and I'd started to shiver. I needed to respond, to say something. Anything.

"This is some really serious shit you're telling me, you know."

"Yes, I know."

What do I say? What am I supposed to say? The scream in my head, held un-screamed, made my voice come out breathy and strangled. "I have to call you later, Theresa. I should be handling this better, I know, but I'm just . . . I can't . . . Can't talk now. Maybe later. I love you and . . . and goodbye."

61 THE SAINT AND THE SINNER

Give a man a fish and he will eat for a day; teach a man to fish and he will eat for a lifetime; give a man religion and he will die praying for a fish.

—Unknown

June 23, 1970
Las Vegas, Nevada

TWO MORNINGS AFTER Theresa's revelation had ripped through my soul, I struggled to wake from an agitated sleep somewhere around noon. I wrestled with a dream object I couldn't make work. I clutched it in a dream hand, urgently squeezing it with my fingers. If it could accomplish . . . something, all the craziness would finally make sense, and I'd be rid of the oily grittiness in my mouth. I clasped and pressed in growing frustration until reality forced me out of my dream world. As my swollen eyes opened, I lay on my side turned toward the nightstand; I noticed the open drawer, and, more compelling, a hand holding my Beretta 9-mm with the gun barrel in my mouth while a finger spasmodically jerked the trigger against the safety. Jesus Christ! *My hand!* I yanked the weapon away, staring at it in shock and disbelief. Only the safety had kept the gun from going off. I'd almost woken up dead!

I threw the pistol to the bottom of the bed gaping at it in horror. Killing myself had never been an option. I would never have considered it. No part of me wanted my life to end. End the pain, yes, stop the ridiculous amount of emotionally-charged, stomach-churning crap I couldn't keep from swallowing, yes. But not death, no, never death.

While I struggled to reason out what had almost happened, my eyes fixed on the cold metal weapon as if it was a coiled rattlesnake. I hadn't vomited since I'd upchucked Blue Hawaiis in Honolulu, but I tasted bile in the back of my throat. Still shaking, I clumsily retrieved the pistol and ejected the magazine, jerked back the slide, so the round in the firing chamber flipped out onto the bedcover, and dropped the defanged Berretta back in the nightstand. The unloaded round, the full magazine plus another in the nightstand, and an open box of bullets went into a paper bag. I left the bag next to the front door. I searched the shelves in my bathroom medicine cabinet checking for anything I might have accidentally ingested because what happened had been an accident. I found a few loose dexies and bennies and dumped them in the toilet. While I was there, I mouth-washed the taste of gun oil out of my mouth. I stood in the center of the living room clothed in nothing but a sleeping tee and turned in a 360-degree examination of the apartment until I was tentatively assured I'd left no easy way to kill myself.

Calmer, but still shaky, I dialed the phone without thinking and called home. Mom answered. I didn't reveal what I'd nearly done; I couldn't begin to imagine how I'd talk to her, or anyone, about something like this. I didn't want her ever to know how close I'd come to completely fucking things up. I managed an inane conversation that, little by little, normalized the horrific experience as adrenaline seeped out of my body. After I'd hung up, the shakes took over. I threw on last night's clothes and took the bag of ammunition out to the car in shaky hands and threw it in the trunk. I didn't want to go back to the apartment, so I drove to the Golden Slipper and ordered a large glass of milk in the dining room hoping to soothe the burning pangs in my stomach. I sat there thinking, *I have to make sure nothing like this happens again.*

Sleeping and waking had been an ongoing problem for weeks, but until now it had never involved my survival. *A will-to-live had saved me from drowning in Hawaii, I guess there's a will-to-die, too.* Too much pain had triggered something inside, maybe that same lizard brain buried deep within my psyche had taken it upon itself to free us both from my miserable existence. From now on, I needed to figure out how to protect myself from myself, as crazy as that sounded.

I'd already tried and been disappointed by the inability of Scientology's techniques to help me, but another temporary fix came to mind as I gulped my milk. A couple of times, when I'd desperately needed a few minutes respite from the unrelenting pressure of loss, I'd slipped into the Catholic Church behind the Sands. I had no specific evidence, but I thought the quiet atmosphere had helped calm me. I paid my bill and drove to the church.

The simple A-frame building let in plenty of light and held comfortable pews for eighty or a hundred people. I eased through the double doors into a sanctuary. I mimicked others, genuflecting and sprinkling holy water around so I could sneak in. I even lit a few candles in the rack near the altar. I didn't see how it could hurt, and who knew, it might help in some mysterious way. The important thing: I was unlikely to off myself in here without witnesses stepping in to stop me. After a while, my fears calmed enough for me to go out in the sunshine.

Over the next few days, I worked out a wake-up routine. Each morning, before I fully awoke, I jumped out of bed and threw on clothes I'd laid out the night before. I would grab my keys and billfold from the table by the door and drive immediately to the sanctuary. I sprinted from the parking lot to the chapel and into the nearest empty row. I'd lean forward, my knees on the little fold-down cushion, and rest my head on the back of the pew in front of me. Sometimes I'd let myself doze before allowing myself to consider the consequence of full consciousness. When the top of the wooden pew in front of me began to hurt my forehead, I knew I was safely awake. Waking this way became automatic, like delivering my paper route at 4 AM in the morning as a kid. Often, I never remembered getting to my morning pew before I awoke.

I wondered how I should tell Theresa what had nearly happened, or if I should tell her at all. I'd promised to stick through to the end, though, and the end had almost happened. Shouldn't she know about that? I decided to play it by ear the next time I was able to get her on the phone. It turned out to be something I needn't have worried about. After a pause in our desultory small talk during our call, I took a breath. "Theresa, something happened a few weeks ago I think I should tell you about it. I'm not entirely sure I want to, though."

"Well, don't, if you don't want to."

"Thing is, I think it's something you should know as much as I don't want to tell you. After you told me about your, ah . . . therapist, you know?" I paused, lightheaded to be even mentioning what she'd done without screaming my lungs out. "Well, I guess I was badly shocked and I, uh . . . I almost shot myself with the Beretta." I hadn't realized how embarrassingly melodramatic and juvenile it sounded until I'd put it into words. I had the urge to apologize for bringing it up.

"You mean like suicide?"

"Well yes, but no, not exactly. I mean, that's not what I was trying to do. It's I, ah . . . woke up from a bad dream and found myself trying to pull the trigger. Treese," I tried to put it into perspective. "I don't want to kill myself. I still believe we're going to get through this."

"I don't know if I should believe you."

"What?"

She sighed, "The therapist . . . before what happened, happened . . . he told me you might say something dramatic like this."

"What did he mean?"

"I don't know. Why? What difference does it make now anyway?"

I waylaid Leonard at rehearsal when we were both free for a moment. I needed guidance. "Hey, Leonard." He looked my way with his bland Leonard expression, impossible to read. "I've been going to your church, man." He lay sprawled out on one of the chairs near the stage. He gazed at me, interested.

"Saint Viator's, on Eastern?"

I made a face. "Doesn't sound right. The one on Cathedral Way, behind the Sands."

"Oh." He sat upright. "That's not a church. You mean the Guardian Angel. It's a shrine."

"A shrine." I shrugged. "Whatever it is, it's kind of helping me cope with things, you know?" I dropped my cigarettes on the table and pulled out a chair.

He cocked his head. "But you're not Catholic." He paused. "Are you? I mean I've always seen you as pretty non-religious."

"No. I'm not, I was raised a Methodist. Do I have to be to go there?"

"No, I guess not. Well, glad if it's helping." He checked his words carefully before he said more. "Is this still about Theresa?"

Obviously, everybody in the band and their wives were aware of my situation with Theresa, if not the details, but this was the first time I'd talked openly to Leonard about it. "Yeah. I know it's a lost cause, but I can't get free of it yet." It was painful to say, but in the harsh light of day, I probably should get used to the idea. I wondered if I could. I flipped open the pack of smokes and pulled one out. "I thought you might give me some hints on what to do when I'm in there." I made a weak gesture. "I lit some candles. Look, I don't have any idea what I'm doing."

He thought for a moment while I smoked quietly. Behind us, Mickey was replacing a string on his bass. His style of playing wore out more strings in a month than most bass players used in a year. Over near the windows, Les worked with Mac and Dave on a new duet.

"You know, there is a Catholic saint for lost causes. Saint Jude."

"There is?"

"Yeah. I don't know much about him. You can ask the priest at Guardian Angel, though."

"Good idea." *But not likely.*

Since I was going to wake up at the Guardian Angel shrine the next morning, I decided it wouldn't hurt to direct some prayers to Saint Jude, but my requests tended to wander all over the place. Lack of focus probably made it hard for him to understand.

On Sunday night, Leonard came into the dressing room with a booklet about Saint Jude. Apparently, to be sure this saint hears you, you have to "pray with all your heart for nine days in a row, using your mind, body, and heart." So saith the pamphlet. And to make sure you're doing your beseeching correctly, a couple of prayer templates were included. Insert the specifics of your particular lost cause into the blanks provided and *pow!* you had the perfect prayer! Cool. Best of all, the prayers came with a guarantee: "For all those who maintain a strong posture of faith that God is always working behind the scenes," I was assured, "a novena to Saint Jude has never been known to fail, with the exception of," and here was the out clause, "some people may receive concrete, visible proof that their request has been granted, while others may receive something that is not what they asked for, but what they really needed at this point in their lives." Sounded a lot like lyrics Mick Jagger would sing.

As soon as I got back to the apartment, I filled in my lost cause plea and the appropriate names into a prayer template on a separate sheet of paper. For the following nine mornings, I profoundly maintained an exceedingly "strong posture of faith" upon waking and put my puny heart and soul into my newly minted prayer. I left the sanctuary each morning positive I'd given everything I had to the effort. *Oh, most holy apostle, Saint Jude, etc.,* insert: *Please intercede with my wife Theresa and show us the way to heal our marriage* and so on I would read and pray.

But, of course, I'm not Catholic, and undoubtedly it was a big ask for a Catholic saint to help me. He probably had a busy schedule. And maybe the pipe was full. After all, it was Las Vegas, where many, many dreams and lost causes come to die. I like to imagine he tried, though, maybe asking his supervisor, "Ah, look I've got this guy here, and he's following all the requirements. I mean he's done his nine days, and he's been outstandingly creative with the part about his wife—ah, ah, wait a minute, got the name right here . . . Yeah, Theresa, good Catholic name, don't you think? Almost brought me to tears. So maybe we should cut him a break? Things have been pretty rough for him this year. What? No can do? Not Catholic enough, or at all? Hasn't really been at the prayer thing for that long either? All right, whatever you say. Let the son of a bitch burn, then.

"

62 RIDING WITH ELVIS

Sometimes you don't realize you're the one that's drowning when you're trying to be someone else's anchor.
—Unknown

July 10, 1970
Las Vegas, Nevada

DAYS SLIPPED PAST like Chinese water torture. I've always needed a lot of sleep, and normally I'd never had much trouble getting it. Different now—my rest was fearful and unsettled. I had a hard time telling the difference between sleeping and waking dreams. On one of our early long breaks, Mac and Leonard decided to go over to the lounge at the International Hotel to renew our acquaintance with Ike and Tina Turner and pulled me along with them. After their show, we lost track of Mac in the huge hotel. Leonard had decided we'd have to catch a cab to avoid being late for our next set when Big Jim Sullivan offered to save the day.

"Look, I've got to get back to the Flamingo for Tom's show. You guys can ride with me. I'll pick you up downstairs in front of the valet station." Mac would have to find his own way back.

Leonard carried on a running conversation with me about how weird Ike and Tina's show had been, but still reeling from the effects of little sleep and a steady diet of anxiety, I found it hard to follow. I nodded a lot and attempted a smile when it seemed appropriate. We exited the hotel entrance about the same time Big Jim drove up in his Cadillac. A uniformed valet opened the back door for

Leonard and me to pile in. It was tight; there was already a large person seated on the far side. The car sped out of the driveway only to come to a near standstill in the sluggish traffic on Paradise Road. The radio was on in the background, and there was a lot of chatter, so I didn't notice right away who was in the passenger seat in front of me until Elvis Presley reached to fine tune the radio.

When he did, B. J. Thomas began breaking my heart again as the car's interior filled with his *Just Can't Help Believing*. As the tears started in my eyes, I wanted to shout, *For Christ's sake! Turn that goddamn radio off! I have to listen to Les burn those fucking words into my brain every night—I don't want to remember her misty morning smiles—or panic when I think about never seeing promises in her eyes again.* Elvis spoke in time to save me from yelling out something jerky.

"Now fellas, this here's B.J.'s version, and I'm not saying it's not real nice. Cause it truly is, and I like it, I really do. As y'all know, I've been rehearsing this tune for the documentary we're filming—least if I could remember the daggone words." He laughed amiably. "Now, I want you to listen here to B.J.'s record, and after, you tell me honestly if my version isn't every bit as good. Maybe even better." The conversation went quiet while we listened to B.J. squeeze my heart. As the song ended, everyone assured Elvis he was right, the way he sang it was way better. When he craned his neck to look back at me, I nodded.

"That's right, boys," he said turning back around. "You bet your bird I do."

I hadn't been to his rehearsal and never heard him sing *Just Can't Help Believing*, and I prayed to God I'd never have to hear that song sung by anybody again. Big Jim turned west on Flamingo Road toward the Strip while I turned inward to a well-worn tunnel of depression and misery.

During a monotone phone conversation where my wife cried continually, and I begged her again to put me out of my misery, she asked me how Joan and Lora were before we ended the call. Then, a few days later, Theresa actually called me.

"Hi." She might have sounded different than she had before. My head wasn't in a space where I could tell or bring myself to care.

"Yeah, hi." What did she want? I'd give her whatever it was. Didn't make any difference. I'd give her anything if she'd just stop killing me. Nothing but pain came from her. After listening to us breathing on the line for a while, she finally said, "Are you okay, Larry?" She sounded kind of pitiful. *Yeah, well me, too.*

"You want to know if I'm okay?" I asked in the voice of a condemned criminal "Why don't I just tell you. Every time I think about you, which is mostly all the time, my heart wants to stop. Sometimes I can't catch a full breath; I feel like I'm being smothered. My brain thinks it's on fire, screaming at me to get up and run— somewhere, anywhere. My body doesn't work right. My muscles don't work together moving my bones around, I walk in fits and starts like a puppet with its strings cut—," I choked, out of breath and energy. There was a long pause before she spoke.

"I wanted to talk to you about Keoki's first birthday. You've been asking me to come back before his birthday. It's only a few weeks away. If you still want us to come, you should make reservations."

What? Am I hearing her right? "You want to come home?"

"I thought that's what you wanted."

"Oh. Sure. Of course, I do . . . I'll call for reservations as soon as I get off the phone." I cringed inside wondering when the punch line would hit. We talked over some of the logistics of the trip to the point where I started to believe she might seriously mean it. I vacillated between scared to death and thinking this could finally be our chance. I'd always believed if we could get together face-to-face, we'd be able to work our way through this. It had been so long since I'd held her in my arms, though. Would it still be the same? Sometimes I was confident we'd find our old selves. But other times, the road out of hell seemed impassable.

63 SKY ROOM FOLLIES

A woman who cuts her hair is about to change her life.
—Coco Chanel

July 21, 1970
Las Vegas, Nevada

THERESA STEPPED OFF the rolling stairs into the heat of the afternoon—alone. *What does that mean?* I shuffled ahead tentatively, arms at my sides. I hadn't recognized her at first; her hair was shorter, and she wore it in a messy bun. I expected at least a perfunctory hug, but she shouldered past me toward luggage retrieval. Unnerved, I tagged along behind until she slowed.

"I guess you noticed I didn't bring Keoki. If you're worried about the cost of the ticket, don't. I canceled it before they charged the Amex card." I was stunned by the tone of our first conversation after more than four months apart.

"Theresa, money's never been an issue when it comes to you guys. I'm surprised, you know, disappointed he's not with you."

She stopped and rounded on me, her stance aggressive. "Are you? Are you really? You've hardly spent any time with him since he was born."

It's not too often I'm caught without words, but this was one of them. I shook my head and staggered backward a step.

She turned back toward the luggage carousel. We wouldn't be kissing or hugging hello. I was an automaton getting her suitcases stowed in the car and heading to our apartment. I tried a couple of times to engage her in conversation, but it didn't go well.

The air conditioning hummed on high as I gave her a quick tour of the home she'd never seen. From the living room, the kitchen was to the left; a short corridor led to a big master bedroom with its own full bath, the main bathroom, and the guest bedroom. Theresa's eyes passed over the flowers on the dresser of what was meant to be our room before rolling her suitcase on toward the guest bedroom door. My heart sank. Not only would I continue missing her physical touch, she'd be sleeping behind a door a few feet away and still be beyond reach. I hadn't anticipated things going so badly. I tried to adjust to her arctic demeanor.

"Look, if you don't want to stay in here with me, okay. Let me move to the small bedroom." She didn't answer and didn't stop.

I didn't like her setting herself up as a guest in our home, but I did my best to accommodate, helping choose fresh towels, sheets, and pillows. I suggested going out for dinner, but she begged off, preferring to take a tuna sandwich to the bedroom claiming she was tired from the trip.

I sat more alone than ever in our living room knowing my precious wife was so close and still so far. Everything I'd been experiencing long distance was suddenly right here in my lap. *What in God's name has happened to her?* I wondered for the millionth time. It was hard to believe her presence here made things seem worse, but it did. Was I reading too much into this? *At least,* I thought, *we'll have a chance to talk face-to-face.*

At the Sky Room, Mac set his rocks glass on my organ cabinet as usual. "So, heard Theresa's back."

I sighed and popped open the keyboard lid and switched the organ on, feeling it's subtle rumble.

"Not so good, huh?" My bruised eyes must have told the story. He nodded. "Well, Joan wanted to know. Wants to see her when she's ready."

"Yeah, me too."

"Wow, it's that bad?"

"If you can imagine worse, than worse. I'll tell her Joan wants her to call. I'm sure she's looking forward to seeing her."

63 SKY ROOM FOLLIES

The sun was bright and the temperature in the mid-nineties when I unlocked the apartment door in the morning hours after work. The guest bedroom door was closed, so I quietly poured a glass of milk and left a note for her to call Joan, including the Brown's phone number, before slouching into the master bedroom.

I lowered the television volume and let an old movie run. Our king-sized bed, which I'd hoped would welcome her, seemed bigger and lonelier than ever.

I woke around noon and searched for a robe. The small bedroom's door stood open, the bed made, and Theresa vanished. A note revealed she'd gone to the mall next to Caesars and would be back in time for dinner.

My wife found me staring at the television when she returned. Uncertain how to respond, I pretended interest in the moving screen and offhandedly said, "Hi."

She bustled into what I'd have to start calling her room and dumped packages on the bed. She came back to fold herself into a chair on the other side of the living room. I turned off the TV.

"I talked to Joan."

"I'm glad." I gave her a tentative smile. "I know she was looking forward to hearing from you."

"It was great to hear her voice." She busied herself, searching in her purse. "The girls are going to the Sky Room Thursday night, I thought I'd go in with you if that's okay."

"Of course, it's okay. You're acting like a stranger in your own home."

"Well, I'm not sure what you think of me."

"I think you're my incredible, fantastic wife. You are who I live and breathe for every day. Nothing will change that, unless . . ."

"Unless, what?" She fished out her own pack of cigarettes and lit one with a throwaway lighter.

She couldn't have forgotten. How could she forget? I glanced at her in consternation. *Why do I always have to remind her? Those four words were my lifeline.* "Unless you want to tell me you don't love me. Don't you remember?"

"Oh, that." She exhaled it away in the smoke. "Well, I'd better catch a shower before we go eat." She stood and stopped for a moment to look at me. "You seem awfully skinny." She disappeared into the bathroom with her smoke, and soon I heard the water running.

We chose the Rio buffet for dinner and conversed civilly but with no sense of intimacy. For anyone observing us, she was gorgeous, and I must have looked as punctured as I felt. I made it a point not to mention anything personal, and that hurt in its own way, but it was better than her open hostility yesterday.

Wednesday was a rehearsal day for the band. Our apartment was under an armed truce, and I couldn't find a way to breach her walls. When I came out of the bedroom Thursday night freshly showered for work, I found a woman waiting on the sofa who barely resembled my wife. She wore a dress to the edge of her ass; instead of hair flowing and loose, she'd blown it out before pushing and hairspraying it into a tight French knot—I desperately missed the long, rippling waves that had first attracted me to her; and she'd put on makeup. Lots of it! Though she'd usually applied a little mascara and light lipstick before we went out, Theresa's natural skin and beauty couldn't be enhanced by anything made by man. Her eye makeup made her look older, harsher. She completed the look with open-backed, fuck-me-twice pumps and a small clutch. I tried to smile through my bewilderment.

I seated her at a ringside table before scurrying away to the dressing room. *Who was this stranger inhabiting my wife's body? Who had taken away my island girl and left behind this slick, overtly-sexy mean girl?*

Little by little the other guys filed in and we dressed for the night. I thought we looked pretty sharp in our pearl-white, long-sleeved turtlenecks and gold John Lieu suits tonight.

"Hey, saw Theresa out there," Mickey said. "Man, is she dolled up." I nodded, cringing with shame. Did he and the rest of my friends see in her what I was seeing? She looked more like one of the high-end working girls who hung around the hotel than the young wife I cherished.

Joan and Lora, and Leonard's new girlfriend, Marie, joined Theresa at the table, but some joker leaned down to talk to her. She laughed, right there in front of me; the wives looking on in indifference. *Shit.* I tried to catch her attention, but except for glancing away once or twice, her eyes never left her admirer. I twisted around to peer behind the drums and cymbal stands.

"Leonard! Hey, Leonard. Is *Close to You* in the first set?"

He glanced at the setlist. "Yeah, third song."

"Skip it." He stared at me. As he opened his mouth, I said, "Leonard, just fucking skip it, goddammit. I can't sing it tonight. Laryngitis, whatever, I can't do the damn thing, so don't call it."

Les overheard me, which I'd been trying to avoid. "Hey, I make the list. We don't skip anything unless I say so."

"Then say so. Find something else. I'm not singing that song, so if you leave it in, you better be ready to sing it yourself." He grabbed the card from Leonard's bass drum with a scowl and took it to his amplifier to make the change. He was angry, but I didn't care.

I'd told her I'd learned this song for her, and she'd barely reacted. Nevertheless, it meant a lot to me, and I couldn't sing it without thinking of her. I thought the breathless and wistful way Karen Carpenter sang the lyrics personified how I cherished her. The melody of *Close to You* may sound simple, but it requires a lot of control to sing in the airy style that made it so meaningful. My breathing was so shallow, my voice so shaky, I could never manage such an emotional song tonight. I took a long glance at her before the first song. *How could this keep getting worse and worse?*

As the night unwound, or in my view unravel, my eyes followed Theresa everywhere. I missed some cues and vocal entries, but I didn't care. When she left the table, I was horrified watching her prowl through the room making it evident she was available to any man who wanted to speak with her. Her attention hadn't always been on me before, but in little ways, she'd always let me know she was mine. She'd never given me a reason to be concerned until now when she was overtly on the prowl.

At the break, I pulled an empty chair from another table next to her where she sat with the other wives. After a few minutes she excused herself, I assumed for the powder room, but when she hadn't gotten back in a while, I strolled around looking for her. She sat at the bar with a drink in front of her, and a guy sidled in between barstools talking the talk. I slipped away; I didn't want her to see the hurt on my face.

I struggled to contain my stomach. Unable to confront her about her reckless wantonness, I escaped as soon as possible to the isolation of the shadowed stage. I would have given anything to disappear entirely, to be anywhere else but here. I crouched behind my organ in disbelief, embarrassed and ashamed. When Les sang Paul Simon's lover's wail, *Cecilia*, midway through the third set, all that registered with me was how it was my heart that was breaking, over and over. As the words steamrollered me, tears streamed down my face, and I bowed my head in confusion, hoping no one would notice. I sang the Archies' *Sugar, Sugar*, knowing Theresa was no longer mine, but having to sing about how I wanted her anyway. Dave closed with the Union Gap's heartbreaker *Woman, Woman*, and Gary Puckett's plaintive question filled me with misery . . . *did the words he was singing describe what she was thinking?* The answer seemed clear enough. I was wrung out as a bar rag when the set ended.

As the night ground on, Theresa worked the club, making advances without restraint, accepting drinks, teasing and flirting without a glance toward me. I tried to find her on each break. I wasn't always successful. On our last break, as dawn threatened to set fire to the tips of the western mountains through the tall windows, we sat together alone. She seemed restless. I tried to engage her in conversation before she lost interest and walked away.

"Who's your favorite singer these days?"

"What?" She seemed impatient with me. "Why are you asking me that?"

"Because we haven't had a normal conversation for months, and it's almost as if we have to get to know each other again."

"Oh." She paused to think. "Englebert Humperdink, I guess. I like the way he sings." He was far from my personal choice. Even so, I resolved never to like anything remotely connected to him or his songs. His tours probably stop in Honolulu. *Is she trying to be one of his backstage girls? God, Larry, stop these raging thoughts!*

"How about songs. Do you have any new favorite songs?"

"*Something*, by the Beatles," she said without pause. I didn't remember it at first, but then . . . I did . . . The melody was haunting and sad. *Does she share this song with someone?* I never wanted to hear this song again. *Why am I asking questions I don't want answers to?*

"You know I hate you like this." Her mean-girl face bored into me in a way so cruel I would have rather had my eyes spiked out than discover the depth of darkness inside the woman I loved. I hurt down through time in a chain of rejections multiplying back to earliest childhood. In that earth-shattering moment, for the first time, I would have given up ever meeting Theresa to avoid the pitiless indifference in her eyes. Damage done, she turned away before speaking again. "Well, hate is too strong a word, but it's hard to be around you when you're so miserable."

A million defensive thoughts jumbled around in my brain. I couldn't think of one I could say to change the trajectory of where things were headed. I did what I have always done when faced with overwhelming force, all the way back to when my father would strap me with his belt: I retreated into a speechless, sullen shell.

After the last set, we drove home without a word. It almost came as a surprise that she hadn't left with someone else. I said nothing as she marched directly into her room without a goodnight. I retreated to the cold bed in what should have been our bedroom. After wrestling the sheets and blanket into rolled ropes and kicking the pillows to the floor in broken sleep, I woke fevered and exhausted to face another day of torment.

64 ROBO-VOICE AND THE FORCE FIELD

Aia a pa`i `ia ka maka, ha`i `ia kupuna nana `oe.
Only when your face is slapped should you tell who your ancestors are.
—Hawaiian Words of Wisdom

July 24, 1970
Las Vegas, Nevada

I SAT OUTSIDE on the patio drinking hot coffee under a large umbrella. After the bone-chilling experience of last night, I let the 110-degree heat bake me into an apathetic stupor. Theresa opened the sliding glass door and stepped out on the concrete slab. She wasn't the woman on the prowl I'd seen last night, but there was no affection in her gaze either.

"Here," she skipped a Polaroid snapshot across the table toward me. "Today is Keoki's first birthday." I'd known, of course, and wondered how we would celebrate it without him here. "I brought you a picture we took of him before I left." She tried to look disinterested in my response, but I sensed her studying me.

A small brown child with the sun in his eyes held a little Nerf football and grinned into the camera. I hardly recognized him; the last time I'd seen him, he'd been a baby. He wore an infant-sized green and yellow striped jersey and diapers, bare feet nestled in sunlit grass. I slammed down on my emotions before glancing at my wife.

"He's lucky. He's got your looks instead of mine."

"What do you mean?" she snapped. "He looks just like you. His eyes are hazel. Can't you see that?"

I glanced at the Polaroid again. The resolution wasn't good, and the little boy squinted into the sun. Whatever color his eyes were wasn't apparent. I nodded noncommittally.

"So, what do you think?" Was I catching a hint of some message in her question? Defiance? Remorse?

"I wish you'd brought him instead of a photo. He's standing up on his own and walking. I've only seen him as an infant. I'm missing important parts of his childhood."

She nodded, seemingly satisfied or relieved. "I want to call Hawaii and talk to him."

I nodded. "Of course." She waited for me to say something more, but I had nothing to say. She went inside while I continued my heat therapy. Perhaps I should have gone in and talked to Keoki, too, but with no invitation from her, I doubted she would welcome my presence.

Theresa came to the Sky Room with me Saturday, and while not as blatant as Thursday night, she had no eyes for me, oblivious when I sang my leads. She accepted drinks and talked with other men but didn't appear to search them out. Without the other wives or girlfriends there, she seemed bored. I took her home early—after our two o'clock show, and she didn't come in Sunday night. The songs we sang continued to pierce my soul, and we remained balanced on a knife's edge.

As Monday, the band's night off, rolled from morning into afternoon, I woke from troubled dreams. The question loomed: what we would do with our first night alone together. We watched television and barely conversed. Around ten o'clock, Theresa disappeared without a word into her room. She'd been here nearly a week. I'd been sure if we spent some time together, we could work through our problems, but the opening for a heart-to-heart talk had never come. I knew this might be a bad idea, but I couldn't stand waiting for the right moment anymore. She cracked her bedroom door partway to my light knock.

"What do you want?"

"We have to talk. We can't let things keep going on like this."

She left the door cracked open and retreated to sit on the bed fully clothed, her face withdrawn and disinterested. I'd seen this expression before. Sometimes it hid nervousness.

I perched on a bamboo storage hamper near the door, unsure of how to begin. *What did you not say?* I wanted to ask her. My mind ran along a frantic track of questions wondering what words would unlock her feelings. *Why couldn't you tell me whatever it was, before whatever awful thing happened, that triggered this long fall into hell? What barrier has grown between us that we can't even talk? What keeps you from telling me what's wrong? What did I miss? What did you need that I failed to give you? Please, please, please tell me how I failed you.*

"Treese," I frantically searched for a way to shape my tortured thoughts, "I don't know where to start. This is the first time I've seen you face to face since you took Keoki to Hawaii. More than four months ago. This is our chance to figure things out. We've got to try."

No response, maybe a facial tic.

"Can you tell me what happened? Everything is so upside down and crazy. "

"I told you what happened. What? You want me to describe the gory details?"

I squeezed the images I'd already stored in my head before they could get started. "God no, Theresa. I don't mean that at all. I don't want that. I meant, where did this start?" I thought for a moment. "Was it the therapist? Or did you meet somebody else? Do you love this guy, whoever he is? Are you still seeing him or something?"

"No," she almost snorted in derision. "Of course not. There's no *guy*. It was what it was, that's all. Something that happened." I didn't have the heart to follow that line any further.

"Honey, is this about Indianapolis? Something with my family? I know you were uncomfortable there. Except for those few days in Las Vegas, before you left, that's the last time I remember us being happy together."

She sighed as if I were wasting her time. "No, nothing happened in Indianapolis." *Why does this have to be a guessing game? Why can't she just tell me?*

Maybe another tack. "Is there anything you want to say, or ask me? Can you give me a chance to make things right? There must be something I've done to cause you to feel the way you do." She turned her head farther aside.

I grunted in exasperation. "God, Theresa, if I only knew what to do to fix this, how to help? If you would give me something to work with. I've told you I'm in this with you for whatever it takes to save our marriage, but you're making it so hard."

She put on her mean-girl face. "What do you want to know, husband?" The disdain she projected was like another presence in the room.

I'll never know why I asked the next question. It hadn't been in my thoughts, just frustration bubbling over into sarcasm. "Well, is there anyone you want to sleep with that you haven't yet? Maybe somebody in the band?"

"Yeah," she said with a smirk, followed without pause by, "Dave."

Before that name had even left her mouth my body rose and my hand moved in a full open-handed slap across her face as I observed it in helpless horror. Those three things—my loose, inadvertent question, Theresa's almost automatic response, and my hand flashing out to slap her—were all attached by cause and effect, moving in series the way billiard balls on a pool table cascade in collision. Click, click, click. Her hand jumped to her face, and her mouth opened wide in surprise. Still holding her face, she looked at me with an expression I'd never seen from her before: loathing. Well, maybe I had recently, but never laced with suppressed fear. I wished I could take back the last five minutes, no, the last year. I considered taking back the whole concept of being born.

I looked at my hand as though it was someone else's. I'd never struck a woman, never conceived of it, let alone the woman I loved. When I glanced again, the mean-girl look had been replaced with the face of a cornered prisoner, veiled hatred, and barely concealed contempt and anger.

My heart continued to plummet as I backed away. "I'm sorry. I never thought . . . I can't believe . . ." I stumbled over something behind me and bolted in total confusion. She'd told me she wanted to sleep with my best friend and somehow here I was apologizing to her. I retreated to what was going to be my bedroom alone forever, now, looking deep into the raw pit of hell. Something didn't ring true about it, though. Maybe she'd been purposely trying to hurt me for some reason. But no matter how I interpreted what she'd said, what I'd done, was too much to bear. I tossed and rolled. I couldn't sleep, couldn't read. There was no way to stop hearing those words or the sound of my hand against my wife's face. In the morning I wasn't surprised that almost the first words out of her mouth were that she wanted to go back to Hawaii to get Keoki. I hated to admit it, but I could barely look at her.

She tried to get my attention when I didn't respond right away. "I need to go get Keoki and bring him home. He can't stay in Waipahu alone."

I stared at her in disbelief. "You're telling me you want to bring Keoki here? The two of you come home?" The lies again.

She glared back in defiance. "That is what you want, isn't it?"

"How soon Theresa? When will you come back?" How could she think I'd believe her? She wouldn't meet my eyes.

"I don't know. How could I know yet? I have to pack everything up."

I sighed. "I'll book your flight today."

Once her flight to Hawaii was set, her relief was obvious, and the wall between us went back up, though she kept alive the fiction that the trip would only be long enough to retrieve our son. I'd been confident we could work everything out if we were face to face. I couldn't have been more wrong. We were further apart than we'd ever been, and the festering knife in my heart had only twisted deeper.

Theresa's plane speared into the hot August sky heading toward Los Angeles and connecting on to Honolulu. I was back to high-functioning catatonia, not feeling anything now—not sadness or sorrow, nothing. I thought of the Scientology tone scale. There'd been something at the bottom, below death itself. It was called Feigning Death, a state of sorrow so low pretending death is the only survival method left. When I first read that, I laughed. What an imagination that Hubbard has, I'd thought. Maybe that was the way I felt, but if so, I was too numb to bring myself to care.

At the apartment, I discovered she had taken anything personal of mine or hers that might remind me of her. She wanted to erase herself entirely from my past, leaving behind no photos, mementos, not a scarf or a used tube of toothpaste, nothing she might have touched or been a part of. She missed two things. One of them was Keoki's picture, probably left behind as some sort of recrimination. The other was a small packet of seven letters I'd put in a large manila envelope and buried in the bottom of my nightstand. She must have overlooked them. I'd kept every one of her letters. Outside of these few, the rest were gone. In two of the letters were four pictures: two of Theresa surfing from after I'd left Hawaii, and two of her at the beach when she was pregnant. Nestled in with them was my little plastic viewer containing a miniature photo of the two of us a few days after we'd met. I held it to my eye: inside, the vivid colors of a spring Honolulu day washed over us as we sat in the back of Leonard's pink convertible outside our mangy hotel. That was it, all that was left of my marriage: seven letters, four pictures, and my little plastic souvenir viewer—and the Polaroid photo of my little, suntanned kid holding a football.

Theresa had to have known I was on complete empty when she left. I couldn't guess where she was. All I could see was her maliciousness and deception; her empty promise to return when, actually, the only thing she wanted was to leave me, Las Vegas, and the whole emotionally super-charged mess behind.

A few days later I thought I should call to confirm her plane had arrived safely as I routinely did. I made the perfunctory call confident I'd only be leaving a message. She wouldn't be the one to pick up, anyway—and she didn't. One of her brothers answered and called her to the phone before I could say anything. It wasn't a long conversation.

I was astonished at how glad I was to hear she was safe and whooshed a sigh of relief. "Thank God you're there safely. I needed to hear you, Treese. I don't care what you say. Say anything, no matter what—just let me hear your voice." *What was I saying? Where were these words coming from?*

She gave me a bitter little laugh. "I don't know what to say."

"Anything. What's the weather like there?"

"It's Hawaii. It rained for five minutes about an hour ago. It got all steamy for a few minutes, and now it's beautiful, like always. What else do you want to hear?"

"I don't know. It's such a relief to talk to you."

"I guess I should finally tell you . . . that Sunday you called, you remember, when you were still in Indiana? When you thought something happened to me, ah?" I held my breath. I didn't want to hear this, but I was transfixed.

"I don't know how you knew, but I did have sex with somebody. A musician, like you, a guy in SOS." She slid this revelation into our conversation like a silver stiletto. There was a roar in my ears, little black dots in my eyesight.

"I thought you wanted to hear me talk, Larry?" So smooth and mean.

"Who's SOS?" I choked out, dazed and bewildered.

"The band. SOS," she said in exasperation. "Society of Seven."

There were probably more words, but I didn't hear them. A newly discovered robot voice took over and eventually said goodbye. The force field it had built filtered everything after that, letting through only the basic things I needed to hear. It felt good to be impervious. I sensed the pain trying to find me, searching for a way to get at me. I watched it flutter around out there beyond me, red sparks and all, trying to hurt me, trying to make me care. But I wasn't about to care. Not about anything. Not anymore.

65 BEDMATES

I hold a beast, an angel, and a madman in me.
—Dylan Thomas

August 8, 1970
Las Vegas, Nevada

MY NEW-FOUND ARMOR had kept me numb from my disastrous conversation with Theresa, but it couldn't keep me safe while I was asleep. The horrors that chased me through the nights were unshaped and vague, made more menacing by their lack of definition. I'd been existing in a kind of waking twilight; finding it nearly impossible to get to sleep and as difficult to come fully conscious. It was going to be worse tonight. If Theresa's first admission of infidelity had brought out my worst instincts, I worried what my lizard brain had in store for me after her latest revelation. But just maybe, Mary, the attractive dark-haired young woman who was still in the Sky Room alone at 4 AM, held the answer to my survival. I dropped into a chair next to her, without a rational plan in mind.

"Hi," I said. I might have smiled. Can't say for sure. Robo-voice was making all the moves. Fortunately, it wasn't shy like me.

She smiled back. "You're with the band."

I grinned back, did something stupid like pointing an index finger at her and making a clicking noise with my mouth.

"You look like you could use some company, sitting here all alone," Robo-voice, that sly devil, said.

"I'm a stewardess for Western Airlines. I'm away from home traveling a lot, and it disconnects me from people." Her eyes dropped to the tabletop. "Yeah, I think I could use some company."

Robo-voice gestured toward the stage. "We've got one more set, what are you doing for breakfast?"

Mary didn't think it was odd that I didn't want anything but a poached egg, a little toast, and milk for breakfast. And it didn't take her long to spot my broken wing and her nursing instinct to take over. Robo-voice was honey-sweet and soon got us home to her place, an apartment about a mile east of the Strip. That was best. I didn't trust my own bedroom anymore.

I was happy to crawl between the crisp sheets that felt almost new. I was tired because—well, because I was always tired. I wanted to close my eyes as soon as my head hit the pillow, but I knew I couldn't yet.

I wished I could explain to Mary that I didn't really want to have sex with her. I would've told her I actually wanted to have sex with my wife, but that wasn't possible anymore, or probably ever. But unless I let Robo-voice handle it, I'd probably cry—and we'd both be embarrassed—worse, I might lose my safe haven for the night. So I left it to Robo-voice to smooth things over with his little lies. With Robo-voice's encouragement, Mary was able to help me rise to the challenge.

Though my body seemed to enjoy itself judging by its lengthy orgasm and intense gyrations, I wasn't much interested. My libido was dialed down near zero. Afterward, I was able to drift away to sweet sleep, cocooned with a warm girl body who would undoubtedly keep me safe through the night. I felt a certain satisfaction in believing, for at least one more morning, I wouldn't wake up dead.

When I woke, around eleven, I snuck out of bed, found my clothes and went out into the world to look for milk and figure out what I had to do this day. I was still tired but more rested than I'd been in weeks. Mary came into the Sky Room again that night, but she seemed unhappy when I pulled out a chair and sat beside her.

"Why did you sneak away this morning?"

"What? Sneak away? I didn't sneak away. I just thought you looked so cute lying there and I thought you needed more sleep, so I was quiet when I left." Robo-voice had all the answers.

"You thought I looked cute?" She grinned shyly. "You looked at me while I was asleep?" Now coy.

"I did. The sheet wasn't entirely covering you. You looked awfully cute and very sexy."

She blushed. "You could have woken me with, you know . . ." She glanced at my crotch.

"Maybe tomorrow morning." Robo-voice was already planning ahead.

"I think that's a good idea." She nodded. "We should do that."

Rinse, repeat for a couple of nights. I was feeling better, and a lot more certain this new mode of living could be the answer. She was a cute girl, and though I was emotionally detached, it was interesting to watch her respond when I experimented with some of the things I knew my body could do.

Mary had to fly and was gone a couple of nights to other cities. I tried to find replacement bedmates for those nights, but Robo-voice failed to interest anyone. I was forced to use my backup routine at the Guardian Angel shrine. Luckily, I woke both mornings safely, but I was relieved to see Mary back in the club. She was pleased to find me so attentive.

The following morning was a Saturday. As usual, I was out of bed before Mary. It had been a strenuous night, so I hadn't felt the need to wake her with more sex and was puttering around in the kitchen making instant coffee. I knew she didn't like me to leave before she was awake, so I had stocked milk, some cereal, and was back to an occasional cup of coffee.

I was thinking about pulling my jeans over my briefs and checking outside for the newspaper when there was a knock at the door. I hesitated, but then opened the door wide. Standing there was a broad-shouldered guy a little younger than me in a cowboy hat. He appeared shocked to see me and looked at me from top to bottom like an apparition from a graveyard.

"Who—who in blue-blazes are you?" he stammered in confusion. "What are you doin' here?"

I shrugged, looking around like, *hey, I'm standing here in my underwear, this is where a girl lives, what do you think I'm doing here?* When that finally sunk in, I think he wanted to confront me physically, but apparently, Robo-voice tries to avoid those kinds of situations. Besides, I was behind my force field, if he had a problem, it was his, not mine. My face gave him a friendly smile.

"Where's Mary?" His face started to thunder up.

"In bed, still asleep I would imagine." He expected me to be mad, or afraid, or to try to explain. Instead, I waited patiently at the door.

"Well, I reckon I wanna come on in there and wake her up." *Fine by me.* I shrugged again and moved aside. As he strode into the apartment, Mary, who had probably been awakened by his knock, shuffled out of the bedroom in her bathrobe. He started to rain down questions and accusations on her, but she held the palm of her hand up to him, and storm clouds to match his rose on her face.

"Now, you shut the hell up for a minute, Gary. Who do you think you are barging in here like this?" Gary went silent and stood there tight-lipped and motionless. "Larry, if it's nice enough, would you mind stepping outside and giving me some private moments with this numbskull?"

I shrugged, grabbed my jeans, and robo-smiled as I stepped outside. Mary lived on the second floor of one of those cookie-cutter apartment units with concrete stoops, metal stairways, and open cement stair-steps. A black, twisted wrought-iron railing was the only ornamentation. I sat there on the top step in the bright Vegas sunshine, thumbing through the *Review-Journal* I'd picked up off the welcome mat, barely aware of the loud voices leaking through the door. I was contented; once again it was daylight, and here I was, above ground and vertical.

Some indeterminable time later, the door opened, and the young man in his tight jeans and two-toned cowboy shirt stepped out with his hat in his hand. He gazed at me humbly, stretched out his hand, and apologized. Robo-voice was running the show, so I found myself smiling and nodding vaguely as he formally introduced himself and asked my name. Suddenly, his face screwed up like a kid about eight, and he started to cry.

Robo-voice told him to sit beside me on the step, and Gary explained how he'd been rodeoing for some years and come to Las Vegas for a big bull riding competition and how he'd sure as hell won it. He's a national champion now, and he's got a big old gold belt buckle or something, that says so, and he wanted to bring it over to show his girl.

"Well, I reckon she's not my girl, as she has just pointed out. It's just I wanted her to be." He turned to me with the most sorrowful look I've ever seen on a man.

"You know what she said to me in there?" I shook my head no. "She told me I was a disgrace to the whole cowboy race." He put his head in his hands.

I think Robo-voice realized this grieving country rhyme was hilarious, but it didn't make me laugh. I figured this was the cue for one of us to leave. But before I could move, he stood, planted his ten-gallon hat on his head, nodded, and tromped down the staircase in his cowboy boots. I went back inside to get dressed while Robo-voice took over listening to Mary. I wasn't sure exactly what was going on, but she seemed upset about me not showing her the affection she thought she deserved. Why didn't I care about her the way Gary did? Why did she have to beg me for sex? What was wrong with her that she cared about me over Gary? I hoped Robo-voice could deal with this because I was drama-averse. As far as I was concerned, the mission for today was a success. Here I was, alive.

I looked for Mary in the Sky Room to help me get through the next couple of days, but she didn't show. I wondered vaguely if Robo-voice might have misunderstood his assignment and said something wrong to her. I'd decided bed partners were definitely a better wakeup routine than the Guardian Angel. While the sex part could be a complication, it was safer. Girls were more likely to intervene if it was needed than any of the elderly parishioners at mid-day. And they were warm and comfy sleeping companions. I met a pert, little Asian girl, though cute was not all that necessary for my purposes, who came home with me one of those nights. Not ideal, as I mentioned; I preferred to be in someone else's bedroom.

At first, I was pleased to see Mary back at the Sky Room several days later until I noticed two older strangers with her. Mary seemed miserable and withdrawn as I sat to let Robo-voice talk to them.

"You're Larry, I understand." The older man was nearly gray and looked concerned, as did the older woman with him. "We're Mary's parents. She called us because she'd become so depressed."

Robo-voice smiled and said nice things about her and pretended to be concerned. I was focused on how well Robo-voice had learned to sing my parts and play the B3. To tell the truth, he probably played better than me.

Her mother leaned forward, eyes swollen. "We're worried about her. She says she can't sleep or eat, only think about you. She seems to think you like her, but we're worried about the obsession she is forming for you. She . . . she's had a problem obsessing over someone in the past so you can see why—"

The force field cut in.

It didn't keep me from recognizing the irony, but honestly, I didn't have it in me to care. Robo-voice tried a couple of times to explain to them why I was sleeping with their daughter, but it didn't seem to make things better. Finally, deciding I couldn't afford any additional baggage, and maybe St. Jude wouldn't like it either, Mary and I bid each other a tearful goodbye. Well, she did. Robo-voice had the right words and managed to produce some moisture in my eyes as a finishing touch. I left the table, already beginning to troll the club for bedmates. I thought I'd seen someone over near the bar who'd given me the eye earlier.

As time went on, I noticed the band seemed dissatisfied with our repertoire, but complained that there wasn't much on the charts for us to learn anymore. We weren't built to sing Bob Dylan songs and not creative enough to figure out how to take songs from the new breed of singer-songwriter and rearrange them to fit our style. The latest music was rougher now, less melodic and the lyrics more about anger and protest, whether folk, rock, or metal.

If I hadn't been so disinterested, I would have found it disheartening. The part of me that was outside my zombie mind seemed horrified to realize I didn't care, but safe inside, I was no longer connected to these problems. My protective force field worked fine isolating me from troublesome complaints about the band's issues. Robo-voice continued to shepherd me through interactions with my bandmates and finding enough bedmates to comfort my nights; I didn't have to think too much about much of anything at all.

66 A HOUSE ON STILTS

Ua hiki maila, he ho'okipa mai.
You have arrived and are welcomed.
—Hawaiian Welcome Chant

September 26, 1970
Las Vegas, Nevada

LISTEN, YOU GUYS. I need a week off. Have to go to Hawaii on personal business."

Mickey eyed me with suspicion. "You're asking can you just up and leave for a week?"

"No, not really. I'm telling you. Is there some part of 'I have to go' not clear? But I'm not leaving tomorrow, not going until we've found a sub. I'm sure Leonard's friend Phil Conti will do it, though, and I can show him whatever he needs to know."

Les wasn't happy. "He can't sing your parts. This is kind of fucked up, Larry."

I made a frustrated noise. "I know you can work something out to cover my vocals for a goddamned week. Look, this is something I'm going to do even if you fire me. I'm not worth shit with all that's been happening with me. Maybe this will end things with Theresa one way or the other."

Robo-voice would've handled this more diplomatically, but I didn't want any doubt about what I planned to do. I'd given it a big shock when I'd called Theresa to wish her a happy birthday a few hours ago.

"You always say you want me to come back to Las Vegas, to figure things out, to talk things over," she'd said after we'd talked for a few minutes. "That didn't go so well."

"You think it would if I came there—to Waipahu?" *What? Did Robo-voice say that?*

"Well, how do I know? Maybe." *Wait. Is this an invitation?* We'd never talked about this idea before.

"Theresa, I'd come there in a heartbeat, you know that. If I thought you wanted me to . . ." Testing the water; I couldn't believe she meant it, though.

After a long pause, she whispered. "I think it might be a good idea."

"Don't kid around about this. I'd have to leave the band for a week or so to come there. None of us ever take time off, not even if we were so sick we puked on stage."

"I don't know, I get your letters, Larry . . . I'm so tired of what's going on. I know you are, too. Maybe you should come and give it a last chance."

"A last chance." I gulped. "Sounds so final."

She laughed sadly but didn't say anything.

"If I do this, it will be a big deal, expensive, and I'll take a major hit with the guys. Not saying I won't do it, I will. But I've got to know there's a real possibility me coming there will be worth it. If you've already made up your mind, tell me. Like I always ask, say those four words if you want to end this."

"How do I know?" Silence. "If you are willing to come, I'm willing to say okay."

Whew. I blew out my breath. *Is this a breakthrough or a death knell?* "I'm going to work in a few hours. I'll tell the guys then." I waited to hear if saying that would change her mind. "It'll be a couple of weeks before I can get there. I need to find someone to sub in for me." I waited again. "Oh, Theresa," I pleaded, "please stop me now if you aren't serious about this." Still nothing.

Christ Almighty, here I am again, jumping off a cliff not knowing if there's a soft place to land. "All right then. I'll call with my arrival information. I love you, sweetheart. Goodbye."

Robo-voice would have never let me go to Hawaii. I'd left my safety zone, but I didn't see how I could pass up this last desperate chance. How long could things keep going the way they were? Over the next two weeks, I gyrated wildly between zombie and scared-out-of-my-mind shitless. Les volunteered to take me to the airport. I was so faint with anxiety the attendant asked him to help me board the plane and find my seat. Apparently, Robo wasn't happy about my decision.

My first night in Waipahu, lying alone in an unfamiliar bed in a house next to a sugar cane field, was unforgettable. The trade winds gently ruffled the thin drapes at the unscreened window above me where a bright, Hawaiian moon illuminated the darkened room beyond my feet. The island smells of Plumeria and fresh aromas I associated with a forest after rainfall perfumed the warm and humid night air. A jet rumbled across the sky on a distant approach to the Honolulu airport. Another rush of rain sheeted through the jungle outside before disappearing as quick as a thought. I was miserable to the depths of my soul, but Hawaii's exotic, alien beauty still stole into my consciousness and connected me to this place.

My first surprise had come when Theresa wasn't at the airport to meet me. The second, was her cousin, Maing Panerio. She'd sent him to collect and deliver me to her parents' house. He was a nice-looking guy, about Theresa's age, and was enthusiastically interested in knowing more about me and the band. Exhausted from the trip and fatigued from anxiety, I let Robo-voice deal with the conversation as we drove along Highway 1 toward Waipahu. I doubt it was very satisfying for him. Her parent's home sat elevated on stilts at the end of a rough, red-dirt track. Maing grabbed my suitcase while I lugged my carry-on to the front door where a woman, who could only be Theresa's mother Willi, welcomed me in with a huge smile.

"Oh, you must be Larry. We have looked forward to see you for so long. Please, take off your shoes and come into our home. You too, Maing. I will fix some food."

"No, Mama Willi, no time. I have to go." He turned to me. "I hope to see you again soon, Larry. I'm happy to have met you." He hopped down from the porch and walked quickly to his car.

As I entered the tiny living room with Willi, a young man and an older one rose to greet me. "This is George, Theresa's older brother. Since he has the same name as his father, we mostly call him Boy. And here is James, her youngest brother."

My brothers-in-laws' appearances couldn't have been more dissimilar. Boy, about as wide as he was tall, looked big as a house, while James, about the same height, was lean. Maybe they'd had different fathers. It shocked me to realize how little I knew about my wife's family.

"Aloha," Boy said, with a broad grin, his pidgin accent strong. "We happy you here, Larry."

James smiled too. "We hope you have a good time while you are here."

I guessed they didn't entirely understand why I'd come. Willi spotted me looking around and gave me the biggest surprise so far.

"Theresa is not here right now, Larry." Embarrassment and sadness crossed her face. "I'm not sure where she is. She went out with her girlfriends a few hours ago and promised to be back in time." She held her arms out—in supplication, I suppose.

"Keoki, that boy, he still asleep. We could get 'im up, but maybe better if you rest awhile, get settled some before we wake him. Boy, take Larry's suitcase and show him where he will be sleeping."

Boy took me down a short corridor to a bedroom on the left with a window looking out toward the road. This was only a two bedroom, well . . . bungalow, actually. I got the feeling this might be his room; I couldn't help but hope we wouldn't be sharing sleeping accommodations. I'd considered booking a hotel, but Theresa insisted I stay at her home since she'd stayed in my parent's house in Indianapolis. Boy left me alone to do a little unpacking, and I sat on the bed trying to collect my thoughts. That didn't go well, so Robo-voice stepped in with the force field, and I clenched my teeth through the shakes and shivers.

After rinsing my face in the one small bathroom serving the whole house, I pattered into the living room bare-footed like everyone else, where a nut-brown European-looking man in a security guard uniform, who must be Theresa's father, George, waited to say hello.

He shook my hand. "I'm glad you're here. We've done nothing but talk about you the last few weeks. It's good to put a face with the name, and, of course, to meet Theresa's husband." Robo-voice took over, but it did get through that her father was sorry Theresa wasn't there to welcome me, and he was sure she would be along soon. And, that he worked night security at Hawaiian Electric and was leaving for work.

I retreated behind my force field for the rest of the day, nodding where appropriate, while the weariness of continually lowering expectations seeped into my bones. As the angled sun filled the living room with vivid light and deep shadow, Willi told me dinner would be on the table soon and "if that girl isn't home then we will eat without her, she can fend for herself."

A little boy child rode into the room on Boy's shoulder. His eyes widened, and he stared at me in amazement and surprise. Boy sat and tried to get him to wobble over to me on the couch, but he couldn't be coaxed from behind one of Boy's tree-trunk calves. Robo-voice assured me this child was Keoki. I accepted the possibility, but honestly, I didn't recognize him and had to let my zombie mind shut off my emotions for the time being.

When Willi called us, we squeezed around a table near the kitchen, and soon my plate was piled with the exotic but pleasant aromas of fish, rice, fresh banana, and what I recognized as poi. Remembering the purple paste I'd discarded at Kapiolani Park and the powdered stuff Theresa had found in California, poi would never be a taste I could acquire. I picked at the food, which I'm sure the family attributed to my disappointment to Theresa's lack of courtesy, which embarrassed everyone. But actually, my poor appetite wasn't abnormal. I asked if they had any milk.

It flustered everyone to admit they didn't, but Willi said there was a store nearby, and James would run for some. I didn't want to impose on them, but I realized it would be best if I agreed. So far, everything had gone about as poorly as it could. This gesture might save them a little face. Willi was right, and James was back in ten minutes with a quart of milk. I drank two glasses in quick succession. Milk would obviously be on the next grocery list.

I barely registered the next few hours; Robo-voice had almost entirely taken over. Keoki was put on my lap a few times, but when he discovered who it was, he cried. He knew I was a phony, that his mother had made a horrible mistake in choosing me as his father. At some point, someone changed his diaper. A good thing, he'd left a wet spot on my khakis. Night arrived suddenly, and as soon as I thought it wasn't too rude, I retreated to my assigned bedroom. Boy, apparently, would sleep on the couch, Theresa's parents in the other bedroom. I had no idea where James went to sleep.

I would have been unbearably miserable in such uncomfortable circumstances if my robotic defenses hadn't given me permission to lock away the crazy inside my own head. I gave thanks for that as I stripped to my boxer briefs and prepared for bed. I wondered where Theresa slept tonight, and before I could block the thought, for a teeny, tiny second, I wondered with who. Only after the house was silent and I was assured the nighttime shadows flickering in the moonlight and whatever brushed against the house outside was merely vegetation, was I able to slip back into the real world to appreciate the sounds and smells of the Hawaiian night outside the window above me.

67 A COUNTERFEIT HAWAIIAN

> *We are what we pretend to be, so we must be careful about what we pretend to be.*
> —Kurt Vonnegut, Jr.

October 13, 1970
Waipahu, Oahu, Hawaii

I WOKE TO a breathtaking Hawaiian morning. The magnificent day gave the humble house a splendor that couldn't be duplicated, not even in California. I thought about Theresa growing up here in these simple surroundings. I knew next to nothing about her life here before I met her, or for that matter, what it's like now. I still didn't understand why, when we first met, she'd been so desperate to leave Hawaii that she'd been willing to risk enslavement and worse. Maybe if I knew more, I would've understood why she hadn't come home last night. Breakfast was fish with pineapple and a slice of fresh bread with a glass of milk from the new gallon container in the refrigerator.

I tried not to look like the sad sack I so obviously was, perched on the couch behind my force field. Should I check to see if I had enough room on my credit card to catch a flight back to Las Vegas? Sitting in my cone of silence in this disastrous situation, I considered how far I'd fallen into this rabbit hole. I pondered the possibility that the mess I'd made of my first marriage was the root cause. I'd failed Pat. In consequence, had I committed myself too far beyond the edge of my own sanity in trying not to fail Theresa? My two wives were very different people. In fact, there was little comparison, but they'd both conquered me with their innocence, their vulnerability. I'd always trusted Pat's gentle nature and assumed it with Theresa as well. I realized how flawed that assessment has been.

I intended to survive my second day quietly reading. Members of the family moved around me, including Keoki. I didn't attempt to spend time with him beyond the most cursory. I couldn't help it, and the way he cried whenever I came near made it clear that even that, was more than he preferred.

"Larry, I have heard from Theresa. That girl promise she be here no later than dinner time." Mama Willi shook her head with such determination I imagined if she had to, she'd chase her down herself. I nodded wondering if she'd actually show and what seeing her in her natural habitat would be like.

Late in the day, Theresa's father stopped by again in his security guard uniform. I sensed he'd like to say something, and I waited with I knew must be a vacuous expression. But he changed his mind, only shaking his head before alerting me he was off for work at the electricity plant.

Not long after, I heard a commotion outside, a car pulling up, and people laughing. Theresa's distinctive voice called out she would phone somebody later. She followed with something in pidgin I couldn't decipher. The front door slammed, and she sauntered into the living room. I drank her in, here in her native home and attire. Very short shorts and a halter-top over a bikini, hair wild, and bare-footed. Her eyes were defiant: she was even more overwhelmingly beautiful than I'd remembered. From the disdain on her face, I realized she might have mistaken me for one of the giant cockroaches that roam the island.

Though I'd been sitting on this couch nearly the entire day, I didn't move a muscle in case I might startle her off. She acknowledged me with a quick nod and sauntered toward the kitchen.

"I'm here, Mama Willi, what time we eatin'?"

"Fish on now. You come so late you miss your father. I think he wanna talk to you."

Theresa shook her hair in annoyance and stepped around the table out of sight to help her mother.

In a few minutes, Willi came to the doorway to gaze at me in sorrow. *Good thing I'm back behind my force field or her face would break me down.* I gave her a vague smile pretending I didn't see the pity and bitter disappointment in her eyes.

"Larry, you can come eat some dinner if you like."

Theresa and her mother must have had words somewhere out of my hearing. She took her place sullen and uncommunicative. There wasn't much conversation at the table. I picked at the fish and rice but skipped the small mound of poi entirely and stuck mainly with milk. *What are we doing to her family?* I thought, well guarded and distant. *She should never have invited me here. Why did she? She seems to be punishing them as much as me. Is there some insight I should take from this?* If there was, I didn't see it.

I excused myself from the table to go to the bathroom. When I returned, no one was able to meet my eyes. Theresa was gone. As far as I knew, she hadn't even ducked in to see Keoki who'd slept through dinner.

Willi sat with me in the living room, her eyes hooded and tired. *There is much more happening here than I can comprehend.*

"I don't know what is going on with this girl, she is crazy in the head, you know. I tell you, her father and I, we don't know what to do with her. We don't know what has happened." She started to say something and stopped for a moment. "I want to say one important thing. I know she loves you. I hope you don't give up on her. She is having a difficult time."

I turned away, trying to find some composure. Tears ran freely down my cheeks, but they were emotionless waterworks. Something my body made happen; I didn't know who was running things in there anymore. I tried to clear my throat.

"I don't know what's happened either," I croaked out. "I hoped . . ." I stopped. Of course, I'd hoped, what an idiot to keep repeating the same hopes and expecting different results. Wasn't that the definition of insanity? Maybe I was insane.

I survived another restless night, relieved to some degree by the amazing nighttime sky in the backcountry of Oahu, far from the bright lights of

Honolulu. I woke again to a dazzling morning. Shortly after breakfast, Theresa returned. I watched her silently. I'd been tortured by her so much, and yet I was still ensnared, enchanted by her every move. I sat on the couch with my book, peering secretively out from behind my force field, unwilling to rise to any confrontation, conversing in monosyllables to anyone who spoke to me. Even Robo-voice seemed speechless. Sometime during the day or evening, she disappeared, and so I did too. In the bedroom, I fell into a dreamless stupor to wake again in the splendor of another Hawaiian morning.

After splashing water on my face, I slipped into the living room and my place on the couch. Theresa played with Keoki in a chair across the room, but she didn't try to include me or encourage us to interact. I watched her warily, the way a mouse tastes the air in a cobra cage, alert for the first sign of abandonment. After a while, she put him away, probably for a nap. A meal or two might've come and gone; Theresa made an appearance for them from somewhere before disappearing again. Her father spoke, looking at me from the wrong side of a deep tunnel. I couldn't comprehend what he was telling me, but no doubt it was about going to work at Hawaiian Electric. *The only time I ever see him is when he's leaving for work.* Eventually, my ferret-like attention wore me out, and I fell asleep on the couch. Someone roused me enough to tell me to go to bed, and this night was so much like the last one I was losing track of how long I'd been here. The time dilation created by the intensity of my bottled-up emotions made me feel like it might have been forever. As I fell into sleep, I wondered if that meant I was Hawaiian now.

68 CASTAWAY

I think the worst feeling in the world is knowing that someone you used to talk to everyday doesn't care about you anymore.
   -- Anmol Andore

October 15, 1970
Waipahu, Oahu, Hawaii

THERESA WAS THERE again in the morning, but her packed carryall bag lay waiting near the door. She wore short shorts imprinted with green ferns, a burnt-orange halter top over a beige bikini, and the ubiquitous slaps on her feet that every local wore. If I'd woken five minutes later, I probably would have missed her. I don't know where she'd slept, maybe on the couch after I left it. Without pause, perhaps spontaneously, she glanced at me.

"Look, I'm going to the beach. You can come with me if you want to, but if you do, we're going to be out all day."

I nodded without comment. Anything I said could be misinterpreted, so I stayed silent. But why wouldn't I want to go? Did I fly two thousand miles to sit on her family's couch for a week?

I changed into the board shorts I'd had made in Waikiki when Stark Naked played at the Lemon Tree and I'd hardly worn since. I threw on an untucked collared shirt and slipped into my slaps. I gathered sunglasses, billfold, and a book. I'd packed a couple of John D. MacDonald paperbacks, but I'd finished them. I picked up Frank Herbert's *Dune Messiah*, my last unread book. Theresa found and threw an extra beach towel at me and grabbed her bag. We walked outside about the same time Charlene arrived in something akin to a Jeep.

"Howzit, Larry," she hollered out at me. I smiled; I could almost believe she was glad to see me.

Theresa's parents' house was out in the country, but the rough road we followed soon degenerated into a winding path through real jungle. Thankfully, we didn't meet anyone on the dirt track; there wasn't room for two cars, or anywhere to turn around. The girls sat in front chattering as though I wasn't there, much of it in pidgin too fast for me to follow. I contented myself with looking out at the fascinating vegetation passing by. Charlene stopped next to a person-sized burrow cut through a wall of bushes and vines. I couldn't make out the passageway's destination through the dim sunshine filtering through the branches above. Judging by a larger, vehicle-sized tunnel a little farther on, I guessed these paths led to some sort of jungle habitation inside.

"You," Theresa said before leaving the car, "wait here." I nodded, and she and Charlene ducked into the entryway. They returned in fifteen minutes or so. Theresa handed me a green-tinted coke bottle with a cork in it.

"For your white skin."

I uncorked the bottle and smelled sweet coconut. "Where did you go? What's out there in the jungle?"

"Kahuna kupua, like a doctor-woman," Theresa said. She and Charlene looked at each other, smiled, and started laughing uproariously. "Well, maybe not entirely like a doctor," she amended, "but she is very powerful."

After a relatively long ride for Oahu, we turned into a parking area bordering a small beach. Not many cars were parked in the rough lot on a weekday in October. The shoreline was as breathtaking as I remembered, and the air so clear I could see to the end of the sky. Out of the car, both girls supervised while I applied the cream from the coke bottle.

"Put this on everywhere except under your bathing suit," Theresa instructed. "Here is a comb, even comb it into your hair, so it will get on your scalp." She took the comb back when my hair had been slicked to my skull. She brandished it like a pointer at me, "Now you must keep putting this on all day long, do you understand me, *haole* man?"

That cracked up Charlene as she got back into the driver's seat and started the car. Theresa opened the passenger door and jumped in.

"What are you doing?" I asked, incredulous.

"We are going to another part of the beach. We'll be back for you later," she said as they drove away. "Don't forget, *haole*, keep putting lotion on your body."

My bewildered astonishment turned to dismay. I sunburned easily, as Theresa well knew. My vampire lifestyle since we'd begun playing Vegas hours left my super-white Irish skin more vulnerable than ever. All I had to protect myself was some weird concoction from a jungle medicine woman.

I wandered around the beach area, considering whether I should walk in the direction they'd gone. *Maybe they were around that point of land up ahead.* Ah, but no. It, of course, would be exactly the wrong thing to do, especially if I found them. I considered going zombie to avoid stressing about it, but with no one to trigger it, my force field wouldn't turn on. A group of surfers sat like a flock of seabirds out where the swells began. There were a few shops along the access road, not all of them open. I replaced my worn and tired rubber slaps with some nice-looking leather ones at one of the shops. I bought a fresh mango and papaya drink from a vendor and slumped into one of the free beach chairs. I reassured myself that the girls would be back soon, this was some kind of hazing.

Surprising myself, I fell deep into the story of Muad'dib's growth into an all-powerful demigod on Dune, though I would have been hard-pressed to remember the details. Hours passed, and I worried about devouring the book without having brought anything else to read as much as I worried about when they'd be back. I tried to pace my reading and made it a point to walk around pretty often, deeply inhaling the island's distinctive ocean smell of salt and sun. As instructed, at regular intervals I coated my skin with the coconut lotion including pomading my hair, though without the comb Theresa had taken with her.

None of the food stalls sold milk, but I got a pork sandwich in the early afternoon and another fruit drink later. I took a break to let the sound of waves cracking on the sand hiss and fizz as they rolled onto the shore. They lulled me into twitchy dozes between reads. There was no danger of me entering the water. I remembered too well my terrifying adventure at Sandy Beach.

As the afternoon wore on, I realized I must be getting dangerously burned despite the homemade coating. The tall palm trees and low bushes here didn't offer much shade from the blazing sun. I liberally slathered the creamy lotion on until I couldn't pound any more out of the coke bottle. As the day waned and the sun dropped behind the horizon, the shopkeepers closed their food stands and shops. My worry turned to alarm: could I put it beyond her to leave me here all night? But finally, as I strained to see up the road, Charlene's car came bumping into the parking area. They didn't have to search for me; if not the last person on the beach, I was the only scarlet-colored one.

"Oh my God! Look at da kine's skin. He burned red like fire." Charlene laughed out loud. "Hop in dis car, red boy."

Theresa glanced at me and snickered. "Oh." She scanned me top to bottom. "Oh my God. You are so burned!"

While they oohed and aahed over the condition of my skin, I began to feel it, too. I was going to have the granddaddy of all sunburns. I already felt a little woozy riding in the backseat. I tried to imagine enduring the rest of this horrible trip with painfully crisped skin. Undoubtedly, this week was aiming to become the worst experience I'd ever had in my entire life.

I couldn't eat much at dinner, my stomach churning from overexposure. I felt so beaten down by the sun I excused myself for bed as soon as I could. I awoke in the middle of the night to sense something changed, something different in the weight on the mattress. I peered over my shoulder and saw Theresa's form, sleeping with her back to me. Whether I was too sore or too wise, I did nothing but groan quietly and try to roll into another position and go back to sleep.

69 BURNED

I just wanted you to know I'd be chasing after you right now, Naked if need required it. But because I'm respecting your need for time and space, I'll force myself to lie here in bed and pretend I'm asleep.
—Nicole Williams, *Clash*

October 17, 1970
Waipahu, Oahu, Hawaii

I WOKE TO brisk breezes snapping the window drapes above. Scattered clouds skittered across the deep sky. High coconut palms dipped and swayed, their little fingerlings flickering in the rowdy gusts. And then, the winds instantly calmed to another perfect day in Paradise.

There was no sign, not even an indentation to suggest Theresa had slept beside me; I wondered if seeing her in the night had been a sun-induced hallucination. Amazingly, my skin didn't hurt. I pinched my arm and felt no pain from my intense sunburn. I could hardly believe it. The face in the mirror looked like me, only brown as a biscuit. I'd been burned to a crisp yesterday, yet today I sported a golden-toasted suntan unlike any I'd had before. Even after being out in the sun all summer as a kid in Indiana, I'd never gotten a quarter this tanned.

After pulling on my board shorts again, to the brown edge of the tan lines matching them, and wrestling on a Tee shirt, I walked into the living room toward some pineapple juice. Theresa stood with our child slung on her hip. She smiled tentatively, but I could see she was going out again.

"I have to go out for a little while, Larry. I have some things I must do. Tell Mama I fed Keoki and I'm taking him with me. I'll be back later." Outside, she took a moment to wave, and turned to strap Keoki into a car seat as she and Charlene disappeared into the day. I exhaled. She'd been so close last night, right next to me in bed . . . Well, what had I expected to happen? Some unrealistic miracle I'd been counting on for months now? *I'm such an idiot!* Soon this fakakta trip would be over, and I could go home to lick my wounds in Las Vegas.

Boy and a new brother he introduced as Stanley shuffled into the living room to ask me if I wanted to go to the "store" with them. They giggled. Stanley, almost as large as Boy, was Theresa's second oldest brother.

"We got one special dinner plan for tonight cause you here wid us, but we gotta go *store* first, fo get some stuff. You wan go wid us, brah?" Stanley turned to laugh boisterously with Boy.

"Yah, bruddah, we going to one special *store*. You come wid us brah, see dis kine *store*."

I barely understood their pidgin, but I could decipher enough to appreciate the hospitality in their invitation. Though the situation was awkward for the entire family, not counting Theresa, they'd treated me like a prince—better actually, as a welcome member of their family. I'd barely been able to respond to their heartwarming acceptance of me. I regretted not getting to know them before everything had exploded between Theresa and me. Not for the first time, I blamed myself for not finding time to come here and get to know my Hawaiian in-laws. I bet the wedding luau they'd wanted to give us would have been incredible.

"Do I have to do anything special to go to the *store* with you guys?" I said, going along with the program.

"No, you brown now brah, you look like one Kanaka. You definitely ready fo go wid us." And they both clapped me on the back, and we laughed together.

We went out to get in an old, jalopy pickup truck that might have been black once and bounced along a two-lane country road for a couple of miles of shore grasses to where the water from Pearl Harbor lapped against green jungle foliage. I hadn't realized they lived so near the harbor. Here, deep inside the bay, the mighty ocean had been tamed, limited to little cat's paw scratches on a shore of sandy dirt. The brothers uncovered a rowboat shoved up into the shoreline vegetation. Together, we pushed it into the water and jumped aboard. Boy pulled three snorkels and a swim mask out of a mesh bag. He gave me the mask and one of the snorkel pipes. Fortunately, I knew how to use it from our excursions to Hanauma Bay two and a half years ago. About a hundred yards offshore we drifted to a stop, and Stanley heaved a primitive anchor made from an automobile wheel over the side.

"Now, you go in water wid us," he said amplifying his meaning with hand gestures. "Jus' cruise on top and watch through da mask. No need dive down. Okay?"

The two of them produced simple, machine-sharpened, quarter-inch steel rods about eighteen inches long and small nets. From the bottom of the boat, they grabbed swim fins, slipped into them and into the water in a single smooth motion. They held the dinghy still so I wouldn't capsize it while I clambered awkwardly over the side and fell into a bright-green, clear-as-glass world in this lobe of the harbor. Within minutes, they'd speared several good-sized fish and popped them into their nets, slipping up to barely break the surface for air as needed, which didn't seem often. These big men seemed like denizens of this watery world; it fascinated me to observe their agile and athletic movements in these surroundings.

They rose up near me, and we broke the surface together. Boy gestured down. "We going to do bottom now. You can follow but stay on surface, cuz it kinda deep. You watch dis time."

In a moment their massive forms moved with supple grace as they turned and twisted like sea creatures diving below. Though I could see the sea floor clearly, the relative size of the brothers' descending bodies showed how much farther it was to the bottom than I'd thought. They flippered over a mossy green meadow of billowing seaweed while I tried to keep pace, dog paddling along above, breathing through my snorkel. Boy jabbed his steel rod into some rocks in the sea bottom and pulled out a green lobster writhing on the end of it. He popped it into his net. Almost simultaneously, Stanley speared another. Within fifteen minutes we'd packed eight of these crustaceans and a good-sized pile of fish into the boat. Not long after, we were dumping our catch on a well-used sideboard next to an outdoor sink in the backyard. We would feast on the spoils tonight.

George supplemented his salary with proceeds from the fish he caught on Saturdays, Willi explained. They took enough fresh food from the sea to freeze for themselves for the week, and he sold the rest of the catch at about a dollar a pound. With a guest, they'd run short of fish a day early, so the brothers had needed to go to the "store," which we chuckled over during dinner.

I watched Willi prepare a creamy casserole with the lobster tails and meat from their claws. As she mixed poi from a canister of dried taro root, she caught me making a face and grinned.

"What's da matter, you no fan of poi? Not unusual. If you not born and raised to it, like here in Hawaii, da flavor and texture is hard to enjoy. For us though, it's different. It connects us to our earliest descendants, gives us life, takes care of us. Most of us can hardly live without it, da more fermented da betta."

I told her about our desperate search for rice when Theresa first came to California, and she smiled in understanding. I'd gained new insight on why poi and the particular rice she needed had been so important to her.

Theresa and Keoki were back in time for dinner. She fed Keoki early, and we played with him together for the first time since the beginning of the nightmare our lives had become. My zombie mind reminded me not to read too much into this and kept my force field handy.

Dinner was a feast by any standard. The seafood was fresh and delicious, the new bread warm and crusty. And there was plenty of ice-cold milk. The family talked a lot of pidgin with each other, but I followed along well enough. Or they may have made an effort to stay intelligible because of me; I couldn't say for sure.

Theresa and I conversed like human beings, and sometimes she translated when she read my face and realized I'd lost my place in the conversation. Finally, she put our son to bed for the night. One by one, everyone found their beds. It became ever more evident Boy was waiting for us to leave; he couldn't sleep until we surrendered the couch.

We were both self-conscious in the bedroom. While Theresa brushed her teeth in the bathroom, I stripped to my briefs and climbed into bed. She turned off the lights when she slipped into the room, but the moonlight silvering her form revealed everything. The local custom of dress didn't require much in the way of clothes, and though I turned away initially, I couldn't help but watch as she turned sideways and reached up to untie her halter top. In a moment she jammed her thumbs into her shorts and underwear and shimmied them off, her figure swaying in the process. I fell back in time remembering the first time she'd danced a hula for me, but quickly backed away from visualizing what followed. She moved like a wraith to what had always been her side of the bed and slipped beneath the single top sheet, all we needed in the tropical night.

She said nothing and turned away from me. I knew her presence didn't necessarily mean anything. Her parents might have insisted she sleep in the bedroom with her supposed husband. I'd gone so long without feeling or touching her, her rebukes had been so stinging—I dared not risk reaching out to touch her . . .

The fact I'd gone flaccid despite knowing she lay unclothed, inches away, confirmed how strongly I'd been conditioned. I was paralyzed with fear and desire; she was all things terrible and beautiful, and she dominated every waking and sleeping moment of my existence. For a few moments I wished desperately to be alone so I could fantasize, get hard, and masturbate, remembering our passionate lovemaking; our greedy ravenous need for each other; our moments of slow, intense, gentle sex, wishing it would never end. Staring up at the moving drapes and bright moonlight, I forced any thought of doing more than listening to her breathe out of my mind and took a long time going to sleep. She wasn't there again when I woke.

On Sunday morning, Willi and George went off to church somewhere nearby. Theresa's brothers were out of the house, too. She stayed home with Keoki and me. We sat quietly in the living room, alone. It wasn't an uncomfortable silence, but my force field had tentatively begun to slide into place. I wanted to talk about us, but I'd tried starting a conversation with her in Las Vegas, and it had gone horribly sideways. I couldn't risk that again. I would be leaving tomorrow morning, and there might not be another chance for us to be alone in the house. But what could I say that would mean more than I'd shown by coming here and enduring all her humiliations?

"Who is playing the organ for you while you are here?" This was the first time she'd asked about anything concerning Las Vegas.

"A guy named Phil Conti. Friend of Leonard's. Good player. Not much of a singer, though."

She nodded. I thought she wanted to ask me more, but she didn't, and I didn't push it. We were on her turf, it was up to her. We spent a quiet afternoon saying little but at least being close. When Keoki was awake, we played with him together, and let him nap between us on the couch.

Dinner was calmer. George had fished in Pearl Harbor this afternoon instead of Saturday since the brothers had brought back fresh fish Friday. After freezing what they needed, he'd sold his hundred-pound catch for over a hundred dollars at the market, and that made it a fine day.

We sat around without saying much, too many of us for such a small living room, but with a comfortable family feeling about it. I could hear the night birds and smell the nighttime smells. It was my last night here, and I was glad Theresa didn't leave. Everyone wanted to get to bed, or go wherever they went, early in the evening. I was leaving for the airport in the morning, so it was a good idea. Things were similar to last night when Theresa and I went to our room to get ready for bed, with one momentous exception. I was just as thrilled and paralyzed to watch her silvery silhouette shuck her shorts off as last night, but when she slid her body beneath the sheets, she didn't turn away. She put her head on her elbow and gazed at me. The molten moonlight streaming from the window above was reflected in her tears. She reached for me, and I sank into a heaven I'd never expected to know again.

70 PARADISE REVISITED

If . . . today is all is left to me, I would love to tell you how much I love you and that I will never forget you.
—Gabriel García Márquez

October 18, 1970
Waipahu, Oahu, Hawaii

WHEN THERESA ROLLED into my arms and turned her moonlit, tear-tracked face to mine, it was me, not Robo-voice, who held her naked against me. I sensed every inch of her, even where our bodies weren't in contact. There was no part of her I hadn't known: tasted, caressed, worshiped at some time or another. She gave herself to me hungrily. At first, I found it difficult to respond, still not sure she wasn't some succubus come for me in the night and that I wouldn't awaken shaking with night sweats. But she quickly convinced me she was very, very real.

In a way I hadn't experienced since the first night I'd entered her body two and a half years ago, I felt my connection with her and this island renewed, and my heart and soul nearly left my body in the rising crescendo we reached. When it was over, I cried without abandon and so did she. We loved each other. How could it be otherwise? The timing was bittersweet, here I was leaving, and now this had happened. I couldn't decide whether to be glad or to wish it hadn't. No fall is so long as the last one.

Everything old about us seemed natural and simple, and everything new, intimate and familiar. We lay together in the night, as we always had: always touching. A leg across a leg, a calf against a bottom, at least an ankle grazing a wrist. Tonight, as I lay on my back, she on her side with a luscious thigh draped across mine, I gently placed the back of a hand on her cheek and spoke quietly into the dark above me.

"What do we do now?"

A long silence. "I don't know."

"My plane leaves in hours. What should I think, Treese? Does this mean anything?"

"Maybe." She sighed from deep inside herself. "I think . . . maybe it does."

"Honey, love of my life, please think carefully before you answer what I'm going to ask. Does this mean you want to try again? Because, until this happened, I figured it was over."

She answered without pause in a hushed voice. "I . . . I think that's what it means. I loved us together playing with our son, our boy. I had forgotten that. And now, this." She heaved a wistful sigh. "As strong as ever."

I tried to think what to do and decided fortune favors the bold. "Will you come with me to Las Vegas tomorrow?"

She took time to think before answering. "I can't go, not right now."

"But you will come?"

She wrestled with her answer. "I couldn't face Joan, Lora, everybody. I don't know. I would be too embarrassed. I feel so terrible. Everything is so messed up."

Another plan popped into mind. A much different one. "Listen, honey. What if I gave my notice to the band, packed up the house, figured out what to do with my B3. . .? What if I came back here to live with you and Keoki? Would that work?" I sensed something changing, softening, and reached further. "If I agreed to do that, would you come back with me for these two weeks while I wrap things up, and then we'd both come back together?"

She tried to hold back deep sobs.

"Why, Theresa, why are you crying?" I'm such a fool. I'd misjudged the situation again. *How can I get back on firmer ground?*

"Larry, please don't leave. Don't get on the plane. Stay with me."

I tried to think how I could do that. It was only for two weeks. I owed that to the band, didn't I? "Treese, sweetheart. I've been playing music with these guys for a long time, some of them six years or more. They've been like my brothers. I'm happy to quit the band so we can be together. But I do need to give them notice."

She said she understood, though she cried and cried, and my heart broke with each sob. I promised her I would give notice Tuesday night before we sang a note. She should count on me being here in two weeks. Think about it, I insisted, plan for it. She nodded, and, emotionally spent, we fell asleep in each other's arms. I slept secure and dreamless enclosed in her comforting aroma.

In the morning, her parents and brothers saw us smiling and touching every moment, the way we used to, though they'd never seen us the way we were before. They were excited and happy to hear I would be back in two weeks. I was going to become a real Hawaiian. After breakfast, I went to pack. Theresa followed me into the bedroom, Keoki athwart her right hip. "Honey, I had asked Maing to take you to the airport before. I still want him to take you. I want to say goodbye here. I think I would die to see you fly away now."

"Okay, but I'll miss every second I'm not with you." Her cousin drove up soon after and we kissed as though a special magic in our lips would seal our hearts together. "I'll be back before you know it, honey. I love you." I blew her a kiss as we drove away. Maing seemed glad my trip here had ended on a happier note than it had begun.

Each mile the plane sped surging toward its cruising altitude and stretching its legs across the Pacific took me further from the miracle of last night. I worried that I should have stayed, grasped the opportunity she'd given me even though I had little money, a lot of debt, and would be abandoning friends and band brothers and everything I owned and knew. What I'd promised to do was crazy enough, wasn't it? Sacrificing everything I'd worked for so I could return to Theresa in two short weeks should surely appease whatever island deity I'd offended.

After all this pain, I thought, *after all the suffering, this is the way it's supposed to happen, right?* I'd suffered through all her indignities, paying perhaps for whatever I'd done wrong. In the end, everything had turned out right. Of course, we had things to work out. Despite our one enchanted night, we would need time and affection to heal the damage we'd suffered. I accepted we might never entirely return to the uncomplicated, romantic life we'd lived before. But we could go on to a more mature and realistic love and life.

I looked at my two hands cupped reflexively in front of me. In them, I cradled the memory of those precious few hours as if it were a little bird, delicate and quiet. *No sudden moves. Don't hold this fragile moment too tightly, but don't let it fly away either.* Here was the storybook ending I'd prayed for. Maybe I'd been living in a fairytale after all. Maybe someone had given Theresa a poisoned apple or pineapple, and the girl I loved had been frozen asleep while someone else took over her body. Maybe last night's magic kiss had awakened my real Theresa, and we'd have our ever-after ending. Maybe—after all hope had been exhausted—it could actually happen in real life. *If I could just believe, if I could hold this moment gently, lightly enough . . .* I'd give my two-weeks' notice and hurry back to my island girl. I didn't know what I'd do for a living, I wouldn't even think about that now. I would keep my mind on the important thing: I had my wife back, my precious girl back, and I wouldn't let this one, and this child, this little family, slip between my fingers.

I lay back in the seat, the rumble of the giant engines fading into a murmur as I tried to think about arranging storage for our furnishings, how to get out from under the financial burden of my damaged B3, what to say to the band. And like a magnet, I was drawn back to re-living that magical night in Theresa's humble home on stilts in the Oahu backcountry.

I changed clothes for my first night back as guys wandered into our dressing rooms at the Flamingo, deflecting questions with banalities until everyone had arrived. I wondered if Robo-voice would take over. I hadn't needed it recently, so when it didn't come, I decided to go it alone.

"Some of you asked about my trip to see Theresa."

Les interrupted. "Yeah, and how you turned yourself brown in a week while we all look like ghosts." There were some grins.

"I know. Freaky, right?" I glanced at my deeply tanned arms dusted with light golden hair. "You won't believe me, but this is from one day in the sun. But I've got something serious to tell you. I think Theresa and I may have gotten some things worked out. At least I hope so because I'm taking a humongous leap of faith." I drew a deep breath and looked around at them. Leonard sat, twirling a drumstick. Mac squinted at me, inhaling from a Marlboro stuck in the corner of his mouth. Mickey seemed uninterested, who knew what he thought. Les was holding his guitar, and he picked at it aimlessly. Dave waited quietly.

"I'm going to move to Hawaii and see if I can make things work with her." I forced out the words I'd never thought I'd ever be saying. "I'm giving you my two-week notice beginning tonight."

Silence, except for clothes rustling as Mickey sorted through the freshly cleaned suits and shirts hanging in the closet.

"You sure that's a good idea?" Mac spoke first. "I mean, it's a big step, bubba. And she ain't treated you so well. You'll be all alone a long way away from home."

"You're right, but I've got to try for two reasons. First, I've got to find out for sure about us, I can't go on the way things are, and second, I can't stand being in the band anymore. I can hardly sing or listen to the music we play. I know you'll think I'm crazier than you already think I am, but every time I sing or hear most of our songs, it feels like catching an arrow in the throat. Look, you guys are my brothers. After all we've been through together, it kills me to say it, but I have to go. I can't do this anymore."

I stood quietly as each of them tapped me on the arm, or gave me a shoulder bump, as they left to walk to the casino. Dave was last out, and I wondered what he would say. He shook his head without comment before leaving. Alone, I finished with my tie and slipped on my coat. I brushed my hands across my face trying to see if the anxious anticipation I was feeling showed in the mirror before I closed and locked the dressing room door behind me.

On stage, I slipped behind my force field; the songs were doubly poignant now. Though numbed to their emotional content, I still had to turn away to hide meaningless, uncontrollable tears. On our first break, I wanted to phone Theresa and tell her I'd talked to the guys the way I'd promised, but it was after ten in Waipahu. I'd be waking the whole household. I forced myself to wait until tomorrow.

The next day, at nine o'clock in the morning Theresa's time, I called Hawaii. My hand holding the receiver shook as I listened to unanswered ring after unanswered ring two thousand miles away across the Pacific Ocean. *Where is everybody?* I waited a couple of hours and tried again, but still no answer. I dialed her number once more before going to work. Considering all I'd been through, my fragile optimism was running on fumes.

Thursday, Mama Willi finally answered. She couldn't hide her concern. She was evasive and uncomfortable when she told me Theresa wasn't there. What little heart I had left, fell through the floor. Whatever was happening, she made clear it wasn't what she wanted. My hopes for a future with Theresa had faded along with my tan when I phoned Sunday. A week had passed since I'd left.

"Why are you crying, Theresa?"

I could hear quiet sobbing. *God have mercy, there's been enough of this.*

"Please," fatigue was cracking my voice, "don't cry, just come out and say it. Obviously, something's gone wrong. Let's not drag it out."

"Don't come back here. It won't work." Her voice was thick with tears. "I don't want you to come here."

I mulled that over pretty dispassionately, considering. I spoke quietly into the receiver. "I've already given notice to the band."

"I don't care," she said, defiance in her voice. "You can't come back. It was a mistake to think I could do it."

"Are you finally letting me go? Are you telling me you don't love me?"

Silence and then, "I can't say that. I don't have to say that." I heard a hesitant breath, a sob, a whisper. "Sometimes things are too broken to fix." There wasn't going to be a magical conclusion to this catastrophe after all.

What I'd taken to be a storybook ending had meant something else to her. The way she'd lit up when she saw me, listened to my long-winded ramblings for hours, the way she'd physically loved me, her long love letters, all the way through having a baby and being apart—all the things that had convinced me I could let go of doubt and accept our romantic fairytale life as real had been unjustified. Maybe, like Orpheus, I'd looked back too often on my flight to LA, and left my Eurydice stranded in an underworld that only seemed like Paradise. Or maybe I'd blown it when I took her from her island in the first place, even though I thought that's what she wanted. Maybe that's not what her island had wanted. I should have accepted our time together while the band played there and not tried to capture lightning in a bottle.

No matter how intense my emotions or powerful my feelings of loss had become, there's only so much emotional energy a person can maintain. Existence in a state of perpetual panic was destroying me. I'd bet my life and sanity our love would get us through this. All I'd asked of her was to tell me she didn't love me. Instead, she'd left me hanging in the traces like a dying dray horse.

The moment I'd feared and denied had arrived. Imagine the most scared you have ever been. Like that moment when the turbulence is so severe, you're sure the airplane you're in will fall out of the sky, and you've begun to negotiate with your Maker. I felt like that and clenched for impact. *How can I survive this? How can I live without her?* I didn't know, but I also didn't know how I could ever bear to have her in my life again, either.

My final words came from somewhere broken and small inside and were barely audible. "Goodbye, Theresa." My failure was complete.

71 SLOW MOTION NOTICE

When you're happy, you enjoy the music. But, when you're sad, you understand the lyrics.
      —UntoldSecrets@mostsecretfacts

October 20, 1970
Las Vegas, Nevada

I WAITED FOR everyone to arrive Tuesday night before making another announcement, this one anticlimactic.

"Guys," I managed a bleak grin, "I'm not going to Hawaii after all. That ship sailed without me." Everybody was smart enough or didn't care enough, to simply nod or at least not ask any questions—except Dave.

"Does that mean you're not leaving the band?"

"I'm still giving notice, but I guess there's no time limit now. I'll leave it to you to decide when it's convenient for the band."

Though my barely functioning rational mind realized my dream marriage was over, my battered heart continued to grieve, trying to hang on to some desperate shred of hope. Even if I wasn't in the band, even if Theresa wasn't coming home again, and even though I couldn't go there, my attention remained pinned on that faraway tropical island. Like a hamster on a wheel, my mind ran through every possible scenario of changing things—past, present, and future. Should I have ditched my friends and stayed in Waipahu? Could we have loved each other through everything if I had? What would happen if I showed up there anyway? Was I being honest believing it was loyalty to the band that made me fly away that day, or had I been too much of a coward to risk staying?

I sat behind the B3 trying to be invisible, avoiding singing at the front mic whenever possible. Everything taking place around me seemed to be happening on the other side of a giant plate-glass window. Song lyrics still overwhelmed me. I despised hearing Dave sing *Woman, Woman* and I loathed Les intoning *Cecilia*. I turned my head to hide the uncontrollable waterworks, which seemed to come without cause. Away from the stage, I no longer listened to music on the radio and walked out of rooms or away from situations whenever I heard the Beatles' *Something*, or the Carpenters' *Close to You*, and other taboo songs that blistered my raw emotions. I was disheartened to find Robo-voice and the force field seemed badly damaged and only appeared intermittently.

Leonard came to me as I was warming up my fingers with some blues runs. "Larry, Vince says he's got something for you from Bill Miller. Sounds kind of important."

The maître d' handed me an envelope with an embossed Flamingo logo. Inside was our formal four-week notification. I stepped back on stage waving the letter around.

"Hey, you guys, we're done at the Sky Room. Who's the leader now? Who do I give the official notice to?"

From the band's reaction, no one seemed to understand what I was talking about. I handed the letter to Leonard. "Your signature's on the contract, so here, I'm giving it to you." I went back to my keyboard.

After the set, Leonard wanted to talk with me in the break room. "Look, we have to figure out what to do."

"No." I looked at him in puzzlement. "Not we. You. You are the ones who have to figure it out. I'm on notice, waiting for you guys to tell me when to leave. The longer it takes you to decide, the more time it gives me to work out some kind of plan, so that's okay I guess. But even though I'm physically here, I'm still *gone*." I'd been daydreaming about what it would be like—being gone. I didn't give a damn about anybody or anything in the world anymore, and that was somehow freeing. I fantasized about finding some tropical Polynesian paradise with fabulous beaches to live on. I couldn't go to Hawaii, of course, but maybe somewhere else. I thought of Tahiti first, but it was French; Americans were only allowed ninety-day visas. I'd checked. But maybe I could find some way around the problem. There were thousands of islands in the South Pacific, and I'd already gone to the library to find out more about them. I still had piles of research to do. Leonard pulled me back from woolgathering.

"You've always been the leader. We talk a lot about you, you know. Everybody is pretty pissed off, the way you've let this personal thing get to you." It wasn't Leonard's nature to be so direct, or critical.

"I'm not real pleased with the band either. I've tried desperately to let you know how hard this thing hit me. Believe me, I didn't want what happened to happen." I let out some of the anger and frustration I'd felt over the past several weeks. "I asked for help from several of you guys weeks ago. I needed all of you to take more responsibility for yourselves. For years, I've been the one to sit with everybody when they had their problems. I held hands or heads while they went through their various dramas. I would try to sympathize, try to understand what they felt, try to let them know I wasn't only a friend but a brother they could count on." I shook my head. "But when it's me who needs help—it pisses everybody off."

Leonard nodded and picked at a piece of lint on his suit. "We've always depended on you to do that stuff. None of us are any good at doing what you do. Now that you're not doing it, there's a lot of unrest in the group, and you don't seem to care. You want to turn your back on it all, and it's making things worse. Your problems aren't our fault either. So, whether it's right or not, I get why everybody's so mad at you."

He stood and looked down at me. "But that's not what this is about. We all know you want to split, so okay. But we don't have any experience in working with Howard or Seymour. I don't know what to say to them. We need to figure out what's going to happen next and you have to help us. Then you can leave."

"Leonard, can't you just pick up the phone and call them?"

"Can't you?"

I sighed and nodded.

Leonard hesitated. "Another thing. I don't want to leave Vegas. I've got a home here now, I want to settle down here with Marie, I want to put down roots and grow a family. We . . . I need for us to find another job in town."

A few afternoons later, I sat in front of the band by the Sky Room windows. As usual, the view was spectacular, but it barely registered.

"Okay, here's what I know so far. Band's here until the second week of November. Howard can get the band into Oil Can Harry's in Vancouver following that. He also thinks he can lock in the Pussycat for January. The problem is the four weeks after Canada and before coming back to Vegas. He says he'll keep looking to fill those weeks, and for something to keep you here in town following the Cat."

"Fuck Vegas," Mac said, irritated and angry. "I'm tired of this damned town. Ain't interested in comin back that soon."

I could see the speculation in Mickey's eyes before he spoke. "The Turquoise Room in Portland used to be home for Sandy and the Vikings. Club owner's a friend of mine. Have to check, but I bet I can get us in there for December."

"Well, it is on the way back from Canada. It could work for you guys." It was their decision; I wasn't going with them. I'd liked Vancouver last time we were there. But we'd driven through Oregon on the way, and for my money, it hadn't looked inviting. I noticed Dave studying me, trying to puzzle out what I was thinking.

"Did you talk to Seymour?" Leonard asked me. He wasn't pleased with Mac's outburst. "I bet he could find some place for us here in Vegas after Oil Can's."

I shook my head. "Can't reach him. He's out of the country with Liberace, in Australia or some damn place. But Howard says he'll try to contact him and see what he suggests."

"What about moving up the date at the Cat? I bet they'd love having us there for the holidays."

"Jesus, Leonard, I don't know." I was more exasperated than I should have been. "Howard's the agent. He'll find out and let us know. That's his job." I glowered at everyone, daring them to question the plan any further. "Well, that's it then. Mickey will check on the Turquoise Room, and I'll tell Howard to solidify the Canada gig." I stood to end the talk.

"Larry," Dave said before I could sidle away, "sounds like you're saying you're done when we close here. Like you're going to leave the band then."

I nodded.

"I think that's too soon. We've only got three weeks to find somebody, even if we do, it will be tough, working them in while we're traveling. I think you should stay with us until we come back from Canada. Until we're back in California or Las Vegas." Dave looked around for support, but there was mainly indifference.

"I don't know, Dave." I wanted an end to this. "Why don't you discuss this with the guys and tell me what you decide. I said I wouldn't leave until it's convenient, but no sense in dragging this out either."

"Howard, like I've already explained. I'm not the leader anymore." I looked out my living room window at the storm blowing in. Sand and intermittent rain rattled against the panes. "I'm just helping out until they figure out who it's going to be." Damn, I'd let myself get dragged into the leader thing again. How hard could it be for one of them to pick up a goddamned phone and have a conversation with their agent? "I agree this is an idiotic decision, but I'm not in charge." I'd warned them Howard would be angry enough to bite nails in half if they decided to take the Portland gig without letting him book it through his agency, but Mickey wouldn't hear of it.

"I'm getting us this gig, and Howard King don't deserve none of it," he'd argued. "If you want to pay somebody ten percent, pay me." I tried to explain to him again why this was so stupid, especially when they were going to need Howard working as hard as he could to find jobs now that the security of the Flamingo and International Hotels was gone. I might as well have been talking to a tree stump, and I didn't have the patience for it. The band still hadn't chosen a leader, no one to counter what Mickey said or did. He'd had the owner of the Turquoise Room send the contract to his address, signed it himself and mailed it back without telling anybody.

I couldn't help but sigh in frustration into the receiver. "I'm sure this mess will settle down as soon as they get adjusted. I shouldn't be on the phone speaking for them. Look, whatever you want me to tell them is fine. I'll pass it on."

His voice was even gruffer than usual. "I don't know why I put up with bands like yours. You guys don't appreciate anything I do. I called the Pussycat like you asked and I've got them locked in for January. Don't worry about what comes after. We'll figure something out." *Why are you telling me this,?* I wanted to say, *I won't be in the band.*

After nearly three years of residence in Las Vegas, it was a big job for some of the guys to get ready for the trip. Joan Brown would stay here with Dani for now, but Mickey planned to drop off Lora with her family in Oregon on his way to Canada. Leonard's misery was evident as he prepared to leave Marie for eight weeks. He held onto the confirmed date at the Cat as a lifeline. I shed nearly everything I owned and took a certain painful pleasure in letting go of the apartment I'd failed to make a home. I packed the B3 for shipping, wondering how it would survive the road trip. Though there'd been some compulsive moments when I'd nearly called Theresa, I hadn't. I hoped I could keep it that way.

72 NORTHWEST PASSAGE

The world breaks everyone, and afterward, many are strong in the broken places. But those that will not break, it kills. It kills the very good and the very gentle and the very brave impartially. If you are none of these you can be sure it will kill you too but there will be no special hurry.

—Ernest Hemmingway

November 17, 1970
Vancouver, British Columbia, Canada

IN MANY WAYS, Vancouver reminded me of San Francisco. Both are kept temperate by warm waters that flow across the Pacific to flow south off the coast of British Columbia and form the California Current. Unlike San Francisco, there were more sunny days and much less rain here. This Canadian city gave off a European vibe with a British flavor, and it was home to the largest Chinatown outside of China. The early fall weather was near perfect for our first trip back since 1967.

Oil Can Harry's, an already-impressive club on Thurlow Street in Vancouver's West End, had undergone a renovation and added a third room, Dirty Sal's, in the basement. The main room where we played was more like a Las Vegas showroom than a nightclub. We adjusted our sets into three one-hour shows nightly to fit the format.

Our first week brought exceptionally large and rowdy crowds: Vancouver's minor league hockey team, the Canucks, had just been elevated to an expansion NHL team and the mighty Boston Bruins were in town. The whole city was celebrating. One night, Bobbie Orr, Gordie Howe, Bobby Hull, and Stan Mikita surprised everyone when they came in to join the celebration. Danny Baceda, part-owner and Entertainment Director of Oil Can's found out and asked us to introduce and bring them on stage in a specific order. It was like bringing on the Beatles; the adoring crowd went wild as each of these legends came out in a following spotlight. I noticed Danny at a ringside table downstairs at Dirty Sal's later in the night. As I walked by, I was thinking how much, not including the John Lennon glasses, he looked like our Dave. He stopped me to thank us for how we had welcomed the hockey stars. As usual in these instances, Mac had done a masterful job of introducing and honoring them.

"Amazing to see all these famous guys here on the same night, Danny. We're pretty hockey ignorant, but even I know who these guys are. Their dentists must love them, too." A couple of them were missing front teeth; they'd displayed the holes in their smiles as badges of honor.

"I'm sure they do. Hey, have you got a minute?" He gestured toward a seat at his side.

"Of course."

"Rumor is you're leaving the band. Is that true?"

I sighed. Nothing stays private long I suppose. "Rumor wins out. Yes, I am leaving."

"You sound a little troubled, sailor. Did you guys fall out or something?"

"Oh, no," I said quickly. "Nothing like that. In fact, the guys have been great. Just time for me to stop performing, I guess. I was never the greatest musician."

He nodded, studying me carefully. He wasn't making casual conversation.

"What are your plans?"

I didn't want to tell him I was searching for some isolated spot at the far ends of the earth, so I gave him my general line. "Can't say for sure yet. Kicking some opportunities around, though."

"If you're interested, maybe you'd entertain an offer from me."

Here was a surprise. "What do you have in mind?"

He smiled, seeing he'd caught my attention. "We're getting ready to open another club in Saskatoon, and we're thinking about two more in the East—Ottawa and Montreal. We want to build a chain of Oil Can Harry's across

Canada. I've been looking for an assistant entertainment director. I'd be interested if you like the idea."

I mulled over Danny's out-of-the-blue proposition as I walked into the Back Room, the dance club on the top floor of the club. A great-sounding band with a female singer called Skylark was playing there.

"Now that there," Mac said, "is a hot band. Something comin for those guys. Talked to their keyboard player, David Foster, says they're goin to LA soon. Told 'em to look us up when they got there, we should get together." I nodded. He was right, they did sound great, but he was sloshed, and we still had two shows to do. Little did we know that Skylark would soon have a top ten hit with *Wildflower*, and David Foster would become one of the most prolific songwriters and producers on the West Coast.

"So, when we finish here, and after the Cat, that's it?" Dave asked. "You're done?"

We sat in the living room of my little apartment after a late lunch at the diner on the street level of our building. We'd rented two apartments for the month in a building halfway between Gastown and Chinatown. Dave had been enumerating the generous assets of a friendly waitress named Dory who regularly waited on us in the diner before he changed subjects. Dory and I had exchanged secret smiles. I hadn't told him my capricious Robo-voice had worked well enough to convince her to be a bedmate. I was still uneasy about sleeping alone, and Vancouver's late-night television didn't provide much distraction. Only one station broadcasted: from sign-off to sign-on a camera slowly swung between a calendar and a clock to the accompaniment of elevator music.

I'd also met a vivacious, if super-spoiled, German girl from Munich named Karin, and though we'd come close, Robo-voice had sputtered and failed to lure her into my rooms.

"I've been done for a while," I told Dave. "You know I'm just playing out my notice until the band finds somebody else." *Why is this hard for them? I only sing a few leads. Finding somebody better than me should be dead easy.* He must have been reading my thoughts.

"Nobody is the leader. Nobody's looking for a keyboard player who can sing. Things are totally screwed up."

I couldn't read his expression. *Is he angry with me?* "Sorry, man, but I can't help that. Been so out of it . . . wasn't doing the job anyway—"

"Tell me again why you're leaving?" Dave asked, interrupting my whining.

"You know why, or at least most of it." I reseated myself on the bed. "This thing with Theresa has killed me. I'm a ghost. When I see the guys look at me, I know they think they know me. But, I'm not who they think I am anymore. I'm empty inside, and they can't, or won't, accept it. I know you try to understand, but how can you? I'm hardly able to talk about it. Even if I tried, there aren't words to explain how truly hopeless I feel, so I'm done with explanations. That's one reason why I have to go; I'm not part of our brotherhood anymore. I don't have the capacity." I got to my feet and began to pace, trying to express the wild thoughts I'd been having.

"The other . . . I've told you the music we play, sometimes all music I think, is destroying me." I walked and thought for a few moments before I went on. Dave waited to hear whatever I wanted to tell him. "I'd never considered how powerful music is. When we play, we influence life-changing decisions in people, even whether to live or die. You know it's true, we hear it or see it often enough. People have fallen in love, divorced, gotten married, gotten angry, or sad, or sometimes even ecstatic because of us. We're like emotional arsonists. We ignite changes in peoples' lives without knowing we're doing it.

"Look, man, when we're not performing, we're rehearsing or looking for new material. Rock and R&B music is meant to be emotional and we're immersed in it, it's the air we breathe, we're submerged in it like fish in water, we sing and play without noticing the consequences." I scrubbed my hands through my hair before gazing at him again.

"We're so surrounded by it, I think we've built up a tolerance for it, become desensitized to its effects." I plopped into a side chair, trying to explain concepts difficult to verbalize.

"Except I'm not anymore. My emotions are raw and out of control . . . I guess I'm oversensitive. I feel like I see and feel music for what it is. A simple melody chokes me up; words and phrases I never thought much about before speak to me of my . . . my failures. They make me feel lost, it's like a knife in the heart or a fall off a cliff, to listen. Words can't explain the torture it is to be drenched in it, to sing and play it, five hours a night, six nights a week."

From Dave's expression, I knew he must see the deep despair on my face, but he didn't have any idea of what I was talking about.

"Anyway, I can't do it anymore," I continued quietly. "I have to leave everything behind that has anything to do with her so I can survive—most of all music, and—my friends—all of them." I lifted my eyes, and we stared at each other, me on the hard edge of hell, Dave unable to fully comprehend, but wishing he could so he would know how to help.

Eventually, the calendar ran out on Oil Can's the way my days as a musician were running out. When Danny brought me our final check, I told him I was interested in the position he'd offered. "I'm committed to two more months with the band before I can say for certain. Can you wait that long?" He said the timing sounded about right, but I should try to make up my mind before the end of January. He couldn't promise beyond then. So, with a potential job in hand, I joined the caravan back across the border. We'd stop at Tumwater, Washington, tonight. We wouldn't be tired, but most of the guys would try to drink the Olympia Brewery dry before heading south.

We arrived in Portland in the middle of a deluge. Rainstorms continued to assail the city through the month of December, switching from a light drizzle to cloudbursts so powerful there weren't individual raindrops, more like a jumbo-sized hose had been turned on the earth. There was no indication of the sun's existence during the entire four weeks of our engagement. It fit the desolation of my mood.

Dave and I had found an apartment to share in Beaverton, across a couple of bridges from the Turquoise Room. As we crossed over one of them on the way to work, Dave peered through wipers whisking at top speed but barely clearing the windshield enough to see ahead a few feet. "Jesus Christ, we're gonna drown in this shit." The rain hammering the roof made us yell to be heard.

"I hate this place. I mean it rained in Indianapolis but never like this. I need the sun. If I lived here, I'd have to kill myself daily, or at least once a week."

Dave grinned. "Got moss or something green growing between my toes. I'm never dry, even when I towel off after a shower."

After a pause, I said, "Looks like Mickey is becoming the leader of the band." The thought added to my general depression. "He's sure acting like it anyway."

"I think he's showing off because he knows the owner, Ron, personally, and everybody else in the place, too. Doesn't hurt that the band's doing well here. None of us are in his face about it, but I don't think any of us want him to run the band."

"How about Mac? What's he think about Mickey as a leader?"

"Yeah." Dave nodded glumly. "He seems okay with it. Mac's been kind of a stranger. I don't know what he's thinking."

"I get this feeling Mickey would like to dump my ass right here in Portland. Make me walk back to civilization if he could."

"Well, that ain't happening. You're staying until Vegas. You promised. We'll worry about finding somebody while we're at the Cat."

My distance from the group continued to grow, which was okay with me. I was on the way out and this unnaturally long notice period rattled everybody's nerves. The Turquoise Room felt like enemy territory. I didn't seem to be able to communicate with anyone without Robo-voice's help, and it only operated intermittently. I trolled the unremarkable Turquoise Room for bedmates without success, not surprising considering my gloomy disposition.

73 REVENGE SEX

Between two evils, I always pick the one I never tried before.
—Mae West

December 20, 1970
Portland, Oregon

LATE ON OUR first Sunday night, the storm hammered the roof of the Turquoise Room in torrents so fierce, there were moments when it drowned out the band. My anger and frustration were rising to match the violence of the downpour outside. Last week I'd turned 29; a year ago, I'd had everything I could have wanted in life, and more. In the last twelve months, I'd managed to let it all slip away for the second time in such a short life. Tonight, I just snapped, barging out into the raging gale to scream from the depths of my soul. I stood there with a raincoat on, my head tilted back, howling into a storm so strong my voice was blown from my lips like a spark in a tornado. I retreated indoors, exhausted, more furious and resentful than ever.

A girl with stringy blonde hair was sitting near the door. I threw my wet raincoat to the floor and plopped into a chair at her table. I was boiling over, and some luckless human being was going to hear about it from me.

"This miserable fucking city is a shithole. Anybody that lives here must be an idiot. It's like living in the bottom of a gigantic toilet that never stops flushing."

"Yeah, it sucks, so?" The girl tightened her grip on a narrow cocktail glass and stared at me with steely-gray eyes. "If you don't like it, why don't you get on the fucking high horse that brought you here and ride the fuck back to wherever the fuck you came from."

Venom knotted my tongue. "Well, fuck you, too," I managed to gasp out.

"Hey! You wanna fuck me, big man, then get in line. Seems like fucking me is what the world is best at. Might as well take your turn."

"What in the hell are you talking about?"

"So, you're not only a moron, you're deaf, too? Guess I have to spell it out. I said if you want to bang me, c'mon over here and do it. You want me to spread my legs here on the table? You need an engraved invitation to fuck me, you son of a bitch?"

I'd found someone as enraged as me, and we fueled each other's fire. "Sure, I'll fuck you. I'm rock hard just thinking about it. If we weren't out in public, I'd be all over you."

"Big talk." She clenched her teeth brandishing her sex like a weapon. "Come with me right this minute, and I'll screw you till all your hair stands on end."

"I have to go back up there," I gestured toward the stage, "but if you're here when I get back, I'll go with you."

The fierce light in her eyes dimmed. "You've blown your chance, asshole. I'm going to screw somebody tonight, and if you leave now, it probably won't be you."

"Do what you want. But I'll tell you this, I'm so pissed off I could chew steel. I think you are, too. Maybe we need each other tonight. Maybe you need someone as angry as you. But maybe I'm wrong." I swept my hand around the club yelling at her and not caring who might hear. "Considering the way people live under a goddamned river here, there should be a lot of pissed off guys in this joint." I leaned over her. "But none of them is as furious as me. My wife has completely torn up my life and pissed on all the pieces. Just being in this hellhole makes me realize what an idiot I've been. I hate you, me, and everybody else in this dirty, wet, shitty nightclub. So, if you want to get it on with me, if you're as mad as I am, be here when I get back, and I promise you'll get screwed like you never have before. If you're not here, I'll figure you weren't as uptight as I thought you were." I turned and stalked toward the bandstand.

She slapped me, hard. "Goddamn, you. I thought you were going to pile-drive me, you asshole." I strained with effort and howled as my anger kept building and my hips pumping. "Harder, harder, you cocksucker," she screamed. "You little girl fucker, you cheating mother—"

I slammed my hand over her mouth, staring into eyes filled with hate and lust. I matched her thrust for thrust as we rode into the night, the rain pounding in fury, and the wind moaning and whimpering at the window of her single-room apartment. Agile and strong, she squirmed from beneath me and pushed me onto my back, mounting me without pause.

She panted and chuffed like a steam engine working her way up a hill to another frenzy. "Come on, you heartless bastard," she wailed into the dark above us. "Come in me like you come in her, you fucker." Her fingers turned to claws that scraped across my chest raising welts that engorged me further. I grabbed her waist to pull her down against my upward lunges, working hard to impale her. I left scratches of my own.

I felt the rise of a monumental orgasm I still wasn't prepared for. "Fuck you, Theresa. Fuck you, you rotten, lying whore," I cried out in an agony I'd never unleashed before, but words weren't basic enough. Guttural noises of a wild animal tore from my throat as I thrashed myself into her, her weight smacking down on me full force, her elbows slamming into my head as she ground against me, shrieking in a tuneless howl. We grabbed each other's hair as our bodies pumped and pulled, grunting like beasts, crescendoing in a mad gesture of defiance at a world that had driven us over the edge. Our eyes locked in those final moments as we fed on each other's pain and despair. As the spasms ebbed, she collapsed across my chest, spent. I couldn't catch my breath, the girl's dead weight made it worse. I'd fallen so deep into oxygen debt I thought I would suffocate and die, and I welcomed it—if it would end this unending misery. But as I lay there, lungs heaving, knowing I would live, I recognized something inside me had snapped like an Achilles tendon, but I wasn't sure where, or what it meant.

In a few minutes, she rolled off me and used a camisole to sop up the wet between her legs as she moved to sit on the side of the mattress. She sat, and I lay spreadeagled for a while. She sighed. "I think you should leave."

I looked in wonder at the angry scrapes on her back and touched them lightly in self-reproach, but she shrugged me away. "I said you should leave."

I shakily turned to dress in some weird false modesty before looking at her. Her eyes were downcast, the fire gone from them and from her drawn face. She was more attractive than I'd thought, but older too, older than me by a few years. None of that had mattered earlier.

"I don't know your name."

"I don't know yours either, so what? If you're waiting for me to tell you what a great fuck you were, then okay, we both got what we needed. But now get the hell out. Please." If she'd found any relief for her pain, it wasn't apparent.

"Will you at least let me use your phone to call a cab?"

"No. You need to go." She turned away. "There's a booth by the drugstore on the corner."

I stumbled through drenching rain to the public phone, energy drained. I felt like I'd been in a back-alley fight, sore everywhere with scratches beginning to sting including those on my face. At least one of her fingernails had caught my cheek and forehead. During the fifteen-minute cab ride to Beaverton, I realized something inside had given way. I felt dirty, as though I'd been swimming in a cesspool. I couldn't stand being this broken. What we'd done wasn't sex, we'd been equal participants in a primitive assault on each other. It was incredibly intense, but I never wanted to mix sex and violence together again. I'd never felt further from being the person I thought I was. In the morning, I deflected Dave's questions about the night past as best I could.

I realized how drained and depleted I'd become. I couldn't express, even to myself, how terribly lost and confused I was. A sadness beyond tears. A sadness that seeps into your being and pools there forever. The feeling for which the word "sad" had been coined—not the cheerless, overused definition of being momentarily uncomfortable.

I mourned of the loss of someone I loved beyond reason, but more than that, the trust in my own judgment. I'd let myself be deluded by a fantasy woven by a master illusionist—myself. It wasn't only Theresa's lies, her sadistic cruelty, and fucking other people that destroyed me; it was the way I'd become an accomplice, accepting a new normal. I'd agreed to degrade myself by sinking to depths I didn't believe I was capable. I'd been so sure I was doing something heroic, honorable, self-sacrificial. I'd arrogantly convinced myself I could be bigger than any pain she brought me, that I could love her through all of it to become her hero, her rescuer. I'd been wrong. Instead, I'd become debased and unlovable. I was the one who needed rescuing.

So, I was surprised, to the degree I could experience surprise, to find that as horrible as this realization felt, it still seemed a small step above the numbness of feeling nothing at all.

No one noticed the red stripes on my face Tuesday night. Except for Dave, and I'd given him as little information as I could about it. To the rest of the band, I was already gone, invisible, even if my body showed up for work every night. The rain continued, and the wooden job of playing music seemed interminable.

A group of girls, four or five depending upon the night, often gathered ringside at the club. I had the feeling they came in to hang with each other no matter what band was playing. I'd become familiar enough with them to be welcome on breaks and allowed to observe them in their habitat, like exotic creatures in the wild. One girl, Liz, made an effort to involve me in their chatty gossip. It was no more than conversation with a girl. I didn't think of it as an invitation to intimacy. The concept of sex, the real kind, felt way too confusing, the last thing I was interested in.

When Liz was away for a few minutes, one of her girlfriends looked at me like she had something to say. She glanced around and leaned toward me.

"If you're trying to get in Liz's pants, forget it. If I hadn't heard different, I'd think she was a lesbian. She's been off men for years." That was the furthest thing from my mind, but I couldn't help considering her in a new light when she came back.

She wore her hair short. Her face was open and expressive. Her last name was French, but I thought I remembered her mentioning Native American ancestry. I could see it now in her high cheekbones. She was striking, I realized. I liked her and hoped she hadn't been screwed up by some man.

On Thursday night of our last week, Portland celebrated the end of 1970. It seemed fitting to end such a rotten year in this wet and miserable place. Wherever Pat and her husband had taken them, David had turned nine two weeks ago, and Danny was seven today. I couldn't imagine where any of us would be this time next year.

On our last Sunday night, while I was feeling the slight reprieve of knowing we'd soon be gone from this godforsaken place, Liz surprised me by inviting me home with her. I knew we would likely never see or hear from each other again and enjoyed the idea of more time with her. She would be saving me from having to stare at Dave's face tonight. For years, we'd often been roommates before this trip, and though we were best friends, I was pitiful to be around. It embarrassed me to inflict my joyless existence on him.

Liz and I sat in the tasteful living room of her one-bedroom apartment and talked easily together, as friends do. I knew she worked in the legal profession, but I hadn't realized she'd intended to go back to school to finish a law degree. She refilled my wine glass and excused herself for a minute. The rainfall outside was steady, and for the first time, I took some comfort in its gentle rhythm.

Faintly, I heard Liz call my name. Apprehensive, I hesitantly entered the short hallway to the rest of her apartment, unsure of how to respond; I liked her, but I didn't see her in this way, and I didn't want this to end badly. Ahead was a closed door, her bedroom. Light flickered into the corridor from the bathroom's partially open doorway. She called again, and I nudged the door open. Candles on every surface illuminated the bathroom. Liz's smile peered from a massive cloud of bubbles in a claw-footed tub. She lifted a wet hand to welcome me in. It was irresistible.

Monday morning, she fussed over me in the kitchen, making me a cheese omelet with several little sausages. She sat across from me watching me devour breakfast and slurp gulps of fresh-squeezed orange juice.

I pushed the empty plate away. "Well. This is not what I imagined happening."

Liz's skin didn't easily show a blush, but I knew it was there.

"Interesting. It was exactly what I imagined." She hesitated, pretending to ponder that thought for a moment. "No, it was more than that, it was exceptional. I knew you were a great guy, but it was so much better to hold you and love on you. I haven't felt like that for a long, long time."

Maybe I'd been a good guy somewhere in the past, but it had been so long ago I couldn't be sure. I knew my face held a puzzled frown. "I'm not a great guy. But honestly, I didn't come here last night intending to sleep with you. In fact, one of your friends told me I shouldn't try. I didn't want to—"

She waved me to a stop. "My only regret is I waited. I knew you were leaving today, and I deeply regret that, but I also have to admit I feel tremendously wonderful. It's like you woke a part of me that's been sleeping. Besides, pretty obvious you're not ready for anything heavy," she said with a bittersweet smile. "Oh, by the way, did you like the bubble bath?"

"Excellent. I was nice and clean when we went on to the next part." I smiled.

"I saw Barbra Streisand in *The Owl and the Pussycat* where she has a bubble bath with this guy. I always wanted to have a bubble bath like that." She gave me a self-satisfied grin. "And I did, except I think mine was way better."

74 AREA 51

It is by no means an irrational fancy that, in a future existence, we shall look upon what we think our present existence, as a dream.
—Edgar Allan Poe

January 11, 1971
Portland, Oregon

THE FASTEST ROUTE to Las Vegas took Dave and me through the Cascade Mountains and across a huge Indian reservation into northern Nevada where we headed south through what looked like the far side of the moon. The high desert got cold out here in the winter; Dave wore a jacket, and I'd pulled on a faded cardinal and gold USC sweatshirt over a collared shirt and black sweatpants. We kept the heater on high. When we were well on our way, somewhere around Winnemucca on US 95, Dave blurted out, "So what are you going to do?"

"That came right out of left field," I slouched back in the passenger seat. "I assume you're talking about after the band?"

He nodded. I took a while answering as I gazed out at the rugged and barren terrain, too harsh for most plant and animal life. All the nuclear bombs they'd set off out here couldn't have altered the scenery much. *Wasn't Area 51 supposed to be around here somewhere?*

"I've had some crazy ideas about what I want to do. I think I'm absolutely going to do them, but then I never do. The line between fantasy and reality isn't all that clear sometimes." I shrugged my shoulders. *Why the hell should it be? Coming to California six years ago started as a fantasy.*

Dave shifted his hands on the wheel bumping his elbow against the window. He wanted to hang an elbow out, but it was too cold. "What are you thinking about, man? What kind of crazy ideas?"

"Well, for instance, I've been researching islands in the South Pacific. I loved being in Hawaii, but obviously, can't go there." Dave nodded, but he hadn't burst out laughing yet. "Since Hawaii is part of Polynesia, I figured I'd look up what other islands are out there. Found out there are two other big island groups in the South Pacific: Micronesia and Melanesia. Means there's a hell of a lot of islands to consider. Tahiti would be my natural first choice, but you can't actually move there unless you're French. Thinking about going to the French embassy to see if I might qualify for some kind of work permit, though the literature seems pretty pessimistic."

Dave glanced at me in disbelief. "You are kidding, aren't you?"

"Well, that's the thing. Don't know if I am or not, but if I am, who is it I'm kidding? I mean who the hell is watching anyway? Can't be fooling anyone but myself. I thought I was serious about it until I talked with Danny in Vancouver. Made me rethink things."

"Danny Baceda? You talked to him about leaving the band?"

I shifted around. "Somehow he knew. Asked me to let him know if I decided to quit the band. Says he needs an assistant entertainment director and troubleshooter for the Oil Can Harry clubs."

"Didn't know there was more than one."

"Me either. Guess they're expanding; they're already breaking ground on another one, and they want to add more, become a chain. So that's a real thing. I mean if I go to some island or something, I get off a plane and then what? I don't know. Can't get past that part of the plan yet. If I were to go to work for Danny, I'd be out of the country, away from all the crap that's happened, and have an actual job."

"You can't do that, Larry," Dave said abruptly.

I looked at him incredulously. "What?"

"You can't leave. You can't take off and leave me hanging. You owe me, you know." He spoke with quiet intensity.

I waited. The longer I waited, the more I realized this wasn't spontaneous. He'd been planning this.

"I've been thinking I might like to be a single artist. I wouldn't want anyone but you to be my personal manager. You could do that."

I shook my head a couple of times, trying to take this in. I hardly knew where to start. I'd told him I couldn't tolerate music.

"How do you figure I owe you? I'm not denying it, I'm sure I do. I'm just curious."

"We're best friends. You always said I could come to you with anything, just like you could with me, and as friends, we'd always do our best for each other."

"But what about the band?" I jumped to the next obvious question.

"There is no band. Mickey's breaking it up at the Pussycat."

"How can he do that? Did you guys make Mickey the leader or something?"

"No, like I said, there isn't a leader. But with you gone and everything up in the air, Mick thinks it's time to start over. He told me last night after the Cat he wants me and Mac to come with him to Portland, back to the Turquoise Room to form an R&B horn band. You know Mac's always wanted a horn band. That's what Mick's promising him. I think the two of them have been hatching this for a while. He's made a deal with Ron to play at the Turquoise Room while we're woodshedding this new band. Mac needs the band to keep working so he can afford to bring Joan and Dani with him. Mickey talked to a bunch of players while we were in Portland. Says they're lining up to audition for a spot in Stark Naked and the Car Thieves."

"Wow." Hell of a lot going on that I'd missed. "What did you tell him?"

"Told him I'd have to think about it. What else could I say? When we pack up after the Cat, he's expecting me and Mac to leave with him."

"What about Les and Leonard?"

"Mickey says he might take Les, but he'd have to shut up and let Mickey make all the decisions."

I made a derisive noise. "Les ever heard that, he'd buy Mickey a one-way bus ticket back to Oregon himself," I grinned. Surprisingly, my face didn't crack. I hadn't done a lot of grinning lately.

"He's not interested in Leonard at all. Says all the drama's gotten to Leonard. Leonard hasn't said it outright, but he won't leave Vegas even if it means leaving the band. Things are so tense, he might just pull the plug anyway. I know he's bugged about the Flamingo and the International not bringing us back. He blames Mac mostly, I think, though Mac doesn't know it. And you, for . . . well, you know why. Anyway, I don't think he'd go with Mick no matter what.

"Larry, I can't imagine Mickey as a leader of a band. I know he was the leader of Sandy and the Vikings, but Jesus, he's the most disorganized, shit-for-brains management kind of guy I've ever seen. He'd just punch people out whenever they disagreed with him. I would never be involved in anything with him as a leader." He shook his head. "I can't see how Mac can go with him."

"Mac's gotten swallowed up by booze. He's not thinking straight. He's about wrecked his voice from liquor and hard living. I hear him say how much he wants to leave Las Vegas, but I've never been able to understand why. Seemed like such a perfect place for him."

"I don't know either. But I know I'm not going to Portland with them. If you don't handle this for me, I'll have to go back to Indiana. Work something out from there. So, I think you owe it to me as a friend to help me figure out what to do," Dave said with finality.

I nodded. "Okay. Got that." I understood his stance. "Has Mickey told anyone else about this plan? Well, you obviously, and Mac. What about Howard King or Seymour Heller? Band's got a signed contract to play at the Back Door in Salt Lake City after the Cat."

"Don't think he plans to talk to them. You know he doesn't trust either of them." He looked at me despondently. "Mick says he's already got a booking at the Trophy Room in Sacramento for four weeks as soon as the band's ready to leave the Turquoise Room. I don't think he ever intends to talk to Howard or Seymour again, not even to tell them the band won't be going to Salt Lake."

"Bad idea on so many levels," I said. "Mickey's going to burn a lot of bridges if he does that. Howard will bury him everywhere he can. He'll fuck up the band's reputation forever, not to mention Les and Leonard need time to find other work." We ruminated for a while before I spoke. "Say, for the sake of argument, I was to manage you as a single artist. I don't know how we'd do it. You have to have players, a band so you can find work. And right away. Unless a rich relative died and left you a bunch of money you haven't told me about, that's a problem."

"Ha! No. Haven't got a pot to shit in or a window to throw it out of."

"Well, me neither, brother. I'm still paying off my busted organ and a billion dollars in phone calls and trips back and forth to Hawaii." I thought about it, I could only come up with one possibility, but it would be a longshot . . .

"So, you'll be my personal manager?"

"I can't promise you that man. Not that I don't want to. I just don't know yet whether I can keep it together. I don't want anything bad to happen to you because I can't keep my shit together. I've never been through anything like what I'm going through. I'm not a well person. I've tried everything to fix it, or get over it, but nothing's worked.

"You're the only one I've told that I almost blew my fucking head off. Goddammit, that's still so fucking weird; I didn't even know I was doing it. That is so fucked up. I'm trying to find a way to save my life Dave, and I don't want to add any more crap to my load by screwing things up for you."

"You won't do that. You're too smart for that. So, you'll at least consider it? Right?"

I sighed. I hoped his confidence in me wasn't misplaced. "Yeah, of course, I'll consider it brother. But we've got some time. Let's see how things go. I need to think about it, and there isn't much we can do until we get back to Vegas. No matter what, I promise I'll do whatever I can."

75 CONSPIRACY

I'm not a conspiracy theorist—I'm a conspiracy analyst.
—Gore Vidal

January 12, 1971
Las Vegas, Nevada

THE PUSSYCAT LOOKED ragged around the edges, like a once-sexy and vivacious woman from the wrong side of the tracks at the end of her days. We were a good match for her because it was a crapshoot whether Stark Naked and the Car Thieves would exist at the end of this gig.

Dave had kept his place in Las Vegas and invited me to stay with him until I figured out what I wanted to do. I repeated what I'd said on our ride through Nevada: "There's no way we can kick off a solo career for you right now. You won't know where your next meal is coming from if the band falls apart. We need to get things under control before that happens. We can't let Mickey hijack Stark Naked."

"No, we can't," he said, frowning. "How do we do that?"

I laid out my tentative plan. "But you'll have to play along with Mickey. We need to keep track of what he's doing."

Our first visit was with Bear. Dave called ahead and asked Les to meet with us before going to the Cat to set up. He and his girlfriend Vicki lived west of the Strip near Sunrise Hospital, where she worked as an RN. When we got there, he opened his apartment door and motioned us in.

Les grabbed his Gibson Les Paul and perched on one end of the couch, picking at the strings. Dave sat on the other side while I chose a side chair. Les curtly acknowledged me and spoke to Dave.

"What's up?"

Dave fidgeted. "There's been some developments I don't think you're aware of. We came by to fill you in."

Les raised an eyebrow. "We?" *Yeah, Les, we,* I thought. *I'm not invisible, I'm just on notice.* I shrugged it off.

"Look, I may be leaving the band, and it may not be obvious, but I do care what happens."

"Hard to believe." He glanced at his strings and fingered his way through a rapid riff. "Well, what is it?"

"Mickey's trying to steal the band after it closes the Cat," I said.

Les stopped playing and forced his eyes to Dave's for confirmation. We both nodded. He addressed me for the first time.

"Steal? How does he plan to do that?" I glanced at Dave, but he was already answering.

"He asked Mac and me not to say anything, but he wants to rebuild Stark Naked and the Car Thieves as a horn band. He plans for us to leave with him after the Cat and go back to the Turquoise Room to add new players he knows there."

I don't often get to see Les startled, but he hadn't seen this coming, and he didn't like that we'd seen that. He was a little paranoid at the best of times; not much snuck up on him. He carefully leaned the guitar against the couch.

"Are you here to tell me you're going with him?"

Dave shook his head with a wry grin. "No, of course not."

Les gave him a short nod. "Good. Because that would be a very fucked up thing to do. I thought for a minute you were here to warn me. Doesn't sound like he even plans to give me two weeks' notice." He paused. "Who the fuck is he to give me notice anyway?" Les was getting angry. "What about Leonard? Does he know? Was he asked?"

Dave shook his head again.

"Just you and Mac." Les's speculative gaze took us both in now. "Mickey's a piece of work. So, what's next?"

Dave leaned forward and spoke to Les. "Bear, do you want to work with me? Do you want to keep the band together?"

"Sure." Les glanced at me. "Why is Larry here? What's his part in this?"

I answered for myself. "To tell you the truth I'm not certain, except to make sure the band goes on. But whatever it is I'm not staying."

"I want him to manage me, to manage us." Dave grinned at me. "He thinks he might want to do something else, but I'm not going to let him." He turned to Les. "Part of the deal. You okay with that? We do this, and if Larry agrees, he'll be our personal manager?"

Les had to think about it. He hadn't had much sympathy for my personal drama, and though I didn't wield my authority as a leader much, he'd always had a problem whenever I did. I was sympathetic, I wasn't great with authority either, which is why I'd tried to lead by consensus. I was disappointed in the way we'd grown more and more distant since we'd settled in Las Vegas. I considered it a good thing that he thought through Dave's proposal before deciding.

"Basically, I'm okay with it, but I got a lot of questions and things to say. Knowing Larry, there's more here than you've told me so far, so let's hear it."

We told him, and he liked most of it. It was the kind of solution that appealed to him.

Leonard, we approached differently. A few nights later, Dave offered to buy him breakfast at the Silver Slipper after our last set. When fresh coffee and our orders were in front of us, Dave got right to the point.

"Mick's breaking up the band after the Cat."

He gave us a mournful gaze and picked at a French fry. I never understood how anyone could eat fries for breakfast. "Guess I'm not surprised. Things have been really rocky. I thought we might come apart before we left town, maybe even out on the road somewhere. Kind of glad something's finally happening though." He paused for a second. "Hey, I don't mean I'm glad something bad is happening to the band, not that."

I chuckled. "Leonard, we know that's not what you meant. But I also know if something did happen, you'd be glad it happened here in Vegas."

He winced. "Yeah, it's been nerve-racking, that's all I meant."

I started in, watching Dave to make sure it was okay. "Mickey wants to take Mac and Dave to Portland and build a new Stark Naked band. And before you ask, no, Dave's not going with him, but Mickey doesn't know yet."

"Mac's going though? Oh, I see. Mac doesn't know Dave's not going either."

Dave nodded in confirmation.

"I feel bad for Mac."

"It's his choice, buddy. If he wants to stay, he can stay."

"What's your deal, Larry? Are you still quitting?"

"Yes. I gave notice to leave, but not to watch our band get destroyed. I don't want to see the name we worked to build dragged through the mud. Besides, what Mickey is doing isn't fair to you and Les. With some work, we can rebuild it without them."

Leonard nodded. "What do you want me to do?"

"Promise you'll stay with the band until after Salt Lake City. Afterward, whatever you want. If we send a reasonable semblance of Naked to Salt Lake—not likely that many people up there have seen the band before—we can use the time to tighten up the act."

Leonard sighed and pushed some egg around on his plate. "I don't want to leave Las Vegas again. I told Marie I'd quit if we couldn't find a job here."

"Figured that's what you'd say. I also figured you'd be willing to sacrifice four weeks in Utah to make sure the band survives."

Leonard's dry grin expressed his feelings.

"Good," I said. "Dave hopes you'll talk to Phil Conti about taking my place in Naked, even if it's only for the short haul. We need you in Salt Lake for those first four weeks to help the new band get acclimated. If Howard or Seymour can't find work for you guys in Vegas, I'll help find a replacement so you can come back to town. At least Mickey and Mac won't be able to run off with the band's name, and we'll be giving them a good chance to survive."

I watched Leonard's gears turn as he considered the proposal. He counted on his fingers. "Les, Dave, me, and Phil . . ." He stared at us. "Who's playing bass?"

We hadn't been back to the Pussycat A' Go-Go other than to hang out, some of us more than others, for more than two years. An excellent R&B group we were familiar with, Seventh Step, had been held over for two weeks as our early band. Pat Mosley, their bass player, was a key to my plan.

I corralled him after their second set. "Hi, Pat. Can you gimme a minute?" Pat wore his reddish-brown hair long and curly. Freckles were sprinkled across his nose and cheeks and he had a spacey smile, but, the most important thing, his voice fit perfectly with the new Stark Naked we were building. He could sing rough or smooth. He tore up R&B and hard rock songs and dripped emotion in tunes like Otis Redding's *Try a Little Tenderness*. He also had a sense of fun and playfulness, sometimes to the edge of distraction. If he agreed to join Stark Naked and the Car Thieves, we'd not only gain a bass player, he could quickly take over Mac's leads, and his textured voice would blend perfectly with Les and Dave. I pointed out a table where a pair of beers stood waiting.

"First, I wanna say, I love Seventh Step, always have. Most of all, I love your voice. You're a fabulous singer and bass player." I lifted a beer glass to him.

"Well, cool," he sat back with a wide grin. I wasn't sure I was reading his expression right at first. Was he genuinely that friendly or was he mocking me? I desperately needed to know if our optimum plan would work as soon as possible, so I got right to the point. "Here's the thing, Pat. Our bass player is leaving at the end of the gig. I wondered if you might be open to coming with us."

He sat up straight, cocking his head. "Join Stark Naked and the Car Thieves? Me?"

"I think you'd be fantastic in our band, and everybody who needs to, agrees. We plan on getting back into the studio again soon, too. You'd be a terrific asset. Consider this an offer if you're interested."

"Where do I sign? I mean I gotta give two-weeks to my band, stuff to work out, but yeah, yeah. I'm in." He thought for a moment. "We close a week from Sunday night. If I don't give notice real soon, I might get accidentally included in Seventh Step's next contract. And they need time to find another bass player. I should tell them right away. Tonight, even."

I grinned in relief, and in the bubbling enthusiasm of our new acquisition. "Okay, full disclosure before you pull the trigger, the band is going through kind of a make-over. Do you know which one of us is Mac?"

"Sure. Your front-man guy."

I nodded. "He and Mickey, our current bass player, are leaving Stark Naked. I'm not going to be in the band anymore either, so we've got a new keyboard player lined up, too. But here's the thing, still the same manager and agent, recording contract, everything. You'll be an upgrade at bass, and with you, Dave, and Les, the vocals will be hot."

There was a question in his eyes.

"I can see you want to ask me something. It's okay, whatever it is, ask away."

"Why are you leaving?"

I sighed and looked at the ceiling. "Pat, it's personal stuff, doesn't have anything to do with the band. Also, let's say a guy's gotta realize his limitations. I'm probably as good as I'm ever going to get and that's not good enough for where this band should go." I paused for a minute. "There's a chance I'll take over the management of the band. That's not for sure, though."

He nodded. "Okay, I'm good."

"Stark Naked doesn't close until two weeks after Seventh Step does. You could be out of work for a week or two."

He grinned. "I been out of work before. Where are we going next?"

76 THE LAST CAT

> *After silence, that which comes nearest to expressing the inexpressible is music.*
> —Aldous Huxley

January 15, 1971
Las Vegas, Nevada

WITH PAT MOSLEY ready to join Stark Naked, we arranged a meeting for him with Dave, Les, and Leonard. I didn't attend. Pat's enthusiasm seemed to give them the spark they needed after the last months of turmoil. Les gave Pat band tapes of our sets so he could work on them while he played out his notice with Seventh Step. Phil Conti was only playing casuals and happy to come onboard immediately. He'd brought his electric piano to Les's, and they'd started working through the song list. The clock had begun ticking on our plan, and on my decision for Danny Baceda.

"So, what are you doing, man? Are you going back to Vancouver? 'Cause I'm going to play my friend card if you think you are."

I grinned at Dave and shook my head in feigned bewilderment. "You know I can't replace Seymour Heller. I mean, c'mon."

"Figure it out. I know you can."

I had a rough plan in mind, but the outcome depended on how the dominoes fell. I was okay with whichever way it went. I was uprooted anyway, a seed in the wind. I might as well let the Universe decide where I landed. "We'll see. I'm flying to LA next week to find out if there's a realistic way to work things out."

It was Monday, two weeks before Stark Naked and the Car Thieves would close at the Cat when Bette let me into Seymour's office. I wanted time enough for him to consider a decision on what I was going to propose, but not enough for a lot of discussion. As usual, she warned me not to take too much of the great man's time.

After we traded greetings and Seymour was comfortably reclined behind his piano-desk, he folded his hands across his belly and gave me his pop-eyed-bullfrog, grandfatherly smile. "Seems as though you boys been going through a rough patch since I've been away. By the way, Lee asked me to give you guys his best wishes."

That was nice to hear. Liberace had always been exceedingly gracious to us. Leonard had become an especially huge fan.

"Are you here about Kerkorian selling the Flamingo and International to Hilton and changing the Sky Room and Crown Room into steakhouses? Nothing to do with you. It wasn't his choice, he managed to get himself too deep in debt building the International. I don't want you to worry too much about that. We want to concentrate more on recording going forward anyway."

"I think you're right," I replied as Seymour led me into explaining why I was here. "Things do change. Las Vegas is changing, so is music, and now, the band is changing, too."

"What do you mean?"

"I'm leaving the band, Seymour."

He moved around in his chair before pulling himself to his desk again. He rested his elbows in front of him and leaned forward. "Why in the world would you want to leave?"

"It's time, and something's happened in my personal life."

"I see." His eyes scrutinized me, calculating. "What are you planning to do next?"

"That's why I'm here. With me leaving there are a couple of options in which way the band may go. The bass player wants to take the band off to the great northwest and leave Hollywood behind. No Attarack-Heller and no Howard King." Seymour had partnered with Eddie Cobb and Ray Harris. Attarack-Heller was what they were calling their record production company.

"That's not good for anybody. That would be incredibly irresponsible," he said, frowning. I took it as a good sign that Seymour hadn't started threatening with contracts. An empty threat with Mickey. He planned to take the band out of the big leagues where Seymour operated anyway.

"Yes, I think so, too."

"And the other option?"

"Well, Dave wants me to rebuild and manage the band." Before Seymour could comment, I went on. "I told him he'd be getting a terrible deal, trading you for me." I smiled at Seymour, he smiled back, but his eyes didn't.

"There may be a best-of-both-worlds solution, if you're willing to consider it," I continued. "I think the choice is obvious, but it would be up to you to make it." I wasn't nervous about what I was about to present to Seymour. It would go one way or the other, and I'd accept whichever path opened up. Nevertheless, what I was proposing was pretty cheeky.

"Suppose I came here . . . to work in your office. Stark Naked would send their commissions to me instead of Attarack-Heller, and I would continue to use your resources to manage them while performing other tasks for you. I'd be learning the ropes of personal management from you, the guy who invented it, a protégé if you like, or an associate if you prefer, and we'd hold on to the band.

He looked at me speculatively. "But you'd get the commissions. And office space here."

I nodded. "Sort of like Jimmy O'Neil and Burt Jacobs did I'd guess. And I'm glad you mentioned more focus on recording. This rebuilt Stark Naked will be improved vocally and musically, and still, feature Dave. And remember you'll get a guy who will do other management tasks for you as part of the deal."

"I'd have to think this over Larry."

"Of course. But I need to know soon. I have a job offer waiting if this isn't what you want. And I'd have to turn down Dave's request to manage him and the band, so I don't know what would happen after that."

"Well, you've made an interesting proposal, I can't deny that. I will tell you this much, if I can see a way to make this work after I talk with Ray and Ed I'll let you know within the week. Is that good enough?"

When I got back from LA, I told Dave about my meeting. "So, here's what it comes down to. If Seymour agrees, I guess I'll be managing you and the band. If he doesn't, I'm calling Danny Baceda and accepting his offer. I mean, let's be realistic, I can't give you what Seymour can unless I'm working beside him. If he doesn't, you still have an excellent group, the band's name, and as good a chance as we've ever had to get where you want to go."

Tuesday, the next steps in the plan went ahead. With Seventh Step's engagement over and Pat's time free, Les scheduled harmony rehearsals with the three of them. Listening to them sing, I ached to join them. I had moments when I wished I could overcome the agonizing impact music made on me; I would've loved harmonizing with their voices, especially in the studio. But every night proved how impossible that fantasy was.

At the first of the following week, Seymour called to accept my proposition and tell me an office was being cleared for me, and he would expect me within the next couple of weeks. I couldn't help but appreciate his good-natured response to my bald-faced blackmail. I didn't have a clue where I would stay in LA yet, or whether my crappy AMC Javelin would even get me to Hollywood. I phoned Danny at Oil Can's and thanked him for his generous offer and told him I was going into personal management. We wished each other the best and hoped for another opportunity to work together.

All that was left was to finish our engagement at the Cat and play out the final scene. Dave had kept his ear to the ground about any changes in Mickey's plans or suspicions, but there were none. The future of the band was so much in question we were no longer rehearsing, so Les's work with our two new Nakeds continued undetected. It had been tense for everyone during these last weeks, but the stress level reached its peak closing night. Mac appeared nervous, drinking even more than usual, fortifying himself before and after each set. Mickey wore a constipated look on his face and played even louder than usual. Nobody complained as we normally would have. Leonard came across as sullen, unwilling to talk to anyone.

Surprisingly, Howard King had no complaint about our plans. He liked the idea of me being in LA and invited me to lunch at the French restaurant beneath his second-story office in Beverly Hills as soon as I got settled. He thought the changes would be good for the band. Every once in a while, he said, bands need to be reshuffled. He encouraged me, telling me not to worry about the Back Door club in Salt Lake. He'd make sure the job stayed solid despite the changes. He added he was close to a deal following Salt Lake at a club in Sacramento where the audience sat around and in renovated antique cars; the guys would absolutely love the place.

I didn't mention that to Leonard right away. Sacramento was pretty close to Oakland, where his family lived, and not that far from Las Vegas so maybe he'd stay with the band for one more engagement. Maybe we could find something for the band back here in Vegas, but whether we did or not, we'd make sure Lenny, as his local friends had begun calling him, had a comfortable way to leave if that's what he wanted. In reality, the new Stark Naked and the Car Thieves would probably never play Las Vegas again unless recording success qualified them for a showroom. For one thing, they were losing Mac. He'd been the showman, the personality and face of the band for many years. When it came to performing, his charisma was irreplaceable, especially in Vegas. But Vegas was changing; live music in the lounges was disappearing, even the Pussycat seemed to be on its last legs.

On closing night, it was time to end the charade. While the guys loaded the band's equipment in the van without comment or conversation, I cashed our final check at the gambling cage and sorted the money into envelopes as I'd always done.

Outside in the parking lot, the early morning darkness was thick with unspoken pronouncements. Mickey's car was packed with his personal belongings including his bass guitar and amp. Lora, who'd flown in to drive back with Mickey, waited patiently in the front seat. It looked like she intended to drive. Mac and Joan had jammed everything they could into their Cadillac convertible, their daughter Dani visiting relatives in Ohio. There was nothing left inside except the remains of my B3 on the stage.

I handed Mac and Mickey their pay envelopes followed by everyone else before they slipped away, as planned. I was here all alone. That's what I wanted. It was my final job as leader, and if I could help it, I didn't want things to get out of hand. I wondered if Mickey would punch me before this was over. My fear rose for a moment before dissipating like morning fog over a graveyard. He'd threatened me before, and under normal circumstances, he could physically intimidate me, though I'd tried not to let him know. But not anymore. Tonight, I didn't care. Since my personal life had exploded, my tolerance for any emotion so flat, fear failed to move the meter. If he did beat me up, at least I'd feel something.

The two of them quickly checked the cash in their envelopes.

After tucking his envelope away, Mickey glared at me with a self-satisfied grin on his face. "Hate to break it to you Larry, but we're not going to Salt Lake City."

"Seriously?" I said calmly. "That mean you're not going to Salt Lake either Mac?"

"Gimme a break, will ya? You're leavin, band's goin under. Anyway, Salt Lake City? What the fuck we doin goin to Salt Lake fuckin City?" Mac fidgeted like he was cold. Poor Mac, he was so nervous. I was giving him every chance to come correct.

"I didn't get that, what about Salt Lake fuckin' City?" I asked him, solemn as a minister in church.

"We don't belong playin in a club there. This band used to have some balls. Ain't got shit no more. Mickey's got some horn players, and me and Dave are going to front a new Stark Naked and deliver some kickass shit." Mac kept moving around.

"Just to get this straight—for the other guys. Not me of course, I gave notice, this is it for me, either way. Les and Leonard, did you give them any notice? Cause if you did, they haven't said anything to me about not honoring their contract in Utah. Don't think this band has ever done that, Mac."

He shook his head like a wet dog. "Like I said, this band's over, done. Ain't no notice due. Nobody owes nobody nothin."

"That's what you think, too, Mickey?"

Mickey had his fighting face on. A smile flickered on his lips like lightning before thunder, and he looked too relaxed and focused. I knew he had a hair-trigger fist. Mickey believed most fistfights were won on the first punch. I'm sure he was right; he'd sucker-punched a lot of people and would know.

"What I think is none of your damned business. Bottom line: Me, Mac, and Dave are leaving. If it's notice these guys want, this is it. Unless you got a problem with that, you should just turn your ass around and walk away."

"You guys don't care if you burn Howard King and Seymour Heller?"

"What have those old men got to do with this?" Mac mumbled. "Bastards just take our money, don't do shit for it." I realized Mac wasn't dancing so much as wobbling. Man, he was shit-faced. I hoped Joan planned on driving tonight.

"Agents ain't none of your goddamn business," Mickey shouted. "I got agents out the wazoo ready to book the new Stark Naked. And we don't have to kiss their asses like you always do, Dunlap." He tried to rein himself in.

"Look, I'm trying to be adult about this. Just tellin' you we're not going to Salt Lake, so no one drives all the way to Utah and finds out we're not there."

"Well damn, Mickey, that's really good of you. Of course, I'm not going to Salt Lake either, you know. I gave notice, in fact, I went way out of my way to give notice, to be fair to the guys I worked with all this time. Something like two and a half months ago." I gazed into Mickey's dead eyes. "If this is any example of it, I'm sure you are going to be one hell of a leader, Mick."

"Shut the fuck up! Where's Dave? We've got to get going!" He looked around for the key to his plan.

"Makes me think of that Cheech and Chong routine," I mused. "'Dave's not here, man. No really man, Dave's not here,'" I said, mimicking Tommy Chong. "And he's not going to be. He honors his contracts; he's going to Salt Lake City with the real Stark Naked and the Car Thieves. So, I guess you'd better get on the road. If you drive straight through, you might make Portland in time for an early dinner.

"By the way, if you thought you were going to take the band's van, you can forget about it. Van's registered in Dave's name, but you probably knew that. Since it belongs to the real Stark Naked and the Car Thieves, it will be staying here. In case you're wondering, it's locked, and Leonard took the keys with him when he left. Hope you didn't leave anything personal in it, but if you did, we'll send it to you care of the Turquoise Room."

Mickey realized I knew everything. I saw his face change and his fist bunch. I'm not saying I looked forward to getting hit. I just couldn't bring myself to care. I smiled, a tired but surely shit-eating smile, and stared back.

"Mac, look for Dave and find out if he's going or not!" Mickey edged up until he was inches from my face. "Why do you always have to be such a goddamned pain in my ass?"

"Don't truthfully know. Thought I was put on this earth for something better myself."

Mac reappeared from his quick scan of the club and got Mickey's attention. He shook his head no and looked my way with regret written in his eyes, or maybe I imagined that. Mickey turned back to me. "So many times I've wanted to punch your lights out, you obsequious little prick. I don't know why I never did, don't know why I'm not now. But you better get the fuck outta my face before I do!"

There was nothing I could think of to say that would serve any purpose other than getting me walloped. I retreated to the wooden bench next to the Pussycat's door to watch the final twitches from Mac and Mickey as they stalked around the parking lot seething. Eventually, Mickey opened his car door and motioned Lora over. He climbed into the driver's side and slammed the heel of his hand on the steering wheel.

Mac didn't say anything at the end. I felt bad for him. We hadn't offered him a chance to renege on his decision, partly because he'd sunk himself so deep into the bottle we didn't know if he could find his way out, and partly because he'd chosen to side with Mickey in breaking the band. If he'd said, "I want to stay," even at this last moment, we'd agreed he would have been welcomed. Instead, he maintained the surly, stubborn demeanor I'd seen more and more from him over the last several months. Once Mickey closed his door and started the vehicle, Mac threw his cigarette to the ground in a splash of sparks and slid into his Caddy next to Joan.

I'd witnessed so much in this town, in this club. One night, I'd found Aretha Franklin lying on this simple wooden bench, dead to the world, drunk. We'd checked her pulse and warned Scottie to find help for her. Jim Morrison had lain battered and raving in the parking lot here. I imagined there were a thousand stories this simple plank could tell. It would soon add another to my personal history. I was witnessing the end of the four musketeers from Indiana who'd struggled to create a rock band six years ago. Together, as the beating heart of the band, we'd found ways to survive and then thrive in the volatile environment of these times and to make a mark in the recording and entertainment industry. We'd come close to having it all. Who knows, maybe it was mostly my fault we hadn't completed the journey. There would be another Stark Naked and the Car Thieves after this one, maybe better, and maybe they'd reach our goal. But they would never be the one we'd built on our common companionship.

I considered Mac and Mickey as they sat there in their vehicles. They'd messed things up royally for themselves and their families, their plans were totally screwed. I took no pleasure in that. I shook my head in disbelief—building a horn band in Portland, Oregon? Mac knew the heart and soul of Stark Naked and the Car Thieves was the voice of Dave Dunn, he should have known Dave would never have gone along with Mickey's ruse. It had been a fantasy, without him they had nothing.

Joan sat beside Mac in their green Cadillac. In the end, she'd proved to be the ultimate survivor. By luck or providence or the grace of God himself, Mac was the beneficiary, because waiting beside him was his partner in life who'd come to terms what "through good times and bad" meant. He'd made a bad choice, but it wasn't his first, maybe not his last, and yet there she was, maybe yelling at him when she thought he deserved it, but always his wife, never deserting him. Hell, there was Lora next to Mickey. I didn't know how long they'd been together. But as much of an asshole as he'd been to me and others of us in the band, she loved and stood by him at every turn as far as I knew. Maybe he was a great human being to her; I knew he was a loving father with his little son. Any satisfaction I might have gotten from this moment disappeared. All I could think of was my own personal failures.

As I sat and watched the disintegration of the band in the chill desert night, wooden in my own loss, I realized they'd retained the most important thing: a person who loved them and would always stand with them right or wrong. Between them and me, I knew they'd won the personal sweepstakes, though I'd never let them know it. My eyes were dry as the shadows in the darkened driveway that swallowed their headlights as they drove out to Las Vegas Boulevard. They didn't need any sympathy from me.

77 MIDNIGHT ON THE MOJAVE

The most painful state of being is remembering the future, particularly the one you'll never have.
—Soren Kierkegaard

February 11, 1971
Interstate 15, The California-Nevada Border to Hollywood

THE MILES SPUN out beneath the wheels of my AMC Javelin beater car, as it bumped and swayed across the moon-goldened desert. The dwindling light from the garish Nevada casinos at the California border no longer glowed in my rearview mirror. The Universe had turned another page in my life.

I was alone, for the first time ever, unequivocally alone. I was no longer part of something bigger than me. In my youth, I'd been part of my family, parents, and sister, grandparents and aunts and uncles, until Pat and I had budded into our own family. In California, the bond I'd shared with my vocal group had expanded to the brotherhood of the band and Marie. In time, Theresa and Keoki had become everything to me until I'd lost them and myself. Now my damaged heart seemed unable to hold a place for others.

Exhausted in every way a person could be, I kept the driver's side window open to the cold, dry midnight breeze off the desert to keep from dozing off. Within days, the new version of Stark Naked and the Car Thieves would begin in Salt Lake City. They would be excellent, in time. The addition of Pat Mosley's voice to Dave's and Les's gave them strong voices. With Les's musical repository of the group's music and a real keyboard player, they'd hardly miss a beat. There was no question the band would miss Mac's bigger-than-life personality—a big but not insurmountable deficit. I worried about Mac and hoped things worked out for him. Despite where we had all ended up and the strained relationships among some of us, I still felt a bond between the four of us. I was proud of all that we'd accomplished. I wished we could have made the transition to reach our ultimate goal as nationally acclaimed recording artists, but we could hardly have been more successful as the performing band we'd become over the years.

My days as a musician were over. My B3, that poor gentle beast, had expired into a pile of broken cabinetry and electronic junk on the Pussycat stage. I'd always suspected I might be an imposter as a musician anyway. Wouldn't a true musician have found solace in channeling his heartbreak into song? I couldn't imagine expressing what I felt in words and music. My shifting emotions were so intense, so personal, I couldn't even think about them directly. My mind was like a kaleidoscope, constantly skittering between images and sensations that barely stood still long enough for me to feel them.

The chill breeze was keeping me alert, but my fingers were growing numb on the wheel. I wound the driver-side window up halfway and turned on the heater.

I thought about the last few days before I'd left. Though the work of rebuilding the band had kept me busy, the loss of Theresa and Keoki never left my mind. She'd been the perfect girl, and then suddenly—she wasn't.

I'd thought I'd known Theresa, but I'd only known what she'd shown me. After a week in Waipahu with her family, I realized I'd barely known her at all. I'd grasped nothing of her life next to the cane fields of Waipahu and on the beaches of Oahu before we met.

Our relationship in those early days in Waikiki and the Surfboard Hotel had been romantically casual, if physically mind-bending—until the foggy morning the collector had come for her. Afterward, she had quietly attached herself to me, entrusted herself to me. She became the perfect girlfriend. Everything she did was to please me, to demonstrate how much I needed her. She would never disagree, always listen patiently, and supply endless varieties of passionate sex. I whole-heartedly accepted that she'd wanted to be with me because I was such a sensitive and enthusiastic lover.

I stopped for gas in Baker. When I realized I was going to be late getting into LA, I called ahead to Thom Keith. He'd offered me a room in his house in the hills above the 101 Freeway at Hollywood Boulevard for as long as I needed. He told me not to worry, there was a key in the mailbox. If no one was awake, use the bedroom with the nightlight on, and he'd see me in the morning.

Back on the highway, I remembered how Theresa had come to me in California—she was the perfect girl—the mythical illusion men believe, in their fantasies, exists. She'd convinced me my philosophical wanderings and long-winded ramblings were logical and brilliant. That me, with my head in a book, was intellectual and wise instead of escapist and nerdy; that my love of board and card games was admirable and brainy; that my wild explorations of mysteries of the mind and obscure philosophies were a brave search for ultimate meaning.

With her pregnancy, my self-examination of our relationship brought me to commit my entire existence to her and our new child. I had failed to fulfill that ultimate promise to my first wife and our sons. This time, I'd vowed, I would never let anything separate me from this precious woman who loved and trusted me with her future and our child.

Our marriage brought us closer; enhanced our loving ways. I believed I'd reached the pinnacle of my life. As my new wife learned more of the ways that brought me pleasure, she became ever more accessible and amenable. She'd convinced me she loved professional football Sundays, lying naked and sweat-sheened on cool cotton sheets all through the day, touching and making love in a surfeit of physical contact. I'd gotten to where I could hardly live without her aroma, without her hands on me and mine on her.

The lights along the highway were beginning to multiply as I entered Barstow, the halfway point between LA and Las Vegas in the high desert. There weren't many cars on the road, even though I'd left late I was making good time. My mind drifted to the thoughts they always returned to . . . when it had all come apart. The perfect wife, the charming island girl I'd loved and married, had been supplanted by an over-mascaraed, cynical, modern girl who would sleep with whoever she wanted whenever she wanted, wife or not, mother or not. A shudder swept through me as they occasionally did these days. I scrubbed a palm across my face trying to wipe away my bitter thoughts.

For a while, I traveled along in a gray fog. I vaguely wondered what kind of reception I'd receive at Attarack-Heller after forcing my way into their organization.

From Victorville, Interstate 15 stepped down from the high desert at Cajon Pass in a series of steep switchbacks that flowed into the 10 Freeway toward LA. The glow from the mega-city lightened the sky to the northwest. I stifled a melancholy yawn. I turned the heater a little lower while managing to rub my eyes without running off the road.

I'd learned some important if difficult things from my experiences. I'd faced the uncertain line between life and death, and twice, when life had seemed harder than living, some fierce part of me chose to live. I guess that qualified me as a survivor.

As a result of my upbringing, I suppose, I'd believed in some foundational way in the possibility of a forever life with one woman. I'd expected to spend a lifetime with Pat until her mother destroyed those hopes for us. I looked for it in even the most casual of encounters I'd experienced. Now I realized that it is too much to expect the people I cared for to stay forever, that people are not monolithic, unchanging beings. People I love, or who love me, will always be moving in and out of my life. I had to learn to accept those losses and make peace with the grief it might bring. And to recognize that I am not invulnerable; I must never allow myself to fall to the depths of these last agonizing months.

In the depths of my despair in Portland, I'd felt something break: my self-respect. I'd always believed that in any circumstance I would always honor, protect, and respect women. Instead, I'd slapped the woman I loved in anger! I'd had violent sex with a woman–though consensual it was inexcusable. And, I'd used women as security blankets to ensure I'd wake safely, regardless of their feelings. Under duress, I'd found that I wasn't any better than anyone else. *If I am not who I thought I was—who the hell am I?*

The dashboard lighter popped out with a snap but with no answers. I pushed the red, metallic glow against my smoke, inhaling deeply. I would figure out how to trust myself and my judgment again. I would start by doing my best for

Dave, and my friends in the band. But in my heart of hearts, I knew I'd always be searching crowds for that perfect girl flipping back her luscious long hair, until one day, though I couldn't say when I won't need to anymore.

Part IV
images

Sheri Schruhl "The Greeter"

Guardian Angel Shrine

Up on the roof

Mac, Larry, Les   Mickey, Dave, Leonard

Oil Can Harry's Vancouver B.C.

Larry 1970

Nakeds on break in the Sky Room
Leonard, Dave, Larry, Les, Mickey, Mac

AFTERMATH (Epilogue)

Your life story is a novel; and people, though they love novels wound between two yellow paper covers, are oddly suspicious of those which come to them in living vellum.

— Alexander Dumas, The Count of Monte Cristo

In real life, there isn't always a straight line to a simple answer for why things happen. In writing this memoir, I have tried not to include or be influenced in any material way by anything that I didn't actually know or experience at the time it was taking place. Though I have never gotten an entirely definitive answer to the mystery of what happened between Theresa and me, there are some elements I can append to update the story:

THERESA

In the shock of a lifetime, after not hearing from her for nearly forty-seven years, or being able to find any trace of her anywhere, Theresa contacted me through a brand-new Facebook page as I was working through a draft of the last section of this book. She instant-messaged to ask if we could talk on the phone. In our first call, she told me she wanted me to know she'd always regretted the events that led to the end of our marriage. Hearing her fight through her own emotions in the voice I remembered so well, to tell me how sorry she was for failing me, failing us, brought us both to tears. I told her how much I'd loved her, and she'd told me she'd loved me just as much. I told her I'd always felt I'd failed us for not finding some way to rescue her and our marriage. This call led to several deep and emotional conversations and messaging. I asked in several different ways why she couldn't bring herself to return to Las Vegas, but she was unable to explain. The incidents she related about what happened after she and Keoki disappeared out of my life made my hair stand on end. Though they involved me peripherally, and partially illuminated certain mysteries, they are a part of her story, and not mine to relate.

In her recollections about our time together it almost seemed as if she were remembering for someone else, and sometimes even referred to herself in the third person. She acknowledged she had suffered from serious bouts of depression and periodic amnesia that required treatment and medication during her life since.

When I'd suggested she seek professional help in 1970, as related in *Enchanted*, I'd begun to suspect she might have fallen victim to some mental disorder. But it was many years later, while researching for this book, that I began to consider her actions after the birth of Keoki, including changes in personality, could be symptoms of clinical depression, possibly post-partum. This is a malady not well understood in the years of this story and still a challenge to treatment today. I am not a diagnostician, but if this is true, as I suspect, I believe it would explain a lot.

Theresa tells me she is living a deeply-spiritual life now that eases her mind and makes her happy. I hope it is true. We have acknowledged our past affection for each other and agreed to remain friends. While I don't know everything I'd like to know, I'm pretty certain I know all I'll ever know and am at peace with that. I appreciate and am thankful for her courage and strength in reaching out and hope she finds whatever happiness she may.

I would like to advise anyone who has experienced symptoms such as those described in this book to find expert professional help. Consider the links below a place to start:

- Depression Hotline:
  www.mentalhelp.net/articles/depression-hotline/
- Symptoms:

www.webmd.com/depression/guide/detecting-depression#1
- Depression in Women:
  www.psycom.net/depression.central.women.html
- Borderline Personality Disorder:
  www.nimh.nih.gov/health/topics/ borderline-personality-disorder/index.shtml
- Dissociative Amnesia:
  www.webmd.com/mental-health/dissociative-amnesia#1

PAT

Pat and her new husband eventually settled in Washington State. She left this world far too early in 2007, a victim of incurable pancreatic cancer. It was devastating to everyone who knew her. She had so much left to offer her three sons and their children. We never spoke again after she flew away in Oakland. One of my greatest regrets is that I was unable to assure her of my undying affection and my unreserved admiration for how well she and her husband, Jim, raised our two boys. Though I've never been able to come to terms with why I was shut out of their lives, I am happy with the parenting that has helped them become stellar men.

MARIE

Though I lost track of Marie pretty early during the years of *Enchanted*, she was my companion through many of my experiences in *Night People*. As mentioned in *Enchanted*, I found we'd had a daughter, and I'm sorry to say I didn't meet her until Marie contacted me about six years later. I fell in love with my daughter, Lori, the moment I saw her. Lori kept communication between Marie and me alive for many years, including the years Lori came to live with me at Marie's request. Eventually, we lost contact, though I understand Marie is happily married and living in Nevada. I am glad to hear that.

SHERI (The Greeter)

I found and contacted Sheri on the internet during the writing of this memoir. I wanted to check with her to be certain I was portraying her accurately, and we instantly resumed our friendship from long ago. She was extremely generous and supportive of my writing, helping me research certain facts for my Las Vegas chapters. She and her husband, Gary, went out of their way to help me, even offering *Night People* for sale in their store in Sedona, Arizona. I believe you'll be able to find *Enchanted* for sale there as well when it is published. She'd looked forward to having her own chapter in *Enchanted*, but tragically, she fell victim to a rapidly-advancing cancer before the book was finished. I'm forever grateful to Gary for allowing me a few minutes to speak with her by phone before she was suddenly called on. She was a genuinely wonderful and generous person who is missed by her husband, her two children, and everyone who was lucky enough to have known her.

THE MEMBERS OF STARK NAKED AND THE CAR THIEVES

DAVID DUNN

Dave continued to sing with various versions of Stark Naked and the Car Thieves for another nine years. He and Pat Mosley, introduced in *Enchanted*, became the featured singers on their 1971 album, *Pick Up the Pieces,* arranged by Les Silvey and produced by Emory Gordy, Jr., which is available on iTunes. It is an excellent album, and I highly recommend it. Dave eventually retired and lives in Indianapolis. I wish more people had gotten to hear his voice. I think his is one of the most special voices I have ever heard. He remains my best friend in this world.

MAC BROWN

Mac's experiment with Mickey in Portland, Oregon, didn't last more than a few weeks before he and his family returned to Ohio. Thankfully we stayed in touch, the friendship between the original four of us outweighing all other considerations. He explained he'd felt he had to leave Las Vegas to save his life. There was just too much temptation for him there. I understand that now very well.

Not long after these events, I helped him form American Headband, a rock band that worked in the same circuit as Dave's Stark Naked and the Car Thieves. In 1979, he was reunited with Dave in one of the most entertaining versions of Stark Naked and the Car Thieves since the original band. Mac and Joan eventually returned to rural Ohio, where they both took positions in a state-run home caring for orphaned children and helping them find new homes and happier lives. They are now contentedly immersed as matriarch and patriarch of their widespread family. Their daughter, Dani, who grew up with us in the band as a cute and precocious little girl, has become a beautiful and kind woman with three sons plus grandkids, and lives near her parents. I've been back to visit them at "Brown's Farm" several times. Our years together will always keep our brotherhood alive.

LES SILVEY

Les stayed with the band for a couple of years after I left, arranging the songs for the next generation of Stark Naked and the Car Thieves. Though their album *Pick Up the Pieces* wasn't initially released due to contract disputes, it was remastered and released by Ron Hitchcock's production company in 2010. (Ron, as has been mentioned in *Night People*, was one of our first audio engineers during our first recording sessions.) It is an excellent album, perhaps the best-sounding recordings of all the Stark Naked and the Car Thieves' sessions. I envied not being part of them. The album is available on iTunes at itunes.apple.com/us/album/pick-up-the-pieces/266056322. Les is retired, happily married, and lives in Nevada.

LEONARD SOUZA

Leonard played with the band for a few months after I left, before leaving to make his home in Las Vegas. He married his love, Marie, and worked diligently to obtain his bartender's license, and in this role entertained all comers at the New York, New York Hotel and Casino on the Las Vegas Strip. He owned a car lot and dabbled in real estate before being taken by cancer in March of 2000. He was deeply loved and revered by his bandmates and the many, many people he'd befriended over the years in Las Vegas and elsewhere. We will always miss and honor him.

MICKEY BORDEN

After the new band he'd hoped to create in Portland failed to materialize, Mickey and Lora settled in their original home of Prineville, Oregon, where he managed his own Ford dealership in nearby Bend, Oregon, until retirement. All of us in the band were shocked and saddened when we learned of the loss of their son Mikey, a wonderful boy, who'd been a member of the band's extended family and his parents' reason for living. We will never stop mourning his passing.

MY CHILDREN

Both volumes of *Things We Lost in the Night* are dedicated to my children. I have told them this memoir is about what happened to their parents, but it does include my accounts of their origin stories. I have tried to protect their and others' privacy by not mentioning their surnames. There may be heroes and villains in what happened in this part of their lives, but as far as I know, there were only imperfect humans.

David and Dan were raised by Pat and a man she chose to be their surrogate father. They grew into smart, amazing, and gracious men, for which I can take little credit, but for which I'm immensely grateful. I was never sure I would get to be in their lives, but they've generously included me. Though I regret what I have missed, I cannot deny the way things worked out might have been best for them. Each of them and their amazing wives have raised two brilliant and beautiful young women, who are already making their marks on the world.

I met my daughter Lori for the first time when Marie, her mother, reached out to find me when Lori was about seven. I wish it had been much earlier. She was a sweet and beautiful child who grew into womanhood too soon. She lived with me for several restless years before striking out on her own. That didn't work out especially well at first, but she seems happy and well now, and I love her and her three wonderful sons dearly.

Keoki had been lost in the world to me for most of his life. But a few weeks prior to publishing *Night People* in 2015, I was able to find and connect with him on Facebook. I wanted to let him, and his mother know about the memoir I was writing, and send him a copy of *Night People*. I wasn't sure if he would let his mother know I'd contacted him, but it's likely that's what brought Theresa to contact me. All our conversations have been by text or email. He hadn't been told as a child that he had a different biological father than his two younger brothers, but he wrote he'd suspected it before it was finally confirmed when he needed his birth certificate to apply for a driver's license. Neither of us know why my identity had been hidden from him. Nevertheless, he made it clear he considers the man who raised him his father and that he wasn't overly thrilled about another one appearing out of the blue. I can't blame him, his mother never mentioned me to him as he was growing up. He told me his grandmother Willi, before she passed, led him to believe the reason his mother and I weren't together was because I thought my career and the two sons I already had were more important than he or his mother. He is a middle-aged man, innocent of all that has happened, and I couldn't think of any good reason to contradict what he'd been told or to cause needless conflict in his life. Nevertheless, he was polite, and I was pleased he was willing to share some of his history with me. He seems happily married, living with his wife and three good-looking and successful children. I hope he will find the time to read my writings and consider my memories of what happened and think a little better of me, but that will be up to him.

LARRY J. DUNLAP

Following my years in the band, I worked in the music business as an associate personal manager with Seymour Heller, helping to establish new rock bands and young recording artists for Attarack-Heller, Seymour's company, including various incarnations of Stark Naked and the Car Thieves. I left Seymour's offices a few years later to form my own artist management company with two partners a few blocks east on Sunset Boulevard near the Roxie and the Rainbow Grill, and eventually owned, helped build, and operated City Recorders, a recording studio housed in the Paramount Studios building at

Sunset and Gower. I continued to represent my old band. There were some very interesting years and events for them: Doug Ingle, lead singer and keyboardist of Iron Butterfly and composer of *In-A-Gadda-Da-Vida* joined them, (replacing me, or so I like to say). I got to hear firsthand from Doug that this title for the hit song he composed came from his drunken slurring of "in the Garden of Eden" when he'd recorded it. Michael McDonald was nearly accepted into the band after he'd left Steely Dan and hadn't yet become a Doobie Brother. At the last minute, the band decided they couldn't afford another player—not their brightest decision. Several other regionally well-known singers and players were members at one time or another until its demise in 1978.

In 1980 I left music altogether to co-found (with Thom Keith, mentioned in this memoir) the first fully digital television network, built to deliver computer games through cable television. A highly successful concept, The Games Network, Inc. went public as GNET on the NASDAQ exchange in 1982 with thousands of potential subscribers on roughly a quarter of the existing domestic cable systems. Sadly, within weeks of the launch of its service and a month before we were to be featured on the cover of *TV Guide*, the company failed from underfunding. It was a highly traumatic ending of a dream that took years to dig out of, but that experience uncovered an affinity for technology in me. After a few years overseeing a film and video post-production house and managing a film and video production company, I accepted a modestly paying job training CompUSA customers how to use consumer software in Culver City, California, and luckily enough, met my wife-to-be, Laurie, in one of my classes. As CompUSA grew, I was kicked from classroom trainer to local training manager then booted farther up to Western regional training manager until I was given the opportunity to design, develop, and then manage a national, high-end training program to train and certify network engineers.

Afterward, CompUSA offered me the opportunity to work as an independent contractor designing national technical training programs for several of their large corporate accounts, which led to authoring a basic computer-training course for Section-8 housing recipients for HUD in Washington, DC. I was recruited into broader technical writing, documentation, and systems analysis, and after obtaining the requisite data management certification, I added database development and system architecture skills to design and develop intelligent information systems and, in the late 1990s, Y2K testing templates for Fortune 50 companies. Laurie and I married about the same time I decided to follow my dream to design and develop multi-player online games. In 2010, I happily committed to becoming a fully-retired, full-time creative author. Now Laurie, the light in my life, and I live quietly near the beaches south of Los Angeles, counting our blessings every day for the life and love we feel so lucky to share.

ACKNOWLEDGMENTS

I'm grateful for the help I've received from so many people. I have to begin with David Dunn, who has read everything I've ever written over the years, including the hundreds of thousands of words discarded during the process. There are surprisingly few details we remember differently and none directly affecting our adventures as I've written here. He's been my rudder, helping me stay on course. I appreciate that Mac Brown and his wife, Joan, the seventh member of the band, whom I treasure as well, have read everything, and recognize this entire story is a *look back in love*, and we'll always be connected through our journey together.

I am especially cognizant that if my fantastic editor Katie Stirling hadn't helped me push through that I might never have finished *Enchanted*. She has the patience of a saint and the eye of an eagle. My long-time friend John C. Clair provided incredible insight and sees layers and subtleties in my words that even I don't realize. I cannot thank him enough for his selfless help and honest appraisal, especially for my Indiana chapters. Finally, I must thank Kristi Bartmess Warren for her final touch-up work.

Rick Stepp-Bolling, my original critique partner for *Night People*, my inspiring friend, along with Linda Moore Kurth and Chris Tunnah who were leaders of the beta reading team. I send my gratitude to Mark Lau and his friends in Hawaii who helped me with the Hawaiian Pidgin in this book; any errors I make with it are my own doing, not theirs. Thank you, Shirley Alapa, for reading my Hawaiian chapters and giving me your insight from those seminal weeks at the Lemon Tree in Honolulu. I'm especially grateful to Sheri Moline, who became a great friend and was notably generous in helping dig out facts from various archives and sources in Las Vegas. Her loss so early in life was tragic. She was a beautiful lady inside and out. I'm grateful to her loving and devoted husband, Gary Moline, for the opportunity to speak with her by phone before her passing. Thanks, Stretch Head, a sublime and polished musician for reading some of my music industry passages.

I appreciate the support I've received from the members of the writing groups I belong to, including the Third Street Writers Ink of Laguna Beach, who gave me the opportunity to try out early chapters of this book in our critique sessions. Special thanks to their founder, Amy Francis-Dechary for her willingness to read and support my effort, and co-leader Rina Palumbo. I've had early reader help from The Orange County Writers and its online leader, Greta Boris. My original and steadfast writing pals, the Coffee House Writers Group in San Dimas, beginning with Christine Marie Bryant, Rick Stepp-Bolling, Steven Hamilton, and many others who have given me years-long help and support from the beginning of this project. Also, the Southern California Writers' Association has provided generous help and encouragement, most especially from P.J. Columbo, Pamela Sheppard, Greta Boris, and Madeline Tighe Margarita.

I'd like to note some writers who influence and teach me through their work as I'm usually immersed in a book whenever I'm not writing myself. As I've struggled to bring to life the years of *Things We Lost in the Night,* I have gained inspiration and standards to live up to from Kiana Davenport, Mary Karr, Amor Towles, Michael Connelly, Dennis Lehane, Robert Crais, Kaui Hart Hemmings, Toby Neal, Susan Shapiro, and Cheryl Strayed who inspired me from the beginning.

As always, my greatest thanks go to my wife and partner-in-life, Laurie. Her patience and the love she shares with me are the primary reasons I've been able to complete this work.

BEFORE YOU GO

Thanks for reading *Enchanted*, the concluding book of *Things We Lost in the Night*. If you haven't yet read **Night People**, the first book of the memoir, you can find it with a simple search by title or author on Amazon.com.

For free e-books and short stories that you can get right now, go to *larryjdunlap.com/readers*, where you will also find current information about the music and people of *Things We Lost in the Night* including links to photos. I appreciate your support and would love to stay in touch.

Would you like a free, signed copy of **Night People**? (or *Enchanted* if you'd prefer.) For everyone who leaves a review on Amazon and/or Goodreads, I do a periodic raffle for signed copies of the book. Just send me an email copy of your review to *reviews@cvppress.com* to automatically be entered.

Even if you don't want to enter the raffle, please consider taking the time to leave a review, no matter how short. Reviews by readers like you are powerful, so powerful that they can make or break a book—especially for independent writers. I'd love to see even a single line of what you thought or felt about this book. I read every one and appreciate them all.

If you want to see what I have planned for my next series of books, and free ARC copies of them (even before they're released), then join my advance readers community at *arc@cvppress.com* where I randomly select up to two hundred readers to get advance, free copies of my new books.

Want to be contacted for new releases only? Join up for alerts of my new book releases. Click/visit *larryjdunlap.com/emailupdates*

You can find me on:

Facebook:

    facebook.com/larryjdunlap.author and

    facebook.com/TWLitN/ for a page dedicated to this memoir.

Website: larryjdunlap.com

With gratitude,

Larry

www.ingramcontent.com/pod-product-compliance
Lightning Source LLC
Chambersburg PA
CBHW030428010526
44118CB00011B/550